The Instrument of Evil

Memoirs of the Unwanted Child

by

Arnaldo M. Montero Sardana

DORRANCE
PUBLISHING CO
EST. 1920
PITTSBURGH, PENNSYLVANIA 15238

Dorrance Publishing Co
585 Alpha Drive
Suite 103
Pittsburgh, PA 15238
Visit our website at www.dorrancebookstore.com

ISBN: 979-8-89027-422-9
eISBN: 979-8-89027-920-0

I dedicate this book to all those who are suffering and are silent in their struggles. To The Underground Kids, my daughter who doesn't know I exist, and to Matthew and Victor, the purpose for all this to happen, and the two little girls who made my monster rest in its prison, Ariel and Khaleesi — I love you both.

Introduction

This is a true and uncut story about a child who was born controlled, grew up fast, and learned how to live with hatred, rage, betrayals, deceptions, and revenge, while becoming friends with loneliness and depression, which led to heartache after heartache, leaving me with an emptiness within my soul.

Families and Society Create.
The Monsters,
they soon come to Fear in The End,
When They cannot Control Them Anymore.
Then they pass judgment and
hunt down what they created like animals.

Chapter 1

I was born on December 12, 1971, at 5:55 p.m. in New York Hospital in Manhattan. My mother gave birth to me by Caesarean section (C-Section) and, according to my mother, she was infected with syphilis by my womanizing father, which resulted in me being born with a heart murmur.

My mother and father were both born in Puerto Rico and came to the United States with their parents and siblings at a certain age. They all lived in New York, and that is all I really know of them. At one time I used to love them.

My nickname on my mother's side of the family is "Macho;" on my father's side, it's either "Manuel" or "Manny." I do not know if I'm a junior because, as my mother told me many times throughout my childhood and teenage years, she had an abortion and I was lucky because she was going to abort me, too.

I start my tale with two memories of my early childhood. I was around four or five years old and remember waking up in a metallic crib in a hospital with my mother and one of my favorite uncles looking down on me and after they hugged and kissed me, they left.

I sat up from the crib and looked around and saw a bunch of little kids sitting around a television watching it quietly like zombies; there was no laughter or playing around. I got out of the metallic crib and sat down with the other children; we were all in hospital gowns, and I looked around again at the kids to see who was playing, so I could try and join but none of them were. I was wondering why they weren't being kids, when my thoughts were

1

interrupted by a Black kid my age who sat next to me with crossed legs, like we were all doing.

I noticed the little Black kid was naked underneath his gown, and was shocked with curiosity by what I saw. The Black kid had a bunch of wooden toothpicks embedded all around his penis and his meatus (the head of the penis). I reached out to gently touch the toothpicks, but the kid stopped me by grabbing my hand and telling me without any emotion on his face that his privates hurt. At that I left him alone. that's all I remember.

The second memory, was again around four or five years old. I was on the Beach with my mother and some of her friends; they had left me alone playing in the sand, while they went swimming, I was digging a ditch in the sand and was interrupted by some white lady, who asked me what was I doing. I looked up at her and answered, "Digging a hole." Then she asked me where my mother was. I answered, "Swimming with her friends." Still looking up at her and digging, I could see her looking around nervously, like she was scared. She then looked down at me and started to compliment me with words like:

"You know you are a cutie," and "You are an adorable boy."

I responded both times, "I know," and before she could say anything else, I heard my mother call out to me and looked towards the direction of her voice and screamed back, "I'm okay!" and when I returned my attention to the lady, she was gone. I again turned towards my mother who was approaching me.

Seeing her, she asked me, "Who was that lady, and what did she want?"

I responded, "I don't know; she was saying I was cute," and the questioning was over.

Now, what kind of child was I? I was a timid, funny, and charming kid who attracted people around me (I still do.), I was also kindhearted, loveable, and curious with a capital C (still curious about everything in life) and don't forget being mischievous, which I still am.

I was a brave kid but avoided fighting at all costs because I feared violence, but if I was pushed to it, well, I would fight back. I was also sexually active and a momma's boy; I was such a momma's boy that when my mother would go out, I would throw some of my toys out of the window just to get her attention, but that only got me spanked.

As I continue with my hateful life story, I wonder where I get the fucking strength to live a life where lies, deceit, betrayals, and being cheated and used is a constant thing in my life, even now.

I ask this question to myself every day, while the thoughts of suicide are on my mind from the moment I wake up to the moment I fall asleep, and sometimes, even in my nightmares. Why haven't I committed suicide yet? The answer that comes back is because the motherfuckers who created these feelings in me will not have the pleasure of being the cause of my death, though there are times, like now, I just want to end the screams in my head of a derange and vengeful personality that fights for freedom, and end my anguish that squeezes my heart to a pulp and end the loneliness, emptiness, and sadness in my soul. And as I write about my demons and how they are trying to destroy everything I have come to love,

I look for the answers which haunt my mind.

What is the purpose of my life?

Why do I continue to fight?

Why can't I end it all?

Will I ever find peace and happiness?

But still, to this day, I have not found the answer to those questions, but one thing is for sure throughout my life, I have been hungry for real love, and all I have is a history of silent tears and rage, which burns within my heart, mind, body, and soul, screaming for vengeance.

I had drafted this book once before while doing time in prison, and even let a prisoner read half the book. Days later, when he returned the book, he told me he became emotional and that I needed to expose everyone who created (Us). But I threw the book away in the garbage because I was not ready to tell my story.

It is a story like no other that has been told, and now, after more than fifteen years, I am ready to expose Us and everyone who created a personality that wants to see the world burn and everyone in it.

I drafted this book to let the good people whom I betrayed and hurt know that at the time I was fighting with myself, and y'all became our target. I am so fucking sorry for everything I did, and I ask you to please forgive me. I also

drafted this book for the hopeless, for those who think of ending their lives and are looking for a reason to not commit suicide, and for the ignorant and blind.

. . .

Who am I? A nobody to the rich, famous, and those of important positions, and to my neighborhood (the real world). A stranger to some, a friend to others, and an enemy to many.

So, sit back and enter my mind and see the demons that haunt my mind, and the suffering they produce, while a maniac lurks in hiding.

. . .

As a child, I always wondered why I was always being sent from my father's custody to my grandparents', and then back to my mother, and as I got older, even to my aunts and uncles; this became a way of life for me until the age of eighteen.

I remember as a child of five years of age, my mother was my physical home schoolteacher and when I was home from school, she would help me with my reading and writing but when I mispronounce a word she just taught me, she would get mad at me, she would become so irate she would threaten physical harm, making me become nervous and scared and making it hard for me to think or pronounce any word, and when I couldn't pronounce it, she would start with the mushing and slapping me on the head and face multiple times, and when the results were still the same, she'd start punching and slapping me all over my face and head. As she would beat on me, she would scream, "You fucking stupid bitch, I just told you the fucking word. Now tell me the fucking word before you make me even more mad." Sometimes the word would come out, and sometimes it didn't.

Her method of teaching got worse when my mother, stepfather, stepbrother, and I moved from the Bronx to North Carolina. My first day fell on Valentine's Day and I was in first grade. My teacher had asked the class to write a Valentine's Day card to welcome me to their school and class. They all did,

and at the end of the school day, I took them all (it was more than ten) and put them in my bookbag.

On the school bus heading home, I kept opening and closing my bookbag to check if the cards were really there; I was surprised all the students gave me one. When I arrived home, I happily showed them to my mother, who asked me to read them to her, and I did—I read every single card but one, it was actually one word in the card I couldn't pronounce, and no matter how hard I tried to pronounce it, it just would not come out, and the crazy thing about it, I knew the word and it was even on the tip of my tongue, but it still would not come out.

I tried hard to concentrate but on seeing my mother's expression turning from frustration to anger, my mind went completely blank, and when she started cursing and threatening me, it made matters worse. But the moment didn't last long because she jumped up from the sofa, grabbed me by my T-shirt quickly, lifted , slammed me on my back onto the sofa, sat on my chest, and started punching and slapping me all over my face, head and upper chest area and as she was doing this, she started cursing and screaming at me, "Tell me the fucking word, motherfucker!"

After a minute or two of this continuous beat down, the word blurted out, "Macho;" my fucking nickname.

My mother was good at whipping my ass. I remember one day in North Carolina, I was playing pretend that I was drowning on the living room floor and whispering like I was screaming for help, and out of nowhere, my mother came from the kitchen and started kicking and stomping me on my back and ribs, she didn't stop hitting me until she got tired, leaving my body sore.

In another incident, I was snorkeling like a pig and my mother straight out punched me so hard in my mouth she busted my lips and nose and knocked out one of my front baby teeth, making me swallow it.

If she wasn't busy beating my ass, she would be fighting verbally and physically with my stepfather, Gus. I remember one night in North Carolina, I was eight years old and my brother Stefano was five, we were awakened by my parents arguing, then the breaking of glass, and then they became physical with one other; that night we fell asleep fearfully with tears rolling down on our faces, like many times before and many to come.

The next day, I saw my mother had her arm in an sling. On seeing the worry on my face, she told me to go outside and play with my friends, I did.

Once outside I spent some time with some of my male friends from across the street where there were a couple houses but I had to walk a little forest with a path to my friends' neighborhood. I met up and started to play with them. One of the boys hit me playfully with a Nerf plastic baseball bat and all I remember was everything going black, and me, watching my body move on its own.

I watched myself snatch the bat out of the kid's hand and start to beat him hard, making him run and cry. I watched myself chase after him, hitting him everywhere I could get him, the head, the face, and everywhere else on his body. I chased him into his house. I just couldn't stop myself from beating him; all I knew was it felt so good. He ran into the kitchen, then to the backyard, and as I continued to chase and hit him, I didn't notice the people in the yard. I chased him into the living room and out to the front of his house, then he ran back in, and I chased him into the backyard again where some lady, who was sitting on a lawn chair, got up. Whatever was controlling me ignored her, and I continued to chase and beat on the kid. I only snapped out of it when the lady snatched the bat from my hands and made me freeze, breaking me out of my darkness. I looked at the white lady who was screaming, "You fucking little savage! Get the fuck away from my kids and never come back!"

I started to walk away but my focus was on her son, who was crying hysterically with welt marks all over his face and exposed body. I still wanted to beat on him.

I walked back to where I lived, but instead of going upstairs, I sat with my back on a fenced swimming pool gate which faced the front of my building. After a few minutes of being lost in my own thoughts, a little white girl my age with long black hair that reached down to her buttocks stood next to me and asked if I was okay. I responded, "Yes," and she sat next to me. I found her quite pretty to the point where I was forming a slight crush on her.

We leaned our backs on the fence that surrounded the pool, which kept people and children safe from harm when it's closed, but since the fence was about four or five feet tall, it made it easy for anyone to climb the fence and

into the pool; when that happened and since it faced the front of the two-story building where I lived, which was on the second floor and my parents' apartment faced the pool.

I could watch whomever snuck in the pool and enjoyed themselves. I don't know why but I started to tell the little girl about the fight my mother and my stepfather had the night before, and how I heard glass and things break, and when I woke up the next morning, my mother had her arm in a sling. At that exact moment, my mother appeared on the porch and I pointed to my mother, telling the little girl that's her arm in a sling.

I changed the subject and we talked about this and that, then we decided to start and play tag and after some time, we got tired of playing, we stopped said our goodbyes, she went home and so did I. At home, my mother got mad at me because she knew I was talking about her to the little girl. My mother screamed to never speak about any family situations to anyone ever again.

· · ·

As time passed by in North Carolina, things started to happen to me that I could not understand or explain, like my defecating habits. I remember like four incidents where I defecated myself: one was in school, and I had defecated on myself and didn't bother to tell the teacher or go to the bathroom to clean myself up. I stood with feces between my buttocks and underwear all day in school, and when I went home, I still didn't clean myself. It was when my mother stood over me to check my schoolwork that she noticed the smell of feces coming from me, and asked if I defecated on myself again. and I answered, "yes." She got mad and screamed all kinds of profanities at me; that's when I decided to clean myself up.

The second incident was a couple days later, actually nights later, and it was late and very dark. I was in my own room and was awakened by something I couldn't explain but as I laid on my bed trying to figure it out, I felt a heat heating my whole body, I felt like I was burning up and it was starting to hurt, I never felt this feeling before and it wasn't lust even though I had a hard-on, my whole body felt on fire and upon feeling my

erection, I pulled my underwear off and started to masturbate until I felt the stinging sensation of ejaculating, I held onto my little penis tightly and I laid there breathing heavily.

I then had an urge to piss, so I let out a stream of hot urine hit me all over my face, chest, stomach, and both of my hands, doing this made me even hornier, so I continued to masturbate and piss on myself, even drinking some as I let the stream of my urine hit my face.

The fire burning in my whole body was hurting me even more but I continued to masturbate and piss, I gotten off the bed and continued to masturbate in different spots of the room and piss on every spot I stood, I even opened a dresser drawer, took out all my folded clothes, threw them on the floor, got in, laid on the dresser drawer, and started to masturbate and piss on myself, I even started to finger myself in my rectum and after a few more ejaculations in the drawer, I got out and went into my closet squatted in a corner and fingered myself until I defecated in the corner, then I stood up like it was nothing, looked for my underwear, put it on, laid on my pissy bed and fell in a deep sleep. As for the burning all over my body, it left as soon as I defecated on the floor.

Like a day or two later, my mother went into my room to clean up my messy room and discovered my shitty mess in the corner of the closet, and started screaming at me that she was going to tell my babysitter, who was a girl in her mid-teens who lived across the hall from us and was a good friend to me. As soon as my mother mentioned the girl, there was a knock on the door, and who do you think it was? The girl from next door. I felt like I was in a horror movie; my heart started beating fast with fear and I felt shame and humiliation. I thought that my mother was going to tell my babysitter friend I defecated in the closet. The girl asked for my mother, and I replied she was busy cleaning my room but she just walked in and went straight into my room. I didn't follow her in because I didn't want to see her expression when she heard the news. I stood outside of view but in good eavesdropping.

I heard Stefani, my babysitter friend, ask my mother what was she doing and my heart went up to my throat, choking me with humiliating fear and the threat of tears, but when my mother replied: "The little one escaped the prison of his diapers and decided to use Macho's closet," I let out a long breath.

My knees became a little weak, so I went into the kitchen and sat down. I felt emotionally relieved and the love I had for my mother intensified. Stefani stood talking privately for some time with my mother, and then she came out of my room. I could see Stefani coming down the long hallway, which led to my parents' room, my room, and the bathroom. From where I was, I could see who came in and out of any room.. As Stefani walked in my direction, I went into a daze and started fantasizing about Stefani and being sexual lovers. I would be the envy of all the boys in the neighborhood. Stefani broke my daze and I came back to reality with a smile. Stefani asked me if I was okay, and I replied, "Yes, why?"

She replied, "I noticed you were in outer space while I was calling out for you."

I answered that I was thinking about something, and we chatted a little longer about this and that, and she left home.

The third defecation incident was one night I was asleep in my room and woke up with an urge to defecate. I jumped out of my bed quickly and ran towards the bathroom, but by the time I reached the bathroom, I had defecated on myself. I walked with my legs spread opened in the bathroom. Once inside, I pulled my underwear off slowly because it was one of those dry hard shits that doesn't need wiping, and seeing no shit stains, I put my underwear over the toilet bowl and flicked it in the bowl, flushed it, then put my underwear back on, and went back into my room and into bed as if nothing had happened.

The final incident, though there have been many close calls after this one, in those moments, I would stand still in a corner and squeeze my buttocks tight to hold my load and after the moment was over. I would continue with whatever I was doing but this night was different. This was a stormy night in North Carolina and the wind was blowing so hard that the trees in the forest were moaning and howling loudly. My mother, brother, and I were in the living room and had the lights off, sitting around a coffee table where my mother had lit a candle on top of it, also on the table was a Mickey Mouse toy camera, it had a white plastic disk that had section of films in each one telling a story of Mickey Mouse and the three ghosts and how the three ghosts were trying real hard to scare Mickey out of the house.

After we all took turns watching the story, we stopped playing with the camera and my mother asked my brother and me to look into the flames and watch how the flames resembled the ghost. My brother and I were so entranced by the flames we didn't notice our mother leaving the living room and going into her room, but all of a sudden my brother and I heard the radio in my mother's room turn on, it had a spooky quality to it, and it spooked us so bad my brother and I ran behind the big couch, where I managed to push my little brother underneath the couch first but when I tried to go under, I couldn't fit. I started to panic so bad that when I tried to call out for my mother, only whispers came out and the fear even made me defecate and urinate on myself—yes, I had the piss and shit scared out of me, After some time with the radio spooking us, it stopped playing. I could hear my mother cracking up and at seeing where we were hiding. She laughed even harder, and when she realized what I had done myself, she didn't get mad, but boy did she pranked us good.

.   .   .

Now speaking of being scared, I remember one of many scary incidents that happened to me. My mother left me home alone to go to the store; she had asked me to peel enough potatoes for all of us for dinner. I was sitting in the kitchen chair facing the hallway, which led into our rooms, also in the position I was sitting in, I could see partway into living room and through the corner of my eyes, I could watch television while peeling potatoes. I was peeling a potato when out of the corner of my eye I saw movement in the living room. I quickly turned and saw a small, shadowy figure running towards the hallway. I followed its movement and it ran into my room. I was halfway scared and feeling silly because I thought it could have been one of my friends, who climbed and snuck in through the porch (which could be done) just to scare me.

I then got up and quickly ran towards my room and froze in fear when I reached the entrance because it wasn't any of my friends and it wasn't a person, it was a black form standing behind the headboard of my bed and the wall and it slid down under my bed. I ran back to the kitchen and sat with my back towards the rooms, scared and shaking. I sat continuing to peel potato and watch

television. I was starting to get comfortable, when nothing further occurred. But the experience still had me a little frighten. I started to pray for my mother to hurry up and come home, and after a few minutes passed by, I heard the lock to the door turn and the door slightly opened. I was thankful, thinking it was my mother. I turned towards the door and that's when I saw the black form run past me and go through the crack of the door, disappearing in a blink of an eye; it just wasn't there, but when it appeared, you see it like you see something out of the corner of your eye. I ran out the door, and it was standing by the top of the staircase that went down and out of the building, and upon seeing me, it ran down the stairs. I ran to the top of the stairs to see where it would go, but it disappeared.

I walked back slowly trying to understand what happened, and as I sat back down and started peeling the rest of the potatoes I could hear the keys entering the doorknob and knew it was my mother. When I saw her, I was relieved but I didn't tell my mother. Why? I do not know. Even to this day, my mother doesn't know about the incident, but what bothers me is why did it wait twice to reveal itself? And how did it know I would respond like I did? And why did he appear to me?

. . .

Another spooky incident was when my babysitter came to pick me up and took me outside to the back of our building where a double set of swings for two was set not too far from our building, and farther down was a dense forest.

We sat in one of the sets of double swings—she sat in one side and I sat with my back to the forest. We were swinging each other without getting up and talking about this and that, and after a couple minutes passed by, I started to feel scared, like someone was watching us, but specifically me. I told Stefani how I felt and we both looked into the forest to see if we could see anyone watching us, but there was nothing, so we continued to rock each other on the swing; she was reassuring me that I was imagining it.

We changed the subject and started asking each other questions about where we lived before and if we like living there or here in North Carolina.

We both chose where we used to live and after more time passed, we both heard running sounds coming from the forest. At first, it sounded like it was coming from a far distance, but the running sounds for some reason sounded like jumping, as it or whoever it was running, would jump, and land closer and start running again, I for some reason became very fearful like someone was only coming for me.

I told Stefani I wanted to leave and she didn't object for when I looked at her, she looked more scared than I was. We started walking with a little pep to our step and it wasn't until we got to the front of our building that the running and jumping noise stopped. Stefani felt comfortable enough to say she wanted to go into the forest and investigate what those sounds were, though I didn't tell her I felt real danger. I begged her not to go and she promised me she wouldn't, and with that, we continued home in silence.

After those two spooky experiences nothing like that ever occurred again until years later. But in the here or now, two tragedies almost happened that if it did, it would of have affected everyone badly.

The first one was on a hot summer day in North Carolina and I was eight and a half years old and my little brother was five. My mother decided to take us to the pool, and once there, we set our towels by the gate and my mother sat my brother by the fence and told him not to move, then my mother and I went in.

We were playing tag to see who could swim the fastest, and while we played, we would check on Stefano (my little brother to see if he was still sitting with his back on the fence playing with some toy of his. Seeing he was okay, we continued to play games in the water.

We lost track of time and my mother stopped playing and asked me where was Stefano. I had stopped swimming but peddling with my feet to stay afloat and looked around; he was nowhere to be seen. I could hear my mother calling out for him. I asked her to lift me, and she swam to lift me. I saw my brother on the bottom of the pool but on the other end, where it was about three or four feet deep, I asked my mother to throw me in the direction of my brother and she did, but by the time I got to my brother, my mother had reached him first and they both were out of the pool with Stefano in her arms. I also got

out quickly and ran towards him; he was okay but red faced, because he was actually holding his breath, he confirmed he was okay with a burst of giggles. With that, the pool day was over.

. . .

I do not know how much time had passed when the second incident occurred, but this one still haunts me with the same fear I felt when it happened. It was late summer, and it was a hot and sticky one. My stepfather decided to take us all to some beach, the drive there was long but we had left early and we arrived there by late noon. The ride over the bridge that led to the beach was amazing because the water was crystal clear; you could actually see the bottom of the beach floor making it seem like anyone could walk on the bottom, but that was a false perception.

When we arrived at the beach's parking lot, Gus (my stepfather) parked at the edge of the parking lot, where we could see the beach area. My brother and I were desperate to get out, so we jumped out of the car as soon as the car was parked and ran down a little sandy path to the beach floor and into the water's edge.

My brother and I had stopped at my mother's voice, "Stay where we can see you both," and we did. We stood at the water's edge letting the little waves splash at our ankles. I spotted an anchored rowboat on the sandy floor floating empty on the water, and ran all the way to the rope which was anchored into the sand attached to some metal pole imbedded in the sandy ground. I followed the rope with my eyes to the boat to see if it can be done, and seeing the beach floor looked no deeper than two feet, I told Stefano, "I'm going to hang by the rope and little by little get to the boat in. Follow me and do what I what I do."

He nodded.

I reached halfway and turned around a little to see if Stefano was following, he was, and as I reached halfway to the boat, but one of my hands missed the rope and I fell in; it was very deep and I fought hard to swim to top side. Once I reached the surface, I could see Stefano had fallen and was struggling hard to stay afloat; it seemed like the more we struggle the harder it was to stay afloat.

I swam to safety onto dry land, spitting out seawater and trying to catch my breath, I turned to see how my brother was doing and he had gone under.

I was scared stiff and all I could manage was open my mouth and let out a shrieking scream, which alerted my mother and she responded quickly by how fast she reached my side. I pointed into the direction where I could see my brother struggling to reach the surface, and my mother ran into the water. After stepping two or three feet deep, she too went under, it felt like hours instead of seconds when my mother reached the surface with Stefano. She got to the sandy beach floor. My mother and Stefano coughed up water and my brother cried I too was crying because I almost lost my little brother, and thank God my mother showed me how to swim, because if she didn't, I would have drowned with Stefano.

Later, after we were all calmed, my mother told me when she went in, she stepped a couple of steps, and she went under, she tried to reach the beach floor with her feet but there wasn't one, and when she grabbed Stefano, she struggled extremely hard to reach the surface.

Chapter 2

Home and Family

"How do you run from evil when it disguises itself as love, goodness, and safety?"

Things between my parents were getting worse—the arguments and the physicals altercations too. One day my brother and I were in my room and we heard them cursing, screaming, and physically fighting, and after a couple minutes of things being broken or thrown, everything went silent until it was broken by my mother yelling at my brother and me to hurry up and get dressed. I knew that it was bad.

When I got my brother and myself dressed, we walked out of the room slowly and I was shocked to see my stepfather hogged tied on his stomach, lying in the entrance of the living room, kitchen, and the apartment's hallway, which lead outside. Gus looked up at me and begged me to untie him. I felt so sorry for him and walked towards him, but I stopped in my tracks and ignore him when my mother told me to leave him alone, then she grabbed us by the hands and left the apartment. Where we went, I do not remember but she drove for hours and when we returned to the crib (apartment), my stepfather was gone; only the restraints remained on the floor.

I do not remember what happened within those days, but late one night my mother came into my room and woke Stefano and me up and quickly helped us get dressed, then she grabbed us by the hands and rushed us out of the apartment. We got in the car and she drove for hours, stopping at a Wendy's to buy us all food, then we stopped at a Grey Hound bus station, where she bought bus tickets. We waited for some time for the bus operator to announce he was starting to board.

Seeing the tension on my mother's face, I decided to try to cheer her up a little. I looked for something I could rip and saw it by the bus station's garbage can on the floor. I waited until my mother was lost in her thoughts and ran quickly to the garbage can area, picked up the paper plate, and ran back to the entrance of the bus station where my mother and brother were standing. I stood beside my mother and took out the paper plate from underneath my shirt but from behind my back I bent down as if I was picking up something and stood up quickly, then ripped the paper plate in half pretending that my pants ripped from behind. My mother heard the ripping and saw me holding my buttocks with pretend embarrassment and started laughing hard; even Stefano was laughing, not because he understood what was happening, but because he saw all of us laughing. After the giggles and laughter were over, I felt happy that, at least for that moment, she was happy.

We entered the bus station because the wait was getting too long and we were tired of standing up. We went into a sitting area that the seats had little televisions on them. My mother paid a quarter for each TV, and I watched a rerun of the original Incredible Hulk, and after she put another quarter in, the bus operator announced that our bus was boarding. We got on the bus, and after some hours passed by, I fell asleep quickly and peacefully knowing we were heading to my grandparents' apartment in Manhattan.

. . .

I don't remember arriving at my grandparents' or being put to bed, but when I woke, I could smell breakfast being cooked and heard my grandmother talking to someone while making breakfast. I ran to her, hugging and kissing her

and my grandfather, who was sitting down by the kitchen window drinking his coffee. I loved being with my grandparents because they were fun and they spoiled Stefano and me, showing us real love.

My grandparents were both religious but my grandfather, well, I think he was a closet gangster (I will explain later in the book). My grandfather was a light-skinned Puerto Rican man in his mid-fifties or early sixties; this 5'9"(I'm guessing because I was too little, and as a child everyone is a giant) 190-pound man, who was like a father to me every time my mother or father dumped me at their house, never seeing them for months or sometimes for a year at a time.

This old man every night would put me to sleep with a Cookie Monster hand puppet using a different voices every time, but in Spanish, or some nights he would tell me stories, or we'd just sit by the window quietly drinking Spanish style hot cocoa with these Spanish white hard crackers when dunked in the cocoa would become so soft it would breakaway and fall into your cup. My grandfather was a pastry maker and a cook and worked in a breakfast and lunch Cuchifrito spot. As for my grandmother, she was a home pastry maker and cook also; she would make bread pudding, rice pudding, flan (a sweet custard), special ordered cakes; she also made exotic drinks like Mavi (a Spanish cold drink), fresh coconut juice, and other refreshing drinks. I was hooked with the Mavi because it was sweet but not too sweet and left me refreshed. and every time my grandmother made Mavi, she would make a gallon for me, which I would devour within a day or two.

My grandmother had a lot of customers, even some cops. As for my brother and me, well, we were in Heaven because it was turning into the fall season and that's when she started the holiday baking and selling. We were like fat, greedy little pigs with all the pastries and other food and drinks we could eat; in my grandparent's apartment we were at peace.

My grandmother was in her mid-sixties, with deep brown skin, who was deeply religious, and every night before my brother and I would go to bed, we would kneel beside her and a say The Padre Nuestro (The Our Father), then she'd tuck us in; or me, when my mother decided to leave me behind, and we'd fall to sleep.

When my mother abandoned me at my grandparents, I really did not care because I was with people who absolutely loved me, kept me safe, and was at peace with myself. Living with my grandmother was fun; she would teach me how to cook many different kinds of breakfasts, lunches, and dinners, she even taught me how to sew with the foot pedal sewing machine and by hand, which I can still do. Sometimes I would help her make all kinds of pastries and refreshing drinks, like Tamarindo (homemade Tamarind juice), coconut juices, Mavi, and other exotic drinks.

My mother had not abandoned me yet, and as days turned into weeks with nothing but fun, Gus started to appear trying to get forgiveness from my mother. When my mother gave in, he arrived at my grandparents' apartment, picked us up, and took us to Coney Island. When we arrived, my brother and I were having fun with the video games and other mechanical games but my main thirst was wanting to get on the rides. After we ate, Gus put my brother and me on many rides, but on the rides my brother Stefano couldn't get on, I was allowed to go but those rides made me swallow my heart and squeeze my butt cheeks tight out of fear, like the Spook-A-Rama. My mother and I got on it, and I thought I was going to die of a heart attack throughout the ride. I closed my eyes until the ride ended and got off with shaky legs and a racing heart. It is funny now but when in the Spook-A-Rama, I was at the point of bolting from the two-sitter ride but seeing a monster pop out, well that was when my eyes closed shut. To make my heart beat much faster, I challenged myself to get on the Dante's Inferno ride, another scary ride but this one wasn't as scary; the ride I was past by some rooms where people were getting killed, then some fucking bitch came out of the darkness and scared the hell out of all the riders. Boy, I thought I was going to faint and shit on myself. When the ride ended, I was more mad than scared (though, as I am writing this part, I am laughing uncontrollably), but all in all, I had fun, and if you think I didn't scream a little when that motherfucker scared all the riders, than you're wrong.

We walked around Coney Island sightseeing until we saw the Disco Inferno ride. My mother asked if I wanted to get on with Stefano, and I excitedly answered, "YES!" While waiting for the ride to end, I could see the excitement on everyone's faces as the ride started spinning frontward and

then backwards, with music playing loudly and the bass of the disco music so deep it could be felt on your chest like a secondary heartbeat.

I was excited, and when the ride stopped and they started boarding, my brother and I were passed through; Stefano boarded first, then me, then everyone else, and when everyone was safely secured, the D.J. asked everyone if they were ready and everyone screamed "Yeah!" The ride started forward slowly with a different song playing, it was "Ring My Bell," and as the ride started to go faster and faster, I noticed my brother was sliding away from me. I reached out and grabbed him by the belt buckle and pulled him closer to me. I decided to let him go when I thought he was safe but then he slid again. I reached out for his belt buckle but it ripped and he slid farther, almost on the verge of hanging on to the rail of the ride. I instinctively leaned towards him and grabbed him by the waistband of his pants. I held on to him for dear life because if he were to slip out, he would land where the machinery was holding the spinning ride and get mangled to death. We were still in forward mode but when the ride slowed to a stop, it would start to rotate backwards. I was about to yell to my mother that Stefano was going to fall off, but I told my brother, "Hold on to the pole, I will hold you too," because I really didn't want to spoil everyone's fun even my own.

After the ride was over, we got off the ride and it was when the fear of what happened and what could of happen hit me. I walked with shaky legs and my heart was beating hard in my chest; yet, I didn't tell anyone (even to this day no knows but my brother; there are nights I have nightmares of what could have happened if my hand missed his pants waistline). With all these emotion running through me, the enjoyment of the Disco Infernal quickly evaporated.

· · ·

As a child, I never believed in ghosts and the supernatural or understood it. Even with my first experiences, I would go to church on Sundays whenever I would stay with my grandparents, like on this particular Sunday.

My mother had abandoned me with my grandparents for the summer and it was early evening and my grandfather was driving, heading to church with

my grandmother and me. He was driving down Grand Concourse Avenue in The Bronx, a mile or so from Clay Avenue, and I was watching the cars pass my grandfather's; I was pretending my grandfather was racing and winning, but there was one car side by side with my grandfather's car. When I looked at the bottom of the car, in the mid-section of the car, I saw it was on fire. At first, I blinked a couple times thinking it might be an hallucination, but it wasn't. I tapped on my grandmother's shoulder and told her in Spanish hat the car I was pointing at was on fire. She looked but replied that there wasn't a fire. I could see the fire was still there but spreading more underneath. I told her again and she looked but responded that if I kept on lying she was going to spank me. I sat quiet but as I watched the car speed ahead of us, the fire was still spreading, I kept on looking at the burning car until it disappeared from view.

We finally arrived at 1275 Grand Concourse Seventh-Day Adventist Church, on the corner of Grand Concourse and East 169th. St. My grandfather had parked in front of this church that had big brass doors and handles. I was the first one out of the car, and ran up the three steps to the church's door and put a hand on the brass door handles to open it, but the door handle painfully shocked me. I quickly let go and tried it again, and after four more tries of the same shocking bolt of electricity, I stopped my attempts and watched some male churchgoer head straight for the door. I didn't say anything to him because I wanted to see if the guy would get shocked, but when he grabbed the door handles and opened the doors, nothing happened to him. I waited for the door to close then grabbed the door handles again, and it again painfully shocked me, preventing me from even holding the handles. After a couple more tries with the same results, I stopped my attempts and waited for my grandparents to open the door and get shocked, but they didn't; my grandmother opened the door without consequences.

In entering the church, it had a dark demeanor to it, with the dim lights like a house in a horror movie. I felt like the church did not want me there and the feeling grew stronger when we picked a bench near the entrance and the bathroom. As we sat down, I started to feel sick—my stomach started to hurt and it bubbled up inside. I excused myself and told my grandfather where I was going. I walked/ran to the bathroom with my stomach hurting more and

more. I pushed through the bathroom door and into a stall. I quickly undid my pants and pulled them down some of the way because I knew I wouldn't make it and just before my butt cheeks touched the bathroom seat, watery feces shot out, and on sitting down, I vomited all over myself.

I vomited all over my chest, stomach, thighs, groin, and inside my underwear and pants. I started to cry like a little baby. I felt so ashamed and humiliated. It felt like hours before my grandfather came to the bathroom, though it was more like a few minutes, and when he saw what had happened to me, he helped clean me up as much as possible, then took me out of the bathroom and church and into the car then left, stating he was going to get my grandmother and go home.

Chapter 3

Home and Family

"I need to think,
Thinking is,
What's killing you"
Cortana of Halo's "Forward Unto Dawn"

I think about these things I am confessing and all the other stuff I am about to reveal and wonder how the fuck I'm still alive. There are times I wish my life was just a dream but the haunts in my head and the screams remind me everything in my life is real and my inner demons are still coming for me.

I will be discussing different eras of my youth, bringing them together as one. This is the era of my sexuality and my many sexual explorations. It was my sixth birthday, and I was hanging out with my eight-year-old male cousin, Chuweto, and we were in the basement where my birthday was being celebrated. Chuweto had asked me to follow him into the backyard of the building, which was connected to a roll of five-story buildings. On the way he explained we were going to play a game of practice. Practice was a game he invented where it was for two players only; he explained it was when two people were going to do fresh things (have sex) and prepare us for sexual play with girls, something I didn't know about—yet.

I followed him into a section in the backyard that led to stairs going farther down to a locked basement where a cemented partition was above us, and it was what covered us completely from anyone looking out the window and catching us. He faced me and pulled his pants and underwear down to his ankles, then he undid my zipper and pants, grabbed me from behind, and pulled us closely so he could rub his harden little penis with mine, which was starting to harden itself. Seeing that I was getting excited, he kissed me on the lips and was teaching me how to French kiss. I was starting to get the hang of French kissing, so we continued to sword fight (rubbing dicks) in tune with each other's humping and kissing. He stopped and asked me to suck his dick, I went on my knees, and he showed me how to suck his penis, and it was like I got possessed I started kissing, licking, rubbing and sucking on his dick and balls, making us go into a lustful mode with his moaning and his passionate lustful whisper saying, "Yes, Macho, suck it like that, oohhhh my dick is yours, I love you." My little body was enflamed with sexual lust, and I continued to rubbed his dick and balls all over my face and lips, he then all of a sudden grabbed me from behind my head, and started humping my mouth, he held my head hard onto his groin as he started ejaculating, he's legs were trembling uncontrollably and when he got control of himself, he stood me up and we started French kissing again.

I did not know the feeling of ejaculating but he wanted more, so while we were French kissing, I masturbate him like he showed me and make him cum, then he asked to fuck me in the ass and I let him, he ejaculated quickly but didn't stop until a couple of more times of ejaculating, then he stopped, began getting dressed. Seeing what he was doing I asked him "How about me?" touching my penis. He responded, "Later," and helped me to get dressed and returned to my sixth-year birthday party.

On another sexual incident, my parents, brother, and I were invited to a party, and Stefano and I were sent into a room with some kids; there were three girls ages nine, eight, and six and one boy aged five. My cousins that I didn't know at that time, the eldest girl locked the door to the room and introduced themselves, except the boy, who was sleeping. Stefano had fallen asleep right beside him too.

Sex started to become a part of my life and by the time I turned eight years old, I was satisfying Chewito in every way he wanted, and with the girls, well in school. When my parents, Stefano, and I moved to Gun Hill Road, I was in school one day eating lunch like a savage, chewing with my mouth open and closing it like a shark, basically enjoying myself in my own pretend world, when I was interrupted by a dark brown-skinned girl of about my age; she approached and asked if I could stop eating like that. I did. She then started talking about this and that and then asked where I lived, how far from school, how did I get to school, and so on. I answered every single one. She finished by asking me if I could walk her home I nodded.

When the school bell rang ending the day, I went to where Monica and I agreed to meet up, then preceded to walk six blocks, the opposite way from where I lived. She then pointed at the building where there were six round pillars that connected other buildings. Because of the pillars, no one from above could see what was going on down below. We were in front of the building, and Monica asked me to follow her to the second pillar, away from prying eyes, and she lifted her dress revealing her privates with no panties, she then asked me to suck her pussy, and I did. I started sucked on that pussy like I was sucking on Chewito's dick. She stopped me and said to follow her into a building. We walked between the front division of the alley of the connected buildings, and she pointed to a building ahead of us and as we headed to the building and greeted some fourteen-year-old Spanish boy. I knew that she had sex with him by the way they greeted each other.

We entered the apartment building she pointed at and walked up a couple flights of stairs when we were stopped by an old dark-skinned old lady who was screaming at the girl, "Get out of the building! I know what you going to do; get out!"

We turned around and walked down to the lobby floor, where she laid on the ground, lifted her skirt and opened her legs. I laid between her legs and started sucking everything that was connected to her pussy, she then stopped me and asked me to stick my dick in her. I pulled my pants and underwear down to my ankles, and was thinking that we were laying right in front of the building's entrance having sex, taking a chance of getting caught; it made me even more excited and hornier. When I stuck my little penis in her, I could

tell that it wasn't making her feel like my tongue and lips did, it must of turn her off because she said that we needed to hurry up and get dress, we got up and by the time I finished fixing myself, she had gone. I walked by where the Spanish teen boy was hanging out, and he too was gone. I left the area, knowing that looking for her would be a waste of time.

A couple days later, it was an early school morning and all the kids were in the schoolyard waiting for the bell to ring so we all could go in and begin the school day. A school announcement was blaring, announcing that a girl from the school was hit by a car getting a ball from the street. The girl was playing with her friends when she was struck.

By the time school ended, I found out who it was—it was the girl whose pussy I had sucked. Weeks had passed before I finally saw her again and she was playing outside with some neighborhood friends. Monica was playing in the middle of the street, and some of her friends were running behind her trying to stop her from going towards traffic. I walked up to her and she stopped but she was acting weird and saying, "I want to get hit by a car again, it felt good." I even chased after her when she started running towards approaching vehicles, which they managed to swerve away avoiding her. A couple of us chased her again, and managed to grab and escort her to her house, which was located behind the block where I lived.

The last time I saw her was on a cold winter night I was coming from the store on the corner of my street and she called out my name. I turned around and she ran to me, and we stood facing each other quietly, then we started French kissing slowly and though the kiss was passionate, it didn't have any sexual overtone to it and after a minute or two of kissing, we stopped, then I watched her run towards her block, never seeing her again.

(Note: she was being sexually abused and her form of escape was sex and trying to commit suicide because her screams for help were being ignored.)

. . .

Life was corrupting me, sending the corrupted children to stain my soul and it was working. Early one evening my uncle Jay, Chewito's father, asked my

mother if she wanted to go to the movie theater and chill. She answered yes, and later on that day, Jay came and picked up my mother, Stefano, and myself and took us to the movie theater with Chewito. Mama (Chewy's older sister) and Marina, their mother.

We all went to see a horror movie, one of my uncle's favorite things to watch, and martial art movies like The Five Deadly Venoms, which is an impressive film. Anyway, we all sat in one row—Stefano was sitting next to my mother, Mama, Chewy, and then me. I was into whatever movie was playing because I too loved horror movies, even though some of them scared me half to death, when suddenly, I felt a hand creeping towards my privates and started fondling my quickly erected penis and balls, I positioned myself more comfortably so Chewito could continue playing with my privates. He stated to my mother, "Titi, Macho and I need to use the bathroom," and not looking at us, granted us permission to go. Chewito and I raced into the bathroom because in reality we really had to go; once there we pissed on all four floor urinals, then around the floor, we then went in one of the four bathroom stalls.

The bathroom stall was much bigger, made for the handicap. We first took some toilet paper from the slot, wet it in one of the four bathroom sinks, and threw them up onto the ceiling. After this, Chewito and I went back into the big stall, locked it, and we started French kissing each other lustfully. We stopped and helped each other with shedding all our clothes off; once naked we started with the sword fighting and the dick humping, I became lost with his flesh, I lick and kissed every section of his neck, going down to his chest, then onto each nipple, I continued down to his belly button and hungrily started sucking on his dick, I made him shoot blanks twice back to back, he then stopped me, positioned himself by toilet bowl, and put one leg on the toilet sit and told me to suck his penis and his balls. I did. I licked and sucked on his dick and balls making him cum many times, then he helped me up and told me he wanted to fuck me in the ass, so I let him, we first did it on the floor on our clothes, then he fucked me with one leg on the toilet seat and then with both legs down but with me standing with my ass up and my upper body bent forward, so he could penetrate me deeper.

We were fucking hardcore and didn't pay attention to anyone coming or going or if anyone did come to use the bathroom, we didn't even know how long we were in the bathroom, and as time passed us by, we continued to have sex, we didn't stop until we heard a knock on the bathroom door and someone screaming, "What the fuck are you two doing there, fucking each other?" It was Chewito's mother and she scared us so bad we must have broken the world's record in getting dressed the fastest. Chewito responded, "We're not faggots."

With that, we didn't hear his mother calling out for us any longer, and finished fixing ourselves properly, and before we left the bathroom, we took a chance and French kissed passionately for a minute or so, then we stopped and left.

We sat back in our places and I noticed the movie was almost finished, in the meanwhile, I daydreamed of how Chewy fell on his knees, when I made cum or how he fingered me and jerked me off, then we made each other cum at the same time, while masturbating each other. I realized the movie was over when Chewy started punching me on my chest, making me wince in pain. I rubbed on my chest breaking me out of my sexual daydream.

We all left the theater, and my uncle asked his wife what was going on with us in the bathroom. She responded "Nothing," but I told him Chewy and I were throwing toilet paper at the ceiling, and he just smiled, with no inkling of what really happened.

Chewy and I always found a way to have sex, either when he visited me or when I would visit him, and we took all kinds of risks getting caught. I remember one day, before Gun Hill Road, I lived on 1015 Boynton Avenue between Bruckner Blvd. and Watson Avenue with my mother, Gus, and my little brother, and my uncle Jay lived a floor below us on the third floor.

It was a hot summer day and school was out. I asked my mother if I could go out and play and she answered "yes," but first I had to go to the store for her. I lived on the fourth floor, and on leaving the apartment, I walked farther down the hallway to press the button for the elevator of the building. When it arrived, I opened the door and when I saw who it was I quickly entered and Chewito and I started French kissing passionately and whispering to one another, "I love you." We stopped kissing and he turned me around and started to dry humping on the ass area (having pretend sex with our clothes on). We

stopped when we reached the lobby floor and left the building; then we turn towards the corner of Bruckner Blvd. where two grocery stores and a number place was located, but instead of entering the store, Chewito stopped me and asked, "Macho, do you want to finish what we started?" I replied, "Hell yeah."

We then walked to the middle of the block where there was a ramp that led to the drawbridge and a bunch of fenced backyard alley ways that were part of the buildings that led all the way up in front of us and down the block, we walked farther in the alley behind the first building and away from street view. I pulled my shorts and underwear down to my ankles, then bent halfway down forward and waited for Chuweto to penetrate me. Once in, he started humping me hard but I didn't care and on the third time of him ejaculating, we heard some lady scream down at us from the hallway lobby of the second floor, "Oye que ustedes estan haciendo," (what are y'all doing?) Chewito quickly abandoned me, dressing quickly because he had his pants and under-wear midway. I didn't have that luck, once my clothes was halfway on, I too ran out of the alley way, and by the time I reach the way Chewy and I came through, I had managed to fix myself completely, almost falling in the process, I ran towards the first store on the corner, scared that the lady would find me and force me to take her to my parents and tell them what I did. I snuck into the store getting my mother's items little by little and when I noticed no one was coming for me, I paid for my items and ran as fast as I could back home.

I got off the elevator and Chewy was waiting by the steps and before I en-tered the crib, we French kissed quickly and I went in. I gave my mother the store items, then I excused myself to the bathroom, where I had gotten naked and started masturbating. I even played with my rectum making me ejaculated twice; once finished, I got dressed and went to my mother and helped her in the kitchen.

The thing between Chewy and me wasn't love—well, on my part, it wasn't. What I loved about it was not only the sex but because we weren't supposed to be doing "fresh things," (male to male sex play) and my mother and grandparents would constantly be telling me they disapproved of me hanging out with Chewy because he was a bad influence on me, but in reality, what they didn't know was that we were a bad influence on each other and any kid in our surroundings.

If it weren't the sex with Chewy, we would always get beat downs by our parents for really being bad, where Chewy and I developed a habit of smacking and punching ourselves on our faces, we would even kneel on the floor and with some force push ourselves forward slamming our foreheads onto the ground.

One day on a family gathering, my parents had moved from Bruckner Blvd. to somewhere on Gun Hill Road in the Bronx and I don't know what the occasion was but Jay's crib was packed with aunts, uncles, cousins of all ages, and my grandparents, Jay had showed everyone what Chewy had done to the shower curtains. I snuck to the bathroom and took a look, the shower curtains were almost burnt completely off their hook.

The adults told all the young kids to get out of their way and stop being nosey and go play. It was Chewy, three other male cousins, and me who all went into the hallway that led in and out of the apartment and Chewy and I had somehow influenced the three boys to kneel in front of the hallway floor and start banging our heads onto the wall; and after we all began banging our heads a couple times hard on the wall, someone in the adult group screamed at us to "stop that fucking shit before I beat y'all's asses!"

We didn't stop. I intensified my head banging on the wall, and noticed my vision was darkening; it was like someone else was doing what I was doing but I was just watching it happen, somehow, we all turned on our knees, facing the apartment door and in unison continued banging our heads but onto the floor. I don't remember how long we continued with this behavior but it was broken when one of the adults threw a bucket of cold water on us. We stopped and my vision became normal, I saw that we all got drenched.

I don't know why we did that but it was becoming bad habit for me; I would spend the day smacking, punching myself and slamming my head either on the wall or the floor. When my grandmother witnessed me doing this, she took me to church where she prayed, and after she finished, she asked me to repeat a prayer as she said it; it didn't work; it was getting worse, so my grandmother took me to the pastor of her church, where he prayed over me for some time and, no lie, it stopped; never to reoccur again.

Chapter 4

Home and Family

"I entered the valley of Evil, and Evil slowly consumes me."

Living on Gun Hill Road was difficult in the beginning for me because I didn't have Chewy around for sex or any of my friends to play with. When my parents, Stefano, and I moved to Southern Boulevard, I started going through changes, like me becoming obsessed with picking my nose and sticking the soft or harden mucus everywhere inside my clothes or wherever I could put it.

Like, when I would go to school, I would wear a favorite sweater and, on the inside, I had it filled with hardened mucus; as the day passed, I would stick the soft or hardened mucus on doorknobs, underneath my desk, chairs, walls, etc., anywhere I could stick it and not get caught.

Then I became the class clown, trying to make everyone laugh, hiding the sadness in me, and also having an older Black kid sexually bully me. It was some thirteen-year-old Black kid in my class who was taller and heavier than me; he would wait until I used the bathroom then write "Dick and Ass" where my name, the classroom's subject, and the classroom's number would be in my notebook. At first, I didn't know who it was until one day I felt someone in class staring at me. I turned around and noticed the Black kid sitting right behind

me staring at me with a thirst in his eyes; the way he was staring made me scared because I knew he was going to do something sexual to me. Here's the crazy shit about the situation: my desk was located right next to the teacher's desk and she never saw him do anything, and I was scared to tell the teacher because I instinctively knew it would make matters worse. I also knew he was going to catch me by myself one day and force himself on me. I was scared to go to school, and for some reason did not want to tell my mother.

He was becoming more daring in class with leaving sexual messages in my notebook, and when I glanced at him, seeing an evil smile as he touched himself, I knew he was going to make his move soon. But then one day, he stopped showing up at school. I couldn't believe it, though on the first of three days of him not showing up, I was scared because I knew if he showed up, he would force himself on me and probably hurt me but he never showed up.

(Remember with what I'm about to say: "When evil strikes, it blinds everyone around you." Throughout my story, I will show you how my statement is true.)

I became friends with some older kid in my class who defended me when I almost got beat up by some older kid for stealing his chocolate candy bar. I was surprised and happy to know he lived near me. Sometimes after school, instead of going to my mother's pizza shop, I would walk with Eddy home, which was a farther distance then my mother's job; from school to my house was like nine or ten blocks, and from my school to mother's job, it was more or less like three or four blocks.

We talked shit and made fun of about everything or anyone, then he dared me to follow him to some high school's yards fence with a cemented base and follow him from one side of the fence to the other end where it would be higher and the drop to the sidewalk was ten feet down or more, but to me, it felt like I was going to jump off a cliff. Eddy instructed me, as I walked sideways with him, to make sure I grabbed the fence securely and when we get to the other end, to watch how he fell on his feet, so I wouldn't break my ankles.

We reached the other end and I watched Eddy jump down. I was scared when I looked down, because it looked like a long way down, especially for my small size. He, on the other hand, was taller than me. My stomach was

developing butterflies making my heart race. I closed my eyes, took a deep breath, opened my eyes, and let the air out, then I jumped like Eddy, and landed on the balls of my feet with my knees bent going with the drop and stopping myself from falling on my ass.

Eddy was proud and he showed it by giving me a pound and a hug. We then continued our walk home and he started talking about girls and how he would kiss them. I never talked to him about girls and I was realizing I had developed something inside of me for him sexually. One school day, we managed to go to the bathroom together, and I told him I wanted to take a shit but it was a lie. I entered a bathroom stall and he sat on a sink facing me. I pulled my pants and underwear down to my knees, letting him see my little flaccid penis, then turned around and bent down pretending to clean the toilet seat, to let him see my fat ass, then I sat down. I looked at him and told him I would like to suck his dick and balls and let him fuck me in the ass. He looked at me and responded that he didn't do that with boys, just girls.

Then the conversation was interrupted by a teacher yelling into the bathroom, "Hurry up and use the bathroom! Stop playing in there!"

Eddy answered we were using the bathroom, and the teacher left it at that.

When he left the bathroom, I got up and fixed myself, and as I was leaving the bathroom stall, I saw some Black kid in the stall next to me with his pants and underwear down tohis ankles. His back was towards me exposing fat round butt cheeks. I made a sound to get his attention to see if we could get something sexual between us, but when he turned around and I saw his face, I got scared. He had down syndrome, but I didn't know that at that time, all I saw was a Black kid my age looking like the character of Jason Voorhees of the Friday the 13th movies when Jason was a child.

I quickly fixed myself and ran out of the bathroom and into my classroom. After school was over, Eddy and I walked home together and he dared me again to follow him and climb on the cemented fence and jump off. I told him no but he wouldn't take no for an answer. He threatened me with, "If you don't do what I say, I'll tell everyone in school you wanted to suck on my dick and balls." That made me change my mind, so I followed him on the fence's edge, but in the back of my mind I was thinking how the school kids would make

fun of me if they found out I liked to have sex with boys. I was scared and already knew we would stop hanging out with one other after today. I followed him to the edge of the fence and when we reached the corner of the fence, I looked down and my stomach began fluttering with butterflies by how high the jump down was. Even though I'd jumped it before, it still looked like I was jumping off the Empire State Building.

I was waiting for him to jump first, when he stated, "Let's go back the way we came." I didn't respond but followed him happily. We took about four sideways steps to our destination, when something in the yard but in the distance caught my eye and it was running towards us; it was a fucking grown German Shepard. My heart froze and I was more than terrified. I screamed out, "Dog!" and Eddy looked at the dog as it ran toward us and we both knew once the dog reached the fence, it would go for our fingers. He jumped almost landing on his ass and I followed right behind him, but landed a little wrong not breaking anything but falling on my ass, sending a painful vibration throughout my body. I looked up at the dog who was barking violently and I caught a flashback of when I was living in the Grand Concourse area when I was seven.

I went to hang out with some neighborhood kids and we went behind our building to where some older kid was doing something behind the back corner of a building, we all had to climb a two-foot embankment to reach the older kid. I didn't know the kid but I was curious to see what he was doing, and that was a big mistake. As I climbed the embankment and started walking toward the kid, I realized he was feeding an adult German Shepard, and when I greeted him, he responded, "Bye," and that moment the dog ran towards me. I tried to run the way I came from but the dog was there in an instant, jumping on me, knocking me off the embankment, and knocking me unconscious.

When I awoke, all the kids, the dog, and the owner were gone. I ran out into the front of the building to where my mother was hanging out by her car, crying hysterically and trying to explain to her what happened. After my mother finally calmed me down, I told her everything, she began checking me over and stated we had to go to the hospital because there was blood coming out from my upper inner thigh by my ball area.

Some of the adults who were hanging outside in earshot went into the alleyway which led to the back of the building to look for the dog. I saw one of the kids that was there coming out of the building next to mine and I pointed at him, letting my mother know he was there. Before my mom put me in the car, I could see some lady who was standing next to us listening and looking at my mother and I interact, the lady seeing me pointing at the kid, went and confronted the boy.

In the hospital, the doctor helped me take my pants off, then spread my legs and looked at the wound. I was watching what the doctor was doing and noticed the wound had a very deep hole. While he was cleaning and stitching up the wound, he was telling me I was lucky because the dog could've bitten off my groin. As I was about to get off the hospital bed and put my pants back on, the doctor stopped me and looked at my back side and stated I had another deep dog bite on my right buttock. After the doctor finished with the wound, I went home.

Suddenly, I was interrupted from my flashback by Eddy, asking me if I was okay. I nodded, slowly realizing I was still looking up to where the dog was barking savagely down at us. We walked in silence towards our building, and I was thinking about how the people in the neighborhood came together, found the dog, and called the cops. We found out that the dog was a stray and when the cops came for the dog, it became aggressive, so it had to be put down.

Eddy and I arrived at our building—he went his way, and I went mine and said nothing to one another and never saw each other again, even in school.

But in school, being in Special Ed., I had many crazy adventures. One day I was eating in the lunchroom, and after I finished, I had to urinate badly. I went quickly into the lunchroom's boys' bathroom, and upon entering, I noticed five boys surrounding one bathroom stall. Out of curiosity, I went to see what they all were all looking at and to my surprise, it was a girl, sitting on the toilet seat taking a piss. I saw her vagina and the urine coming down. I wasn't sexually aroused but curious because I never saw a girl take a piss, and I already knew that girls didn't have horizontal vaginas like some of the kids in school were saying, claiming to had seen one. Now the boys in the bathroom looking at the girl were asking each other what the hell she was

doing in the boys' bathroom. It wasn't until one boy asked her. "Hey, do you know where you are?"

She responded, "Yes, the girls' bathroom."

We all said no unison. "No, you're not, you're in the boys' bathroom."

I could see her demeanor turn to fear, then some other boy ordered us to leave her alone. We did, then the same boy told another boy to get a teacher quickly and the boy ran out of the bathroom fast but the rest of us stood looking at her. After she managed to fix herself properly, it didn't take long for a female and male teacher to run into the bathroom and remove all the boys, myself included, out of the bathroom.

We waited outside the bathroom for the teachers to escort the girl out and find out what happened, but were told by the male teacher who was now standing outside of the boys' bathroom that the girl had forgotten her glasses at home, and made it difficult to see anything, then the teacher left to catch up with the female teacher and the little girl.

I'm not going to lie, the boy who gave us the order saved that girl from something bad happening to her. You see, I wasn't sexually aroused but curious, but in some of the boys' expression and physical demeanor, I could see it wasn't that of saving the girl, they were going to fuck her, and because I loved sex, I would have joined them too.

· · ·

Time passed, and in school, we had a new girl in class and every day she would pull down the back of her pants and panties, exposing her creamy round buttocks. She would have all the class laughing, but with the boys, she had all of them in heat; some would touch themselves as they were sitting in their seats and others would go to the closet to jerk off quickly, while others exposed themselves to her; it got to the point she was letting some of the boys fuck her in the ass in the classroom closet.

This sexual activity was being done with the teacher being distracted with either her back to us while writing assignments for us to complete in class or with one of the boys distracting her. While the sexual activity was happening,

there were two girls being bullied, a long blond haired Spanish girl of about nine, who had half an arm amputated, making some of the kids tease her with, "Everybody, do you know the real reason why she lost half of arm? It was because she was masturbating and when she came, her pussy bit her arm off," making the little girl shed tears The kids in class had many fucked up reasons why she had her arm amputated, making her cry all the time. It had gotten so bad she never came back to school.

As for the second girl being bullied, some Black kid and I had a girl sit between us and would each take turns slapping her glasses off from her face and dirtying them. We both threatened her that if she told on us, we would make it even worse for her. Though she never told on us, the bullying did get worse. We would tell her she was ugly, a disgusting unwanted human being, then, we changed our tactics by forcing her to eat notebook paper and a lot of it too. I was already thinking of making her do something sexual to me and I knew if I did something sexual to her, the Black kid would join also but on the next school day, she didn't come and she never returned to the school.

Since I was in a Special Education class, I had to see a guidance counselor who would ask me all kinds of uninteresting questions or asked me to take an inkblot test "Rorschach Therapy" and tell him what I saw within the picture cards with the different black shapes. I looked at him as he was explaining the inkblot test, but in my mind, I was saying, What the hell is wrong with this dude? I always felt uncomfortable seeing the guidance counselor with all the personal questions being asked in different ways, and the way he was observing me, I realized then what it was he wanted to hear, so I looked at the card and told him the boy was sad over a dead butterfly and other misleading imaginations I could create. I couldn't tell him the vicious beatdowns by both my mother and stepfather, and after a few sessions, he terminated our meetings.

· · ·

My mother then started to take me to an outpatient facility to see a therapist. On the way there, I was thinking about my day in my classroom where we had watched a movie called Rocky with Sylvester Stallone. I was telling my mother

about the movie and how I wished they'd make a couple parts to Rocky, and she responded, "How about I punch you in the face and kick your ass?" With that, I stayed quiet all the way to therapy. She took all the fun out of me. I was hurt and was looking out the window feeling really lonely (To this day, I do not know why I was going to therapy).

· · ·

The therapy sessions ended abruptly when the summer vacation arrived. I couldn't wait because I wanted to hang out in the pizza shop and help my mother and my uncle Jay with whatever I could. The other reason I loved going to the pizza spot, was because of all the free pizzas and beef patties I could eat.

At my mother's job, I would help in wiping the small round tables with two sitting stools on each side or any other minor chores, and when their wasn't anything to really do, I would help babysit my little brother, Stefano. My mother would allow us to go through the back of the shop and play in the backyard of the business parking lot. My mother's business was also connected to other stores and they too had access to the lot that was secured with a chained and lock. The parking lot had two exit or entrances at both ends with secure gates and the only way in and out of the lot was either you own or work in one of the businesses having the keys or climbed over the fence.

Early one summer afternoon, my brother and I were allowed to play in the back and were having fun playing tag, then we found a discarded empty box that was able to conceal us both, and used the box to play pirates; through the little holes of the box, I was able to turn on each side without touching the box's interior and see my surroundings.

The box was situated a couple feet from my mother's job and I decided to turn and look at the other end of the parking lot. I saw a door swing open from one of the stores and froze in pure terror. I saw a guy let a medium sized Pit Bull loose. I slowly turned around and wrapped myself around my brother tightly and whispered in his ear, "Don't move; some one let a big dog out and if we move it will bite us." Stefano didn't move or say a word but I was so

scared I started to cry quietly. The dog got near the box and started sniffing around the box. I held my sobs in but the tears were still flowing down my face. The dog took a piss on the box and it kept on sniffing, then I heard a whistle and the dog ran towards the whistler. I let go of Stefano and looked through the hole of the box, seeing the dog go in the store. I was relieved but it left me drenched in sweat and tears. I burst out of the box, grabbed my little brother by the hand, and walked/ran into the pizza shop, never to play back there ever again.

• • •

Summer was moving forward and it was busy at the pizza shop, so my mother left me, an eight year old, home alone with Stefano and all we did was watch television and play around. We stopped playing around late noon so I could make something to eat for the both of us. Afterwards we went into the living room where Stefano, the rats, and I slept on a large sofa, and in the middle of the living room was a wooden coffee table with a glass top. We decided to run around the coffee table and play tag; we were doing fine until Stefano slipped, hitting the glass with one hand and breaking the glass. He didn't get injured but we were terrified because that was definitely an ass whipping by my mother. I tried to hide the evidence by folding the laundry and putting it in a way that it would hide the missing glass. We then sat in the kitchen chairs by the table quietly and watched television. I didn't know about my brother, but I was hoping and praying she didn't beat my ass.

When my mother arrived late that night, she went straight into the bathroom, came out, approached the coffee table, and picked up the folded clothes. When she saw the broken table glass, her demeanor changed to straight-out anger; she looked at me and my heart froze with fear, and asked, "Who the fuck broke the glass table?"

I answered in shuttering, fearful words, "I was folding the clothes and slipped on the table." I waited for her to come charging at me but she didn't; she turned around and went into her room.

. . .

I've mentioned the rats before, and boy those motherfuckers were bigger than an average Chihuahua—well, to me anyway; I was small and those bitches were big and they didn't care who was around at night when the lights were off. I remember one night sleeping on the sofa with Stefano when I was awakened by the rats chasing each other and running on top of us to get away from each other as they played with one another. On those nights, I would try to stay up as long as possible because I knew they could bite one of us while we were sleeping, and at other times, I would be awakened by the sounds of the rats eating underneath the big sofa Stefano and I slept on, and that was scary, hearing them crunching on the bones or crab shells.

My mother had taken us to her job the next day, where an old lady was waiting to pick up Stefano; she sometimes babysat my brother and me when my mother and Gus would go out. I liked her and was always happy to see her, but that day, she was there for Stefano.

As for me, well, I went across the street to where the Projects were to see if I could find some kids to play with. I found a boy about my age who was swimming in a parking lot overflowed with water from rain the night before. I asked the brown skinned Spanish kid with black curly hair if I could join him. He responded, "Yes," and I jumped in and swam with him. We played tag in the water for a while until some adult guy approached us and told us to get out of the water because it was dirty. We complied, and the kid told me there was a swimming pool in the middle of the Projects not far from where we were, and asked if I wanted to go; I answered "Yes."

We walked maybe half a block into the middle of the Projects, and I could see a secured fenced swimming pool. The kid explained there was an illegal opening in one of the side fences of the pool for those who wanted to sneak in and take a quick dip. It was a hot summer morning and all I wanted to do was refresh my body and keep it cool.

We entered the pool and quickly jumped in with sneakers and all, played swimming tag, then changed the game play to who could last the longest underneath the water. Afterwards, we took a break in one of the corners of the

pool and just talked kids' stuff and after we regain our second wind, we resumed chasing each other around the pool, jumping in and swimming to the other end. I purposely let him tag me sometimes because I was a better swimmer than he was and it was hard for him to catch me. We took another break, and as we went back to playing and swimming around, I didn't notice a heavy set Black kid entering the pool and watching us play until the Spanish kid announced his presence. The kid was about thirteen or fourteen years old; he approached us and asked if he could join us in the swimming games. We both answered "Yes," but the Spanish kid looked uncomfortable and a little scared. After a couple minutes playing with the Black teen, the Spanish kid left, and instead of playing with the Black kid and me, he got out and sat on one corner of the pool just watching us play.

I continued to play with the Black kid, and about five minutes into the game he started to get rough and dangerous; instead of playing tag, he would grab me and hold me under the water with both hands, and I would fight him to let me loose, but he'd grab me again and hold me underneath. I would fight his grip again, managing to escape. After a couple times of doing that, I asked him breathlessly to stop or I would leave. He agreed. I looked to see if the Spanish kid wanted to play but he was gone. I really paid no mind to his absence and continued to play with the Black kid, but he started to repeat his gameplay of pulling me under the water and holding me there. I managed to escape from his grip, but as I was going to tell him I was going to leave, he grabbed my head and hair and pushed it under and held his grip tightly so I wouldn't get out. I was starting to panic and struggle hard. I exhaled some of my air from lungs but they started to scream for more air.

Fighting was useless, so I calmed myself a little and thought of a way to get out of his grip, and it came. I put myself in a fetal position and with all my strength kicked him in the chest, using that momentum to swim backward as fast as I could and out of the pool and, being that my mother showed me how to swim, I swam to the other side very fast, making it very difficult for the teen to catch me. I grabbed the edge of the pool and used the rest of my strength to climb out. I was catching my breath and I looked at the Black kid, whom I could see swimming towards me. He kept asking me, "Why are you leaving?

Let's play," but the way he said it over and over and how he was looking at me, I felt a cold chill run down my spine. I ran towards the way I came in. As I was walking away, I could see the Black kid looking at me and inviting me to play with him. I kept going towards my mother's job, never going into or around the Projects again.

. . .

The summer days were hot and I didn't have any money to buy candy and I didn't want to ask my parents for any either, so one day I noticed The Number Spot on the same block as my mother's job but on the other side of the corner of the block, I walked in to be nosy and saw a big statue of Mother Mary with a large bowl filled with water. Inside the bowl was lots of coins. I developed a plan of waiting for The Number Spot to get somewhat packed with people and sneak by the statue and see if anyone would be watching me; if I saw that nobody was paying any attention to me, I would grab a handful of wet coins, put them in my shorts' pocket, then look around to see if I drew any attention. Seeing that no one was looking at me, I took another handful, put them in my pocket, and walked out the numbered spot slowly, then buying a lot of candy in the store next to it and whatever money was left, I would buy a toy.

I kept on hitting The Number Spot for more than a week, until one day, when I thought I was slick, escaping without getting caught earlier that day, my greed got the best of me and I went back to The Number Spot and positioned myself like I always did, right by the statue and the bowl. I looked around to see if anyone was paying attention. Seeing none, I grabbed a handful of wet coins, put them in my pocket, and started to walk out, when I was grabbed by the owner, who gently took me by the arm and escorted me to his office.

Once there, I was seated in a chair, and the owner asked, "Who are your parents, and where are they?" I didn't answer but burst into tears. He questioned me again about my parents, getting the same response from me. He left me in the office for more than fifteen minutes alone and when he returned,

he told me he was going to let me go, but to never return to the numbered spot. Still sobbing, I promised I wouldn't return and I kept that promise.

. . .

The summer had made me get into all sorts of trouble. I remember a couple days after The Number Spot incident, my mother had left my brother and me home alone again, but this time she told us to be ready for when she and Gus return, as they were going to take us to the beach.

When she left, I put on my beach attire and helped Stefano with his, we then sat in the kitchen and watched cartoon until there weren't any left on the television. I switched the channel to see what was on and I saw a Godzilla movie playing and left it there. I was a fan of Godzilla, and when the movie was about King Kong versus Godzilla and somehow King Kong drowned Godzilla (something impossible because it's how he travels but I didn't know that then). I started to sob that King Kong had won and my brother, seeing me cry, started to cheer for King Kong. I became so enraged that I picked up a pair of scissors and threw them at him, embedding itself in the front section of his foot where the ankle joint is located. He looked with fear and shock on his face and seeing that it was stuck in his foot, he didn't move but started to sob loudly. I, on the other hand, didn't feel any emotion but a calm within me, then I quickly snapped out of it and pulled the scissors out and wiped the blood from his wounded foot.

I sat him on the chair and put on whatever he wanted to watch. I would have done whatever he wanted as I was scared and worried what would happen to me when Gus and my mother returned. A couple hours passed before they arrived and Stefano started to sob harder and told my mother what happened. She turned to me and asked what happened.

I answered, "He got me mad."

My mother didn't beat on me but she gave me one of those looks. "Move, motherfucker, just move."

Gus told Stefano not to worry because the beach water would clean his wound and cure it. Well, for the rest of the day, I did my best to behave and avoid getting my ass whipped.

Living on the first-floor house in Gun Hill Road was good with not too many people. The owners had a backyard with a patch of grapevines, and they explained that no one was to go back there, as I would listen.

My mother was working late one evening and I was home alone with Stefano again, contemplating how to steal some grapes from the grapevines again; it was my ninth try and somehow, I couldn't figure out how the hell they knew someone was in the yard. Every time I try, they would wait until I either got next to the grapevines or picked a grape, then someone would scream "HEY!" scaring my soul out of my body.

But this night was different; I watched, planned, and hoped I would get away with getting some grapes. I opened the kitchen window and started to play loudly with my brother, then I slapped the ground of the yard with both hands making it sound like someone was in the yard, then I waited after a couple minutes, then turned the lights off in the kitchen and sat in the kitchen with Stefano looking out the yard. I whispered to Stefano to be quiet because I was going to steal some grapes for the both of us. He nodded with understanding. We stood quiet for a couple more minutes, then I got up and walked by the kitchen window and listened, hearing nothing. As quietly as I could, climbed out the window and ran under the shadow of a tree, then snuck into the grapevine patch and started to pick and pick until I filled two of my pants pockets, then checked if the coast was clear. Seeing that it was, I snuck back the way I came and shared the sourest grapes I'd ever tasted with Stefano.

· · ·

It was the beginning of August and I was still getting into trouble, and the ass whipping by my mother were getting worse. I remember one day I was outside walking around the neighborhood in my own world of make believe and on the corner of my block there was a red pole where, in case of an emergency, you could either press the red button for the fire department and the blue one, for the police department. I had the habit of pressing the fire department button and running away, then watching from afar when the fire trucks arrived.

What was the point of this? Not getting caught by anyone? One day, I thought I was slick and went outside to play as usual. As I was walking toward the emergency pole, I was observing my surrounding to see if anyone was outside. Not seeing any one, I went to the pole and pressed the fire department button. I waited for an operator to announce her presence and lied, telling her there was a fire, and just as she was going to ask me where the fire was located, I heard someone scream out to me to stop what I was doing. I looked down on the other side of the block and saw some dude in the middle of the block doing something with his car, looking at and walking towards me. I ran back to my crib hoping he didn't see where I went.

Everything was okay until five or ten minutes later when someone started knocking on the apartment door. My mother answered and was speaking to whomever was there; I couldn't see who it was and couldn't hear what was being spoken, all I heard was the end when my mother said, "Thank you," to whomever she was speaking to, and closed the door. She then went into the bathroom and came out with a plunger.

She rushed me with the plunger stick, striking me first on the side of my head, then she went crazy and began beating me with the plunger, hitting me over my upper body, but her main aim was catching me all over my head. As I tried to escape her assault, I would run from the living room, to the kitchen, to her bedroom, where I ran under her bed but that didn't stop her, because she grabbed the bottom of her bed, flipped and flung it to the other side of the room and continued assaulting me. I had managed to get up as she was beating and run out of the room but she was right there behind me, hitting me. One of the hits struck me on the back of my skull, making me become so dazed I couldn't block the two other hits on my skull.

As she was doing this shit to me, I would plead, screaming and crying, "Mommy, I'm sorry, I won't do it again," but my pleas didn't stop her. She continued beating me until she got tired, then she screamed at me to go take a fucking shower. The beating stopped in the living room and my body was throbbing painfully; it was worst while walking to the bathroom. Once in the shower, the water drops falling on my body were making the pain a burning stinging sensation. I was still crying and my sobs became worse when I passed

the palm of my hand on the back of the head and it came back bloody. I screamed out for my mother and she came. I showed her my bloody hand, she looked at the back of my head, and stated the beating was my fault for being bad, and when I went to school if anyone asked what happened to my head, to say I fell down.

After the shower I went to sleep, but the next day, going to school was extremely painful. Every step I made was like fire running throughout my body. When I arrived in my classroom and sat down, the pain exploding from my buttocks was so intense it felt like my mother was still beating me.

Doing the classroom assignment was very uncomfortable; I would clench my teeth in pain because my fingers were stiff from all the blocking I did. It was very painful to write, and when the teacher stood over me to check on my progress, I hid the pain, but when she put one of her hands on my shoulder, I pulled back wincing in pain. In pulling back, one of her fingers got caught at the neckline of my sweater and she sucked in air at what she saw.

The teacher told the aide she was escorting me to the principal's office. Once in the office, the principal and the teacher asked me to take my sweater off. I refused and the teacher then took off my sweater herself and they both sucked in air at seeing bruises all over my upper body. I was almost completely covered in black and blue in the stick's form. Luckily, they didn't ask me to lower my pants or they would have seen more bruises. The principal asked me what happened, and I told her I fell down playing. She responded that I didn't fall and to tell her the truth. I was nervous and started to cry those tears, which were hot, like they were burning my face. When the principal assured me it would be okay, they had to wait a few minutes because of my uncontrollable sobbing. I calmed down enough to tell the principal that it was my mother.

The principal asked the teacher to provide her with my home phone number and I thought I was going to die; my heart was beating ridiculously hard and fast, making it hard to breathe. I continued to sob uncontrollably, begging the principal while hiccupping not to call my mother, but she ignored me and called my mother. The principal introduced herself to my mother. I was so scared that I became deaf and didn't hear anything until the whole conversation was over, and the principal threatened my mother with, "If he ever

shows up to school with anymore bruises, I'll get the cops involve," then the principal hung the phone up.

At the mention of the police officers, my crying subsided a little, though I was thinking that the abuse would stop. When the school bell rang, ending the day, I walked home with butterflies in my stomach from fear of what might happen when I got home. I arrived and did not get a beating, but my mother threatened me with, "If you ever tell on family problems again, I will kill you."

Chapter 5

Home and Family

Before I continue further into my life, I have to take some time to calm down because what comes next will make my hatred and rage ignite like a nuclear bomb. My soul is damaged beyond repair with the tears of innocence lost, creating a personality that wants to see the world burn with everyone in it, and it stays on; its constant screaming in my head, so I could let it free and let it get revenge on everyone, regardless who you are.

There are times I look up into the sky and let my inner pain scream its anguish cries to the angels above to announce my presence to God, but what I see through this journey of mine is a solo one, and not even God can help me, or has he?

· · ·

We moved to Southern Boulevard and life there was boring. Summer had turned into autumn, and it was getting cold. Because of the change of the weather, I hardly saw any kids outside. In my neighborhood to one side was five to six six-story buildings connected to each other and across the street was a long endless stretch of a forested park with a stream which led somewhere.

One day, while playing by myself in the park, some older kid approached and told me to be careful because some time ago some kid was playing by the stream edge and was swept away in a flash flood and died. I took his advice and was careful not to play around the stream's edge. Being that it was a nice day, I decided to get my bike and ride on the paved path of the park's walkway. I happened to notice a mountain of piled fallen leaves from a distance, so I decided to ride as fast as I could and rush through the leaves and see them splash into the sky. Boy, was that a mistake. I was peddling fast feeling the cool breeze hitting my face and body, making me feel real good and picturing how the leaves would explode when I went through the pile. I entered the pile at full speed and my bike hit some obstruction and I was ejected into the air; my bike tumbled a distance and stopped. I, on the other hand, was still airborne and landed farther than my bike. I hit the concrete floor, tumbling and rolling uncontrollably, and when my body stopped tumbling, I was face down on my stomach in pain, breathless and dazed. I painfully turned onto my back and just lay there until I was able to get my bearings in check. Some stranger who was driving his car had stopped, gotten out, and asked me if I was okay. I lifted one arm and gave him a thumbs up, letting him know I was alright. He left, and I lay there for a minute or two and painfully got up.

I went to the pile of leaves to see what the hell made me fly off my bike and it seemed some dickhead had put a big stone brick in the middle of the pile. I went and got my bike and saw that the front wheel was bent and flat.

I walked home slowly and never went bike riding again. It was a good thing because a couple days later, I was watching the news with my mother and some kid's head was decapitated when he was riding the bike in the same park some faggot had tied a fishing line from one side of a tree too another and when the kid was riding fast, well. I don't have to say anymore.

· · ·

Some weeks had passed and I was getting excited because my tenth birthday was around the corner and my mother was pregnant and she was almost due. Some nights my mother would let us lay with her, so we could see and feel the

baby kick. My brother and I would laugh with happiness and be excited we were going to have another brother or sister.

Things didn't change in the house. My brother and I still shared the big sofa, my stepfather was drinking and doing drugs, and I was still getting my ass whipped whether I was good or bad but this time my mother allowed Gus to whip on me too.

I remember one time Gus asked me to go the store, I did and was late getting back because the store was packed. They were mad at me and didn't want to hear anything I had to say. My mother started to beat on me and after she finished, my stepfather jumped in and punched me all over my head and face, and in one of his punches, he hit me so hard on my forehead I lost my vision. I could feel my eyelids blinking a hundred miles per hour. I managed to somehow reach the big sofa in the living room and, sobbing uncontrollably, I lay down where I could fall asleep. As I was falling sleep, I could hear my mother telling Gus he hit me too hard on my head that the next time he beat on me to hit me anywhere else except my head, and that's when I passed out. I awoke sometime later, still my vision didn't return but as my eyelids to continue to blink rapidly, my vision was starting to come and go, the blinking didn't stop until my vison returned to normal.

Gus's drinking and drugging was getting worse and there were nights where my mother would be arguing with Gus and accuse him of cheating on her, which he would deny. One night Gus came from who knows where; my brother and I were lying with our mother playing with her stomach gently, and every time we would see the baby rise, we would gently touch the risen area and laugh. After some time my brother had fallen asleep, and I decided to use the bathroom before I did. I finished in the bathroom and was stepping out when I saw the door to the apartment fling open from Gus kicking it, then he went into the closet by the entrance of the door and took out a big oak table leg. Seeing the look on Gus's face, I quickly hid in the bathroom and when I saw he was coming towards me, I screamed as loud as I could for my mother.

He passed me and I ran out of the apartment in my pajama bottoms, tank top, and bare footed, ignoring the cold I ran two or three blocks to the gas station and a payphone. I went to the phonebooth and dialed the operator to

make a collect call to my grandparents, but being that I was hysterically sobbing, the operator couldn't understand what I was saying; it took her some rime to coax me until I was able to calm down and tell the operator in hiccupping sobs that I needed to call my grandparents. She calmly asked me for the number and I gave it to her and I started to cry again because I thought my mother and my little brother were dead. I was even picturing my stepfather beating them to death with that oak table leg. I heard my grandmother's voice and I broke down again. It took some time for her to calm me down and I told her everything. She told me to go back home that she'd take care of everything. I hung up and started to walk back home. I looked at the cold floor as I walking and with corner of my eye I could see people who were either putting gas in their car or walking in and out the gas station store. Why? Why couldn't they see or hear me?

I reached the corner of my building and started praying that everything would be all right but it still didn't comfort me enough to stop the burning river of hot tears running down my face and the picture of my brother and mother dead. I entered my building and saw the apartment door was still opened. I walked in and everything was silent for a moment, then I heard my mother call out to me. I ran into her room and into her arms where she was sitting on half of the bed set.

As she was calming me down, she was telling me when I screamed, it woke her up and in time for her to get in between the two bed set made as one and grab the table leg as it was coming down on her. They had tussled for a little until she got the upper hand, making Gus run out of the room and the apartment. That night she secured the apartment door so no one can get in. My brother and I slept with our mother, but the very next day, my mother allowed Gus back in, acting like nothing had happened, acting like my stepfather didn't try to kill us while in a drunken rage.

• • •

To understand what happened next, I must take you back to the days of Chuweto and me. When I briefly lived on Bruckner Blvd. in the Bronx, Chuweto and I

had a fascination with playing with fire, it made us sexually aroused to the point that we would fuck each other rough and hard. When Chewy would come to the crib, I would put on the TV for Stefano to watch, while Chuweto and I would have fun, the games we played was when my mother left me and my little brother home alone.

One summer afternoon, home alone with Stefano again, Chuweto came to my crib and we all played home tag, then we went after my mother's cat, we all took turns grabbing it by the tail, swinging it like a lasso, then letting go and watching it slam hard against the wall, we kept on doing this until the cat became the aggressor, he arched his back, hiss and I could see the claws were ready to tear flesh, so we left the cat alone.

We then started to play a game of "The Falling Airplane;" we took of some of my mother's old newspapers stacked on the kitchen floor by the window, which faced the back ally of the building. Chuweto and I would take turns balling up a stack of newspapers, lighting one end on fire, then throwing them out the window, and watching the fiery falling newspaper hit the ground. It was my turn and I rolled up the newspaper, lit it, and threw out the window, but this one didn't make it to the ground, it landed in the apartment below us. I thought when it hit the window sill it turned off, and since Chuweto and I couldn't have sex because Stefano was really being nosey, Chuweto left. Sometime later, my mother returned from work and not five minutes after her getting comfortable, there was a knock on the door. My mother started speaking to someone and they had a long conversation. When it was over, my mother turned around and looked at me. I knew then I was in deep trouble.

She said, "So you want to play with fire?" she asked, making my body freeze in fear. She approached me quickly and punched me straight in my face, knocking me down, then she started kicking, punching, and slapping me over my face and body. As she was beating, she was telling me the newspapers Chuweto and I were lighting up and throwing out the window, one of them landed below us and it lit the kitchen curtain, almost burning the baby that was sleeping by the window. After the ass whipping, I was grounded from going outside for a long time. As for Chuweto, he too got his ass whipped by Jay.

. . .

Now back to the present age of almost nine years old, and we were living on Southern Blvd. My mother had left Stefano and me home alone again, and we were watching TV in the kitchen until my mother returned. She entered the kitchen and asked if I was playing with fire. I answered truthfully, "No." She then asked Stefano, and he answered that I was playing with fire. My mother grabbed me by the arm and took me roughly into the bathroom. She started screaming at me to get undressed, get in the bathtub, plug the drain, and fill it up with hot water, and left the bathroom. I was filling the tub up with as much hot water that my body could handle and then sat down, waiting for my mother to return to the bathroom.

My mother returned and reached down, and touch the water; she then unplugged the tub to let the water out, then plugged the tub again and started to fill the tub with only hot water. I was standing in the middle of the tub, but when I felt how hot the water was, I started moving back little by little until there was nowhere to go. The hot water made my feet numb, and when she forced me to sit down, the pain I felt in my butthole, my privates, and the rest of my body was unbearable. I was sobbing uncontrollably. My mother then smacked me hard on the face, pulled out a steel pipe, and threatened with beating me to death if I didn't stop crying. I was hiccupping my sobs in silence and when the water reached my chest, my mother turned the water off and told me before she left the bathroom, that if I got out before the water turned cold, she was going to beat me to death.

I didn't know how much time passed, but I had fainted from the pain and in that unconscious state, I started dreaming about being in an amusement park and on line so I could slide down the water slide. I could hear the kids scream out in delight, and when I entered the slide and let go, I was yelling in excitement also. As I was reaching the end of the slide, I was screaming at the kids and the adults to move out of my way, but all sudden they just disappeared and when I splashed into the pool, I could see something in the deep dark end of the pool quickly changing into a something that resemble of a human being.

I realized it was coming for me by how it was looking at me. I began to swim to the surface in fear, with the knowledge that if this thing grabbed me it was going to take me into the darkness. Just as my head reached the surface, it managed to grab me by the ankles and pull me down. I gave it a hard time and fought like hell. I even fought my mother splashing water all over the floor. After she was able to calm me down, she left the bathroom, and I started to dry off and put on my night clothes.

I then went into the kitchen where my mother was preparing dinner and sat down and examined myself; my skin was a hot pinkish color. My mother was telling me I was lucky because she thought I was playing around in the bathtub, ready to whip my ass but then she saw I was drowning in my sleep. I told my mother I never played with fire, that Stefano was lying.

She looked at me and asked, "Why didn't you tell me?"

I did, many times, and like always, she never listened to anything I said.

. . .

In another incident with my mother's brutalities to me, I remember one time, my mother went the store to get more beer, she had left one open and when she returned from the store, she took a sip of the open twelve oz. can and asked me if I touched the beer. I answered, "No." She continued to say to stop lying; it got to the point where my mother accused me of drinking some beer and putting water in the can to replace what I drank. Though I continued to deny her accusation, it had gotten her so mad she grabbed the can of beer and threw it at my face, hitting me spilling all over me.

Chapter 6

Home and Family

*Some memories were meant to be forgotten but I am cursed to re-
member Pain, how dare you use that word, what you think of as
Pain, is only a shadow, Pain has a face? allow me to show it to you,
I Am Pain.*

Pinhead of Hellraiser 4: Bloodline.

Before I move on in this chapter of my life, I would like to mention this, I have
so much shit buried in my head that it takes me some time to try to organized
my memories, they all run wild, crazy and in different directions without any
order, it's like a movie projector in my head, which never stops showing me
everything I went through, and therefore I will forget certain times in my life
but will intertwine it with whatever chapter I'm in like the one I'm about to
mention, I was four or five years old and my aunt and her family came over to
visit and my mother decided to use me as the entertainment by tying me to a
door knob of a closet that faced the kitchen and the living room and though
my aunt protest against this, my mother ignored her, she went so far as to serve
every one food, then she served me but told me, if I could reach the plate of
food that is on the floor, then I could eat it, no matter what I did, I couldn't

reach the plate of food, so I was left there until my aunt and the rest of the family ate, chatted and then left, which was hours later.

Now as we return to the present age of nine years old, almost ten in three months, I was still living in Southern Blvd. and things were going to go from bad to worse for me and as I begin to write the part I'm going to mention, I feel a wave of sadness, rage and hatred, erupt in my chest and spread throughout my whole body. It starts with my stepfather, who I tried very hard to please as a real son would but no matter what I did, it was never enough, so I let it be, and since my mother was working at the Pizza shop, Stefano and I was left home with Gus.

My mother was pregnant with her third child, working, and would cook when she got home, while Gus did nothing but get high and drink. One night while my mother was working, I was watching TV with my little brother Stefano in my mother's room, when I hear Gus call out my name. He was in the kitchen sitting by the refrigerator and told me to sit down on the chair opposite of him. He was drinking his Greek wine, smoking cigarettes and his smoking thing that had a sweet smell to it, (it was cannabis but at that time I didn't know it), plus he had a Ziploc bag full of the sweet smelling stuff on the table and two joints rolled up. He then gave me a cigarette and told me to take it and that he won't tell, so I took it and he gave me a cup of his wine. I tried to smoke the cigarette like he was, but all I managed to do was choke on the smoke.

Gus took the cigarette from me, turned it off, got up and went into the closet that was connected to the little hallway by the apartment door that led outside, and pulled out a movie projector. He then set it up in the kitchen table facing the wall above the sink, and asked me to check on Stefano. I did, and he was sleeping when I returned to the kitchen and told Gus the news.

I had to sit down fast because I was feeling dizzy and when Gus finished hooking up the projector, he had asked me to sit on his lap. In my head, I really thought that he accepted me as his son, and what he put on surprised me. It was a black and white video of a woman getting fucked doggy style by a man.

As I sat on his lap, he whispered in my ear that's what he wanted to do to me. I could feel his hard-on rubbing on my butt cheeks. He then started rubbing my inner thighs smoothly with both hands and he took me off him. I

watched as Gus undid his pants zipper, whip out his penis, and start masturbating in front of me. He asked me if I wanted to do what he was doing, which was masturbating. I answered yes, and then he asked me if I wanted to masturbate him and I replied "no", but he noticed my little erection, and took off my underwear. He then stood me up on his lap and started to sucked me off. He quickly stopped to put me back on the floor, where he began to masturbate me. I was in heat and when he told me to masturbate him, I did.

He then stopped me and asked me to suck his dick. I did, though it was big, he was telling me what to do, and sometimes I would gag. He would then take his dick out of my mouth and rub it all over my lips and put it back in my mouth. I knew he was cumming by how his legs were trembling and when he ejaculated it filled my mouth and made me gag to the point of vomiting. Gus saw that I was going to throw up , so he opened the refrigerator, took out a two liter of soda, opened it and told me to drink soda. That night I sucked his dick until he was dry. Every time he came he forced me to drink his sperm. After he dried up, he took me into the bathroom and asked me to masturbate while he took a piss, When he saw me ejaculate, a stream of piss shot out falling into the bathtub and Gus gave me five dollars and told me to go to sleep. I did.

The next day, I awoke on the living room floor surrounded by my own vomit. I could hear my mother and Gus argue about what he did, (gave me wine). My mother cleaned me up and that day, I had spent the money in a store near the Pizza shop. I bought candy and a toy and played all day outside the pizza store. Later that evening, I was taken home by my mother but she had to leave again and wouldn't be back until later that night, and my stepfather took advantage of that. Once my mother left, he put Stefano to sleep in the living room, and we went into the kitchen and he started rubbing my inner thighs until he reached my penis and started masturbating it. Seeing that it was erect, he sucked on it for a little and then made me suck his dick.

I thought that it was a way to be accepted as a son, so I did everything he wanted. He even tried to make me deep throat. Making me gag, I was already aroused by what he was doing to me that I performed oral sex on him until he was empty of all his cum. What I mean is, I made him ejaculate more than five times and every time I had to drink his cum.

During that week, he had me suck and drink his cum. I remember on the third night, my mother was working late, and Stefano had fallen asleep in the living room. Gus got me naked as he undressed himself and we went into the bedroom that Gus and my mother shared. We laid on the bed and he had me doing the same shit since the beginning, suck his dick, make him cum and drink it. But after drinking his cum a second time, I vomited all over the bed and on him, so he asked me to help him change the sheets, which I did. He went to the bathroom to clean himself, but once he returned to the room, he made me suck his dick again for hours.

On the sixth night after Gus tried to fuck me in the ass, all he was doing was rubbing the head of his dick on my rectum and making me suck his dick for hours. After he was done getting pleased, he asked me to go to the kitchen, which I did, and sat down by the kitchen table. I watched him go into the closet next to the apartment door and pull something out and then put it on the table. It was a Gun.

He picked up the gun again, pointed it at my face and threatened me. "I will kill you, your mother, and your brother if you tell anyone what we did." He returned the gun to the closet and went back into the kitchen, where he had me preform more oral sex until his dick couldn't stand up. He then told me to go to sleep. I did but with fear in my heart.

The seventh night Gus put Stefano to sleep in Gus's room, then he laid nakedly on the big sofa and made me perform oral sex. After a while, he asked me, "what would you do for twenty dollars?" I responded, "I'll let you put it in my butt." He replied, "it's going to hurt." I responded back, "I don't care." He sat me on his erect dick, trying hard to penetrate me but my butt wouldn't let it. All he was able to do was rub his dick on my rectum, but then he told me to suck him off again and I did.

One morning my mother went into labor and knowing that she was going to be in the hospital, I started sobbing uncontrollably. I didn't want to stay around my stepfather but I was too scared to tell her anything. I begged my mother to let me go with her but she responded that I couldn't be in the hospital while she's having the baby. When I returned home, my stepfather had a sexual party with me. That night, he put Stefano in Gus's room, had me sit on

the edge of the sofa nakedly, and suck on his dick. This time he had me suck on his balls too.

The next night was the same, but I asked Gus if he was going to do to Stefano what he did with me and he responded," I'm thinking about it." I decided to make sure that it did not happen.

The next day, he had me do the same thing. After making him cum a couple of times and drinking it every time, he told me that I was going to my grandparents in Clay Avenue of the Bronx. I was happy because I was tired of feeling disgusted for preforming oral sex with a grown up and with myself, there were times that I had to pretend I was doing Chuweto in order to please Gus.

We arrived at my grandparents on 343 E. 173 street between Clay Avenue and Topping Avenue in the Bronx, I was overcome with emotion but happy to not be with Gus.

· · ·

While staying with my grandparents, I found out that my mother had a baby girl and I became friends with a Spanish family that lived across the street from us, at 347 E. 173 Street on the third floor.

The memory of my sexual experiences with Gus evaporated with hanging out with the two boys of the Spanish family, my grandparents allowed me to play with them either outside or in the home.

My friend Alex was the oldest boy of us three, he was eleven going on twelve and his little brother Henry was eight going on nine years old. I was nine going on ten. Both boys had black hair in a crop cut style, and they had a tannish skin complexion like I did, and they were mischievous pranksters.

We would spend days playing Tag, Freeze Tag, go skateboarding or just talking shit in front of their building. Since the weather was cold with no snow yet, we decided to go skateboarding early one morning. We were going up and down the hill of 173 street, and it was my turn. I went to the street side, while the cars were waiting for the street lights to change into green. I went down the hill and was picking up speed and just as I was reaching the corner of 173 St., my skate board ran into a pebble, ejecting me off my feet, and the

skate board went under a car that was waiting for the light to change to green. I was airborne and landed underneath the car that the skate board went under. The tire of the car was between my neck and shoulder, and I had quickly gotten out from underneath the car before the driver got out, see me stand up, and asked me if I was alright. I gave him a thumbs up and got on my skateboard for the last time and rode up to my giggling friends. I didn't giggle right there and then because my heart was still beating fast from the fear of almost being ran over, but later on, I laughed with them.

A couple days later, I was looking out the window and I heard Alex call me from his window. He was wrapped up in a towel and he screamed out at me, asking me if I was going to his birthday party. I replied that I'll go ask my grandmother. I left the window and asked my grandmother who was washing dishes in the kitchen. I asked her and she answered yes, so I went to the window and Alex was standing waiting for me. I gave him the thumbs up, and he then unwrapped himself, shook his waist side to side, so his privates could swing side to side. I gave him the middle finger and bent my hand to signal to him that he was gay.

I took a reluctant shower because showers and I didn't get along. I usually faked my showers. I would lock the bathroom door, turn on the hot water on the shower, and let it steam cover me making my body damp, and then I would splash a little water on my face and on my chest. I would then dry off the wet spots. It's the only way I could fool my grandparents.

I got dressed and went to the party. I didn't have to worry about my grandparents because the family were church-going people, who went to the same church as my grandparents. Once at the party, I started to play with my friends and their friends. I felt so good, I didn't have to worry about having sex. The boys and would I chase the girls, hoping we could get kisses from them, then we tried to dance with the girls only managing to stepping on their toes. We then changed it to pranking one another. Afterwards, we played other games, we were going to finish with joking on one another but then the food was served. After we ate, the cake and ice cream was served. We all ate, and all of the kids began playing for a little while longer. Then they started to leave either one by one or in groups. I stood a little longer playing with Alex and Henry, then I too went home.

. . .

My birthday and the holidays were arriving, and I could not wait. My grandparents and I would spend the time watching their favorite shows like Hawaii Five-o, Magnum P.I., Remington Steele, Mission Impossible, and MacGyver and Kojak, which was my grandmother's favorite show.

My grandmother wasn't into television much, she was truly a dedicated church going lady, who's main focus was doing good, spreading the word of God, and loving and saving souls. Beyond that, my grandmother was an awesome woman. She was a heavy set black-skinned woman, who didn't watch much of TV, but when I ask her if she could watch a movie with me, she'll do it even though the movies I watched were horror movies and it scared her and boy, was it fun watching them with my grandmother. She would either cover her eyes on scary parts, yell a little prayer on the victims getting killed, or pray to banish the killer or questioned, "why would they make a cursed movie of devils destroying humanity?" After every movie, my grandmother would ask me to kneel next to her and pray to God "The Our Father" in Spanish, I would repeat every word after my grandmother, who would say a sentence, then wait for me to repeat her and after we finished, she would go to sleep and I would watch television in the living room until I fell asleep.

Besides my grandmother being a church going lady, my grandmother like my grandfather were both professional cooks and pastry makers. Throughout the holiday season, my grandmother would make from scratch bread puddings, rice puddings, flan (a caramel custard cake) and other kinds of cakes. Some was for family and the majority was for selling to people on the street that my grandmother knew, people from the building, and people in the church. If she wasn't making the pastries, she would make Pasteles (known in English as Pastelles) and the healthy tropical drinks like Quanabana (which is from the apple family known as soursop fruit) fresh coconut juice, tamarindo juice and my favorite mavi (a part of a bark tree from the maubi tree and fermented with other spices to make it drinkable).

I was so addicted to mavi that I used to tap each bottle and drink a little from each one of them. My grandmother somehow knew, and she would always make a gallon of Mavi just for me, which I used to drink quickly. I will say within two days, all the food, cakes, and drinks my grandmother sold helped with the rent and save some money for other things. As for my grandfather, he was a mid-fiftyish light-skin man with curly hair, who worked early in the morning in a Cuchifrito restaurant, making fresh bread and different kinds of donuts or special ordered cakes. Though he was a professional cook, he only made the breads and pastries. Every weekend my grandfather would wake me up and ask me if I wanted to go with him to work. I responded by jumping off the sofa and I was quickly getting dressed. I then quickly brushed my teeth, washed my face, ran to give my grandmother a kiss and left with my grandfather. Once we arrived at his job, everyone greeted me. They knew me from when I used to go there during school vacations, when my parents abandoned me to my grandparents.

The Cuchifrito restaurant, specializes in breakfast and lunch specials like variety selections of beans, rice, meats, soups, sandwiches, cakes and pastries, bread and donuts. I used to help my grandfather pour and mix the ingredients for either the bread or donuts. My grandfather would mess with the machinery parts, and after the dough was completed, my grandfather would take it out of the machine and put it on a big table. He would sprinkle the flour on the table. This technique was to make sure the dough wouldn't stick on the table and made it easy to cut the dough and mold it to make hero-size or long Italian-size bread. After the whole process was done, the dough was left sitting so it would rise before putting it in the oven.

While waiting for the bread to rise, I'd start to help my grandfather with the dough for the donuts. After it was taken out of the mixer, he'd put it on the table that was prepared with flour, and my grandfather would give me two different round metal donut makers. One with a hole in the middle and the other with no hole. I'd start with the one with a hole and I'd make some trays and put it in the tray holder, then I'd do the same with the other donut maker.

Meanwhile, my grandfather would be putting the trays of risen bread dough in the ovens. Once he was finished with the bread, he would make donut

twists and other different kinds of donuts. Once we were done and the donuts had risen, my grandfather would then throw trays of donuts into a big pot of boiling oil. Once the first set was fried, we'd put them on a big strainer, drain as much oil out of them, and then my grandfather and I would make sugar and glazed donuts and for the donuts without the holes, we'd fill them with jelly and different custards like vanilla, chocolate or strawberry. Then we'd do the same with the donut twist.

My grandfather and I prepared three big batches of bread and donuts and when helping to put the hot bread and donut trays in the tray holder, I have gotten a few burns on my arms and hands. Some of them almost brought me to tears. The cooks and my grandfather said that my burns were cooking badges.

If I wasn't working with my grandfather every weekend from 3:00 a.m. until 1:00 p.m. in the afternoon, or if it was a busy day, until around four in the afternoon, my grandfather, grandmother, and I would spend the day in church. Afterwards, my grandfather would take us to eat Chinese food, then he would take us to a park so I could play with other kids. I really didn't like church because I didn't understand what the teachers were teaching us. To me it was a regular fairytale story, not real, plus I was starting to worry more about what my stepfather was going to do with me when I returned home.

The church wasn't an interest to me. The only time it had some importance was when someone told the church people that I killed my friend's cat. They were all trying to make me feel guilty, but it didn't work. All I felt was ashamed for getting caught. They never asked me why I killed the cat, and they didn't know I killed the cat out of curiosity but it was more out of revenge.

It was one day, I was chilling in the building and I went to the last floor to see if the kid that I saw in the church was out and he was. He was petting a cat that he claimed was his, and the cat was sitting by the hallway window and I too started petting it. Then some other kids from the building came upstairs to join us. After a few minutes of petting and joking, the kid from church invited all the kids except me. At first it didn't faze me and I went back to the third floor, my floor, and looked out the hallway window spacing out. I don't know how long I was spaced out, but when I came to, I was back on the fifth floor, sitting on the windowsill of the hallway. I started to pet the cat, and after

it was calm and trusty, I grabbed it by the back of its neck, put it on the edge of the window and shoved it out of the window. I thought it fell but it managed to use its claws to hang onto the edge, where I couldn't see it until it jumped up onto the edge of the window again. I then pushed it off completely, and watched as it fell unto his death when it hit the ground. I even stood there for a minute or so as the cat's blood was visibly coming out of the side of the cat's head.

I am not going to lie, the cat did put up a fight, but my intention was to kill it for two reasons: one was because I wanted to know if it could fly as I saw in the Tom & Jerry cartoons, and the second reason was that the kid didn't invite me to his crib.

Every Sunday the church class would teach us that killing is wrong and it felt like they were directing those comments towards me, and I did not care. I really did not feel any emotion about the cat, the situation, or the church or God. I did not believe in them.

• • •

Though I did not believe in God, it was my Grandparents love for me, one another, and dedication to the church that made me feel guilty about going to hell for my actions. It is their love that has kept my personality in prison and not burn this world and everyone in it.

One of my fondest memories with my grandparents was every night before I would go to sleep, I would pray to God with my grandmother and then my grandfather would make hot cocoa. We'd sit by the window quietly looking at the cars passing by, drinking hot cocoa, and consuming it with some water crackers. I would fight to keep the crackers from becoming so soft that it would crumble and fall into the cup of hot cocoa. Many of the nights, I would lose the battle and just pass out.

Every night these were my rituals with my grandparents. Before I would go to sleep, my grandfather had a Sesame Street hand puppet, which I believe was Big Bird or Cookie Monster. He'd wait until I was covered with the blankets, and then he'd pull out Big Bird from the edge of the bed and in different voices he'd make jokes or question me if I was a good boy. Which I would

answer "yes" with giggles. On Thanksgiving, Christmas and the other holidays, my grandparents would take a big dish, surround the edges of the dish with Ritz crackers and in the middle of the dish would be small slices of goat cheese and Guava paste with three cups of hot cocoa on the coffee table in the living room. We would sit together either watch a holiday movie or listen to my favorite record for the Christmas holidays, The Nut Cracker Prince.

Things were good for some time, but it started to turn bad. One day, Alex invited me to his crib to play, I asked my grandmother for permission to go over Alex's crib and she said "yes," I shot out of my crib quickly and went to Alex's to play.

In Alex's crib we played wrestling until we got tired, and then we sat in a corner of the room making up scary stories trying to scare one another. Afterwards, we got up and returned to wrestling, we got tired again and we went into the closet. We started conversing about this and that and a few minutes later, Alex stood up unzipped his pants and whipped out his erect penis. He then asked me to suck it. I got on my knees and sucked him off, and then his little brother sat next to me and asked me to masturbate him. I did, and we were so into it that just when Alex was about to ejaculate, we didn't hear his mother enter the room until she opened the closet door. We all jumped and Alex and Henry quickly put their erect penises back in their pants, and their mother stood in shocked silence for some time. When she came to, she told us, "boys don't do things like that with other boys", then she asked me to leave. I left a little embarrassed behind getting caught, but was really more mad for her interruption. I was so horny that I was going to let Alex fuck me in my ass with his long skinny dick and suck on Henry's dick while getting fucked.

Some time had passed by and my life turned from bad to worse. It was nighttime, I'll say around six o'clock p.m. and I was chilling on the fire escape looking down at people and cars passing by, when some black kid looking out of his window from the building where Alex lives was trying to catch my attention. Once my attention was caught, we started gesturing through hand gestures then screaming out loud, he went in and came back showing me a picture of butt cheeks. I went in and drew a picture of a big dick on a piece of notebook paper, went back out on the fire escape, and showed the black kid

the picture and we both started laughing. He then yelled at me "you want to be friends?" I screamed back "yes", and he then asked me if I could come outside. With one of my hands, I signaled for him to wait. I went in and asked my grandmother if I could play with a friend from Alex's building and she answered "yes". I returned to the fire escape not knowing that a young predator had me in his trap. I screamed out that I was coming outside.

My uncle jay was chilling outside in front of our building and asked me where I was going. I replied to my friend's crib, and he let me go. I met the kid inside the lobby and we sat side-by-side on the windowsill that was underneath the staircase leading to the second floor. There were two apartments side-by-side one another on the lobby floor. The black kid and I was blocked from anyone seeing. The conversation started with our likes and dislikes in school and in teachers. Then he asked me my age and I told him I'm almost ten. He told me his age being thirteen years old, and he then changes the conversation to girls. He asked me if I had ever kissed a girl, and in trying to impress him, I answered that not only did I kiss a girl but I had three of them suck on my dick at the same time. He then asked me if I jerk off. I shook my head up and down in reply to yes, though I had slowed down, which was the truth. It was almost nonexistent, due to what Gus was doing to me, it killed the mood.

The black kid continued to question me with if I had ever kissed a boy. I lied and told him "no", and he then kissed me on my lips quickly. I didn't say anything and he kissed me again. I was becoming aroused and I responded in return. We started French kissing passionately, even moaning. He then stopped, got up, stood in front of me and pulled his pants and underwear down mid-thigh and stuck his erect penis in my mouth. My whole body became enflamed with lustful fire. I was performing oral sex on him, hoping that I can make his dick a part of my mouth and then I caught a flashback of what Gus was doing to me and I stopped as well as my lustful fire completely extinguished. I pushed him away from me, then got up and started putting on my sweater. Once finished, I started to leave from underneath the staircase. He grabbed me roughly by the back of the shoulders and forced me to the ground on my knees, got in front of me and forced his exposed penis in my mouth but

I wouldn't let it enter my mouth. I had clenched my teeth tightly, all he was doing was fucking my teeth and lips. It didn't bother him that my teeth was clenched, he just kept on fucking my mouth hard. I again tried to push him away but he had a firm grip on the back of my head. I began moving my head side to side making his dick hit me all over my face. As we were struggling, he was telling me aggressively, "you're going to suck my dick and finish what you started." I managed to break free from his grip and stood up. He punched me on my face and kicked me so hard that I flew backward almost three feet hitting the wall with my back. I fought him the best way I could and while he was beating me up, I was telling him that I'm not going to do shit to him.

He grabbed me by the back of my sweater and started to pull me under the steps. I fought and managed to run halfway towards the entrance of the building. He managed to reach me and grab the back of my shirt, choking me, and then he started swinging me side to side on each side of the hallway wall, making me bang hard against those walls. He was able to drag me back towards the steps and tell me, "you're going to suck my dick." That's when I fought harder and was able to get free of his grip and run as fast as I could towards the lobby's door. He chased me and kicked me on my back hard making me fall on my hands and knees, and again grabbed me by the back of my sweater. He began dragging me towards the stairs. I was crying loudly and as I was starting to stand he was punching, smacking, and kicking me all over my body. This time I made sure I didn't fall on the floor. I pulling him towards the exit of the building, while he was beating me, trying to stop me from leaving the building. His assault continued, even after I reached the door knob and held for dear life, he had kicked me again hard and in doing so, I was able to turn the door knob. The black kid seeing what just happened let go and left me alone, disappearing further into the building. I fixed myself as best I could and dried my tears and headed home to my grandparents, my uncle Jay was still chilling in front of the building, and on seeing me, asked me if I was alright, I replied "yes".

I went home and slept, I didn't get to see the black kid again until the summer school vacation and I was still living with my grandparents. It was early in the morning, Alex and Henry was calling out to me. I looked out the

window, and they asked me if I wanted to play in the park. I told them to wait asked my grandmother for permission she said yes, and I ran out the apartment, down the stairs and met them.

Alex, Henry, and some other kids walked around the corner and climbed the hill that led to Clay Park. We could have gone through the other side by the actual entrance but where's the danger to that. We were going to play hide and seek tag, (what is known today as Man Hunt), I wasn't worried about the black kid because since I didn't see him around, I assumed that he moved away. The side of the park that we all entered was behind my building and all the other buildings and when it was time for me to hide, I decided to go to the hill we climb and hide behind a big tree with bushes. After a couple of minutes of hiding, I heard movement and I looked to where the sounds of footsteps were coming from and my heart stop, when out nowhere the black kid appeared in front of me, grabbing me by the front of my t-shirt and slamming my back hard onto the tree. He then put a steak knife onto my throat and threatened me with, "if you ever tell anyone what I did to you, I'll find you and kill you." And to prove his point he put pressure on the knife cutting me on my throat. He then asked, 'do you fucking understand me? I will kill you." I couldn't speak, I was speechless with fear. I responded by shaking my head" yes" and he disappeared. I never told a soul and I never saw him again but I was always watchful. When I was at my grandparent's or when I was outside, my stepfather came back a couple of days later because my mother was about to be released from the hospital with my baby sister and to break me in, he put me to suck his dick and drink his cum.

Then one night after Gus put me to sexually satisfy him, he left me and my little brother home alone. Then my father called, hearing his voice I couldn't speak. My throat had clogged with a knot of emotions, and after not hearing a response my father asked me what was wrong. I started sobbing uncontrollably and all I was able to say to him over and over again was, "Papi come and pick me up, I don't want to live here anymore." He asked me to calm down and tell him what's going on, but the only thing I told him was that they are always hitting me for no reason. He reassured me that he was coming to pick

me up soon. We said our goodbyes in Spanish and I hung up. Later that night, Gus and my mother arrived home with my baby sister Patricia.

My father was true to his word. He came a couple of days later, to pick me up and live with him. As soon as I saw him, I hugged him tightly and started sobbing because I thought I was safe and going somewhere to be okay and safe, boy was I wrong.

Chapter 7

Home and Family

Fal. Nietzsche once said.
"When you look long into the abyss, The abyss looks into you.
But I say 'The abyss has already chosen, for its why it lurks'"

Before I continue with my story, I want to mention that writing my two-part book of my life was very hard, especially when dealing with personal disappointments and tragedies. In writing this book, I did some research by reading autobiographies and biographies to know how I should write my story and how it would be felt by my readers. I decided to write my books without high vocabulary words, so the readers could continue reading without stopping.

Also in my research, I noticed that some of these authors, would tell half truths or leave out the most important parts leaving the readers clueless. My story will be different, I want you all to experience what my mind goes through every day and the thoughts of suicide that are on my mind from the moment I wake up until I fall asleep.

Many authors tell of one or two traumatic experiences. I am a forty-nine and a half year-old man and I am still going through fuck up shit and though I battle my Mental illness, which is trying to make me completely insane, I

battle my personality who wants to be free, so it can see the world burn by his hands. I battle my suicide tendency, which as I said before, is on my mind from the moment I wake up until I fall asleep. I also battle all the people, who pretend to be my friends or good caring decent people but secretly wanting to see me fail. I battle my physical health. Since the beginning of both books, I've had three amputations and been in the hospital more than six times for emergency basis.

In writing certain chapters, each one took time for me to write, like the last chapter, it has taken me almost six months to write because it makes me so enraged that I want physical vengeance for what was done to me. So I stopped writing and started to do research about revenge and what happens in the end, and I've learned that vengeance cannot give you the satisfaction you seek but adds onto your troubles. So my only form of vengeance is by telling my story of what was done to me and to all those who created the demon in me, you're lucky because it was going to first kill my family members, whether it was men, women or children, then turn on society for they too had part in creating it.

Lastly, for me to write freely, I have to get high, like I am now high on Cannabis. It's the only way I could express myself truthfully and freely. Returning to my story, when my real father came to pick me up from my mother and Gus's crib, I felt so relieved that words couldn't even come close to described how I felt, no more being physically and sexually abused.

·   ·   ·

I moved in with my father, somewhere in the Marcus Garvey section of Brooklyn, where all the apartment complexes, were five stories each. We lived on the fourth floor. My father introduced me to his new family, a fourteen-year-old stepdaughter named Janet and his soon-to-be wife Sandra. They were planning to conduct the wedding in two days.

The apartment had two bedrooms, one was Janet's, which was right next to the bathroom, and the other room was my stepmother and my father's. I slept on the sofa bed, which was very comfortable, nothing like when I was

living with my mother and Gus. The whole apartment was well furnished with plants, little statues of saints, figurines, different types of paintings, and they also had a big fish tank.

The new family treated me good, and I was happy. On the wedding day, I became a boyfriend to a girl my age and became the center of attention to my actual family from my father's side that I didn't know existed, some of his friends and Sandra's family too.

There was too much going on and it had me excited. People filled the living room dancing, drinking, and conversing. In the kitchen, there were at least three or four females cooking different kinds of food. It filled the air with delicious smells and the teens and younger kids were running around playing or trying to steal alcoholic drinks left on the table. But what I was doing was running around to certain spots out of eye shot of anyone to meet up with Christy and start French kissing. When the kissing moment came and left, I would go by the kitchen to investigate what was being cooked and to smell the food coming out from the kitchen making me weak and drooling. I just couldn't wait until they finished. I found out that they were cooking rice with Gandules, Pasteles, Pernils(pork shoulders}}}, tostones(fried plantains}}}, platanos dulce (fried sweet plantains), potato salads and different kinds of alcoholic drinks for those who can't take the strong stuff. There were also beers, juices, and sodas.

The music was booming loudly and almost everyone was dancing to either Spanish music or English music, especially the slow dancing ones. The adults and the kids were separated at times. We were put in Janet's room but some of us boys would sneak out to get a dance or two with the older females, the dancing filled the whole apartment from the living room to the hallway leading to the apartment door and outside the apartment.

It was a beautiful experience, the kids were dancing with one another and I was still on the mission with Christy, sneaking around to French kiss. We stopped kissing because we felt like someone was going to catch us. And in one of our missions, we got caught by Janet and Janet was acting creepy following us where ever we went, hoping to catch us but we had stopped. I didn't let it spoil the fun I was having, it was helping me forget what I went through. When they mentioned that the food was being served, I was one of the first in

line, I grabbed my plate which was filled with food and went into Janet's room and ate like a pig. Since there was enough food to serve more than a hundred people, I went for seconds leaving enough room for the ice cream and cake after the ceremony.

Everyone was eating, the music was lowered while people were finding somewhere to sit. Some managed to sit and others stood standing up and ate. After everyone was done eating, the wedding ceremony started. the Priest was positioned in the living room, as was my father, then Sandra in her wedding dress came out of her room, entered the living room, and stood by my father. The Priest said his part and my father was married. I really didn't care about the marriage ceremony, I was waiting for the cake and ice cream.

Once the ceremony was over, the music began blasting loudly and everyone was dancing and drinking. The kids were served the cake and ice cream first because it was getting late and the party got so hectic that a couple who was dancing happened to knock down my father's fish tank, which was full of fish. There was water, fish and pebbles all over the floor leading into the living room and the kitchen floor. I was told to go to Janet's room with the other kids, while the mess was picked up.

It was after midnight when people started to leave. Everyone left except my little girl friend, who was staying over. Her parents had decided to leave her with my father's and Janet's permission. She, Janet and I shared the same bed in Janet's room, and we didn't go straight to sleep. We stood awake joking on each other, talking kids talk and Janet wanting to see Christy and I French kiss and do some sex acts. We refused and after some time had passed, Janet was the first one to fall asleep, then Christy. I, on the other hand, remained awake enjoying the silence and the moment. My thoughts were disturbed by Christy waking up wanting to go the bathroom. She reached the bedroom door and opened it, my father was standing in front of the doorway and for no reason, my father grabbed Christy by the top of her long blond hair, lifted her up, and slammed Christy violently sideways on the wall. I was frozen with shock and fear, I couldn't even scream for him to stop. But when Janet awoke to the commotion, she started to scream, making me find my voice and scream with her. He managed to slam her violently against the wall a couple of more

times before he let her fall on the television that was on a TV stand, which fell on her when he let Christy go, then he left closing the bedroom door.

Janet jumped out of the bed to help Christy up. She was sobbing uncontrollably. Janet brought her to the bed and calm her down. After some time Christy stopped crying and said "he's a big monkey like King Kong", and we all started giggling silently as possible, then we all fell asleep. (Even to this day, I do not know why my father did what he did).

· · ·

Time passed and things were good even after the incident with Christy. My relationship with my father was good, he spoiled me with love and with whatever I wanted though I never asked him for anything because all I wanted was to be loved for real and he not only gave me love but gave me protection, too. And after three weeks since the wedding, my father announced that we were all going to Puerto Rico for their honeymoon to spend time with my father's and stepmother's family, people I did not know.

On the day that was decided to head to Puerto Rico, we packed enough clothes for a month, then we all went to sleep early so we could wake up early and get to the Airport on time. The next day, one of Sandra's family members arrived at the crib ringing the doorbell very early in the morning waking all of us up. I don't know who answered the door because I went back to sleep. A few minutes later, I was awoken by father and after we all got prepared and ready, Sandra's brother drove us to the airport.

Once seated in our assign seats, I was excited with anticipation and wonder because I have never flown before, did not know that Puerto Rico existed, and to find out, I had family in Puerto Rico. I was dying to meet them, being that it was my first time flying, I was not scared even after we hit some rough turbulence, making the plane shake from side to side and up and down. After three hours in the air, we landed.

Getting off the plane, I felt the heat and humidity hit me. My father seeing that I was a little uncomfortable explained to me that Puerto Rico is always hot because it's a tropical island and all the animals, insects, fruits, and trees

depend on this type of weather. I wasn't really paying attention because I was fascinated in being in another country and how different it was, when comparing Puerto Rico to New York.

We were being waited on by one of Sandra's family members, who were happy to see us and invited us to stay in his house. We were heading somewhere in the town of Fajardo. I don't remember how long the ride was but my amazement had the better of me. I was seeing houses made out of tin metal, the coconut trees, mango trees, some roads in gravel form, and kids running around either in underwear or naked on the gravel floor, chasing goats, chickens and or horses. My father told me that what I was seeing was Campo life (country lifestyle).

A lifestyle I used to read about in the National Geographic of other countries and it was something that I secretly fantasized about in school of how I wanted to live in whatever country I was reading about and explore it, though I never read anything on Puerto Rico. So to me, it didn't exist but being there and passing through or by mountains, beaches, and seeing some richer parts of certain towns, where the houses were built with cinder blocks, painted and made to look like rich people lived there.

We finally arrived at Sandra's male family member's house, which was built with cinder block, cement and painted. This man whom I would call Alex because I never knew his name and I never heard my parents address him by his name. He was a deep brown skin complexioned man either in his fifties or sixty years of age.

One could tell that Sandra and Janet were families with this man, by the similar features and skin complexion. As for my father and I, well he is white skinned with green eyes and I had tannish skin with brown eyes. My skin complexion gets darker when in the sun. Anyone knowing my father and I would assume that we weren't related. I remember as a child, when kids used to roast each other, someone would come out saying "your mother is white, your father is black and they call you a zebra." But for me it's the other way around. I am a Zebra, whose stripes change in the sun.

Anyway, once inside his house, he had dinner prepared. All he did was warm it up and serve it. After we all finished eating, we all sat in different sections in

a well-furnished living room, where Sandra introduced my father and me, and then they started conversating about adult stuff. As for me, my eyes were getting heavy and Alex noticed, so he escorted me into one of the three bedrooms he had. I was to share the bed with Janet and as soon as I laid down, I quickly fell to sleep.

The crowing of the Roosters early in the morning woke everyone up. Alex and Sandra fixed breakfast, and afterward, we all went into the backyard, where some of the grounds of the backyard were paved with cement but the rest had grass and dirt. There was a table and Alex was there cutting up green coconuts and making drinks for me and Janet and adult drinks for my father and Sandra.

We hung out in the yard and I noticed that Alex had an adult male goat tied to a tree in his yard. I asked Alex if I could pet it and he responded "yes." I had never seen a real goat and when I rubbed my hand on his horned head, to me, it felt like petting a horned dog. It started to make its bleating sound and I laughed at how funny it sounded. While petting the goat, I overheard Alex tell my parents that the goat is going to be killed for dinner. I pretended not to hear and after some time with the goat, I went back inside and started watching whatever was on the television. As soon as I sat down on the sofa, my father enters the house and approaches me, explaining to me that the goat was going to get killed and that he didn't want me to witness it. I asked him why didn't he want me to witness the killing and he answered in Spanish that I was too young and if I witness the killing, I would have bad dreams. Also if I watched and felt sorry for the goat, it would take the goat a long time to die.

According to the mataderos, mataderos are certain farmers that are called to kill hogs and other animals for eating, selling their meat, and for celebrations. It is said that if anyone with a soft heart witness these killings and starts to feel sorry, it would take the animal longer to die and Alex and my father were skilled mataderos.

By the time the early afternoon approached, my father came back in and told me not to go out to the backyard because he and Alex were going to kill the goat. I agreed not to go but as soon as he left to the backyard, I ran into the room I shared with Janet because It overlooked the whole backyard. I peeked through the corner of the window to see what they were doing.

Alex and my father had tied the goat's back hind legs together, then Alex helped my father tie the goat upside down from a tree, leaving the goat hanging freely, while they fixed a metal contraption on the ground. Then they tied the front legs to the contraption, making sure that the goat couldn't move, while they were doing this the goat was bleating loudly. Then I saw Alex take a small sharp machete and pierced the goat through its neck and pushing it deeper into its heart, I was hearing the goat gurgling and seeing it thrashing side to side, trying to escape from his imprisonment. I was starting to feel sorry for the goat, almost to the point of crying. After more than ten minutes, the goat was still thrashing side to side and I duck back in because my father was telling Alex that someone was watching and feeling sorry for the goat with that I ran back into the living and pretended to be into some Spanish show, just as I got comfortable my father entered the house to see if it was me, seeing that I was watching TV, he returned to the yard. I ran back into the room and watch them take a bucket and let all the blood drain into the bucket, then they skinned the goat and they started to cut the unwanted pieces into the bucket. Then they cut up the rest of the goat and placed the pieces that was going to be used in plastic wrap and aluminum foil, then put in the freezer.

Sandra and Janet had returned back from wherever they were and as Alex and my father were preparing dinner, my father was telling Sandra what happened and how they could not figure out who had felt sorry for the goat. Though I felt sorry for the goat when it was being killed but when it was prepared, my sorrow left me as I ate the delicious meat. We all sat in the living room and ate, my father and Alex were the only one's eating and talking about adult stuff. As for me, I was enjoying a meal I've never eaten before and after we ate, Alex had made Flan and Sour sop juice. The juice made my mouth feel like it was in ecstasy. We all finished eating and my father announced to Janet and me that we needed to sleep early because we were going to another of Sandra's family members' house. Being full, I had no trouble falling fast to sleep.

The next morning arrived with the sounds of the roosters crowing. My father, Sandra, Janet, and I washed up and got dressed. Alex had prepared breakfast and we ate and left. It was incredibly early in the morning, I'll say around four or five in the morning, and the ride to one of Janet's member's

house was exceptionally long but adventurist. We drove past many mountains and hills, where my father would stop the car, so we could pick up some mangoes that had fallen from the tree. My father knew which ones to pick and I would help him pick them. We ate some and saved some for the trip. My mouth was again fascinated by the exotic taste of fruits I've never heard of, let alone eaten.

We arrived around eight or nine in the morning, and Sandra introduced my father and me. We were greeted with hugs, kisses, and my cheeks being pinched by all the females. Oh, how I hated my cheeks being pinched. That shit hurt.

I was told to go to the big backyard, where the family's kids were playing. I was too busy looking around the property. Sandra's family house was built with cinder blocks and cement and as my eyes could see, all the rest of the houses surrounding Sandra's family house were either built out of wood or wood and tin metal.

I went to the front of the house to continue my observation of my surroundings. I could see children running around either in underwear or naked. They were either playing with one another or chasing chickens, pigs/piglets, goats, neighborhood dogs, and they even were some boys climbing up coconut trees or the mango trees. I had the urge to take off all my clothes and run with them but I was ashamed because things like that don't happen in New York and New York kids especially the boys would call me a homosexual.

Still observing, I noticed vines around Sandra's family house and in the gates of the backyard, they had some type of round fruit the size of tennis balls and they had different colors, somewhere green, orange or orange-red. One of the kids saw me looking at them and a boy of about eight or nine approached the vine, ripped an orange-red ball, gave it to me, and told me that it is Parcha (passion fruit), a delicious fruit. He gave it to me and told me to bite down hard on the fruit because the skin was kind of hard and not edible, only what was inside. I bit down hard for the skin felt like rubber, I ripped a corner of the Parcha and this sweet liquid that was inside with little seed like sacks burst into my mouth and was amazed by the taste it left in my mouth. It even smelled delicious, one of the grown up's called on the kid to go help

them and he left. I was still looking around at all the different types of fruit trees, trees, and palm trees.

The air had all kinds of smells and aromas, some cooking smells, some fruity smells and fresh air, nothing like New York. My concentration was broken when both adult females and males were carrying cooking supplies: large pots, knives, a couple of five gallons, and empty buckets. Some of the kids were even helping, someone had built a fire on a pit, so they could put one big pot of water on the fire to boil. I was curious about what was about to happen, when some older kid seeing my curiosity told me that they were going to kill a hog for the marriage celebration.

I followed the kid and saw my father and a couple of older adult males enter a big hut that housed many big hogs. My father and some of the men choose the hog which would be slaughtered. Then they took the hog almost to the entrance of the hut where they had the contraption ready for it. My father and the men worked together to tie the hog the way my father and Alex tied the goat. After the hog was tied properly, the men left the hog hanging until the water boiled. One of the men approached me and told me not to feel sorry about the hog because it would take long for the hog to die, I assured him that I wouldn't.

The hog must have known what was about to happen to him because it was screeching loudly and in that moment one of the ladies screamed out to the men that the water was ready. At that my father took a small thin machete, which was sharp as hell and he pierced the hogs neck and pushed the machete deeper until it pierce its heart. It was gurgling and I could see blood coming out of its snout, mouth, and the hole in its neck and that blood was falling into a five gallon bucket. There was a crowd of men and children watching the hog screeching and trashing uncontrollably. I again felt sorry for the hog and the hog took a long time to die. I saw one of the men observing everyone around the hut, to see if he could see who had the look of guilty sorrow of their face. Seeing none he returned his attention to the hog that stopped its gurgling squealing but still was thrashing violently. It took more than five or ten extra minutes before death finally took over and the funny thing that happened, all the grownups were trying to find out who was the one feeling sorry for the

hog. They all turned around and looked at me, even one of the men asked me if I was the one feeling sorry for the hog and with a straight face, I lied and answered him that it wasn't me but I think they knew it was me.

The hog was dead, and all its blood drained into the bucket. My father cut the hog from the neck down to the middle of his body until he reached the hog's butthole. One of my father's helpers had cut the butthole out and tried to give it to me, telling me that if I put it on my ring finger like a ring, it would bring me good luck. At that all the men started laughing, even my father. I looked at every one not understanding the joke but many years later reminiscing about those days, it hit me, the guy was trying to prank me in wearing the hog's bloody butthole.

Once the hog was cut down the middle, one of the men started cutting out all its organs even its intestines and putting it in another bucket. Then it was brought to the women, where two females with a hose started washing the intestines inside and out with water, lemon juice, vinegar and something else. Once the intestines were cleaned, another lady took it inside to make Morcilla's (blood pudding). As for the other organs they were taken inside. I don't know what they were going to do with them.

Meanwhile, two men had gotten the big pot of hot water and brought it to a big, long wooden cutting table where the hog was laid out, then one of the men with a smaller metal pot started scooping up hot boiling water and started pouring it on one side of the hog not only to clean the skin but to make it easier to either pull out the hog's hair or scrape the rest of the hair out with a sharp knife.

After that process was done on both sides, another man started poking deep holes in certain parts of the hog's body with a small knife. Then he took a big sauce pot placed there by one of the ladies and, filled it with a thick saucy seasoning. He then started spreading the seasoning everywhere on the hog, even the insides and all the small holes. Once done on both sides, he called out in Spanish "that it was ready". At that, another guy came towards us with a long thick metal pole and started forcing one end of the pole through the hog's mouth until it reached the other end, where another guy placed metal clamps on the lose skin where the rectum used to be, then

with bigger clamps they would clamp the back and front legs, even the whole underbelly was clamped.

I was not only fascinated but curious as to why they tied the hog like that, so I asked one of the men and he explained to me in Spanish, "it was to keep the seasoning inside so it's cooking the meat from the inside out, while the top seasoning would cook it from the outside in" and he had also explained to me that by tying the hogs underbelly, it would keep the seasoning and the juices from seeping out.

Once they finished tying the hog, the same two men lifted the pole on each end and took the seasoned hog to where they had prepared the pit fire. There were two contraptions on each end of the fire pit, where they can place each end of the pole that held the hog. Then one of the men put a metal crank on one end of the inside of the pole's hole, so one of the men could sit on a chair, turning the pole with the hog on it, and it would cook all the way around evenly.

Seeing the men were finished with the hog and it would take hours to cook properly, I went inside to see what the women were doing. A few were preparing the Morcilla's, they had mixed the hog's blood with cooked rice and other ingredients, then they would stuff the mixture inside the large intestines and tie them up to make them look like large sausages. It would be passed to another woman, who would put them inside a big boiling pot of water.

I watched in silent wonder, this experience was so much different than New York life and the way everyone was doing something to help, the adults drinking, listening to music or taking time to dance, or the women inside the house singing in tune with whatever Spanish love song came on. I felt my soul become clean and really happy for the first time in my little life. Still inside the house I was watching what was to become of the Morcilla's, she left them there for a few minutes, then put them in a hot frying pan filled halfway with boiling oil.

The first batch was for tasting and once some were fried, I was given a piece of fried Morcilla's, it had a chewy but crunchy consistency almost like a sausage but the taste was delicious. I had asked for more and was given another piece. I could see that they were cooking rice with Gandules and in two different large plates were cut up plantains and sweet plantains ready to get fried but not until the hog was completely cooked.

Satisfied with my snack, I went outside to see who was turning the hog and it was my father. I stood beside him and after a couple of minutes of me watching him, I asked him If I could turn the hog and he let me. Though I knew what to do, I was very careful. Every time one of my arms got tired, I would change to the other or I would stop to brush the outside of the hog with the thick seasoning. I continued to spin the hog, when I noticed my father taking pictures of me and of my moment.

I resumed to turning the hog and after some time, another person took over. The hog was almost done, as it had been cooking for more than three and a half hours. The hog's skin was red and hardened just the way it's supposed to be and after another hour, the hog and all the food was ready to be eaten. One of the men took care of cutting up the hog and I could see that not very much cutting is needed because the meat literally came off the bones.

I was served a little bit of everything: the hard, crunchy and flavorful skin, the hog meat, fried plantains, fried sweet plantains, rice and Gandules, and potato salad and gravy. I began to stuff my mouth with a little bit of everything on my plate, making my mouth explode with all these different and wonderful flavors. when I was done, I was asked if I wanted more and I answered "yes", I ate so much that I didn't have room for the Pasteles and dessert, which was bread pudding. When everyone was finished, we just sat down and let our food digest for about an hour, and then my father told Janet and me to get ready and that we were about to leave. I was in the car, and I could see that my father and Sandra carrying two big bowls each.

The bowls were safely put away in the trunk of the car and we headed to Alex's house. Once there, the bowls were left on the table for Alex to enjoy and we could have something for tomorrow. We all sat in the living room, listening to Alex tell us stories of his adventuristic youth. I didn't last long as my eyes were losing their battle to sleep and as soon as my head hit the pillow, I fell into a deep sleep.

For the next few days, my father took Sandra, Janet, and myself to explore Puerto Rico. We passed and went to different beaches, especially the most famous one The Loquillo beach, then we spent time in Fajardo, Sabana Seca, San Juan. We passed El Morro and a San Juan National Historic site.

We arrived back at Alex's and just before I went to sleep, my father announced that we were all going to see his side of the family.

. . .

The next day, my father drove to a little town called Areciebo and we went to a little mountain called El Cerro de Maravilla, in Hatillo, Pajir. There weren't any sidewalks or streets, everything was gravel and dirt and since my father's family lived up in this little mountain. The car had to be left at the bottom because it wasn't strong enough to go up.

We walked up the steep hill and by the time I reached the top, boy not only was my legs crying out in pain but I was a little out of breath too. I noticed six or seven houses made of tin metal and wood and they were all almost covered by different kinds trees, some fruit and some ordinary trees. Also six of the seven houses occupied by people were family and the last one was friends of the family.

There was a large group of people waiting for us. My father introduced all of us and hugs and kisses started but when it got to me, the damn pinching of the cheeks started and by the end of the pinching, it not only hurt but I was very annoyed. I didn't know I had a lot of family, I had two married aunts, one aunt Wanda with shoulder length black hair and a chocolate brown skin complexion and infant male child named Willy. The other aunt was a light skin women with dirty blond mid-back hair length, who had my grandmother's grey eyes and my grandmother's first name Pilar, and lastly my uncle Nelson and his wife Alba both were light skinned like my father. They had a male child of about five years old named Juan Pablo, then you have my grandmother Dona Pilar light skin like my father, with long white mid-back hair length and she always had one of those strong tobacco wrapped cigars, which stinks like hell.

I had asked her where was the bathroom and she escorted me to the back of her house, where she pointed to a little shed made of tin metal and the toilet was made of cement with a hole in the middle for defecating and urinating and a little away from the toilet was a homemade shower. I thank God that I didn't have to defecate because as I was urinating a couple of big water bugs

came out of the latrine hole. I ran out of there zipping up my pants outside and as I went to the front of Dona Pilar's house, my grandmother called me to the side and asked me in Spanish, if I knew who she was to me. Looking into her grey eyes I shook my head up and down, in a yes response "mi abuela", then she continued asking questions like how old I am, how long I have been living with my father, all to which I answered. Once she finished with the questioning, she turned her attention to my father, so I went and played with my little cousins.

I ran around playing with my little cousins and I noticed them running around barefoot on the gravel, so my dumb ass thought that I could do the same thing. I took off my sneakers and socks and boy did I regret it. I tried to run around like my cousins and the bottom of my feet felt like I was walking on glass. It hurt so much that I wanted to cry from the pain. I went back and put on my socks and sneakers and waited for the pain to subside, so I could continue to play with my cousins. By the time the afternoon came, my grandmother Dona Pilar had called out to the family that was outside and announced that lunch was ready. It was sandwiches made of Italian bread but this bread had a better taste than the bread of New York, this bread was called Pan de Agua(water bread) and it was so soft that even when they made the sandwich toasted with melted cheese and cooked pork, the inside was still soft and we all consumed the sandwiches with some tasty coffee. I ate in silence and listened to the grownups speak on adult stuff and all of a sudden I started to feel a surge of renewed energy. It was the coffee but I didn't know it at that time. After I finished eating lunch, I went out and played with my cousins until dinner, which wasn't anything exotic. Afterwards, my father told Janet and myself to get ready that we were going back to Alex's house.

We arrived at Alex's and all we did was sit down in the living room, eat fruits, and listen to Alex reminiscing about some funny adventures he had as a youth. I was eating a passion fruit and my father decided to prank me. My father was asking me why was I eating the Parcha fruit without taking the seeds out? (The seeds were exceedingly small and edible). He continued to tell me that because of me consuming the seeds that a tree was going to grow in my and eventually I was going to turn into a tree and no one could help me. I

started to panic and tears started to flow down my eyes, and I ran into the room that I shared with Janet and slammed the door. My father screamed at me and entered the room, took off his belt and started beating me. As he was hitting me, he was stating that the reason for him beating me was because I was disrespectful in a strangers house. I didn't speak to my father the whole next day.

In the final week in Puerto Rico, my father took us to many different places, eating exotics fruits and foods and on the last night in P.R., Alex killed a rabbit and cooked it in beer and other seasonings(fricassee style). And when the food was completed, Alex explained to me to be careful eating the rabbit because its bones are brittle and can do damage to my intestines. We ate and when we were done eating, we went to the backyard and drank exotic drinks and ate fruits. Then we went to sleep for the next day would be a busy day.

Early the next day, Alex took us to the airport and after saying our good-byes we headed to our assigned gate and got on the airplane and after three hours, we landed and headed home to the beginning of a renewed hell for me.

Chapter 8

Home and Family

False Safety
"How does one bandage a child's heart,
when it has taken, twisted, and left to represent the evil of those
who broke his trust and heart, draining his soul?"

We were back in Brooklyn, New York in the Marcus Garvey projects, things were good for a while and I was happy. The only time I got depressed and started to cry was when one night I was watching a Smurf movie and a friend of Smurfette, which was a goose, had died and it made all the Smurfs sad and tearful. My father walked in the living room, where I slept and upon seeing me crying, he asked me what was the matter. I responded nothing, I didn't want to tell my father that I was crying because a cartoon character had died. He would have probably laughed at me, but he questioned me no more.

The next few days were good until one early afternoon, I was allowed to go outside to play with the kids of the neighborhood. We all went into the basketball courtyard, which was positioned in the middle of the Marcus Garvey buildings that are attached to one another. My father's apartment windows faced not only the front of the building but the back of the building also and

there were many entrances and benches with walkways and some trees that stood tall behind the benches blocking the sun. Some of the walkways, lead to one side of the block to another from many different directions of the projects.

In the basketball court, I was with kids of all ages and we were having fun trying to play basketball. It was a nice summer day and there were adults outside watching us. The teens and older teens were waiting for us to get hot and tired. We were having fun running around trying to look like the big kids. Some of the bigger kids were laughing at us but in good nature. While playing, I heard a couple of pops. I thought that it was someone playing with firecrackers but then I noticed everyone young and old that was around the outside of the basketball court or hanging around the front or back of the building (depending how the building was situated) running into the buildings. Some of the adults were calling at the kids and myself to hurry up and leave the courtyard and come to them but I stood in the middle of the courtyard watching everyone running into the nearby buildings and wondering why was everyone running. Then all of a sudden, some white male with long dirty blond hair ran by the end of the courtyard and stopped at the walkway that lead to the street and started shooting up in the air. He then ran out into the street and disappeared. While this was happening, people young and old were calling out to me. I ignored them because I really didn't understand the situation and didn't have the fear that everyone else had.

I don't how long it was before an officer came up to me and asked me if I was okay. I answered yes, and the cop continued to question me about what I saw and if I could describe the guy with the gun. I don't know why I did it but I gave the cop a different description. I told him the guy was white with a different set of clothing. I didn't tell the cop that the white guy had long blond hair or that the gunman threw the gun into one of the bushes by the corner of the building leading to the street.

After everything was clear and people were starting to come back outside, I found out that the white guy had shot someone who was sitting on a bench further down the walkway. I wasn't told if the guy that got shot had died or not, but out of curiosity, I went down to where the incident happened and saw a big puddle of blood. When I went home and told everyone what happened,

I wasn't allowed to go outside again unless I was with Janet. But because of me not running when the guy was shooting up in the air near me, some of the kids respected me and I developed a crush on a girl who had hung out with the boys. Though I couldn't go outside alone, the girl and I became girlfriend and boyfriend and to show her that I was really serious, every time my friends would call out for me, she would be with them. I would steal Sandra's gold necklaces and some gold medallion, which symbolize love and gave it to her but it didn't last because I wasn't able to go outside and Janet didn't want me to go outside either.

. . .

Time passed and I was starting to feel sexually aroused. I would try to ignore my urges but one day home alone, I was in the kitchen looking out the window, which overlooked the front side of the building. I had squeezed between the stove and the window, and I was looking out watching people and cars passing by. I don't what overcame me but I started feeling aroused and not thinking that I could be seen by the people upstairs from their windows, I pulled my shorts and underwear down onto my knees and slowly started masturbating. My body started to become enflamed with lust and I was masturbating quicker and just as I was about to ejaculate, I heard the keys entering the door and I quickly struggled with my clothes managing to fix myself before they entered, I was ashamed and somewhat panicky because I thought they knew what I was doing and when they didn't ask me what was I doing, I left it alone but I believe someone saw me and because of my actions, it almost cost my life.

. . .

It was probably a day or two later and I was left home alone again. I was in my underwear only and it was early in the afternoon. I'll say around one or two o'clock, I was watching TV and someone was knocking on the apartment door. I answered the door without asking who it was or properly dressing myself. I opened the door and it was a black teen of about fifteen or sixteen years of age.

He asked if I had any notebook paper. I replied yes and invited him in. I closed the door and guided him into the living room and gave him a tour of the apartment. Then we went back into the living room and I noticed that he was looking at me and my almost nakedness. I wasn't teasing or flirting with him, I just didn't know the danger I was in and making matter worse, I had fat round butt cheeks like a well-developed girl. I went into the closet in the living room, took out one brand new pack of loose leaf note paper and gave it to the black kid. After a few minutes of chatting and him asking me questions about, where were my parents, and when they would return, I answered both questions, letting him know that they would be back later in the evening. Satisfied with my answers he left my crib, but no more than five or ten minutes later, there was a knock on the door. I was about to open the door, but something made me put the chain on the door and that was what saved my life, I opened the door and flinched back when I saw the bat go between the crack of the door and hit the chain hard, I tried to closed the door but it was jammed with the bat, this infuriated him and he started screaming and cursing at me angrily to open the door, which I refused but then he started to push hard at the door trying to break the chain. I leaned on the little wall of the hallway that separated the entrance of the apartment, the kitchen, and the living room. I then slid to the floor and used both legs to try to push the door closed to keep him from breaking the chain to the door. He was going berserk on the door and screaming and cursing at me. I was scared out of my ass but I had the advantage on him by using the wall, my body, and legs. He managed to pull the bat from the door's crack and the door closed. I quickly got up and secured the door with the other two door locks but this didn't stop him. He started to hit the door with the bat, screaming and cursing for me to open the door. The door secured, I ran into Janet's room and hid underneath the bed. He was going at it for a few more minutes, then silence. I was so frightened that I didn't come out from underneath the bed until I heard someone using keys to open the door and to my relief it was Sandra's voice at the door. As she was knocking on the door because the chain was still secured, I left from under the bed and ran to the door and opened it. She started questioning me with why did I lock the door with the door chain but I didn't answer. She continued with what

happened to the door and the peep hole. Again I played ignorant and they entered the apartment and I went outside to see the damage to the door and I saw that the outside peep hole was completely broken off and there were many deep dents all around the door and like all the bullshit in my life, no one bothered to intervene but it was the last time I saw the black teen. It's like I said before the devil blinded everyone to what was happening around them.

. . .

After that incident with the black teen and me not telling anyone about what happened, I was left home alone but this time with Janet and she spent most of the time in her room, while I was in the living room watching TV. After a couple of hours, she came out of her room and sat down next to me for few minutes. Then she stood up and asked me how can she get her buttocks big like mine. I replied that I didn't know. She then asked me if I wanted to do an experiment and I answered yeah. She then said to follow her, so I followed her to the outside of her bedroom and she told me to wait outside her room. I watched her go in and bring out a little plastic school chair, and she put it on the floor by the entrance of her room and asked me to stand on it. She then took my underwear off and started playing with my penis. When my penis became erect, she pulled her pants and panty off from her behind and asked me to put in her ass. I did, it penetrated her asshole but not by much and after a few humps, she told me to stop. I did, then she told me to turn around. I did, she then started rubbing and massaging my buttocks. She then told me to stand still while she rubbed her buttocks with mine. After a minute or two, she stopped then went into the bathroom to masturbate. How do I know she went to do that, well one, she was in the bathroom for a long time and after a while I could hear her moaning. While she was in the bathroom, I nakedly went into the living room, laid on the sofa, and masturbated quickly. When I was finished, I went to where the little plastic chair was and picked up my underwear and put them on. I could hear Janet heard her moan real loud. When everyone was finished with relieving themselves, she went into her room until her mother came back from wherever she was. One thing is for sure, she did have

a flat ass and later that night, she tried to tell me that she felt her buttocks getting fatter, which was a big fat lie.

My stepsister was not only ugly but she couldn't get a boyfriend no matter what she did and even though we had that sexual encounter, I wasn't what she wanted and we never had sex again but she started to mistreat me. It first started when my father would give us money to buy whatever we wanted though the limit was ten dollars each, she instead of giving me my cut. She would buy me a cheap item, tell me that it was an expensive item, and that I didn't have any change left over. She thought I was stupid but I didn't bother to play her game. Then one day, we were home alone and she had broken one of Sandra's figurines. Her mother returned and Janet had told her mother that it was me. I tried to tell Sandra that it wasn't me but she didn't believe me and she punished me by making me write 500 times " I shouldn't touch or break anything that doesn't belong to me".

Then a couple of days later, Janet not only stole something that belonged to Sandra but whatever item Janet got it from, it broke and Janet told Sandra that it was me. I was again punished by writing a thousand times "I will not steal, touch, or break anything that doesn't belong to me and lie about it". Writing that shit took me all day and night to write and when I was finished not only did my fingers hurt but the tips of my fingers were black. I couldn't even masturbate because of the pain. Janet had slowed down with getting me in trouble because my father started questioning her but she always had the perfect lie ready, Then I realized that Janet was doing those things because she was jealous that I had a girlfriend and she couldn't get a boyfriend. I figured that out one day, when my stepmother took Janet and I to Christy's mother's apartment to hang out. We all chilled inside for a while and Christy's mom decided to hang out on the front stoop of her building. We all followed her. I was playing with Christy and we decided to sneak upstairs to kiss and do some sexual things. We sat on Christy's bed and started French kissing, she started touching my privates and I hers, seeing that we could fit underneath the bed, we went underneath, she pulled off her short's and panty down and I pulled my shorts and underwear down unto my ankles. She then started to touch my erect penis and started to masturbate it. I feeling on fire, started playing with

her vagina, even sticking one of my fingers in her. We had gotten each other so horny that she requested that I penetrate her with my penis. I struggled a little to fit myself on top of her. She helped a little by opening her legs making it easier for me to position myself and penetrate her, my penis was in her and just when I was about to hump her, Janet came out of nowhere and screamed "ah ha". We both jumped from the fright of being caught but Janet told us "don't be scared, let me watch". Christy and I responded in unison " no, that's creepy " and we got out from under the bed dressed ourselves properly, then we went down stairs like nothing happened.

A couple of days later, my father was off from work and he had some male friends over. I decided to sit with them in the kitchen and listen to them talk adult stuff and my father turned to me and said to me in Spanish, "I heard you was doing fresh stuff with a girl" though when he said it, he said it with a smile on his face. I denied it ands he didn't bother me with any more questions of my sexual conquest. I knew who the snitch was and she thought that it would get me into trouble. It didn't, so I developed a plan to get even. I waited until I was home alone and I went into her room and looked around to see what I could do to her and it came to me, she has a lot of dolls, especially some she loved the most, which were dolls almost my height. I wanted to piss on it but I knew she would know, so I took one of her favorite dolls, undressed it, seeing that it didn't have a hole, I went into the kitchen, got a steak knife, went back into her room and made a hole in the vagina area big enough for my penis to enter. I got aroused and humped the hole until I ejaculated, feeling I had to urinate I did it in the doll, then placed the doll where Janet always left it, hoping that she wouldn't know, she didn't and every time I was left home alone, I would have sex with the doll, then urinate inside it, after a few times I stopped because one, having sex with the doll did hurt my penis and second, Janet was trying to figure out where the smell of rotten piss was coming from in her room and that was vengeance enough for me.

My stepmother was leaving me with Christy's mom instead of leaving me home alone or with Janet, Christy and I stopped trying to have sex because Janet would watch us and hope she would catch us, so she could be a spectator. What Christy and I started doing was going outside and playing with the other

kids of the building and the neighbor kids, which were all boys. We would play tag, freeze tag, hide-and-go-seek and a game of dodge the rocks. I advise Christy not to play dodge the rocks but she insisted on playing. We had went around the block of Christy's building, which was connected to an abandoned lot, where a building used to be but what was left in the lot was a mixture of garbage, dirt, some bricks and rocks of all sizes, and a fence that surrounded Christy's building's backyard. On the other side of the block was all fenced up with rubble of where buildings used to be also. I was on one side with a team of six. I stopped talking to Christy because she chose to be on the enemy side, though I wasn't going to throw any rocks at her but my teammates, that was another thing. I hit two of the enemy on their chest with rocks and they stood to the side, rubbing themselves. I noticed that my teammates were aiming at Christy, I tried to stop them but it was too late because someone on my team managed to hit her right on the forehead with a rock. She fell on her buttocks and started crying loudly. We all stopped playing and we all ran to her. We looked at her forehead and she had developed a knot the size of half a golf ball. We tried to console her but she got up and ran to where she lived. Almost all the kids left except two boys, brothers ages twelve and eight years old. We stood behind and the twelve year old asked me if I wanted to hang out in his and his little brother's club house, which was actually an abandoned car in the fenced backyard. I shrugged my shoulders in a I don't care manner. We then climbed the fence and went to the abandoned car that had back seats only, there were no tires or car windows. We all sat in the back and talked about Christy and her getting hit with the rock. We continued to talk about kid stuff until their mother called out for the them from out the back side of their apartment window.

A few days later I was left at Christy's mother's crib, so I decided to hang outside and see if I could find some kids to play with but once outside, I went around the corner to where they hung out, even going by the fenced backyard to see if they were there but no one was there. I climbed the gate and went into the abandoned car and sat down, thinking about how tired I am of my parents leaving me either home alone or at Christy's mother's crib. It was hard enough that I hardly saw my father. My father worked at an auto mechanic shop and he would arrive at home around eight at night, then he would shower, eat, spend

maybe half an hour with me, then he would fall asleep. My thoughts were interrupted by the two brother's mother's screaming at them that they were faggpts and that they probably like it up their asses and then there were silence. I was used to hearing parents bring down their kids, it's like parents not only have forgotten what it's like being a child but get mad at us because they failed in life and somewhere deep in their mind, they hate us because we have a chance of changing our lifestyle and succeeding. I got tired of thinking and being alone, so I left the lot and went up to Christy's and watched television with her and her mother. It was some Spanish soap opera and I watched them until my father came to pick me up, and being that Christy's apartment faced the front of the building, I heard my father call out my name and beeping his car horn. I left running out of the apartment and down the first few flight of stair cases until I reached the top of the first flight of stairs entering the building. I froze because standing between the stairs and the outside door was a big German Shepard, unchained and looking at me. My father didn't know about my last confrontation with a German Shepard, which landed me in the hospital with deep dog bites. He was urging me to hurry up, he couldn't get in on less you have the keys or someone opens the door. My legs were stuck, I couldn't move and the dog knew because every time I managed the courage to sneak a step, he would bark continuously at me. Tears were rolling down my cheeks from the fear, and I saw my father hit the door with his body, opening it without breaking the door. A trick my father told me, later on in the car, my father was holding the door open, and I ran as fast as I could down the stairs and out of the building. All I heard while running out was the dog barking, the door slamming loudly and my father laughing. He told me going as we headed towards the car, that the reason he is laughing is because the dog is actually friendly and that he was just messing with me, if my father only knew my fear.

· · ·

Summer was quickly turning into Autumn and I was finally spending some quality time with my father. He had asked me one day if I wanted to go out with him somewhere. I responded yes and that I was ready. We left and I sat

in silence enjoying the breeze the car is producing as my father drives to his destination. We were passing a Spanish neighborhood and my father asked me if I was hungry. I replied yes and he stopped off at a Spanish restaurant, the restaurant was on the middle of a hill and my father parked across the street from it and told me to stay in the car. I did but before he left he asked me what I wanted to eat and I replied beef stew with white rice. My favorite dish even to this day, then he left. I was kneeling on the driver side window looking at the direction my father went and watching the passing cars go up and down the hill. After some time I got bored and decided to go back to my seat on the passenger side, in moving to my seat, I didn't notice hitting the stick shift of the car until I was seated and I felt the car reversing slowly, I then saw some guy rushing out of the restaurant towards the car and me, he quickly followed the rhythm of the car and jumped in and pressed on the brakes and stopped the car from going any further.

When the guy got out of the car, I saw my father run out of the restaurant with the bag of our food and approach the guy. The guy explained to my father what happened and my father thanked him, then my father got in the car and asked me if I was okay. I responded yes, then we rode to his friend Jose's neighborhood, chilled and ate our food. My father was the first one who finished eating, so he left me in the car and hung out with his male friends. I was watching him interact with his friends, then he did something that I never seen him do before and it fascinated me. He got on a motorcycle and started doing tricks with the bike until he was out of sight. I wasn't worried about being alone and unprotected. His friends and the people of the block watched over all the kids in the neighborhood and if that wasn't enough, all my father's friends spoiled me with anything I wanted.

• • •

I was being left home alone less and less and spending more time with my father. I would go with him to his auto mechanic job and get dirty on purpose doing nothing but sometimes my father would ask me to help him change a tire or assist him in getting the tools he requested. I would gladly help him

and because I was the only kid in his job, I was the life to everyone in his job. Everyone loved me and even spoiled with gifts or anything I wanted though I never took advantage or asked for anything. I was good.

If it wasn't hanging out with my father at his job, I would hang out with him in his friends neighborhood and it got to the point that I made friends with kids my age or a year or two older than me. I became close friends with a twelve year old boy, who loved to exercise. Sometimes he would ask me to join him. He would start with pushups, after he was done he would urge me to do it and boy that was a struggle because I was only able to do one push up. David the twelve year would help me do more. I would be in the push up position and he would stand over me with one leg each side of my waist, then he would put a hand on each side of my chest and assist me in doing some more pushups. After my struggles with pushups, he went and asked me to sit on his back. I didn't voice my doubt on him lifting me up, so I sat on his upper back area and to my surprise not only did he do one perfect push up but he completed nine more in perfect form. And every time I'm the neighborhood with my father, I would hang out with David. If it wasn't doing pushups, David would teach me how to fight or better yet use me as a punching bag. In one of his physical training, he wanted to teach me how to take a punch on my stomach. He instructed me on how to make my stomach firm and hard by doing it himself. He then asked me to punch him a couple of times on the stomach area. Seeing my hesitation, he assured me not to worry. I balled up my fist and hit him as hard as I could one time on his stomach. He took the hit, and seeing that I stopped, he urged me to continue. I did; I hit him a few more times then I stopped. He then told me that it was my turn, I did as he showed me and he started to punch me on my stomach but on the third hit, I couldn't take it. It felt like he snatched the air out of my lungs, making me double over, I was trying to get my breathing in check, when his mother saw what happen and told him to stop being a bully. After I finally was able to regulate my breathing, I explained to David's mother that he wasn't bullying me but teaching me how to take a punch. Satisfied with my answer, she then told him to come inside and take a shower. David mother's invited me to the apartment. David was already inside and I followed his mother to where she said his room was, the

door to his bedroom was closed but one could see inside because half the door was made of glass. His mother announced my presence to David and he appeared in bikini underwear, which were tight and as his mother walked away, he started to do body building poses but my eyes were glued to his crotch area and was wondering where the fuck is his dick and balls? What I was seeing was some small little thing hardly noticeable and the more he flexed the more I found myself getting aroused. I wanted to enter his room, pull his bikinis off and suck him off. I didn't realize that I had grabbed his doorknob until he's mother appeared right next to me and said in Spanish "tu eres un maricon", then switch to English "showing your body to a boy, you must be a faggot ". At that, he stopped flexing his body, and went further into his room and got dressed. The moment was ruined, I knew he knew that I was looking at his crotch area because he kept on doing certain poses to make it look like he had a bigger dick. I told David that I was going outside and left, and I saw my father by the car and he screamed out loud to me that it was time to go.

. . .

The next day, my father announced to everyone that we were going to his friend Jose's neighborhood for a block party and to be ready by twelve in the afternoon. Once twelve p.m. arrived, we were on our way. It was a thirty minute drive and when we reached our destination, I told my father that I was going to hang out with David and some of my other friends, he said go ahead but to be careful, I replied okay and left.

David was outside in front of his building steps with some other kids getting ready to play some game. Upon seeing me, he asked me if I wanted to play tag. I replied with shaking my head up and down in a yes gesture. I arrived close enough to place both my feet with the other little feet getting ready to see who will be chosen to be the first tagger. It wasn't David or I , so we ran behind a car, that was parked further down the block. We waited until it was time to run around and avoid being tagged. We played the game for a while, then changed it to freeze tag. We played freeze tag until we got tired and every one decided to go to their cribs to eat and rest. David invited me to eat at his

crib. I followed him to his crib and we ate rice and beans with steak cooked in onions and fried plantains and after we finished eating, we sat in the living room quietly watching TV until we heard the music outside started to play.

We ran out of his crib and the building and into the streets, where there was a crowd forming in front of the DJ and it was a big crowd mixed with adults and kids dancing with one another. We were doing or trying to do the electric boogey or break dancing to Afrika Bambaataa's and Soul Sonic Force's "Planet Rock"(in those days it was peaceful, it's not like it is now, where a block party is thrown and you have to be worried about being raped, molested, get into a fight, stabbing or shoot out), it was a fun moment, where neighbors and people came together, whether young or old danced to music. There were kids dancing or challenging one another and the adults were doing the same thing. Then kids started to dance with the adults, even challenging some of them in electric boogey dancing, the DJ switched the music to "The Message" by Grandmaster Flash and the Furious Five but before the song ended, he put in "White Lines ,{don't do it}" by Grandmaster Melle Mel, and as I was dancing with some grown chick, I was also looking around the block and seeing that it was packed with people dancing and having fun. When the D.J. mixed in New-cleus's "Jam on It", everyone started shouting out their excitement and the dancing got deeply serious, it was like everyone was hypnotized. The better dancers were challenging dancers on their level, which was okay by me. I didn't know how to dance anyway. All I was doing was what everyone else was doing, failing at that but the others were pretty awesome dancers, even some of the kids were doing some awesome dancing moves too. It got so competitive that everyone with the heart to challenge one another did so, even the kids partic-ipated in competing. The DJ interrupted the music by asking every one loudly "is everybody having fun?" , and you could hear and feel every one yelling their reply of "yes" . The D.J. announced that he was going to turn the mood down a little and played "Love Come Down" by Evelyn Champagne. I was dancing with another female. I knew the only reason the older girls danced with me was because as they put it, I was "adorable". The song was almost fin-ished when the D.J. switched it to "Walkin' on Sunshine", by the Rockers Re-venge. I was having fun and I danced for about an hour or more before I felt

the tiredness sneaking in, and I decided to dance my way away from the crowd and head towards the car where I could see my father was hanging out with some of his friends. As soon as I entered the car and sat on the back seat I passed out and wasn't awake until I got home.

. . .

Days later, I was left at Christy's mother's crib, and I had stopped hanging inside the apartment thanks to Janet's creepiness. She knew that Christy and I wanted to have sex but Janet wanted to watch and tell Christy and I what to do, so I decided to go outside, hoping to bump into the two brothers, which I did. They were sitting on the building's front stoops, and seeing me they jumped up and gave me a pound (a ghetto hand shake) and a hug. We chilled and talked about nothing, then I heard some kids laughing in the back of the block. I went to look and there were a group of six or seven boys playing in the fenced back yard of the two brother's building. We climbed the fence and walked towards them and asked them what they were doing and can we play with them. They said to come and join them. We walked towards the abandoned car with no windows, no tires, and no engine, just the driver, passenger side, and the back had their seats. They were some boys playing in the car. They were pretending to play cops and robbers and were escaping through the windows, while some of the other boys were running around playing their own game. We were with the others in the car talking about kid stuff, then one of the older boys changed the subject to sex with girls. They weren't talking about what they did with them, some were talking about what they wanted done to them, and I was getting aroused and before I gave in to my lust, I screamed out "let's play tag" and that broke whatever it was that was building. Many of the kids replied "hell yeah". We played tag, then freeze tag, and after some time, kids started to leave until those who were left stopped playing, myself included.

Soon the only ones left were the two brothers and me. We were sitting in the back of the car doing nothing but talking shit and relaxing. The youngest brother left due to having to use the bathroom. Once he was out of sight, the

twelve year old turned to me and asked me if I ever did it with a boy. At first I was going to say no, but when he whipped his erect penis out of his pants, my answer was by grabbing his penis and masturbating it. He then stopped me so he could finish undoing his pants and underwear. He helped me with mine and in the process we would French kiss passionately. Once we were naked from the waist down, I laid on my back with my legs slightly open, and he then went between my legs and started dick fucking me and French kissing. He wanted to change position and while we did, we were French kissing like if our life depended on it. He laid with his legs open and as I was bending down to suck his dick, and from the corner of my right eye I saw movement and when I looked to what caught my eye, I froze with fear. It was a dog. The twelve-year-old tried to assure me that the dog is friendly but I didn't want to hear it, I got dressed and told the twelve-year-old that we could finish what we started but not here, with that I ran towards the fence and climb it, I waited for the twelve-year-old and he was right beside me quickly, we went into the empty lot where there was all kinds of garbage and debris, it was beside his building, and in that debris was a standing refrigerator, we managed to open the fridge and position it where no one from he's building could see us, he told me that he wanted to suck my dick, so I let him undo my pants and bring them down with my underwear unto my knees, he pulled my fore skin down and started kissing and licking the head of my dick, then he started sucking, I was feeling good and super horny, when all of a sudden, he bit my dick, not hard but enough to make me jump back, he did it a couple of times apologizing, I stopped him and told him to stand up that I would show him how to suck a dick, he complied but no matter how many times I showed him, he always managed to bite it lightly, so I told him that I was going to finish sucking his dick and got on my knees again and started sucking his penis, the twelve-year-old was moaning and I knew he was about to ejaculate, I was lost in lust and sucking on his dick, I came out of my trance when I heard my father call out for me, I quickly got dressed and told the twelve-year-old to stay there that I didn't want my father catching us, I looked around the refrigerator and saw that my father was walking around the lot, I jumped out of the hiding position of the refrigerator and walked very rapidly towards my father, he asked me

what was I doing and I replied" nothing, just playing by myself ", we walked to the car in silence but in the car, I was fantasying about what was going to happen between me and the twelve-year-old, when I saw him again.

. . .

At home, my father told me that we were going to visit his sister Rosa, who lives at 182 street on Bathgate Avenue in the Bronx, so she could get to know me. I didn't know whom he was talking about but I was anxious to meet her. Before going to Puerto Rico I didn't know who my family was on my father's side and I didn't know that some lived in New York.

The next day, the drive to my aunt was done in silence. I was being entertained by the passing cars and me pretending that my father was racing cars as he was passing them. The drive was also a silent escape from the torments of my stepsister and stepmother. We arrived at my Aunt Rosa after an hour or two. She lived in a three-story building, not counting the basement. My aunt lived on the first floor and before entering the building, we walked up five little steps and entered a two-door entrance, where the only way in was to have a key or ring the bell for someone in the building to open the door. My father rang the bell and after a minute or so, a light-skinned plump mid-thirties woman with long black hair opened the door. She greeted us with hugs and kisses and we followed her into her apartment, walked a long hall way, which lead us into the bathroom, kitchen and the first bedroom. We followed her into the kitchen, where we sat down and my father and aunt were reminiscing about the good times. My father went to the bathroom and my aunt started to ask me question about me and where I lived before my father. I answered them all, she continued to question me about other things and my father having come back from the bathroom, answer them, I learned through my aunt that I had four cousins, two girls ages eleven and nine-years-old and two boys ages five and two-years-old and they were hanging out in some other family members crib and that I have other family members in the neighborhood. My father reassured me that we will meet them all later on in the future. My father talked with my aunt for some more and my father

announced that we were about to leave, five minutes later, we were in the car heading home.

. . .

Like I said before my relationship with both my stepmother and stepsister had gotten bad, every time I am left home alone with Janet, she manages to steal and break things that belonged to her mother, then blame it on me. Sandra, instead of listening to my side chose to believe Janet and punished me with the writing, which I hated and now she had me write three thousand times "I shall not steal and break things that doesn't belong to me". I literally wrote all day and night and the next day, there were times late at night when Sandra would come into the kitchen just to wake me up and make sure I was still writing.

A few mornings later, my father nudged me awake and whispered to me to continue writing before my stepmother wakes up and gets mad at me and left for work. I didn't stop writing even when my father returned from his job and saw me still writing. My hand was numb with pain and my fingertips were black and I still had a lot to write. Some minutes after my father arrived, he approached me and told me to get ready and that we were going out to talk. I was ready within minutes and after he was done taking care of whatever it was he was doing, we left. My father said that we were going to his friend's Jose neighborhood and on the way there, he bought Burger King, a whopper for me, at that time and age, those fucking whoppers were humongous in a child's hand. We were nearing Jose's neighborhood, when my father broke the silence with " you need to respect your step mother" , I don't know why but I didn't tell him what was really going on, I decided to go with whatever my step-mother was saying, and apologized to my father and told him that not to worry, I will respect Sandra and he left it at that. Once we were in the hood, I went to play and he chilled with his friends. After a couple of hours, my father called out for me, letting me know it's time to go.

I really don't know why I didn't tell my father what I was going through when he is at work but my stepmother took advantage of that and became more cruel to me. She allowed her daughter to join in whatever Sandra wanted

her to do to me. I remember one of many times of Sandra calling me into the living room and Janet following right behind me, as soon as I entered the living room with Janet behind me and Sandra in front, Sandra would start by slapping me all over my face nonstop, while Janet would grab me by my hair with both hands pulling on it and making my head thrash from one side to another. After they finished beating on me, Sandra would grab me by the back of my shirt and pull me dragging me into the kitchen, where she would get a couple of hands full of raw rice, pour it in a corner on the floor, and make me kneel on it for hours and threatening me with a more severe ass whipping if I got up.

Each day would be a different form of a beat down from both of them and afterwards kneeling me on raw rice for hours with my face bloodied, I did notice that every time before my father would come, they would take turns looking out the window and clean me up. Whenever they see him coming towards the building, Sandra would then threaten me with, " if you tell, we'll say it's a lie and that you're saying that because you were disrespectful towards me and misbehaved badly" , I stood quiet.

Because of staying quiet, the abuse got worse, and as the days passed by and they'd put me in between them and they would start with the slapping and the pulling of hair, then with the punching me all over my face, head, and body, and after a few minutes of them beating on me, Sandra would grab me roughly, dragging me into the kitchen and making me kneel on raw rice for hours with my face bloodied all over. Then when they would see my father they would take me into the bathroom and clean me up, then change my bloodied shirt and threaten me "if you tell your father what we do to you, I will say it's a lie and when he leaves for work, I'll kill you and make it look like an accident, do you understand me". I could only shake my head up and down, in a "yes" response because the way she said it scared the hell out of me.

This tag team of physical abuse towards me was an everyday thing, then there would be quiet times, free of being abused, then it would start again but this time it was more vicious. They would do all the hair pulling, slapping, and punching me all over my face, head, and body. Now they included the kicking. Janet kicked me on my back sending me flying into Sandra and Sandra responded by kicking me back to Janet, all I felt was hands, fists, and feet hitting

me all over my body. I couldn't even run away or put my hands up to block the hits because Sandra threaten me that they would do much worse if I did.

Then one day in mid-October they gave me a bad ass whipping and had me kneeling with blood coming out of my busted lip and nose. Every time they would beat on me, my shirts were becoming bloodier and bloodier, it never crossed my mind, if my father was noticing my face or the abuse but after that day in mid-October, he came from work, I heard him call Sandra, they quickly ran me into the bathroom and cleaned my bloodied face and change my shirt. Janet was cleaning out what ever blood spots she could find over my face, head and body, when I heard Sandra respond to my father and him replying for her to send me down to him, Sandra came to me, grabbed me by the front of my shirt and said in threatening voice, "remember what I told you before, if you tell, we would kill you". Then she mushed my head so hard that I almost fell forward into the sink.

I quickly rushed out of the apartment, down the stairs, and stopped when I reached the lobby. I walked out calmly and entered the passenger side of the car. I couldn't look at my father or even greet him with the "benediction" I always said to him after he came from work. He looked at me and asked me if I was okay, I answered yes by shaking my head up and down with a tear running down my left side of my face. My father saw the tear and asked me again if everything was all right. I couldn't speak anymore. All I was able to do in answering the question was to shake my head up and down or side to side for an answer. He asked me again, assuring me that he wouldn't be mad at me and I told him everything with hot tears rolling down my face, he sat quietly in the car for a few minutes before starting up the car. I looked up to their window and they stood grilling me until my father drove away, driving to his sister's Rosa crib.

Chapter 9

Home and Family

"Daddy did not give affection and the
Boy was something that mommy
Would not wear king, Jeremy the
Wicked ruled his world."
Jeremy by: Pearl Jam.

Before I continue my story, I want to say something about this book. I hate everything about it and I also noticed that there is something that doesn't want me to tell my story. Why? I don't know, but I'll say this: since I've started writing and editing the first part of this book, certain pages would just up and erase itself on my flash drive. I'll give you an example, pages I to 80 I began writing in a shelter. I bought a flash drive and as soon as I got to page 60, somehow the next day, my work wasn't in the floppy disk. It was erased that was in 2006, and I decided that I wasn't ready to tell my story due to all the complications.

Then in 2015, I had a nineteen-inch Toshiba laptop, and I decided that the world needed to know what was done to me and every time I reached page 70, the next day, twenty or more pages would be erased. I took the laptop to the computer shop and they told me that there isn't anything wrong with the

laptop. Then one day when I woke up to continue writing, it happened again. The different files I had my work saved in, started erasing. I got so upset that I smashed the laptop into a million pieces.

Later that year, my therapist bought me a note book laptop after telling him what happened to my last laptop. I restarted writing the book, then one night, I was on page 60 and I was deep in writing when all of a sudden, my apartment lights started flickering crazily on and off causing my laptop to shut down. When the flickering stopped, I tried to turn on the laptop and it didn't go on. I then took it to the computer shop to get it look at but I was told by the specialist that it just burnt out.

Then in 2016, I decided to buy a typewriter and in getting it, the letter E didn't work, so I used the number 3 as a substitute. It wasn't until a couple of months later, when I decided to get it fixed, I already had written a couple of pages, but as soon as I got to page sixty and up, the typewriter burned out and it was fixed by the assistance of one of my therapists.

While waiting for the typewriter to get fixed, I bought a Lenovo laptop from one of my friend's friends, which was not only stolen but the volume didn't work. The battery wasn't working properly, the laptop seemed to be completely messed up, though I was given a bargain. I took it and felt bad for them because a few days later, I was curious to see what would happen if I reset the laptop and to my surprise, everything started working properly. I used the Microsoft Word Office application and since I only had somewhere around fifty pages, I decided to rewrite everything on the laptop's Microsoft app. I made four different files again just in case it doesn't appear or it gets erased again. I started working hard on my book because I was excited that three publishing companies were interested in my two-part book, I had written 73 pages when I called it a night, so I could get some rest.

The next day I woke up with enthusiasm and I hit the laptop. I opened one of the four files and started typing. I was an hour into typing when I started to see three of my of my four files, one by one simply disappear, I knew that if I tried to look for the files and leave the file I was working with, it too would disappear but my fears came true when right in front of my eyes, my file closed

and disappeared. I was so upset but I decided to go to the same computer expert and it came down that the files couldn't be retrieved or found.

My suspicion of some entity being around me, following me, and not wanting me to write my story was confirmed, when I decided to take a break from writing for the day and went out to visit a friend, who is like a son to me. He lived with his family, his girlfriend, and his newborn daughter and as soon as I entered the apartment, heading to my friend's room, the baby woke up screaming hysterically in sobs. At first I thought nothing of it, but every time my friend, his girl, and the baby would come to my apartment. They would put the baby in my room and the baby would wake up screaming in sobs and would react the same way she did at their crib. Also, since the beginning of the book, I've been hospitalized many times, I've had three amputations on my feet, I almost caught septic poisoning three times and I had two bad side effects from medications and when finally my being hospitalized slowed down and I was able to retrieve my type writer, I started to type where I left off, page 56 and all of a sudden my hands and arms started to cramp up and hurt. Then I started to hear strange noises around my apartment, but no matter what complications or what interruptions crossed my path, I am determined to finish my story and no entity whether supernatural or not will stop me from completing the first part. And this goes for all the negative situations confronting me and all those who have backstabbed me, abandoned me and wanted to see me fail, just know it's not me that you have to worry about. Y'all are going to deal with an entity way more powerful than y'all are, God the creator and the Creator's son, Jesus Christ.

· · ·

Returning back to when I was ten years old and my father and I, left Sandra's crib and moved to my aunt Rosa's apartment at 2239 in Bathgate Avenue on 182 St., in the Bronx, my father and I were introduced to her husband Pipe and I was further introduced to my newfound cousin's that I did not know existed but heard of.

Pipe was shorter than my aunt by a few inches and suffered from baldness. He was a white-skinned, skinny man, who looked older than my aunt's mid-thirties.

then there is five-year-old Junior, who is a white-skinned kid with black straight hair but cropped cut, he looked like the kid from the Superman movie when Superman crash landed in his pod as a baby and grew around five or six years of age. The resemblance was amazing to everyone but me. I really didn't give a fuck. He had a disgusting habit of taking different foods and mixing them together, and then eating it. I had tried one day to mix the foods he mixes. Well it made me gag. His three-year-old brother Anthony was different. He was a three-year-old, who snitches on everything he sees and nosey as hell, he was a tannish-skinned boy with black curly hair.

Then there's the two sisters, eleven-year-old Maria, who has long black shoulder length hair with a white skin complexion and a flat face, and was very sexually active. I didn't find this until later on but her nine-year-old sister Emma, she had long dirty blondish hair that reached the middle of her back, she too was white skinned but was the quiet one and a good girl. As for Emma's looks, well she was beautiful, nothing like her ugly sister Maria.

. . .

As I mentioned before about my aunt's building, one has to walk up five little steps, then go through a two-door entrance of the building. My aunt lives in an apartment that has two forms of entry, one is located as soon as one passes the second door to the entrance of the building but on the left side, and the second one is more or less forty feet from the entrance of the building. Everyone enters the back door because the front entrance to the apartment, which faces the front of the building, is where my aunt's and Pipe's room is located, but before anyone enters the back way, there is the staircase, which leads to the upper floors and the basement.

Once you enter the back of the apartment, you have to walk another forty or fifty feet into a long hallway, where the first thing you see is the bathroom, and connected to it was the kitchen and the living room. As you walk further into the living room, it connects to the three bedrooms, the first one is where the girls sleep, the second room is where the boys sleep and the last one was my aunt's.

I need to continue with describing my aunt's building because it's important to my story. now the other occupants in the three-floored building was an old black lady, which every one called Grandma and she lived on the second with two mentally ill children: a black teen of about fifteen or sixteen years of age and a black girl about thirteen-years-old and they didn't bother anyone and Grandma was a sweet lady, who always loved to pinch my cheeks whenever she saw me. As for the third floor, it was completely empty and no one went up there, and the basement had a small studio apartment in the front section of the building. The rest of the basement had two other rooms, one room was small which was the boiler room and the last room was big enough to hold fifty or sixty people and still have room for more but this room was filled with old furniture and very organized junk all around the room. Also before I forget, the stairs that takes you to and from the basement had a little spacious compartment under it, though it wasn't being used. The back yard too couldn't be used because Pipe had a vicious adult male german shepard and he was the only one that went to the yard and dealt with the dog.

Back in the apartment, I was assigned to sleep with my male cousins and my father slept with the girls and like all things in my young little life, everything starts off good and then it transformed into something else. An illusion of love and happiness. I got along with my cousins and we always play with one another. Sometimes we would all manipulate and hustle my father and Pipe to see who could hustle the most money from them, afterwards no matter who won, we would spend all the money on different kinds of candies and potato chips, putting all the different kinds of potato chips in one shopping bag, mixing the chips together and in another, all the different kinds of candies, then we would all sit in the living room, either to watch cartoons, our favorite TV show like "The Little House on The Prairie" or a movie and while watching whatever was on TV, we would share all the chips and candies until they were gone. Sometimes we would save some for after dinner to enjoy. As it was getting late, my aunt ordered us to start taking a shower because dinner is being prepared and it was almost ready. One by one my cousins took their showers making me the last one and when I was finished, dinner was ready and being served and after we all ate, my cousins and I were told to go to sleep.

. . .

Time passed and Halloween was around the corner. Maria told me that my aunt practices "Santeria"(white Magic) to protect us from evil and evil people. I really didn't care because I didn't understand and didn't believe in any of that bullshit but one thing is for sure is that a lot of spooky and supernatural things were happening in the apartment and in the building. I remember one day of many, it was Maria, Emma, Junior and I, we were sitting in the kitchen, talking about an incident concerning Anthony, when he was taking a shower.

Maria and I were chilling in the kitchen and we decided to check on Anthony while he was in the shower just to make sure he was okay. We approached the bathroom and the door was closed, when it should have been opened, we heard Anthony speaking and laughing with someone, Maria opened the door quickly to see who Anthony was speaking too, Maria and I were curious because Emma and Junior were in the living room watching TV, in the bathroom it was covered with steam from the shower's hot water being the only thing turned on, Anthony was sitting nakedly on the toilet bowl, looking at us with an angry expression on his face. Maria asked him, why was he mad and who was he speaking to. He replied that he was speaking to his friend and that we scared him away. Hearing his response, she continued to question him about his friend. "What friend are you talking about?", he answered, "my friend, who comes and plays with me when I'm alone". Maria and I looked at each other in silence. We returned our attention to Anthony and Maria questioned him again and asked him "what does your friend looks like?", he answered still with that angry expression on his face, "he's a boy small like me, he is dressed in shorts, t-shirt and a baseball hat" and just when Maria was about to finish the story, a broom that was lying on a ninety degrees angle on the wall next to the kitchen sink, stood up by itself and fell on the opposite side of the wall. We all ran out of the kitchen and into the living room, scared out of our wits.

. . .

Then on the early morning of Halloween, my father and I shared the girl's bed, and the girls slept with their brothers. Maria was waking me and as I was trying to get fully awake, I was hearing a commotion in the building's hallway. I went into the living room, where Maria was waiting for me with a look of fear on her face. We spoke in whispers because we didn't want to wake up the adults and the rest of the kids. Maria was explaining to me that she was awakened by the noise in the hallway of the building. I told Maria to be quiet that I wanted to hear and identify the noise she was talking about. Within a minute of Maria being quiet I heard the noise and was able to identify it. It was someone stomping heavily up and down the staircase of the first floor leading to the second floor and whomever was stomping up and down the stairs, they were also dragging chains. I started to giggle at Maria and called her a scaredy cat. I told her, "it had to be Pipe trying to scare us because it's Halloween. I'll prove it to you, come follow me", we walked past her and her sister's room, then her brother's room, and finally to my aunt's room, which had double doors made of glass with curtains that prevented anyone from looking into their room. We had tip toed to the door and opened it just enough to see them. I wanted to prove to Maria that it was Pipe but when I looked into the room, Pipe was snoring loudly and my aunt was passed out.

We returned to the living room quietly and I explained to Maria that it had to be Grandma's son. I told her to follow me into the hallway of the apartment, so we could peek into the peep hole and catch whoever it is making that noise. The noise would stop then return again and every time it did come and go, it sounded like it would get nearer and nearer to the apartment door. It had stopped for some time then it started again. I went to look into the peep hole and Maria grabbed me by my arm. Scared for both of us, she didn't want me to investigate but I wanted to prove to her that it wasn't a supernatural event. We waited by the door for the noise, the stomping and the dragging of the chains got nearer, I quickly looked into the peep hole and all I saw was a pair of boots and a long chained curled around the old muddy boots on the first three steps leading up to the second floor, at that I opened the door quickly and ran towards the stair case to catch Grandma's son but there was no one there. I then ran up to the second floor to see if he was hiding but again

no one was there. I walked back down and went back to the apartment, where Maria was waiting by the door and as soon as we closed the door, the stomping and the dragging of the chains started again but this time I could hear the stomping and the chains going up and down the first floor hallway loudly. I looked at Maria and told her that when it got close to the door, I'll open the door and we'll catch the person trying to prank and scare us. The stomping was getting closer and closer to the door and when it got close enough, I opened it quickly and to my frighten surprise, there was no one there but the muddy boots and the chain curled around the boots in front of our apartment door. After I closed the door, it started again but after some time had passed it stopped and here's the funny shit about the incident. As loud as the stomping and the dragging of the chain was, no one was awakened by the noise besides Maria and me.

· · ·

Then a few days later, around November 5th or so, it started to snow very hard. Maria, Emma, Junior, and I were looking out the window, praying that it snowed so hard that school would be canceled, and it did. It had snowed all day and night and the next day too. I really can't remember how many days it snowed but when it stopped, the snowfall had reached five feet or more, many of the cars were buried under the snow but other cars could be identified only by the top of the hood, which was the only thing visible.

My father and Pipe went outside to shovel the snow from in front of the building and the side walk. Junior and I were looking out the window looking at kids and teens of all ages, climbing on the hoods of the cars and doing back flips into the snow. They kept climbing and flipping into the snow and laughing. Seeing that they were enjoying themselves, Junior and I ran to my aunt and asked her if we could go out and play in the snow. She replied go ahead but be careful, the snow is very deep. Junior and I were the first ones of the kids to go outside. My father and Pipe had the front of the building and part of the side walk already cleared but as for the other buildings connected to my aunt's they weren't shoveled, so Junior and I climbed unto the unshoveled snow

of the stairs of one of the buildings. The snow almost covered us completely but it didn't stop us from diving into the snow head first. We played for a little, then Pipe and my father asked us to help shovel some snow from a building next us. We did as much as we could and after we finished helping them, Junior and I decided to make snow tunnels. I saw the girls and Anthony playing snow ball fight in front of the building but after some time, they all went inside except Junior and I. We were having fun making tunnels, we made a long tunnel that passed two buildings but as we were trying to go further, the tunnel collapsed on us burying us completely. I struggle hard to unbury myself but when I didn't see Junior, I screamed out loud to my father and Pipe and told them what happened and where Junior was buried. They went and unburied Junior, who was very pale, shaking uncontrollably, and crying that he was too cold to move. My father picked Junior up and took him inside but I stood outside playing until I couldn't feel my hands and legs.

I went in and joined Junior in my aunt's bed, where Junior was covered from the neck down with three quilts, I laid next to him and chilled until I was warm enough, I was thinking about going back outside but changed my mind and stood on the bed and watched TV with Junior, who had his color back and his body heat was normal. We didn't go back outside until the snow was gone and on the news, the reporter reported that bodies of some kids and adults were found buried in the snow, when the plow truck cleared the streets of the Bronx.

Thanksgiving was slowly creeping up and Maria and I were getting very close. It got so deep that we started going around the apartment, out of the view of the adults and the kids and French kiss and feel each other up. There were some mornings, when the adults were sleeping, Maria, Emma, Junior, Anthony, and I would chill in the kitchen, waiting for Maria to cook breakfast for us and while she was cooking, Maria and I would speak in codes on how we would fuck each other.

One early Saturday morning, when everyone was asleep except the kids, we were all in the living room watching cartoons but Maria and I had other plans. We were horny and we wanted to fuck, so we told the kids that we wanted to play mother and father and they would be our kids, we gathered

some quilts and made two beds on the floor, one for Emma and her two brothers and the other one for Maria and me. We told them to pretend to be sleeping until Maria and I told them to wake up, as soon as they covered themselves from head to toe, Maria and I did the same thing but we started French kissing. As we were kissing, I would put my hand inside her panties and start to play with her pussy and in return, she would put a hand in my shorts and start masturbating me. My penis was so hard that it hurt. My body was on fire and I whispered into Maria's ear that I wanted to stick my dick in her pussy, at that I pulled my shorts and underwear down onto my knees and Maria pulled her panties down too and just as I was about to get on top of Maria, Junior pulled the sheets off us so he could see what we were doing. I froze and so did Maria. Junior was the only one who could see Maria and I almost naked. He was mostly looking at my hard on. Maria and I thought that Junior was going to scream and tell on us but he didn't make a sound and didn't tell either, Maria and I dressed ourselves properly, and we stopped playing mother and father and watched TV quietly. We were scared and paranoid throughout the whole day worried that Junior would tell on us to his mother or father and when the adults woke up and he didn't tell on us, Maria and I were relieved.

But that still didn't stop us, we would sexually tease each other every day, hoping for the opportunity to actually fuck one another. We already had it planned out. She wanted to suck on my dick and I told her that I wanted to stick my penis in her pussy. Then one evening, I'll say around seven or eight at night, my aunt had washed clothes on her washing machine early in the morning and hung the clothes on a rope fashioned as zip line in the basement, and left them to dry. She had asked us to go downstairs in the basement and get the clothes, Maria and I hid our excitement and walked slowly out the apartment but as soon as the door was closed, we ran down the stairs into the basement and in the last room with all the furniture and junk but instead of having sex, Maria and I got curious of the junk all around the room. Maria then told me that Pipe had a barrel full of marbles of different sizes and colors.

Maria showed me where the barrel was and I went to it and started picking out some Marbles. Maria told me not to take too much because Pipe needed them to make designs around the bath tub. I was rummaging through the barrel,

when all of a sudden, I started to hear several voices whispering my name at the same time. It sounded like six or seven voices. I was about to turn around to see where the voices were coming from when Maria grabbed me by the arm and told me not to turn around and look for the voices, to ignore them. At first I thought that I was going crazy but when Maria told me what not to do, I knew that I wasn't the only one hearing the voices and no matter how hard I tried to ignore the them, their whispering of my nick names "Manuel, Manny, and Macho" had me entranced almost hypnotized. I was lost in their calling. I then felt some one pull on me roughly, pulling me away from the room, breaking me out of the trance. I looked to who it was and realized that it was Maria. She was forcing me out of the room. She was telling me that if I responded to the voices and look in the direction of where it was coming from, something bad would have happened to me. She was still pulling on me until we were in the first room by the stairs. Maria grabbed all the dry clothes from the rope quickly and pulled me towards the stairs breaking me from the trance. I was scared out of my wits, and I ran up the stairs fearfully ahead of Maria and she followed right behind me. We were by the door of the apartment. Not only were they still calling me by my nick names, but they were telling me to go to them. At that we entered the apartment and closed the door, shutting out the voices, and we didn't tell anyone because we knew that no one would believe us.

· · ·

With all this supernatural shit happening to me, I really didn't put my mind to it or fully understand it, to me it was part of life and as I was experiencing these events, I started to notice my aunt always complaining about everything I do. As for my father, he was staying less and less in my aunt's apartment. I was told by my aunt that my father met some female and was staying over in her apartment. I was seeing less of him and when I did, it was like I was with a stranger. It felt like he didn't want to be here with me and my aunt.

Because of his absence, my sleeping arrangement was switched yet again. Instead of sleeping with my male cousins, I was sent to sleep with my female

cousins, and early one morning, I awoke drenched from my chest down to my legs with what I thought was water. Even Maria was wet, I thought that Maria and Emma played a prank on me, making it look like I wet the bed but then the smell of urine hit my nostrils, I still refused to believe that I pissed the bed, and asked the girls, "why did y'all wet me with water". They responded that it wasn't water but piss and they denied that it was their urine. I was thinking to myself, how could this be possible? I never pissed the bed before. Maria broke me out of my thoughts by her running out of the room and screaming to her mother that I pissed the bed. My aunt Rosa came into the girls room and inspected the bed and when she saw the big wet stain, she went ape shit. She started to yell and scream that the bed was brand new that my father and I didn't have enough money to buy a new one. She went on ranting and raving almost all day. I stood in the room because one, I was too embarrassed to show my face and two, I didn't want to be in the presence of my aunt because she would continue to scream and yell at me.

My aunt was in a bad mood all day and once in a while, she would come to the girl's room and scream and yell at me and threatening that she was going to tell my father what I have done. My father was working and he wasn't off until the evening but when he did returned home, the first thing that fucking bitch of my aunt did was scream at him about what I did for at least fifteen minutes straight then she stood quiet and I thought that the moment was finally over.

I heard my father call out to me and I thought he was going to talk to me and punish me. I ran happily to where he was by the entrance of the bathroom. As soon as I reached his side, he grabbed me violently by the back of my neck, almost lifting off my feet and snatched me further into the bathroom, slamming my head face first into the bathroom sink, which was filled with running water. He held my head under, and I started to struggle violently but in doing so, I was inhaling and swallowing water from mouth and nostrils. I was starting to feel the darkness slowly creeping up on me and I knew that my father was going to kill me. I knew that if I didn't try to get out of his grip, I was going to die, so I relaxed a little and with both hands on the edge of the sink, I mustered all the energy I had and pushed upward. It worked and I was able to let

out a piercing scream before he slammed my head face first again into the sink drowning me that scream was what saved my life because my fucking aunt heard it. As I was slowly losing consciousness, I could hear my aunt screaming and pulling at him, to let me go. At that he let his grip on my neck go, and I raised my head spitting out water and gasping for air. I could feel the tears mixing with the water coming down my head and face and from that moment on, my hatred and rage was born. I started to hate my father and every living thing, though I kept it hidden.

Later on that night, Maria told me that she witnessed her mother physically beat my father with one of those home landline phones of the 1980s a couple of times and it was what made my father stop from killing me. I had lost all love and respect for my father, it had evaporated like water being boiled into steam and every day after that my father became physically and mentally abusive towards me.

. . .

After that incident with my father, I started to see even less of him, the only time I would see my father was when he and my aunt planned to baptize me on my eleventh birthday. My father with my aunt's direction, bought me a white suit to wear on my baptism day. I was punished with two weeks of me not getting out of bed because one day, Maria and I was home alone, and Maria was feeling superior than me and she was making it be known by all the name calling. I defended myself and started name calling back and this upset her real bad that we started to physically brawl, we started in her mother's room, all the way into the kitchen, where I pushed her so hard that she slammed onto the stove, overturning a pot of hot water that was used to cook some hot dogs onto her. She started screaming and thrashing all around the kitchen and all the way into her mother's room, where she continued to cry for a while. I went into the kitchen to investigate the temperature of the hot water that was left in the pot after it spilled and it wasn't hot enough to make me cry, I returned to her mother's room to inspect her burns and she didn't have any, only a little redness. She had stopped crying but threatened me on telling her mother and

she did, when Rosa returned from wherever she was, she started to scream, yell, and curse at me and threatening me that she was going to tell my father and that she wasn't going to intervene if my father started to bug out on me like he did the last time.

I was really scared, and I even prayed that he didn't go crazy on me, and when he did arrive at my aunt's crib after work. I had butterflies in my stomach from the fright of what was to come, I heard my aunt scream at my father about what I did to Maria, he then came into the boys room where I was chilling, and in a threatening voice, told me "lay on the bed, do not sit up on less it is to use the bathroom, take a shower, or eat food", he continued with "if you do anything other than lay on the bed, I am going to beat you to death.

Not only did my hate for everyone intensified but I was starting to hate myself to point that I wanted to die. I felt like I was the only one who was suffering in the world and I didn't understand why God didn't help me and the more I laid on the bed, the more I thought of how it would be to run away or just fucking die. I felt that I wasn't wanted, unloved and during the two weeks confined on the bed, I tried to scheme on how to stay out of the bed for as long as long as I could, sometimes my father would be around when I do this and he would bang on the door and tell me to hurry up and if it wasn't him, my aunt would make sure that I wouldn't take long and when the punishment was finally over, I tried to get off the bed, I fell on my knees and no matter how I tried to stand, my legs were too weak to hold my body. It was Maria and Junior who helped me regain the strength in my legs by helping me stand and get my balance.

· · ·

Then December 12th arrived, my eleventh birthday and the day I was to get baptized. I was starting to forget all the bad shit I went through with the Spanish music playing and the smells of the different foods that were being prepared. The smell of the food had me hypnotized like in the Tom and Jerry cartoons. I tried to sneak into the kitchen and partake in a taste test but was thrown out and barred from the kitchen by all the females that were helping with the cooking of the foods.

My aunt and the other ladies were cooking Pasteles, Pernil, Rice, Gandules, and other Spanish foods and as the evening was approaching, people I didn't know were coming to the celebration. Some were family members I didn't know existed until I was introduced later on and the rest were friends of the family. My aunt told me to take a shower that soon, I will be going to get baptized. I did and when I finished showering, I put on the white pants but decided to finish getting dressed in the room because the bathroom was too humid, making the clothes feel uncomfortable. I stepped out of the bathroom and I was frozen with embarrassment because when I went in to shower, there wasn't any kids but Rosa's kids and standing right in front of me, was a little girl of about my age, looking at my shirtless body. I quickly ran into Maria's and Emma's room and finished dressing. I then went into the living room, where the adults were either dancing or drinking and dancing, and saw the little girl who saw me shirtless and I asked her to dance with me. While I was dancing, I could hear my aunt telling someone that I danced like a robot and the person who she was talking to responded with, "he's doing okay, remember he's just a kid" and the conversation was over.

Eight in the evening arrived and so did my father and the woman he was dating. Pipe and my aunt were ready, and we all left to the church on 183 between Bathgate and Washington Avenue, which served as a school for elementary kids and once the baptism was over, Pipe and my aunt became my Godparents and we all returned to my aunt's apartment.

Man the party was awesome, it made me forget everything bad that has happened to me. Even the negative feelings I felt of myself were gone. The living room was filled with people of all ages dancing and in the middle of the living room by the wall was a dinner table with my birthday cake and decorations all around the table, even on the wall around the table and the ceiling.

Dinner was announced that it was ready and my aunt and all the ladies that helped started serving. I was served first and I made sure that I didn't get any food on my all-white suit. I ate with gusto and even went for seconds. I made sure that I left enough room for the cake and ice cream and after I finished eating, I started to dance again with the girl who saw me shirtless.

By the time eleven at night arrived, it was time for the birthday cake to be cut and served. I went behind the dinner table and faced everyone who had surrounded the front of the table and started to sing happy birthday in Spanish to me. When they finished singing, I cut the cake and cake ice cream was served. When everyone finished eating, Spanish music started playing again and we all started dancing. After some time passed, people started to leave little by little. I, on the other hand, was losing the battle to sleep, so I went into the girl's room and changed my white suit into my sleeping gear, and laid on the bed and fell quickly into sleep being that it was the last time my birthday was ever celebrated. I remember that my birthday was only celebrated around four other times before my eleventh birthday.

• • •

Days later, my father came to my aunt's apartment with the lady he's been dating, she was a big-boned light-skinned female with long dirty blonde hair that reached the middle of her back. She lived two buildings down on 2243 on 182 street. I don't know why I did it but when my father introduced me, I kissed her on the lips, which she gently pushed me away. After they spent some hours in my aunt's apartment, I found her kind of cool and everyone accepted her, but I was cautious. I already knew that people change after they are comfortable. Carmen was her name and she stood a little while longer, and then she left with my father.

I didn't see my father for a while and I was wondering if he abandoned me. I was getting very uncomfortable living with my aunt/Godmother, besides her treating me like shit, like some unwanted child, the paranormal activity was getting more active. I remember days after my father's visit with Carmen, his new girlfriend, some real crazy shit happened. I woke up somewhere around past midnight and I had to take a real bad piss. I was switched again to sleep with my male cousins, so I got up from the bed carefully not to disturb Junior or Anthony, and went into the bathroom. As I was urinating I heard piercing screams scaring me so bad that I not only did I almost jump out of my skin but the scream made me piss on my hand, underwear, the toilet seat

and the floor. I fixed myself and ran to where the screams were coming from, and it was Junior and Anthony crying hysterically in their mother's arms.

According to Junior and Anthony, Anthony had awakened as soon as I got up from the bed to go to the bathroom but stood in the room until I came back from the bathroom when all of a sudden the bed started to levitate. Junior continued saying that as the bed was rising something pointy was pressing on his back that's when Anthony witnessing the activity, started to scream out of fear. It had taken a couple of hours for everyone to calm down and fall right back to sleep but the next day, no one spoke about what occurred but Maria and I. We were in the kitchen and above the ventilation system which is above the stove, was a statuette of a Witch sitting on a rocking chair with a broom stick in one hand. Maria noticed that I was looking at the witch and she began telling me that the witch is protection against evil since my aunt practices Santeria. After Maria finished explaining the witch to me, I was thinking to myself, how can it represent good when a lot of the spooky shit is happening, especially to me is evil.

· · ·

The Christmas holidays were around the corner and I already knew what to expect, nothing. During my young life I've received presents two or three times and they came from my Grandparents and being that I was being sent from one household to another, I never had the joy of opening presents and now living with my aunt/godmother, I knew that I wasn't getting anything. When Christmas arrived, just as I said, I didn't get anything but my cousins did and the feelings of jealously and a sadden silent anguish pain squeezing my heart was all I had as a present. Then the New Year's came and went but I didn't celebrate it. Oh don't get me wrong, I pretended to be in a festive mood but deep inside I not only hated everyone but the holidays too. I had to hide the sadness and hatred that was almost overwhelming my heart, mind, and soul, making me want to die and to make matters worse, my father didn't come to see me until a few days after the New Year holiday and it was to take me to meet Carmen's family that lived two houses down.

The next day my father came and picked me up and we went to where Carmen's apartment was, and it had the same layout as my aunt's apartment. Entering the apartment from the second door was the long hallway that connected the living room, bathroom, and kitchen. Carmen introduced me to her mother Milagros, who is a white-skinned older lady of about fiftyish with long dirty blond hair like her daughter and big-boned like Carmen too. She then introduced me to her two children, who to my surprise they both resembled my father. One is a five-year-old female with long dark brown hair that reached the middle of her back with hazel eyes that changed when she was in a different mood, then there was the second child, a male of seven-years-old with blue eyes like my father with short cropped-cut dark brown hair and they both were white skinned, like my father.

The girl is called Puri, and her brother Pito, and Milagros was screaming at both of them about something. Milagros had Pito by the arm, pulling him into the living room, where Milagros had him kneel on the floor, next to the window in one corner next to the big couch I was sitting on. Milagros then left and went into the kitchen, where my father and Carmen were waiting.

I could hear them having a conversation, not really paying attention to what they were saying, my attention was at Pito. I felt a connection due to him being on his knees as punishment. I was thinking how I used to be put to kneel on raw rice, he then did something that had me transfixed on him. He whipped out his erect circumcised penis, which was longer than mine. I had the urge to just grab it and play with and the urge became more powerful, when he started to masturbate and look at me. My trance was broken when my father, Carmen, and Milagros entered the living room, I looked over towards Pito to see if he was still masturbating but he had put his penis away and after an hour or so, my father took me back to my aunt/godmother's crib.

Days later, my father brought his girlfriend and her two kids to my aunt's crib and seeing Pito, I was still curious as to why Pito was punished. While Pito, Puri, my cousins, and I were playing, I pulled Pito aside and asked him. He responded by saying that he was having sex with his sister and got caught. I was left speechless because I knew that having sex with your sister is not only wrong but disgusting but in the back of my mind where my darkness

had laid the thought of fucking Puri and having sex with Pito, but I had to wait when it was the right time, we went back to where the other kids were and started playing.

We played many games and we all agreed to switch the game to wrestling, Puri tried to put me in a choke hold and being that she was young, I responded in a way, as not to hurt her while playing I noticed my aunt/godmother watching me for a while and then she left. I continued to play until my father announced to Pito and Puri that they have to get ready because it was time to go home. While Pito and Puri were getting ready and my cousins left the play area, my father pulled me aside and explained to me that Rosa told him that she saw me rubbing on Puri's butt cheeks. I was too shocked to deny that it happened. In my mind, all I could think of was why would my aunt would lie to my father about something like that. All I was able to do was nod my head up and down, in a yes motion to let my father know that I understood and that it wouldn't happen again. I was very upset but like all my other emotions I kept it hidden. I did the same with how I was feeling towards everyone and I was thinking in my mind, why didn't my father take me to live with him and his new family?

· · ·

Spring was upon us and I was still living with my aunt/godmother. I hardly saw my father and I was tired of being around my aunt who I had a suspicion is trying to harm me. She was giving me all kinds of things to cure me from illnesses she caused with her Santeria elixirs, then one late afternoon, Maria had taken a nap and she woke up crying hysterically. She came into the living room sobbing and I asked her what was the matter and she answered "I had a bad dream about you". She stood quiet for a minute, then continued "mommy sent you to the store and you asked her, if I could go with you and she said no and when you went to the store, you got hit by a car and died". I reassured her that nothing was going to happen to me that she just had a bad dream and dreams don't come true. I stood by her side the rest of the afternoon and the part of the evening just to comfort her and show her that

she is acting silly over a dream but I could see that she was still worried through the whole time.

Later that evening, I'll say around six or seven at night, my aunt had called me into the kitchen and told me to get ready to go to the store and get some things, so she could finish cooking. As I went into the living room to go to the room to get dressed and put on my jacket because it was still chilly outside, I saw Maria crying and after I finish getting dressed, I approached Maria and told her to stop bugging out over a dream. I then went into the kitchen to ask my aunt if Maria could come with me, like she almost always does, but my aunt told me no. I didn't make an issue of it. As I was leaving, Maria met me by the apartment door looking nervous and with tears running down her face. Before I left, I reassured her that everything was going to be alright.

I stepped outside and looked down the long stretch of the block that made two blocks. Now on my aunt's left side of the block, there were five to six three-story buildings, then a partition that separated those buildings with a private house and a big tree that created a shadow that covered half of the middle of each side of the block. Then further down were a couple of abandoned buildings, which were connected to a six-story building at the end of the block, which was occupied with people but I didn't walk down this side of the block because it was too dark and in that era, it wasn't safe because of the drug dealers almost always in a shoot-out with one another or the fiends lurking and looking for money to feed their addictions.

I crossed the street to the other block, where there was two very old three-story family buildings privately owned by two different unrelated black families and it was connected to an abandoned fenced lot, where buildings used to be and was replaced with tall grass that a child or an adult could get lost in and it stretched almost all the way down the block attached to a ghetto mechanic garage where cars go and get their cars fixed by unlicensed mechanics, some who are better than some professional ones. The garage gate was locked with a chain and lock, and connected to the lot, was a five-story building with part of the building on top of a grocery store, which the store and building were located on the corner of the block, which was my destination. As I was walking by the grassy fenced lot, I was fantasizing that I would jump over the fence

and appear in a jungle getting ready to hunt dangerous beasts. I neared the locked mechanic lot, and my attention was reverted back to the real world. I saw a car parked horizontally, where half the car was on the street and the other half on the side walk. The front of the car was facing the locked gate. I looked into the car to see if anyone was in it because the engine was running but there was no one in it. I started to walk between the car and the gate and all of a sudden the car moved forward slowly, I quickly jumped backwards and the car moved back. I repeated my steps my forward and the car did the same, I again jumped back and the car moved back also, it didn't hit me right there and then that when I first looked into the car it was empty, hell no. I was getting mad, I moved forward again and the car did the same, I jumped back and the car did the same. I then looked into the car again but this time, the inside of the car was completely pitch black and it still didn't hit me that car was empty. All I wanted to do was curse the motherfucker out but decided against it because I didn't want to get into trouble. I stood for a minute or more to see if the car would leave but it didn't, so I decided to walk between the car and the gate again and the car did the same thing and when I moved back, so did the car. I said to myself, "fuck this, just walk around the car", I walked behind the car but at a farther distance and the car backed up, following my footsteps and not allowing me to pass behind it. Realizing that the car wasn't letting me get through, I went back to the front but this time I planned to trick the driver, I was going to walk between the car and the gate and when the car follows me forward and it backs up, what I'll do is, time the moment and run forward as fast as I could not stopping. I repeated my steps forward and the car did the same and when I moved back and the car follow suit, I dashed forward as fast as I could and the car's tires screeched as it switched to go forward but this time I didn't stop, I kept on running and managed to pass the car but the car sped forward through the locked gates, busting and breaking the gates, I continued to run towards the corner store and inside, I was scared and wondering, why would someone want to run me over.

While getting the items for my aunt, something was bothering me and had me very curious. There were people hanging out in front of the building on the steps and no one asked me if I was okay or bothered to help me or get

involved and check out what the hell was all that about. They were blind to the whole incident and after I got all the items for my aunt and paid for it, my heart started to beat fast with fear as I walked out the store but this time, instead of walking the way I came from, I walked on my aunt's side of the block and as I was heading towards my aunt's crib, I glanced towards the garage area to see if the car was there and I froze with confusion because not only wasn't the car there but the busted gate wasn't busted. It was locked and undamaged. Seeing that, I ran all the way home never telling Maria or anyone else, until many decades later, as a Halloween story to scare friends of a kid I was mentoring.

. . .

As the Summer was slowly approaching, I was getting more ill in my aunt's crib and instead of taking me to the hospital, she would give me a liquid that was in a little bottle with a red ribbon wrapped around the tip of the bottle. It was something made by her and one of her female friends done on the down-low and every time she would give me that little bottle, she would always have the same woman in her crib. Who she was a mystery to me and as for my father, he was in the blind to all of this. He and his new family moved from Milagro's apartment to 2293 on 183 street in Bathgate. I was excluded from staying with him, and only allowed to visit, which I did one day. I walked up to the fifth floor of the building to where they lived because there wasn't any elevator. I knocked on the door and was answered by Carmen's sister Candy, who had shoulder length black hair, a trim body and men found her attractive. She let me in and told me that no one was home but Puri who was sick. Candy was kind to me at first but as time went by her true colors came out. She was a gossiping bitch who had a hateful demeanor. I walked into the apartment and walked a long hallway that took forty to fifty feet before I came across the first bedroom on my left side and a couple more feet forward was a comfortable living room and further down was another bedroom, which belonged to Pito and Puri and on the right side of the entrance to the living room was the bathroom and the kitchen. The apartment was big but not as big as my aunt's and Milagro's.

I went into Pito and Puri's room to chill with Puri and keep her company, since she was sick and bedridden. We started to play cards and after some time, we got tired of the card game and started to talk kid stuff. Candy was busy watching her soaps and wasn't really paying any attention to us. Puri and I were talking and joking for a while, when she pulled down the quilt that was covering her and keeping her warm unto her knees, she then whispered to me to play with her vagina. She pulled up her dress up, exposing her panties. At first I was hesitant but then Puri grabbed one of my hands and placed it on her pussy. I then slowly put my hand inside her panties and started to first play with her pussy lips and her clit and after I started to feel her getting wet down there, I popped two fingers in her and started finger popping her slowly at first, then a little faster. I became so horny that I stopped the fingering and got up, I sat a on the bed but a little distant so I could be comfortable while suck on her clit and pussy lips. After a minute or so, I forced myself to stop because I didn't want to get caught and as I was pulling up the quilt to cover her, Candy walked into the room and told me to go to the living room, what Candy did was inspect Puri's private area. After she finished, Candy didn't say anything to me and sat down to continue watching her soap's. After a while of sitting in silence in the living room, I decided to leave the crib and head back to my aunt's crib.

At my aunt's, I was scared that Candy would tell my father. I knew that if he found out, he'd probably whip me to death but by the end of the day and my father didn't say anything, I knew that Candy stood shut about the ordeal between Puri and I. I got to see my father at the beginning of the summer school vacation and it was to take me to my grandparents, which was fine by me because my grandparents were the only ones giving the love I needed. Not that fake shit everyone was showing me and because my grandparents spoiled me, I never disrespected them for they never gave me reason to. And like all the other times with my grandparents, every Sunday was church day and after the church service was over, my grandfather would take us out for Chinese food, then go to a park and eat the food in peace while watching the people and kids in the park and once I'd finish eating they would let me play in the park with the kids that was there. And if it wasn't Chinese food, my grandfather

would take us to City Island, to eat fried shrimps, clams, or fish sandwiches with fries. Then we would chill outside quietly, listening and watching the seagulls scream in the air begging for food or snatching food from the ground, tables, or people.

Sometimes, we would go to the beach and spend the entire day there and afterwards, we would get something to eat and chill somewhere my grandfather would take us and if it wasn't spent outdoors, we'd be home and while my grandmother would be making one of her specialties, my grandfather and I would be watching something on TV.

Sometimes on the weekends, I would go with my grandfather to his job at the bakery, and help him make bread and all kinds of donuts and when I would get tired, my grandfather would allow me to take a break. I would go down to the basement where the boss of the Cuchifrito would be counting money or doing paperwork. While he's doing either one, he'll tell me stories about people doing crazy stuff in his job and if I wasn't hanging with him, I would hang out with the Mexican cooks who would make me part of their jokes by asking me in Spanish, "tu eres un chingao" or "tu chingas", and even though I didn't understand what they were saying, I would answer "yes" and they would all crack up laughing. What they were asking me was "if I was a fucker", and "do I fuck"?, and though they were joking, they always made sure that I was safe and fed, even sometimes they would show me how they made the meals for the day.

• • •

One of my many fondest memories with my grandparents, is where every night, my grandmother would ask me to kneel next to her and recite word for word the our father prayer or my grandfather would have a hand puppet, and before I go to sleep, he'd tell me jokes or ask me funny questions. Making me giggle like crazy, he would go on until I finally fell asleep or the many nights when my grandmother would make hot cocoa from those thick cocoa bars, and my grandfather would cut pieces of Guava paste and a cheese that is wrapped in a red wax covering, place them on a large dinner plate with water

crackers surrounding the snacks, then we would all sit in the living room together, watch TV and eat the snacks.

· · ·

As the summer vacation was almost ending, my father came to visit me, only
to tell me that I would be staying with my grandparents until half the school
term. I really didn't give a fuck but I pretended to be sad but when he left, I
was back to my happy self and when half the school term arrived, my father
came to pick me up to live with his new family.

Chapter 10

Home and the New Family

"The Devil has put a million on my Soul and those, who are blinded by his lies has corrupted my soul, developing Hatred in my Heart and Rage in my mind, hoping I become like them."

The new family, what a crock of shit. I was the male version of Cinderella and what made matters worse was the fact that my step siblings had my father's features and there was favoritism because of it and as an introduction to the new family on my first day being there and to show me that I was unwanted. My father for no apparent reason just straight out punched me on the face as I walked through the living room while there being visitors. I went into Pito's and Puri's room, where I was going to share a bed with Pito, and stood in the room because I was too embarrassed by what my father did to me and since I was alone in the room, I got bored and wind up falling asleep. Later on that night I was awaken by my father beating on me with a pair of rubber slippers, at first I was being beaten on my back, head, and arms, which was what woke me up and when I turned around, he continued to beat me all over my face, chest, and arms.

Carmen ran into the room and interrupted and stopped my father from continuing his assault on me, she then asked my father why was he beating on

me, which he answered in Spanish that Pito and I were doing homosexual activities, Pito interrupted my father and told Carmen with tears running down his face that my father was a liar. He explained that he was hot and uncomfortable so he took off his t-shirt and shorts staying in his underwear. I on the other hand didn't know Pito did that, I was dead a sleep, they believed Pito but anything I had to say was paid no mind.

. . .

A few nights later, there was a knock on the apartment door and I was told to answer it. I ran to the door and without asking who it was, I opened it, and froze with horror, it was my father's ex-wife and her daughter, Sandra and Janet. I thought they came to kill me. I slammed the door closed and ran into the living room and told my father who it was. Carmen and my father got up from the sofa and went to the door and handled the situation, I could hear Sandra speaking loudly that all she needed was for the divorce papers to be signed, to finalize the divorce, when everything was done and Sandra and Janet left. My father was the first one to enter the living room, he looked at me and told me in a threatening voice to go in my room.

My father was always finding an excuse to beat on me or torture me and he made an issue of me returning late from the store. I remember one day, I came home late from the store because the first one was packed with customers, so I decided to go to the other two stores that are located underneath my building but they too were packed. When I returned home, my father was so angry that he made me go up and down the buildings five flight of stairs. He wanted me to go all down way down and out the front of the building, where he could see me and go all the way up and report to him inside the apartment. I had to this over and over again until he decided it was enough.

I don't know how long I was going up and down those steps. I lost count after the fourth time, my legs were starting to shake painfully making it harder to climb up the stairs and it was taking longer going up and down the flight of stairs. It was Carmen after seeing me walking funny that stopped my punishment but told me to go to my room and stay in the room while she dealt with

my father, who was pissed off after finding out what Carmen did but I listened to Carmen and stood in my room and didn't make a peep. I only came out to either use the bathroom, take a shower, or get my food, which I ate alone in my room.

. . .

My father always found ways to ignore my existence or blame me for things I never did and I don't know why but he always thought that Pito and I were having sex, when in fact it never crossed our minds while living there and since my father accused me for things I never did, I decided if I'm going to get my ass whipped, tortured, and punished, might as well to do everything, I even told Pito, how I felt and he agreed.

The first sexual activity happened a couple of days later, after the up and down stairs incident, my father was in his bedroom, watching TV and I was watching Pito play with Puri's vagina, her panties were halfway down her thighs. Seeing that her pussy was wet, my penis started throbbing hard in my pants but I held on to my urges and asked Pito in a low voice, "why do you do it with your sister"?, and they both replied that they were boyfriend and girlfriend, she even went as far as saying that she has another boyfriend named Sammy, I asked them, "who the hell is Sammy?", and they both answered, "our cousin".

Puri then asked me if I wanted to be her boyfriend and without letting me answer, Pito started fondling my erect penis over my shorts. After a couple of seconds, Pito put his hand inside my pants and underwear and started to masturbate me slowly. I was in heat and I wanted to get naked and have sex with both of them but after a couple of minutes of Pito messaging my balls and jerking me off, I pulled out his hand from inside my pants and told him to stop that we were going to get caught. They listened to me and fixed themselves and as we started to play wrestling, my father appeared in front of the room's doorway and stood there and told us to stop playing and making noise. That was another thing my father didn't approve of me doing, playing or playing with anyone. Carmen would intervene and send all three of us into the room and play, while she dealt with my father.

Sometimes we would play as quietly as possible but eventually our giggles and laughter would overtake our silence, making my father scream in Spanglish "callate la fucking boca" "shut the fuck up". We would try to be quiet but it was hard because we would be making fun of my father or quietly imitating him but all our giggles and laughter would stop when my father appeared at the front of the bedroom door and glared at us angrily, knowing what that meant. Pito, Puri, and I would go into the living room, and watch television quietly until it was time for bed.

My father in making me feel invisible only acknowledging me when he found excuses to beat on me, torture me in every mental way or ignore me, like in going to school, he had me dressing bummy with holes the sizes of half dollars on the side of my sneakers, while my step siblings were dressed fashionable and to make matters worse, I was in special ed. The special ed kids were the joke to the regular students of the school, especially those of us taking the yellow submarine or the banana boat a.k.a. the school bus. I had to take the school bus because from where I lived to P.S.62, which is located on Fox street between Leggett Avenue and Avenue St. John was far away and though I was in Special ed, I didn't mind because I was surrounded by kids like me with issues.

.   .   .

In school, I became friends with a kid in my homeroom class named Lazaro, who happens to be the target for bullies because of how he walked and sat down. He walked like a girl but tried very hard not to and when he sat, he sat like a girl. He would sit on one foot, where the heal of that foot would go between his buttocks, the school bullies would always tease him for it and some did it to impress the girls that sat around us, the boys would ask him, if he was a fag and if he like it up his ass. Because of the way he sat, I got mad and defended Lazaro by stating to the bullies with "oh you'll just jealous because no one is fucking you in the ass", that made the girls and some boys laugh, as for the bullies, well they stopped bullying him but except for the one's in our class, they were too many and he wouldn't even defend himself.

The bullying in my class on Lazaro started because he was speaking to the teacher and instead of the teacher taking Lazaro somewhere to talk on a one-to-one basis, she spoke to him in the back of the classroom, where everyone could still hear the conversation. Lazaro was telling the teacher that he stood over at a family members apartment and one night, one of his cousins seduced him into having sex. The kids in my classroom started laughing thinking he had sex with a female cousin but I knew different, so I kept it to myself, and it made him emotional and a little mental and because of the experience he couldn't concentrate on school work unless he was given a break, to do what he wanted. I had gotten up to go to the bathroom and as I passed Lazaro, who was busy doing something else besides school work, I was amazed by what he was doing. He had taken a break and started to draw, and he was drawing the Statue of Liberty exactly as she looks with a different background which made the whole drawing look beautiful. When I complemented him on his drawing, everyone in the class got up and went to see his drawing, even the teacher and the teacher's aide participated in surrounding him and they all complimented him with oohh's and aahh's.

The next day after lunch, my class was walking up the stairs, heading to the classroom and Lazaro and I were the last one's in the line. I was behind Lazaro and he stopped at the top of the flight of stairs, facing me as I was going up. He was looking at me in a different way that I knew but I pretended not to know, I ran up the stairs saying to him "the last one up, is a rotten egg" and together we raced all the way to the classroom.

In the classroom, I was thinking of the look he gave me, letting me know that he was interested in me sexually. Why I didn't show interest in him? Because one I wasn't looking for homosexual activity and two he was too easy, I'm not going to lie, he did look very handsome with his low cut cropped straight black hair and his tannish skin tone. He was taller than I was by a few inches and every time he looked at me with interest, he would look at me biting and sucking on his lower lip, making me sexually aroused. I would fight the urge to respond because he wasn't really my type, it was the bad boys that I was interested in and the challenge of me finding ways to seduce them to have sex with me. It feels strange writing this because I sound like a homosexual

and due to the violation done to me by my mother's husband, I find myself having sex with males just to corrupt them and when I look at Lazaro, I felt disgusted with myself and with the thought of me waking up to a male, even the bad kids I seduced or other boys who wind up wanting to have sex with me. I felt disgusted after I was done with them but once the urge was satisfied, I wouldn't be interested in male sex, only being with girls but Lazaro was making it hard for me because it made me fight with the part of me that wants to be evil and corruptive and fuck his brains out but when the teasing on him got worse, he was moved into another classroom, which was fine by me but the teasing didn't stop there, other kids started bullying him and it didn't stop until he was transferred to another school and the another reason why I didn't find a way to have sex with Lazaro was because his eyes had a demented look to him. He looked like he was going to kill someone, he really scared me but fascinated me at same time.

· · ·

Then a few days later in school, I was headed to another classroom when I saw a Spanish kid being jumped by two black kids. Knowing that the fight wasn't fair, I involved myself and jumped in and helped the Spanish kid. We fought them from the long stretch of hallway that led to other classrooms all the way down into the staircase. We fought hard managing to get the upper hand on both kids and once we were in the staircase, it's when we fought the hardest making the two black kids back down. They couldn't take any more of our hits. The Spanish and I made them escaped by running down the stairs, never bothering him or us again and during all that fighting, not one teacher or aide came to separate us or stop the fight and because of me, helping the kid, we became best friends.

As we were walking, I come to find out that the Spanish kid was lost looking for his assigned home room classroom, which was the classroom I was in, I introduced myself as Manny and he said his name was Audaliss, when he found out that we would be together in the same classes, he was happy and we sat next to each other. We got so close that we began to prank one another

and the girls, the girls were crazy about his almost mid-shoulder length dirty blond hair, and his tannish skin tone. He wore glasses and was taller than me, making him look more handsome and I believe he was having sex with some of the girls in school. He and I were pranking the girls constantly. The girls didn't mind me pranking them because they saw me, as an adorable little cutie because of my height and my innocent looks.

As the days passed, my relationship with Audaliss became stronger than friends, we became brothers but then he got sick and was out for a week and through that time, I got into a fight with some big fat kid in my class. The heavy set kid for no reason got up from his seat and came to where I was seating at and suckered punched me on my face, while I was busy doing my school work, then the fat motherfucker turned around and went back his seat, I got so enraged thinking that he thought that I wasn't going to retaliate, I was so mad that I tasted blood in my mouth, I then ran to him and faced him, so we could be face to face and straight out punched him twice on the face, then I quickly grabbed a chair and swung it as hard as I could, hitting him on his face and chest. With that, all the fight in him died and that's when the teacher decided to intervene, the fat bitch was escorted out the classroom and was suspended. As for me, I was given an assignment to write one hundred times "I should not fight with anyone in school", the assignment was easy but what wasn't easy was that I had to get the assignment signed by my father. If I did that, he would of beat my ass because he didn't want me to fight with anyone, even if it was to defend myself. What I did was, since he had signed a permission slip some time ago, his hand writing was that of a small child, I used my left hand to sign his name making it looked exactly like his sloppy hand writing, so when I took the signed assignment letter back to my teacher, and I gave it to her, it passed with no question of suspicion.

The last few days of school before the summer vacation was cool, Audaliss my brother from another mother was back. I started to call him "the blind bat with glasses" and continued where we left off with the pranking each other and the girls. We would be in the school lunch room and we would go around snapping bras and running away, making the girls playfully chase us, It used to be funny, watching them arch their backs forward in painful surprise before

they chased us and even though we were pranking each other and the girls, we always kept our grades up and respected the girls.

On the last day of school, we weren't given any assignments to do in our homeroom class, so the four eye faggot decided to prank me, even though we had a truce, the motherfucker was sitting next to me like usual and was busy writing a letter, he asked me to go into the right side of his pants pocket and get the letter he had there, I told him "no, why doesn't he get it himself?", he responded "I'm writing a letter to a girl and I don't want to lose my frame of thought" and my stupid gullible ass believed him, I went into his right inside pocket looking for the letter and I didn't feel anything but something rubbery, I started pulling on it and then it hit me, I was not only holding his dick but I was pulling on it like an idiot. I couldn't scream out because we were in class and in doing so, the class would know what I did and call me a cock holder or other messed up things. Audaliss was giggling and his giggling were becoming louder and louder, I took out my hand out slowly and on the down low, not to draw attention because some of kids and the aide was looking at him, as I took out my hand, I told him that I will get even. I was a little mad at him for pranking me that way but I was even madder because I had to wait after the school vacation was over to get my revenge but for now, we chilled, talked shit wishing we lived next to each other, so we could hang out all summer long together.

After the school day ended, we stood in front of the school, and spoke a little more, then we gave each other our secret handshake, then we hugged each other and said to one another to have fun and be careful, then we departed. He went his way and I went mine, then a few days later, my father took me to my grandparents, which was a relief, a relief from being around my abusive father and worrying about being beaten or being mentally tortured by him and also from being around Pito and Puri, why? Because they wanted to have sex with me.

• • •

My father thought that abandoning me at my grandparents was a curse, but it wasn't because of them and their love for me, I am able to keep my personality

in prison, and even though deep down my personality and I both agree that society needs to burn and die. Yet I am still grateful when he brought me to my grandparents because little by little I was being corrupted more and more by the temptation of sex, which disgusted me but keeping me fascinated and exciting to me that's why living with my grandparents was awesome. I was free to be a normal kid and if it wasn't working with my grandfather on the weekends or home with my grandmother making bread pudding, Mavi, or other exotic drinks or spending the day in church service or in the parks and beaches, or we would spend it at home chilling watching TV and eating or just watching television in silence.

When I am at home with my grandmother, she would teach me how to season and cook all kinds of different meats and foods or how to sew clothes and other things or how to properly wash clothes. She once told me that I needed to learn to do these things, so I wouldn't depend on women for anything, that if necessary, the only thing I would need a women was for procreation. It never was a bored day in grandparents' home, I was always learning something every day and my brain was drinking it all up. Part of me was excited with the learning, it was and still is, a strange feeling in me, to wanting to learn more than normal Human Beings and now at the age of 50 years of age, the extra knowledge that I have acquired, is now killing me slowly, mentally, spiritually and emotionally, for as I am writing this, my birthday is in a few days, making me a half of century-year-old and a year-old, and I sit alone, where everyone has abandoned or betrayed me and even some who I used to care the most, has tried to get me hospitalized three times , so I could get my feet amputated. This individual has been blinded by his mother, who practices Santeria, which is actually worshipping demons, who disguises themselves, as angels or God and these Santero's create potions to actually control all of the families they want to control. This individual talks to me like he has helped me or stands by my side but actually he has never helped me in anything in his fucking life. Anyway , I am sorry but I went a little too far into my future, I am smoking a blunt and I am letting my heart and hands do the telling. So we left off with me being eleven-years-old with my grandmother telling me that I only needed women was for procreation, my grandparents were teaching

me survivor living skills. When all the teaching for the day was over, I would ask to go outside with the kids of the block. My grandparents would allow me and it would be adventurous and dangerous but it was still fun with the neighborhood kids. My grandparents didn't know that the kids I hung out with were a little off, (mentally ill), though we never did anything bad, we were just a mischievous bunch.

By midsummer, my mother came to visit me and take me clothes shopping. We spent the whole day going from one store to another, then we would take breaks to eat either pizzas or hot dogs, then return back to shopping. After all the shopping was done, we returned back to my grandparents, where my mother didn't stay long, for a moment I was happy that I spent some time with my mother, I didn't care that she spent a couple of hundreds of dollars on me, no, what mattered was the quality time we had together but I got depressed because she had left and it seems like that was all she came to do, buy me clothed like if it was an act of love. All I really wanted was to have a real family, instead of being dumped to my grandparents and to make matters worse, later on that week, my father came to supposedly pick me up and take me home, I was even excited, even though he treated me like shit, my excitement was evaporated with the news that I would be staying with my grandparents a little while longer, I asked myself this questions. Why doesn't my parents love me enough to want me to live with them? and why do they keep on hurting me? but the only answer that came back in the form of my emotion was rage and hatred, which I kept well hidden.

Don't get me wrong, I love my grandparents but what I was hungry for was the love of a mother and a father, something that all the kids around me were getting, except me.

.   .   .

The summer vacation was over and I returned back to school, while staying with my grandparents, every Monday through Friday my grandmother would wake me up, so I could take one of my fake showers, and while in the bathroom my grandmother would make me my favorite breakfast, French toast, which I

would eat quickly, so I won't be late for school but there were times, I woke up late and instead of showering. I will grab the breakfast my grandmother made, which she wrapped up in aluminum foil and she'll give me a couple of dollars to get me something to drink and some candy. Back in those days, candy was way cheaper, like the Tootsie rolls, two for five cents or many other sweets with that same deal. I had bought a whole bag of Chan's bubble gum, which was one of the kid's favorite candies, and when I arrived in my home room class, I started to chew on a few pieces of gum on the down low (on the down low, means doing it in secret), but somehow the teacher realized that I was eating something and she asked me out loud "what are you eating?" I responded, "nothing". "I just saw you chewing on something" she retorted. I was starting to get irritated by her interrogating me in front of my classmates, so I answered in a sarcastic manner "gum". She continued questioning me "didn't I stated that there's no eating in class on less, you have enough for the whole class". I looked her directly at her eyes, the whole class was looking at the confrontation between us, then without taking my eyes off the teacher, I went into my book bag and grabbed the bag of Chan's gum, pulled the bag out and slammed it on my desk. At that the whole class started to laugh, I got up from my seat and gave every one in my class five sticks of gum and sat back down, the teacher not only didn't stop me from giving out the gum but she didn't bother me through the whole day, though after that incident, I never brought candy to the class ever again.

·   ·   ·

I loved school. It was an escape from the troubles in my life but in all honesty, some teachers can be fucking assholes and a pain in the ass. I remember one teacher, who was an old European lady, she would tell me every time I would go to her class that the meaning of "Mr." is actually Master not Mister and when I address an adult male I should address them as Master. In my head, I said to myself "who the fuck does she think she's fooling", but I responded "yes ma'am" and left the class. Now mind you, in school the teachers really didn't teach the true history of the horrors of slavery. They never went into

details and I never knew anything about racism but when that old lady made that statement to me, I knew there were something wrong with what she said but like all things I dealt with, I just let it fly and ignore it.

If it wasn't the asshole teachers, it was the Guidance counselor, who I would see once a week. He would question me about me and a whole lot of other stuff but instead of me saying the truth. I would lie and he would then put me to do the Inkblot test and I would carefully watch what I said to him because I knew what he was looking for and I couldn't tell him my secrets because I felt that if I told him all the bad things done to me and things still being done to me, I would get into trouble and so will certain individuals in my family but I did tell him while doing the Inkblot test that I was sad but not the reason for my sadness.

•   •   •

Somewhere around August or October, my father decided to come and pick me up and take me home, I had learned how to put on the mask of false emotions when around him and the emotion that I use the most is that of happiness. I knew what was going to happen to me living with my father but this time, I was going to do everything he accused me of, especially having sex with my step brother Pito, which was the main thing he accuse me of, my thoughts were disrupted when we arrived in 183 street, instead of going to 2293, to the building where they lived, I followed my father to a three story building, half a block away from 2293, and stopped at 505 east 183 street, where they had moved to and lived.

There were five little steps in front of the building before entering inside the building was one long flight of stairs which led to the third floor apartment, where we lived, and as I was going up the stairs, I saw that there was a Spanish family of seven that lived below us, five boys ranging from the ages of eighteen, eleven, nine, five, and a infant of about two or three-years-old and their parents, now the second floor is actually on the first floor and the basement is where the first floor apartment was located, as for who lived in the basement apartment, I never paid any mind to who did.

The apartment we lived in had three bedrooms, two big ones and a small one. One of the big bedrooms was located forty to fifty feet from the entrance of the apartment, passing the living room, the bathroom was across the room and they both were connected to the kitchen, and it was the bedroom I would be sharing with Pito and Puri, where they slept on bunk beds and I on a regular single bed.

The other two rooms were located once you enter the apartment, and you make a left into the apartment entering and passing the living room, which was where Carmen and my father slept, and the small bedroom is connected to my parent's room but not the living room and those two bedrooms faced the front of the apartment.

The apartment was an improvement than the last one, but the one thing did not change was my father's treatment of me, it had gotten worse, now it wasn't only beatings, torturous punishments or humiliating me. No, now he was using cruel words to beat on me.

I remember in one of my father's torturous behaviors towards me before he started to verbally assaulting me was when one Saturday morning, it was Pito, Puri and I, we were preparing our sugarless Kellogg's cold flakes cereal and I was putting some sugar on my cereal and Puri, who my father spoiled and treated her like if she was made of diamond, started rushing me to hurry up and finish using the sugar, instead of her just standing next to me like Pito was doing, no that little bitch started making a big deal about it, so I tuned her out and ignored her bad mistake. She went to my father crying and complained about me, making my father get up from his bed and take the five pound bag of sugar that Pito and I had used and poured more than half a bag into my bowl. He then threatened me with "if I didn't eat everything in the bowl, he was going to beat me to death," it was around nine in the morning and I was still eating the bowl of cereal full of sugar. Somewhere around one in the afternoon, the taste of cereal was so disgusting that it made me gag and it was Carmen, who told me to go and throw the cereal away and go to my room and stay out my father's face, which I did, I stood as quite as a church mouse because I knew that my father was very pissed off and ready to take it out on me.

. . .

Then to make matters worse, I started to wet my bed again. I was able to hide my actions for some time but the pissing on my bed got worse, I hid my actions by changing the bed sheets and my clothes but the bed started to smell bad and my father found out and he started calling me names and saying things to humiliate me, especially in front family members, he even had Pito and Puri teasing me and calling me "piss pot" and other names.

The teasing and the name calling had gotten so bad that I would stay in my room, listening to my walkman that my grandparents had gotten me before I left and ignore everyone, especially Pito and Puri but one day Pito took it a little too far and scream out loud that I was a faggot, it had gotten me so mad that without thinking, I threw the walk man with all my might at Pito as he was running away from me, hitting him on the middle of his back, causing him to not only fall on the floor but to cry like a little baby. He was sobbing so loudly that Carmen came to check on him and asked him what happened, he told her that I threw the walk man at him for no reason, I interrupted whatever else he was going to say and told Carmen, what really happened, instead of her becoming mad at me, she turned to him and told him that's what he gets for bullying and teasing someone. I was lucky that my father wasn't at home when that happened because it would have been a different outcome, by the time night fall arrived, Pito and I made up and became friends again, Pito, Puri and I even started playing as quietly as possible until it was time to go to sleep.

. . .

It was late at night, when I felt some one tapping me to wake up, I awoke to see that it was Pito standing nakedly and with an erection next to my bed, I could tell that it was late at night because everyone else was sleeping and by how quite it was, seeing him naked with a hard on, made me became aroused. I got up from my bed and got naked with him, my little penis was hard and Pito stood very close to me and we started sword fighting our dicks together,

he stopped playing with both our dicks and laid on my bed and asked me if I wanted to fuck, without answering him, I laid next to him but on my back, he then got on top of me and positioned his and my penis between each other's legs but in the groin area and started humping me, I didn't have to do anything because it felt like we were both gyrating in sync (moving at same time) with one another.

After a couple of seconds of Pito humping me, I join in the humping with him because I was about to ejaculate. I grabbed Pito by both buttocks and held him still so as not to make me cum, he laid on me without moving and when I was able to calm down, I told him to get off me, so I can suck his dick. He did and laid on his back, I spread his legs open enough, so I could lay between his legs and start sucking his dick like I was starving. After a minute or two I took out his penis from my mouth and started sucking on his balls. I let myself go with the moment, letting all my stress and the bad shit I felt about myself and the shit I was being put through by my father, take over me and it felt good. As I continued to perform oral sex on Pito's dick and balls, I was getting more and more aroused. My body was burning on fire with lust and in that mode, I did something I've never done before, while sucking on Pito's balls. I took the tip of my tongue and tasted his rectum and when It had no taste, I told him to turn around and lay on his stomach, he did and I started kissing and licking on each of his buttocks until I reached his rectum. I tried to put my tongue as far in his rectum as I could, then started sucking and nibbling around the skin of his rectum, I continued to perform oral sex on his rectum for a long while until I decided it was time for me to cum. I stopped sucking on him and lifted myself a little and moved myself on top of him, so I could penetrate him.

The world around me was invisible and the only thing that matter was the sex I was having. I had penetrated Pito and was humping him like a rabbit, I started to feel the power of ejaculation sneaking up my balls and when I finally erupted, my entire body felt like it was hit by a bolt of lightning, making me feel electrified as the last bolts of ejaculation passed my body. I stood perfectly still on top of Pito and after I was able to control my breathing and calm down, I rolled off Pito and laid on my back nakedly. Pito had gotten up, dressed, and

climbed onto the top bunk bed and fell asleep, I stood up on shaky legs, got dressed, laid back down and fell asleep too. When I awoke the next morning, I felt relieved, new and happy.

. . .

I was in a good mood all the next day and after school. Pito and I didn't speak on what happened last night but then Puri, I don't know if she was awake, when Pito and I were fucking or if he told her but she asked me, while in the room doing homework, if I wanted to fuck her. Just the mention of sex made me horny. I answered "yes" but told her to wait until night fall when everyone was sleeping, she responded okay and we left it at that but later that night, Puri and I waited until everyone was sleeping and the apartment was quiet with the distant sound of my father snoring, I got up from my bed and went to the bottom bunk, where Puri slept, she was not only awake but was already naked, I too got undressed and sat in the middle part of the bed and with my right hand starting to fondle her vagina and clitoris. When I felt her get real wet and slippery, I opened her legs wider, laid between her legs and started to hungrily suck on her pussy lips and her clit, my little penis was throbbing so hard that it was hurting. I stopped sucking on her vagina and quickly got on top of her and penetrated her at first I started humping slowly but the lust in me couldn't contain itself and I started humping her hard and fast, it didn't take long for me to reach my peak but when it did, boy my body felt like it blew up, my ejaculation was more powerful than what I felt with Pito. I laid on her until my body stopped trembling and I was able to control my breathing, I rolled off her, so she could get dressed, and I did the same but on real shaky legs, I then went to my bed and fell peacefully asleep again.

. . .

The sexual activity between Pito, Puri, and me was almost an every two or three night thing and I've learn that Pito can't ejaculate and I was still inexperienced when it came to girls because I didn't know that girls can get orgasms.

All I knew was that girls could get horny, I thought that only some boys could ejaculate. The sex between us was my escape from what was going through my mind and life, I was getting different urges, which I hid and controlled. I wanted kill everyone in my family and everyone in my path, especially those who represented happiness, there were times, I would be in the streets just walking around and when I see kids and their parents or family members sharing happiness and love, the hatred in me became a physical knot in my throat making my whole being feel on fire, I wanted to destroy everything that represented love, happiness and goodness and sex was my only way to calm those urges.

As I mentioned before, school was also the other entity that helped me escape me, giving me the ability to contain my emotions, and when that happens I'll start to feel guilty for having these chaotic feelings and thoughts. I felt like my little life was going on over load and it was even worst with my constant bed wetting, every morning the school bus would come to pick me up and I would wake up completely soaked with urine and instead of taking a shower, I would either change my under clothes or leave them on and get on the bus and once in the school bus, I would wish that the smell of piss wouldn't come through my outer clothes.

On the bus, I sat next to some kid named Domingo and hoping that the smell of piss didn't protrude (come out) from my clothes, he was a little skinny Spanish kid, the same age as me and as we introduced each other, we came to find out that not only were we in the same school but in the same class and in the class he spent most of the time drawing, he was like Lazaro, an awesome artist and since I haven't seen Audaliss, Domingo and I became friends.

Domingo was a hyperactive kid and we were always getting into mischief, especially in the school bus, whether going and coming from school and because of our always fooling around, we were always sent to sit in the back of the bus for the misbehaved kids and given a written ticket of our misbehavior for our parents to sign, it was the perfect excuse for my father to beat my ass.

I remember one of many incidents, where Domingo and I were messing around in the bus and the aide got angry because we weren't listening, we were sent to the back of the bus and the aide gave me a ticket to get signed by my

father. At home my father was sitting in the living room when I gave him the ticket, he had signed it and returned it to me but as I walking to my room, he threw me with one of his slippers, missing me but hitting and breaking the glass of the China glass door. He then threatened me "to stay in my room and stay out of his face and not make a sound or he was going to beat me to death".

The next day I told Domingo that I had to chill and he agreed with me, saying that he got in trouble. I replied that I too got in trouble but I didn't mention about my father's threat, which I knew my father would do. We chilled in the same classroom before Domingo and I went in the bathroom we would make plans on what we were going to do, then we would ask the teacher permission to go to the bathroom and when she allow us, we would walk out of the classroom in a slow pace but once we close the door, we would run into the bathroom and let out our pent up steam, by pissing on the toilet seats and the floor, then we would wet as many bundled up toilet paper as we could and start throwing them on the ceiling, wall, or at each other and once all the wet toilet paper was gone, we would run out of the bathroom and into the classroom, the teacher would ask us, why were we running and we would both answer breathlessly "racing up the stairs", satisfied with our answers, she left us alone.

Then one day, I wasn't allowed to go to the bathroom with Domingo, and he took some time in coming back, when he returned, the teacher asked him, if he washed his hands after using the bathroom, he answered "yes", but for some reason the teacher made an issue of his answer and didn't believe him, so the teacher sent another student, to go the bathroom and check, if any of the toilet paper had been used but the kid that the teacher sent was known to all the student in my class of being a pathological liar, the kid went and came back and told the teacher that Domingo was lying that all the toilet paper had sneaker prints on them, the teacher then asked the aide to escort Domingo to the bathroom, so he can wash his hands. While the teacher was asking the aide to escort Domingo, I was trying very hard not to let the giggles out, even when he returned I still held my composure but after class, oh, man did I let out my laughter and I made it even more funnier, when I mimicked my teacher by saying "Domingo, did you wash your hands?" Touching your dirty dick is a crime", making us both start to laugh out loud.

On the bus I reminded Domingo about us behaving and that we had to be good because Christmas was around the corner. He agreed and we even spoke of what we wanted for Christmas but a few days later our pledge of being good on the bus was broken. We were heading home and Domingo and I decided to see if we could sneak from one seat to another. We were getting away with the sneaking being that the bus was somewhat empty, the aide didn't see us but the bus driver did and he told the aide, she then turned to us and told us to go and sit in the back of the bus. We did but we had to sit separate from each other, so we wouldn't get into more mischief, the aide then told us that she wasn't going to write us up because of the holidays were around the corner.

We sat separated making jokes and giggling, the bus was almost reaching my neighborhood and Domingo asked me if I ever played with myself, I answered "yes", he then unzipped his pants and dug in his pants and whipped out his very small uncircumcised penis. He asked me to do the same, I did, our penises weren't erect and we weren't aroused or trying to get aroused, all we did was compete to see who could stretch our foreskin the farthest, making us laugh, then we started flapping our penises every which way it could go, I then told Domingo to lets pull our pants and underwear down, so we could be comfortable, we did and we continued to flap our flaccid (limp) penises all around and make jokes of our dicks, we were so entertain with our game play that I didn't realized that the bus had reach my neighborhood until it stopped in front of my building, I quickly fixed myself and so did Domingo, then I gave him a pound(a quick ghetto handshake), and told him that I'll see him in school but it was the last time I saw Domingo.

At home, my father and Carmen not only did they have the Christmas tree fully decorated but they had the Christmas tree surrounded mid-way with presents. I was secretly excited and could not wait for Christmas to come, Pito and Puri was excited like I was too.

A couple of days later, on the school bus Domingo didn't show up in the bus or school. I was saddened by his absence but it still didn't take me away from the excitement I felt from seeing all those presents and after I came from school, Pito, Puri, and I were left home alone. We decided to investigate to see how many gifts we were getting, as we were counting, we made sure not

to make it look like we were searching through the gifts, we had stopped counting after we all realized that we were all getting more than nine gifts each, even Sammy and Carlos, who I haven't met yet, who were Pito's and Puri's cousins. They too were getting gifts.

. . .

My twelfth birthday arrived and I was hoping it would be celebrated but as the school day came, I fell ill and by the time school ended, I arrived at my crib with my illness much worse. I had a migraine headache but I did not know it back then, all I knew was that the light, sound, and even walking was making my head feel like someone had something embedded in my brain and was stabbing at it crazily, making me feel nauseous and dizzy. I went straight into my room and laid down with the pillow over my head. Two minutes didn't go by when Carmen came into my room and asked me to go to the store. My head still under the pillow, I replied that I didn't feel good and I refused to go. Instead of her trying to see what was wrong with me, she said "since you refuse to go to the store, your birthday won't be celebrated". The pain I felt in my heart with what she said, made me sob so hard that I passed out because of the pain in my head plus what Carmen told me was too much and it was what made me pass out but when I awoke later on that night and no one said happy birthday to me, my whole body was consumed with a fiery darkness. What I mean is that my body was on fire but it was my eyes that felt mostly on fire making my vision turned into a greyish black darkness and the hatred and rage I was feeling became more powerful than it ever was. I put on my emotional mask and looked at every one in the apartment, hoping they would all die suffering. I was even imagining that I was the one that killed them. I was afraid that they would see my true emotion, so I went and took a tearful shower, then went to sleep in anger.

. . .

Days after my birthday I was still enraged and sadden but I kept it hidden, though the thoughts of suicide started to sing through my mind. I started to

think, would I be missed if I die but somewhere in the back of my mind, a whisper answered "no", that night when I thought everyone was sleeping, I decided to punch myself on the nose to make myself bleed. I suffer from nose bleeds, and if it gets too hot, or if I rough play with someone or if I get a real bad headache, I start to bleed from my nose, as soon as I had punched myself on the nose, I started to bleed and I let it fall on my pillow, my blood was covering my pillow, so I got up, took off my t-shirt, covered my bleeding nose and went into the kitchen and grabbed an empty large butter bowl and returned back into my room, where I laid on my stomach with my head on the edge of the bed and my face facing the floor letting my blood drip into the bowl.

I watched my blood drip dropping into the bowl reaching almost a centimeter high in the bowl, Pito saw what I was doing and he quickly ran to my father and told him what I was doing. My father entered my room and grabbed me roughly by the arm and dragged me into the bathroom and told me angrily to lie on my back in the bath tub, underneath the faucet of the tub. He then turned the faucet on, where the water was splashing in my nose, mouth. and face. I was choking on the water and as I tried to get away from the water, my father threatened me with a pipe he had in his hand and said that if I got up from underneath the faucet, he was going to beat me to death with the pipe, I was choking and drowning on the water and I was trying very hard not to breath in the water but it was no use, I saw Carmen enter the bathroom and scream at my father to get out of the bathroom, she then turned the water off and told me to go to my room, I did but I stood out of my father's presence for that whole week.

. . .

Christmas Eve arrived and I believe it fell on a Saturday. Pito, Puri, and I were overjoyed. Early in the morning, around nine or ten, we were invited to an adult Pool Hall, somewhere near 2170 east 181 St. in Bathgate Avenue, where the owner and the adults made it child proof, and on top of the Pool tables were wrapped little gifts, where every child was told to take two gifts. I took my two little gifts and said my thank you's, then I went and chilled with Pito and Puri,

Christmas music was playing loudly and the adults were serving cake, can soda or hot chocolate, I took a piece of cake and chose the hot chocolate because chocolate was and still is my favorite sweet poison even now as an a adult.

There were many kids in the pool hall, getting there gifts and eating and drinking, snacks were provided to everyone, Pito went to hang out with two male children and I went to where they were, Pito introduced me to his two cousins, Sammy a ten-year-old, who had tannish skin complexion, dirty blond straight hair, which was a little longish and he had a habit of biting the middle of his right first finger, I found out later on that the reason he bites on his first finger is a nerve thing that helps him control his emotions, then there is Sammy's little brother Carlos, a five-year-old light skin complexion kid with straight close crop dirty blond hair, we chilled for a little while in the pool room and Pito, Puri and I, followed Sammy and his little brother Carlos to where they lived further up on the same block at 2195 181st. in Bathgate Avenue on the fourth floor, which faced the front of the building and the park, and the park was connected to P.S. 23 and the school's yard, the school that Pito, Puri, and my two cousins Emma and Junior went to.

Sammy and his brother Carlos lived with both parents, his mother Nancy who had mid shoulder dirty blond hair with a light skin complexion and was a sweet and kind lady. Now her husband Pedro was a big boned man with short curly black hair and he had a short beard and a bad temper and they all lived in a two bedroom apartment. Upon entering their crib, there was a little hallway that connected the kitchen, which was on the left of the hallway and on the right of the hallway was a big living room. Once you walk further into the living room was a small hallway that connected the bathroom which was on the left side of the hallway and straight ahead was Sammy's and Carlos room and on the right of the hallway was his parents' bedroom.

Carmen, Candy, and Nancy were in the kitchen cooking. They are all sisters, Carmen had stopped me and introduced me to Sammy's mother Nancy. We said hi to each other and I answered a couple of questions, then I followed Sammy, who was standing behind me with Pito, Puri, and Carlos waiting for me to go to his room, once inside, all we were able to talk about the presents and how we couldn't wait to open them.

Someone had put on some Christmas music and after some songs were played, it was changed to Spanish dancing music. Sammy and the rest of us, agreed to go to the living room to dance. We left the room and I could see that people were coming to the party and they were filling up the big living room, Pito introduced me to his three uncles Angel "little man", the tallest and the second oldest. He had shoulder length black hair with a light skin complexion, and like his little brother Tito, who was around eighteen or nineteen years old at that time they both were dangerous but respectful, and lastly Spanky, a hard belly that protruded like a basketball, he was a dark tannish man, who was the relaxed one and was always besides his skinning girlfriend, Maritza who had long mid back black hair and had the same skin complexion as Spanky.

They were all dancing to the Spanish music and so was I. I was enjoining the moment because I knew I had presents coming to me and this was the first happy celebration without being without, after the Spanish played a little while longer then it was changed to English Electric Bogie music. They were a couple of good dancers but Tito was out doing every single one on the dance floor, I found out later through Sammy that he was in The New York City Break Dancer crew, a group of professional break dancers.

The food was served around six in the evening and what was cooked was a couple of Pernils (pork shoulders), rice with Gandoles, cooked together, red beans in sauce for those, who just wanted more gravy, Pasteles and many different salads and homemade Flan (sweet custard) and don't forget, other the food and other deserts as well as salads that came from some of the visitors and after every one had eaten everything, the adults started drinking or some would try to sneak and smoke a joint in the living room or doing both but one thing was for sure, everyone was dancing and having fun.

By nine at night, the Christmas party was at its peak and still the adults were smoking and drinking and I watched to see who would forget their alcoholic drinks and leave it around, giving me a chance of sneaking one to taste. I waited and spotted an adult filling a cup mid-way of alcohol and some tannish creamy substance, then he took a sip and put on a night table that was in one corner of the living room and went dancing. When I saw that he didn't pick

up his drink, after dancing two songs, I stood next to it and pick it up without drawing attention, then walked fast into the bathroom and locked the door, I sniffed at what was inside the cup and it lightly smelled of alcohol but it was dominated by the smell of coconut, the first sip tasted good but on the second bigger try, I had to spit it out because it burned my throat. I threw the rest away in the toilet bowl, flushed it and returned to where Pito, Puri, and Sammy were trying to dance but it did not matter, everyone was having fun.

By eleven, people started to leave. My father, Carmen, my step brother, and sister and I, followed suit. We were all walking down the lobby steps, exiting the building, when Tito appear and walked up to my father and hit my father on the forehead with a stick, making him bleed, Carmen got in between my father and Tito, to stop Tito from continuing assaulting my father, Milagros was the one that escorted me and my step sibling's to where we lived.

My father and Carmen didn't arrive at the crib until a little after twelve midnight and it was when Milagro decided to give out the presents, she sat by the Christmas tree and started calling out the names that the presents belong to but so far, all I kept seeing was that Pito and Puri were the only ones getting presents. I felt like something was squeezing my heart and as I fought the tears that threatened to burst out of my eyes, I couldn't hold them any longer after I saw them received five presents each but on sixth go around, it's when I received my first and only gift, I watched in complete breathlessness mixed with a profound sadness, how Pito and Puri received nine gifts each and Milagros searching the Christmas tree for my presents and didn't find any. The pain that washed over me, infected my heart and soul. It felt like my whole being was not only in pain but sobbing, I was crying so hard that I could hardly breath. I walked into my room with my soul burning from the tears. I laid on my bed with the pillow over my head to hide the loud hiccupping cries coming from me. After an hour or more, my crying had slowed down, I heard my father tell Milagros, Milagros's husband, and Carmen that it looks like someone broke into the apartment and stole the presents. I don't know if they believe that crock of shit but I didn't. I believed my father had something to do with it and the truth came out a week later after New Year's, Tito was in the living room of my crib dancing and teaching me how to break dance, while

trying to mimic what Tito was teaching me, I asked him, "why did you attack my father?", and he answered that "it was my father who paid him, to not only steal my presents but to do whatever he wanted with it", the hatred and rage that filled me became a calm darkness and it developed an urge in me. I wanted to kill everyone in the crib, I wanted to make them all suffer for hurting me but didn't know how too and get away with it.

The urge transformed itself into a voice that screams in my head to "make them all suffer". Even till this day, it screams to be released. It loathes everything that represents good and happiness and wants to destroy it but somehow I've learned to keep these urges imprisoned because it has the ability to take control of me, as for my father, all I had for him was pure hatred, I lost the little love I had for him.

· · ·

This new family was a good one because they showed each other love and I started to like them, especially Tito and Angel, they were gangsters not like the fake wannabe gangsters of this era and when they committed crimes, most of the time, they would do them solo, but there were times they would do them together or with trusted friends and they loved to fight with those who thought they were tough. Angel a.k.a. 'little man" was always picking on me physically and I knew why he was doing it, to make me tough, there were times while he was picking on me, he would say to me "I'm going to make you tough," and I would fight him as hard as I could but with frustrated angry tears.

Spanky, Angel, and Tito would come to the crib to hang out every day and watch channel U 64. It was a channel that showed hip hop music, while they listen to what ever music comes on Tito would practice his breakdancing routine, while Lil' man, Spanky, and Maritza smoked chiba, which what they called Cannabis a.k.a. marijuana back in my days, in my room, they really came to check on their sister Carmen making sure that my father wasn't abusive towards her but then a time came when Spanky and his girl came to hard times and they came to live with us for some time. I don't know how Spanky and Maritza did it but they both managed to sleep together on the bottom bunk

of the twin beds, while Puri was moved to and slept in the little room connected to my father's and Carmen's room and after a couple of days living in the crib, Spanky brought something to the crib that I feared, a dog and not an ordinary one, this one was a pitbull which I've heard that wasn't friendly and vicious and to make matter worst, the dog was tied to the banister in the middle of the hallway on our floor and every time I would go to and from school or to the store, Lady is what the female dog was called would smell my fear and act like she was going to attack me. It would take me a long time to muster enough courage to run down the stairs, sometimes making me miss the school bus and when those moments happen, I would walk to school, it took weeks before I got used to Lady and she even stopped acting like she was going to bite me.

There were times that Spanky didn't walk Lady or pick up after her when made her mess. My father would do it, and he told Carmen to speak to Spanky about picking up his dog's mess. He started doing it but one night, Lady wasn't taken out and she defecated and urinated on the hallway floor. My father was mad and instead of speaking to Spanky, my father took it out on me and made me lay right next to the shit and piss and threatened me that if I moved from that spot, he was going to beat me to death. I laid there for hours, I even fell asleep, I awoke when my father was screaming at me to clean up Lady's mess, I did and I went and took a shower because I had gotten a little bit of dog piss on my t-shirt and ever since that day, Lady fell in love with me to the point that one day my father was beating me with a belt with spikes on it and Lady witnessing what my father was doing to me started barking until Lady became so enraged that she broke free from her restraints and went after my father's arm that he was using to beat me. If it wasn't for Spanky, who was trying to stop my father from beating me with that spiked leather belt, Lady would of bit and destroyed my father's arm but that still didn't stop my father from continuing beating me with the spiked leather belt. He beat me so bad that he manage to break a big sections of skin on the right side of my shoulder making it bleed.

The next day my shoulder was not only on fire with pain but it was swollen and when I put on a sweater to hide my injury, it made my wound throb like a heartbeat. In school while in my class doing school work, my teacher came to see how I was doing with the assignment she gave us and she happened to

put a hand on the right side of my shoulder, I cried out in pain, she then asked me what was wrong?, I responded that it was nothing but she didn't believe me and pulled the right side of my sweater to one side and winced at seeing my wound, she then restarted questioning me and I explained to her that my father got into a fight with someone and I tried to stop him from fighting and I got hit with the weapon that my father was going to use on the individual, at that the teacher stopped questioning me. But back home, the fear of Lady was gone and I came to love her and every day I would go to her and kiss and hug her and when I was allowed to take her out for her walk, she wouldn't let anyone get next to me. Even the dog's owner Spanky, she'll start growling warning anyone that they were about to get attacked, my father feared Lady and he had stopped beating me for a while.

Lady loved me so much that when she gave birth to her puppies and Spanky touched her puppies, she ate every single one except one and she only allowed me to not only touch her puppy but let me play with it, Spanky would put her and the pup in my room and close the door to my room as Lady stood guard by the bedroom door letting no one in and if someone tried to open the door she would start growling letting the intruder know that she was about to attack, and once the puppy would fall asleep from playing with me, she would grab the puppy by the neck gently wait by my bedroom door and once the door was opened, she would go to her bed that was made in the hallway and lay there with the pup.

I say about a week or two later, I went to school and when I returned Lady was gone, when I asked Spanky where was Lady, he told me that my father made him give her away. I ran down the stairs and outside with tears flowing down my face, I didn't know where she was taken to or where to look for her, so I went around my neighborhood looking for Lady but I couldn't find her and for next few days, every time I would come from school, I would go outside and around the neighborhood looking for her, I would even scream out her name, hoping that she would respond to my calling but none came, then one day I stopped looking for her, it made my father happy because he knew that with Lady around, he couldn't beat on me and with her gone, I didn't have anyone to protect me and my father didn't have to worry that Lady would attack him when he started beating my ass again.

. . .

Back at school, Domingo and Audaliss never returned to school. I found out that they were transferred to another school, I missed them but I wasn't worry about them because I was going to graduate to Junior High school and I was very happy though it got close for me not to participate the graduation ceremony behind a fight being expelled, it happened two weeks before my graduation day with my arch enemy, who I fought twice before. It was some black kid, who was a school bully and he thought that I was the one to pick on, the kid was taller and heavier than I was, and I don't why he had it in for me but every time we fought, he lost.

I remember the first fight; it was on the school bus. He just attacked me for no reason, he probably thought that I wasn't going to fight back but I did and it got so intense that the bus driver had to stopped the bus on the corner of 182 street and Bathgate Avenue, it was right next to P.S.23 and where my aunt Rosa lived, the bus driver yelled at us to get off the bus and fight outside and we did but we fought all the way off the bus and kept on fighting outside the bus. The kids where all yelling their excitement at the fight, the black kid couldn't handle me defending myself and he turned around and ran to picked up an empty forty ounce glass bottle, seeing him do that I ran towards him before he could use it as a weapon but he saw what I was going to do and he threw the bottle at me as I neared him, I quickly side step the bottle, which whizzed right by my head by an inch or two and I then commenced punching him all over his face and stomach, while we fighting the bus a driver instead of stopping the fight was watching us like the rest of the kids, who were cheering me on and after five or ten minutes in battle, someone from the neighborhood, intervened and broke us up. The kid was forced back on the bus where the bus driver left without me but thank God that I was in my aunt's neighborhood, all I had to do was walk a block and a half to where I lived.

The second fight was on the stair case of the school and he was coming up the stairs and tried to grab my leg to trip me and make me fall down the steps. I grabbed the hand rail and lifted that same leg and kicked him on the

chest knocking him down and leaving him breathless, I stood on the top of the staircase and looking down at him, watching him get his breath back and when did, he threatened me with "I'm going to kill you the next time we meet" and turned around and ran down the steps. I stood watching just in case the pussy decided to turn around and sneak attack me but he didn't.

The third fight which I mentioned before, where I almost got expelled, was when I was walking to one of my assigned classrooms and all of a sudden, someone hit me from behind. It didn't affect me the way he wanted, I turned around and saw who it was, I instinctively hit him on the jaw making him stagger, he came at me and fist were flying, he knew that it was useless fighting hand to hand combat with me, so he rushed me and brought me down on my back, he was on top of me, hitting me all over my face and chest, I quickly covered my face and managed to wriggle free and get on my feet, I then grabbed his shirt and twisted him slamming him on his back and all he did was cover his face from the assault I was bringing to him but then a teacher seeing the commotion on the steps broke us up and threatened us that if we continued to keep on fighting, we wouldn't participate in the graduation ceremony and that made me stop, he ran down the stairs and I never saw him again after that.

But then a couple of days later, my teacher was upset at me and told me to stop acting like a little faggot and I responded by calling her a fucking bitch. She was so surprised by my response that she ordered me to apologized to her or I wouldn't be in the ceremony. I didn't, and after school when I went home I told my father and step mother, what had happened between me and the teacher and the next day my father instead of going to work, he went to my school and confronted my teacher but the bitch lied and said that she never said those things to me but that I cursed at her for no apparent reason. He believed her, and I began to cry at her lying and when my father left, she wanted me to apologize but I didn't every day after that she wanted me to apologize but I refused and because of my actions, I wasn't allowed to participate in the graduation ceremony and even to this day, if she ordered me to apologize, I wouldn't apologize to that lying bitch and it was a good thing to because my father told me that even if I did go, he wasn't going to buy me any graduation clothing but Pito and Puri did graduate that year too

and my father spent over a thousand dollars on graduation clothes, regular clothes, and gifts for them.

Ah man the emotions that ran throughout my body and little mind was that of hatred becoming a thirst for vengeance and in my room I laid down envisioning how I was going to kill them all and after some time passed in my chaotic day dreaming mind, I calmed down, I started to feel guilty with what I had thinking. The thought that came to me was first to stab them all to death while they slept, starting with my father first , then the rest but after I calmed down, I was extremely ashamed with that thought and I knew there was something wrong with me because there were times that a darkness would overcome me, making my vision lose color and it was like I was looking through someone else's eyes.

I realized this one day, after Spanky and Maritza left the crib and moved to Milagros's apartment and Carmen had let a female friend and her two kids live in our crib. I was left home alone with the three-year-old Alex, who had curly dirty blondish hair and a tannish skin complexion and was in diapers. All I know was all of a sudden everything went dark, leaving me in a colorless world and my body was being controlled by something in me, all I could do was watch what it was going to do, it had opened the apartment door wide open and sat on the couch, which faced the entrance door, it knew that the baby was going to go out the door because his mother had told me that he had went out the door one day and almost fell down the stairs and was saved by someone in my crib but this time, I was waiting and hoping that the baby would go into the hallway fall and break its neck. I wanted to watch when the baby fell, I could feel its excitement and anticipation, it even played with the baby until it got bored, then it ignored the baby, which was trying to get our attention.

After many tries to get my attention, the baby gave up and started to play by himself, he then started to run around until he reached the entrance of the crib, he stopped and looked outside, I got up and stood by the doorway and watched the baby stand on the first step, then falling down the steps. As the baby was falling and crying loudly, it looked happily but then it heard Ariel's mother scream at me to stop the baby and it was what brought me back to my regular self and I jump into action by jumping down the steps two or three at

a time until I was able to jump over the falling baby, stopping him from further falling, he was crying hysterically, and I picked him up and started to consoled him as we went up the stairs, I then gave him a warm bath and a warm bottle of milk and put him to sleep.

As the baby was sleeping, I could see that he had some bumps around his head and scratches with some bruising around his face and body and when his mother returned from wherever she was, she saw the baby and asked me what happened. I lied and told her that I went into the hallway to get something and that I didn't realize the baby was behind me until he started screaming and falling down the stairs, she believed what I say to her, leaving no suspicion but the thing in me was raging with pure hatred and rage because the baby didn't die, I on the other hand felt guilty.

. . .

I don't know what's the limit is on hatred and rage but all I know is that it was consuming me completely and it got worse. When Ariel and his two brothers invited me to play outside with them, I asked Carmen and she allowed me to go but told me not to go to the swimming pool. I reassured her that I wouldn't, even though that it was a hot summer day but then once outside and playing for hours, we decided to go to other neighborhoods and start trouble. We kept on until we realized that we were in front of the swimming pool located at 800 east 180 street. Ignoring my stepmothers request, I followed the three brothers into the pool. Ariel, a twelve-year-old with light skin complexion and short crop black hair, he was a normal size kid but had an evil streak like his little brothers, something that excited the darkness in me.

Ariel and I went into the adult section of the pool, while eight-year-old Carlos who had the same skin complexion as Ariel but had dirty blond short crop hair and six-year-old Raul, who had a deep brown skin complexion and curly black hair that almost resembled an afro. They went into the kiddie pool, Ariel and I was swimming and playing hide and seek tag, being that the pool was packed, after some time, I lost interest with the game and so did Ariel, we split up and I started to play with some other kids, while Ariel went swimming

by himself, I was having fun and decided to swim under the water until I could reach Ariel and grab his foot and pull him under, as I was nearing him, I noticed that he was standing still but behind a little six-year-old girl, who was holding on to the edge of the pool, I came up got my breathing in control and went under again but this time I wanted to see what he was doing because he was a sex freak and we had French kissed and had sexual intercourse one time in his crib, when he was home alone and as I got closer, I could see that he had his erect penis exposed rubbing on the little girl's back side, I could see that the little girl was scared at what he was doing to her.

I swam up next to him and looked around to see if any of her family members were watching her but no one was and I could see that Ariel was pulling down the back side of her bikini bottom to butt fuck her. I then grabbed his erect penis and whispered in his ear, for us to go to the shower area, so I could suck his dick and let him fuck me in the ass and without hesitation, he fixed himself and we both left the pool area. As he got out, he realized that his hard on was noticeable, so he pinched the head of his penis with the edge of his swimming trucks, once we entered the bath room and went into a shower stall, which had doors to give the swimmers privacy. As soon as I closed the door, he had already had his swimming trucks down onto his knees and I did the same, we sword fought (rubbing each other's dicks together), then I stopped and went onto my knees and started to suck on his dick and balls. I was in super heat and didn't care if someone caught us. I stopped and took off my swimming trucks, leaving me completely naked. I then turned around bent a little and let him fuck me in the ass. We kept on with this activity for a couple of minutes, as I was going from getting fucked to sucking him off, someone had taken a big shit on the stall next to us and the feces managed to come to our side but I didn't care because the fiery lust that was burning my body was making the stress, hatred, and rage disappear, as the sex with Ariel got intense someone knocked on our stall's door making us both jump in fear, we started to put on our clothes on and stood still and opened the door to see if the person who was knocking saw us and decided to scream out that two boys were having sex but nothing was said, so we left the stall and went and got his two younger brothers and left the pool, once outside, Ariel told his brothers to go ahead of

us that we would meet up at the crib. They listened and Ariel and I walked two blocks from the pool, we were surrounded by occupied apartment buildings and a grocery store. I don't know what got into us but we stopped in the middle of the block and Ariel pulled his short's down onto his knees and I got on my knees and started to suck him off like if we were in secluded from view. We didn't give a fuck about someone seeing us though there wasn't anyone outside or in the window looking out that we knew. I continued to perform oral sex on his dick and balls until his body shook from him ejaculating and shooting blanks(ejaculating without sperm or pre-cum), I got up and waited for him to fix himself. Once he finished, we went back home.

At home Ariel went to his crib and I went to mine. As soon as Carmen saw me, she became upset at me because I disobeyed her order not to go to the swimming pool. She sent me into my room and told me that she going to tell my father when he returned from where ever he went and after an hour passed by, he returned home and I heard Carmen tell him, he got so enraged that he got a wooden cane and started beating me all over my body. I tried to escape his beat down by running from one room into another but he still managed to hit me. I then ran out of the apartment door, down the stairs and out the building, I continued to run all the way into the corner of the block and sat bare footed on some small steps that led into a closed down adult club and sobbed.

Ariel and his brothers came to where I was crying and I called Raul a fucking snitch because it was him that told Carmen. She had told me when I tried to lie, Ariel on the other hand gave me a strong brotherly hug to calm me down, then he asked me if I wanted to kill my father. I looked at Ariel to see if he was joking like his two little brothers were, who were laughing and mimicking with what Ariel was asking me but I thought that he was serious and I answered "yes" and it was the truth in my part and after some time planning on different ways on how to kill him. Ariel started to laugh and told me that he was only joking. I was disappointed and depressed because I really wanted to kill my father but I didn't know how to and plus I was too small not able to do it alone. I was left with a rumbling in my head, overcome by a deep hatred and a burning rage, which was blinding me, after some time passed by Pito

came to where I was and told me that my father wanted me upstairs and in my room, which I did.

· · ·

As the days passed by, I became bitter and angry, so I took it out on five-year-old Michael and his three-year-old brother Alex, when the three of us were left home alone, I would beat them both with a balled up towel. Once they started crying, I would wait until they stopped, then I would man handle them to the point of them crying again. Afterwards when they calmed down and stopped crying, I would realize what I have done and I would console them both, then I would even make something for them to eat and play with them both but things between Michael and I, well I took it into another level, one night, he was put to sleep nakedly next to me, and I pretended to be asleep and when his mother left the room, turning off the light's, I woke up and started to play with Michael's dick and balls, when he caught an erection, I first started to masturbate him and when I thought it was safe for me to suck on his chocolate brown dick and balls, I did, and since he couldn't ejaculate, I continued to perform oral sex until my mouth and jaw got tired. I was so into preforming oral sex on Michael that I almost didn't hear Carmen and her friend Candy talking as they were approaching the room. I quickly covered him, turned my back to him and pretended to be asleep, I wasn't worry about them realizing what I was doing with Michael because his privates didn't show the evidence of having sex, unless his penis remained erect but he turned to one side, where he was facing the wall and I turned facing the other side and as Carmen and Candy entered the room, I was praying that his penis became flaccid.

I was frightened and was hoping that Carmen and Michael's mother didn't hear my heart beating hard and loud, I felt Candy uncover us picking up Michael and I could hear Candy tell Carmen that she had forgotten to come back into the room and put a pair of underwear on Michael, hearing that instead of asking Carmen why would his penis be erect, I was relieved. Candy had laid Michael back on the bed with me, covered us and turned the lights off and

when I felt sure that both Carmen and Candy had left the room, I turned to Michael and reached over to see if he still had an erection but he didn't and I turned with my back facing Michael and went to sleep.

. . .

As Candy stood longer in the crib, things started to get freaky between Candy, Pito, and I, every time she would take a shower, she would still be in a towel and come into our room and ask Pito and me to rub lotion on her legs. Pito and I would take a leg each and rub lotion on her leg. One day Pito and I agreed to see how high she would let us put lotion on her legs and see if we could touch her pussy lips that night, she came to my room and asked us to rub lotion on her legs. We were rubbing and getting higher and higher and since she didn't tell us to stop, Pito and I looked at each other with a smirk on both of our faces and crept up higher and higher until we were inches away from her pussy lips but then we heard someone coming and we stopped and she left the room. We were both hoping that she would have let us play with her vagina.

Pito and I were so aroused that we both went into the big closet in our room, got naked and we started fucking each other hungrily. I sucked him off and let him fuck me in the ass, then after a couple of minutes of him fucking me, I got up and turned him around and fucked him in the ass until I ejaculated. I wanted him to suck on my penis but the last time he did, all he was doing was biting it, he couldn't even French kiss without using his teeth, though that night we waited for everyone to sleep, leaving Pito, Puri and me up, Pito and I was still sexually aroused, so we involved Puri, who got naked with us and we fucked. Pito and I fucked her one at a time and then Pito and I would fuck each other again, then we would go back to Puri. We were fucking for a long time and when I ejaculated in Puri, we had stopped having sex and got dressed, I wasn't worry about shooting sperm in Puri because I was still shooting blanks, after we finished dressing, we all went to asleep.

I was escaping more and more into sex, even masturbating whenever I had a chance to escape my father physically abusing me. It made me relaxed. Like one day, my father sent me to the store, I went to all three stores in Bathgate

but every store was packed. I went back to the store that I first went to on the corner of 183 street on Bathgate Avenue and waited to purchase my items, as I was waiting I could see my father leave the building that we lived in with a two by four in his hand, he had crossed the street passing the store I was in and not seeing me, instinct told me that he was looking for me, so after I purchased the items, I ran back to the crib gave Carmen the purchased items and went into my room and sat down on the bottom bunk quietly, he always got mad at me for coming late from the store, even though I told him that it was packed, he would still beat on me.

After a couple of minutes went by my father burst through the apartment door, slamming the door on the wall, and went straight into my room, I got up from the bottom bunk in time to take the blow from the two by four on my left side of my ribs, the hit sucked the air right out of my lungs, he then lifted the two by four with both hands getting ready to hit me again but on the head. Carmen heard the commotion that my father made coming into the crib and she started screaming at him, then I saw just before my father almost bashed me on my head, Carmen running into my room and throwing the wall phone at my father hitting him on the head, it made him stop and he then left my room.

I started getting my breath back but the tears of my pain, inflamed my soul with the rest of the hatred that burned my being and all I could of done was vowed to myself that when I grow up, I will get my revenge and kill everyone in my family regardless if they were innocent or guilty but in the meantime, I was going to escape into my own world of sex and the fantasy of being with a real family that doesn't abuse me but truly loves me but living in a fantasy had its limits because it was a false world and no matter how much I tried to escape, the real world was out to get me, I felt like I wasn't meant to be happy or safe, it felt like some unseen entity was working hard to destroy my soul and find a way to corrupt me in order to control me or possess me.

Like one day, Maritza was babysitting me and the phone rang and I answered it. A man started to speak to me and I could tell that it was some Caucasian man. He started to ask me questions like "if I was home alone?", "how old am I?" and other non-sexual questions, it was really spooking me out, so I

got Maritza's attention without him knowing it and she took the phone and started to speak to the man but whatever he said to her, creeped her out and she hung up the phone. I had asked her what he said but she didn't repeat what he said though I could see that it made her real frightened.

A couple of days later, Maritza came to the crib and asked me if I wanted to go somewhere with her. I answered "yes" but she first had to ask Carmen for permission, since my father was not around Carmen allowed me to go, Maritza and I left the crib and we walked on 183 street to 3rd avenue, then walked all 3rd Avenue until we reached 180 street and Monterey Avenue, Maritza had noticed some one following us and she told me not to react but that we were being followed by some white guy, I asked her how did she know we were being followed, and she answered that every time we would cross one block to another, he would do the same, she then explained to me that we were going to zig zag from one block to another to make sure and as we were zig zagging, I happened to see the white guy Maritza had described following us, he was in his mid-thirties to early forties (I'm able to describe him now because everything that has happened in my life, is like a movie projector that repeats itself over and over, never stopping, even things said and smelled), and just like Maritza said, this bitch ass guy was following us and he made it known not caring if Maritza and I knew it, I didn't know if Maritza was scared but I wasn't, it wasn't because I was brave, it was because I didn't really understand the situation and the danger we were in, we reached the corner of Lafontaine Avenue and headed up to 179 street, there she advises me to walk faster and I did, by the time we reached half the block, the white guy stopped and watched us move on without following us.

Maritza and I walked a little further to her destination, we went to one of her family members apartment so she could take care some personal business. We stood in the crib for more than an hour, then she told me that it was time to go but ten minutes on our walk home, Maritza noticed the same white guy that was following us earlier was following us again. Se asked me to put some pep to my step, and this time I could see the fear on her face so I walked faster but I still wasn't afraid thanks to my ignorance, I didn't see the danger but seeing her fear, I knew that something was very wrong and once we reached the

corner of La Fontaine and !79 street, I knew where we could go, we walked further down La Fontaine to where the gang known as The Chingalins hung out and lived, people were afraid of them but I knew for a fact that they would help a little boy and a female, I could see that the white guy was getting closer but he didn't know what was about to happen to him.

I told Maritza not to worry and follow me. She didn't fight me on my request, she followed me until we reached 180 street and La Fontaine, we walked a little further until I saw two big giant white guys with long dirty blond hair and beards with a little grayish on them, they were talking to each other and I excused myself, they both became quiet and looked down at me, I told them what was happening to us and when I turned around to point to where the white faggot who was half a block behind us was, he was gone, they in turn escorted us a couple of blocks down to our neighborhood, and we thanked both men and headed safely to our hood in Bathgate hoping the white faggot happened to somehow find us and follow us, all I had to do was tell one of the drug dealers in our hood and they would make him disappear for good.

(Note: before I continue with my story, if you have children or are planning to have children or are a person, who loves and wants to protect children, teach the kids of the human creatures that lurk in either in broad day light or in the night and how they come in different disguises, as a Family member, friend, stranger, teacher, etc., etc., for if you don't they will be blind to these creatures and won't be able to see and defend themselves from them.)

• • •

Maritza and I were safe in the neighborhood but my neighborhood really wasn't all that safe, my neighborhood was infested with drug dealers and the drug fiends and every one of them were scheming against each other and the gun fights, which was a constant thing in my neighborhood, whether it was the drug dealers trying to be the number one drug dealer in the hood or the drug fiends, who would rob each other or try to rob the drug dealers and sometimes the fiends would rob from the people in the hood. They were many times the gun fights occurred early in the morning, while I'll be waiting for

the school bus and when that happens, I would duck behind a car and wait for either the school bus or the gun fight to stop, so I could stand safely. I wasn't the only one ducking, the were other children and adults, who would duck until it was safe for them to continue their day. Sometimes when that happened, I could hear the bullets whiz by trying to find someone to imbed themselves but thank God, no one visible was ever hurt.

The summer came and went and things in the hood cooled down but my father's abusive wrath didn't. His physical, emotional, and mental abusive behavior towards me heightened and I would escape with having more sex with Pito, Puri, Ariel, Sammy, and Juan Pablo, my cousin. I remember one night, it was my father, Carmen, Pito, Puri and myself, we were walking back from visiting one of Carmen's family members crib and they were both having a conversation, I decided to walk a little ahead of all of them, like a quarter of a block, enough to block all of them, all of a sudden objects were being thrown at me but missing me, I didn't turn around because I knew who it was.

My father was throwing bottles, rocks, or whatever hard object he could get his hands on, just to cause me injury and as he was throwing these objects at me. He would be screaming curses and demeaning insults at me. I would continue walking my pace fighting the tears that was starting to over flow my eyes burning a trail down my face, I felt like someone was squeezing my heart harder and harder and the hatred for my father was flowing through my body making my body burn with fire, even the thought of committing suicide was singing in my head and as I continued to walk, other thoughts were appearing in my head but in questions, I was asking to myself, why is this happening to me?, why isn't anyone helping me? Or other questions, which shouldn't be in a child's mind and when school started, it was a relief because it was an escape from my father and sex with my step siblings, their cousin, my cousin and the boy downstairs. I felt pleasure but I was disgusted about having sex with boys but being that it was the only other way besides committing suicide, I continued with the sexual activity but school stopped all that.

I started to go to school at Junior high school 118 known as William W. Niles school in 179 street between La Fontaine and Arthur Avenue and I did not need a school bus because it was walking distance. It was a good walk and

every time I would go to and from my new school, I would pretend that I was someone else going to a dangerous adventure. I would walk up 183 street to third avenue, where I would turn on 180 street up La Fontaine and Arthur Avenue, to the school's backyard.

Every day was a different episode in my adventures to school but there were times, it wasn't an adventure that was in my mind. It was my life. I would be thinking about the things I'm going through and how my whole life was filled with hatred and rage. I even swore that before I die people will fear and hate me after I get my revenge against everyone, and as these things were happening to me, it had me feeling despicable and even hateful of myself, I would envision myself going to an unoccupied and unpopular area and find a dark corner and just curl up and give up, in those moments I would look around and wonder, what would happen, if I committed suicide, would someone stop me?, would someone miss or cry for me or would I be the unwanted burden finally giving what everyone wanted, being freed of me and other times I would feel the unwanted and the disgusting lustful emotions of wanting to be with the mischievous boys, just to have sex with them, sometimes while in school, I would see a boy that looked good to me and I would go to the bathroom and masturbate in a fantasy of having sex or preforming oral sex with the boy, and when I started to develop pre-cum, it made me even more lustful, I wasn't worried about being caught in school masturbating because the pre-cum made me ejaculate quickly and if I did get caught, I was hoping it would be with a boy who wanted to get his dick sucked and though I felt disgusted by these sexual feelings with boys, it was the only way for me to escape from the things happening to me.

Other times while walking to school my mind would explode with thoughts of wanting to get revenge on everyone by making them suffer before I killed them all and though these negative fantasies and thoughts were on my mind, school somehow made me feel relieved and in control from all these thoughts and feelings, replacing them with something I really yearn for, hope for a family who would really love and protect me from everyone or anything.

My school subjects also helped me escape even more from my thoughts and feelings with all the activities in school like typing class. The teacher

taught the students how to type and how to make designs, while typing. Then there was the wood shop and it's there that I found out that Maria my cousin was a slut, sucking dick and letting boys fuck her. I was approached by some Caucasian kid of fourteen and he started off talking to me about how his babysitter and her female friends would always play with and suck on his dick until he ejaculated, then he explained to me that a friend of his told him about my cousin Maria and he wanted me to hook him up with her, I was sexually aroused with all his sex talk and seeing that the kid was in tight pants, I could see that he had a long skinny dick like Pito and since we were sitting in the back of the classroom together, sharing a school desk for two, I on the down low reached out and grabbed his dick and balls and whispered to him that if he let me suck his dick, I would hook him up with my cousin, which was a lie, he responded that he doesn't do it with boys but then the bell rung before I could try to persuade him to let me pleasure him, what I did was go quickly into the bathroom to masturbate.

By the time I reached the bathroom, my penis became flaccid so I didn't masturbate I just took a piss instead. But little did I know, someone was watching me urinating but didn't know it until the next day, when some thirteen-year-old Spanish kid with curly brown hair and light tannish skin complexion who was taller than I was approached me and introduced himself to me as Joseph and stated to me that he was looking at my penis as I was urinating the day before. I looked at him without responding and knew that he was a little boy fiend like Gus. I brushed his comment aside and we chilled on the school's staircase next to the school's lunch room doors waiting for lunch, the staircase was getting packed with students waiting for the doors to the lunchroom to be open, while Joseph and I were making conversation, a black kid of the same age as Joseph and tall like him, interrupted us, the black kid introduced himself to me as Eric and said he was Joseph best friend, we shook hands and as they started talking, I managed to slowly slip away without them realizing it and waited with the other students for the door to the lunch room to be opened, so we all could eat lunch.

I avoided Joseph and Eric for a while due to Joseph's sexual lust for me and when I decided to hang with them, it was always at lunchtime and in the

schoolyard after lunch, and since the school teachers allowed the students to go to the candy store on the corner of Arthur Avenue and/or hang out outside school property with some students sneaking to where they lived across the street from the school. Joseph, Eric, and I would hang out across the street from the school on La Fontaine Avenue, leaning or sitting on a parked car, just talking and chilling, when a bunch of grown men ranging from the ages of eighteen to twenty-one years old approached us. The group of six or seven of them proudly introduced themselves as The Hue Boys, they were known in the school as violent bullies and they loved to attack little kids, especially if the school kids had Lee pants, they would target those kids and rip out the Lee patches from the back of their pants, sometimes beating up the little kids on the process.

The purpose for them snatching the patches were because in that era, if you had over ten patches, you could get something free from the clothing store and at that time Lee clothing was the trend. I even had a couple of pairs of Lee pants , which I would wear to school but with a long shirt that would cover my waist and the Lee patch. I was scared every time I wore them but I knew that if they beat me up, Tito, Lil 'man and their gang of friends would go over to my school and beat them down or worse but still I was scared and that day thank God none of us had any Lee clothing on but for some reason they targeted Joseph and threatened him for acting tough, which he wasn't, they were looking for an excuse to be violent and when they thought that Joseph was acting tough, they grabbed him, lifted him up and slammed him on the hood of the car that we were all chilling on, then they started making fun at him and cursing him out and after more than five or ten minutes of bullying Joseph, they left him alone and left the neighborhood, I was so fucking angry inside that I couldn't defend Joseph, I even wished to be big, so I could show them how it felt to be beaten up and because of that incident I felt sorry for Joseph and all three of us hung out more after lunch.

Joseph, Eric, and I were in special ed but in different classes, and one day all the students from special ed were taken on a trip to the botanical gardens in the Bronx and we decided to stick together. We imagined that we were in a forest, surrounded by Dinosaurs and we had to move around quietly without

making any noise after all the student visited almost all of The Botanical Garden, the teachers decided to take all the students to the park that was around there, which was filled with a bunch of screaming little kids of around the ages of eight and nine and they all occupied all of the playgrounds.

Joseph, Eric, and I went to a big slide with a bridge connected to it. I got bored and tired of going up and down, so I went and sat down next to one of my teachers on the bench. She was speaking to three little boys quietly, so I was able to overhear the conversation they were having. What those little kids were telling my teacher was that every time Joseph would go up the slide through the bridge, he would rub himself on their backsides or grab their private parts, the teacher reassured the little boys that she would speak to Joseph and take care of the situation.

She then called Joseph over and asked him why was he touching the little boy's private area, he got up and responded angrily that he didn't do anything. He kept on denying it and getting more upset that he even started screaming at the teacher, then he left the park and went home. I suppose, as for Eric and I, we joined a group of our schoolmates, who were getting ready to play tag, after putting out feet next to theirs and the leader of the group was picking who would start the tagging with the "ennie Minnie mynnie moe", Eric and I weren't the ones to be it and when the leader finally finished with the last kid to be it, the chase started.

It was a group of about ten of us playing and we started running around the park and trees, some of the kids and I ran into a forested area full of trees and a semi-dried up pond. It had no water and I didn't expect to go through what was going to happen to the ones who entered it, it was muddy as hell and we couldn't run. I saw some of them fall on the mud, while some lost a sneaker or two, I didn't realize that I was robbed of my sneakers until I was out of the pond, we were all laughing at the moment even after we went back to the section, where some of us lost our sneakers, I found both of my sneakers and walk to a bench where Eric was sitting and laughing at me. I sat down next to him laughing at the whole thing, I took off both of my socks, threw them into the garbage, then we went to where the teachers were because it was about that time to go home, the teachers told the students, who ever wanted to go from

the park to their crib can. Eric and I choose to leave on our own, Eric and I walked and talked for a bit and then he went his way and I went mine.

. . .

A couple of days later, I bumped into Eric at school and asked him what was up with Joseph Eric responded that Joseph was jumped by the Hue boys and that they beat him up with a bat. Hearing this, my mind was saying to itself, these fucking grown men are happy and proud of jumping little kids, why couldn't they pick on someone their own size. I realized then that the school was becoming dangerous for us kids, whether coming and going to school or hanging out in the schoolyard after lunch, and things in my crib were about to hit the fan with Candy.

One night Pito and I was still rubbing Candy down with lotion and we had gotten so close to touching her vagina but we were scared that she would stop us from ever putting lotion on her and every time we would finished, she would leave the room, leaving Pito and I with a hard on noticeable through our shorts but one day while rubbing her legs, Pito and I decided to go for it and touch her pussy but just as we were almost there, my father's brother Nelson's wife Alba busted in the apartment door screaming out Candy's name, she quickly left us and went into the bathroom to get dressed. Pito and I stood in the room because our hard on was noticeable to anyone, who was there, we sat on the bottom bunk and pretended to be playing tic tac toe in one of my note books, it was to distract us from going in the room's closet and fucking each other. My uncle's wife Alba was still screaming Candy's name out and looking for her at that moment Candy came out of the bathroom and they both started brawling. The fight only lasted a minute or two because my father and Carmen got in between them and stopped the fight but they stood screaming at each other and my uncle Nelson also tried to stop them from screaming but my aunt Alba took it out on my uncle and started smacking and punching him and around his face. The whole fight was about Candy trying or doing something sexual with my uncle, my uncle and his wife left the apartment arguing and my father and Carmen told Candy that they will give her some time for her to find another place to live.

A week passed by when she left the crib but two days before she left, the darkness in me appeared, I went into the bathroom to urinate and I saw the baby was taking a bath but he had fallen asleep and was struggling to breathe. In my darkened state, it wanted to see him not only die but how long it takes for the baby to drown, the thing in me was telling me that we were going to watch the baby die and it was happy with excitement when it said that something made me snap out of my darkened daze and I grabbed the baby out of the bath tub, took him into my bedroom, dried him up, change his diaper and made sure he was okay, then I put him to sleep on my bed. I felt so guilty with what happen and I was trying to figure out what the hell was wrong with me but after a couple of hours trying to find the answer, the incident was brushed out of my mind, I was afraid to tell anyone about what I was going through because I knew they would treat me even more shitty than before.

The things I realized while writing this crazy and demented book is that I was never loved and wanted and though they treated me like shit for some reason I didn't tell on them, I kept their torturous behavior towards me a secret and in doing so, I had sacrificed my soul making me want to die. Every day I woke up suicidal feelings would sing in my head and continue throughout the day until I fell asleep.

I thought that everyone was blind to my father's abusive behavior towards me but then I started to realize that Spanky and Maritza saw it and they would sometimes ask my father permission to take me to Milagros crib to do some work, which was a lie, like one day Maritza was visiting my crib and my father was starting his abusive nature towards me and Maritza waited for the right time and asked my father if she could take Pito, Puri, and I, to a family members house to help them clean up a room. My father allowed her to take me, as long as it was for work, he didn't want me to have any fun.

Maritza took us to a family member's apartment to chill, have fun, and escape my father's wrath. She told Pito, Puri and I to go play with the other kids in the living room but not to touch or break anything and not to make too much noise. We went into the living room where there were four or five other children of mixed ages, two were my age but the others were around Pito and Puri ages. We all decided to play WWF wrestling were having fun, when all

of a sudden, the stereo in the living turned on by itself and the volume went from low to max drowning out our laughter. Maritza and some other adults came running into the living room, asking all of us in a screaming voice "who was the one playing with the stereo?" We all stood quiet, while the adults was trying to turn off the stereo but then as it turned on by itself, it went off by itself too and when Maritza went to unplug the stereo, she was stung by what she saw, she turned around and showed all of us that the stereo had always been unplugged, Maritza asked the adults "how can a stereo be unplug and play?", but no one had an answer and after an hour, Maritza took us home and she left to Milagro's crib.

• • •

I also realized something about writing about my life, the presence that's been following me is making sure that not only do I suffer but that those who see the abusive nature of my father are blinded this goes also for anyone who helps me in my trials and tribulations of my life, I am left to deal with it all by myself, now the incident with the unplugged stereo turning on by itself was a warning to Maritza, at that time I didn't know it until now while editing my book, as you keep on reading, you will see what I mean and know that whatever is following me do influence people to change their positive ways into negativity.

The warning was unknowable and the consequences for them providing a positive escape for me almost costed Spanky's life. One day Spanky and Maritza came to the crib to hang out and chill outside in front of the building with my family, Ariel, Ariel's father, mother and his brothers were outside too but Spanky for some reason told Ariel's mother that if it wasn't for her husband he would fuck the shit out of her that made Ariel's father so enraged that he pulled out one of those Barber's shaving blades and sliced Spanky from the top of one side of Spanky's shoulder all the way down onto his tail bone. Ariel's father went for Spanky's throat but Spanky ran down the block and around the corner and Ariel's father ran right behind him and so did Ariel's mother to stop her husband from killing Spanky and she succeeded because no more than five minutes later, both Ariel's mother and father returned back to hood and

went into their apartment. As for Spanky well my father got into the car and went looking for him to take him to the hospital to get staples because the cut with the blade was very deep and because of that incident Spanky and Maritza couldn't come back to the hood.

· · ·

While editing one of those forgotten memories appeared in my head and I know now that when I was five or six years old my mother wanted me to get kidnapped or worse, she had told me to go outside and play but it was passed midnight and I was just chilling outside in front of the building where I lived with no one watching over me and after more than an hour or two later, some guy approached me and asked me "why are you outside by yourself?" I answered "playing", he then told me to go back to my apartment because being outside by myself was very dangerous for me, I didn't understand the danger he meant but I listen to him and went home. I want to thank that stranger for giving me that advice as a child and like the being who seems on making me suffer there were always, some one positive intervening, whether I knew it or not, but my bitterness, rage and hatred made me blind to it, even now as an adult editing my life.

· · ·

Back to my present age of twelve years old and after the Spanky incident, my father was free from pretending to be nice to me in the presence of people and reverted into putting me down and beating on me.

In school there was a twenty four stay at a camping trip for the special ed. students in my school and I was hoping that I was given permission to go. I couldn't ask my father because like I said before, he didn't want me to have fun, so I asked Carmen in front of my father, if she could sign the permission slip so I could go but my father quickly intervened and responded "no" but Carmen told him to let me go and he became angry at her and a heated conversation started between them and after sometime later and everything was

calm and quiet, my stepmother gave me the signed permission slip. I was so relieved and happy but I didn't show it because my father was ready to beat the shit out of me.

On the day of the camping trip, I pretended it to be a normal school day. Carmen gave me some money, so I could buy some snacks, which I did and while waiting for all the students and the teachers that were going to the camping trip to get on the school bus, I showed my happiness and I was already planning mischievous pranks that I was going to do to the girls and other students and teachers too but I was going to wait to see, who would share the tent with me, so I could influence my tent mate and do it together after we all sat around the camp fire to tell scary stories.

Once everyone was in the school bus and accounted for we were on the road to I believe was the Bear Mountains. I am not too sure because I did not ask where we were going, and I never heard the teachers speak about it in front of me. The ride to the camping site was going to take a couple of hours and a teacher told the students on the bus that in the meantime to kill time, all the students were to sing songs with the teacher, we sang songs and afterwards the students started doing their own thing with a selected group, I happened to sit with a group of boys that were planning to do what I was going to do after the camp fire story telling was over and after a couple of hours later, we arrived at the Camp site and about time because I and the other boys had to urinate and as soon as we all got off the bus, some of us, myself included walked because if I would of run I would of peed on myself, some of the boys walked with me but we had to go around the building and urinate where ever we could because the boys bathroom was packed, and after we all relieved ourselves we ran back to where the other kids were with the teachers, who were asking the students to line up, so they could count heads and make sure no one was missing.

Everyone was accounted for and the teachers started helping the students build the tents, I was to share the tent with two other kids, at first we tried to build our own tent but failed so one of the teachers seeing our struggles helped us and when all the tents were put up, the teachers announced that food was being served inside the one-story brick building, where the bathrooms were also located.

With food in our stomachs, all the kids did different things. Some went to their tents, some hung outside in selected groups talking about kids' stuff, while others hung out with the teachers. I was with the group that was planning to scare everyone, I couldn't wait, I wanted to hear the teachers and the students scream or cry out in fear but then clouds started to form and as the clouds started forming and darkening, I started to fake pray that the clouds would disappear but it didn't. It started drizzling then it changed to pouring rain. I went into the tent and the two kids that shared the tent with me were dead asleep. I was in between both kids, on one side was a heavy set kid that could make two of me and the other kid was smaller and skinner than I was. I was thinking of doing something mischievous but the sound of the rain hitting the tent and the ground was starting to put me to sleep. I fought my sleep and went into my book bag and took out a pack of those wannabe Oreo cookies that you buy two for a dollar and it had three rolls in a pack. I looked at the two boys wanting to wake them up and share some cookies with them, as we spoke on kid stuff but the silence was peaceful, and as I laid on my back and ate some of the cookies, I really felt peaceful within. I didn't have to deal with my father's mental, physical and emotional abuse towards me and I also didn't have to escape into sexual situations with Pito, Puri, Ariel, and the other boys, my mind was completely blank of the negativity that surrounded me, all I was focused on was the thunder, lighting and the rain falling on the tent and the ground, I was so peacefully calm that I too fell asleep.

Early the next morning, the teachers started waking up all of the students, they announced that after everyone finished getting their hygiene in check, there would be breakfast waiting for us in the camp's building. I went and washed my face and brushed my teeth and after I was finished, I started to get a strong urge to defecate but I couldn't use the bathroom because I was afraid of being made fun of by the other boys and it felt like it was about to come out, so what I did was go around the building, stand very still and squeeze my buttocks tightly until the urge to defecate went away, I didn't eat any breakfast so I went an hung out with the other kids, who didn't want to eat breakfast either and when noon arrived all the students and teachers mounted on the

bus that was waiting to take us back to the school, where the regular school buses were waiting for the students to take back home.

Once I arrived at home, I ran to the bathroom and took the biggest shit in my young life afterwards it felt like I lost twenty pounds and soon things went back to normal with my father ignoring me and abusing me and me escaping into sex with Pito, Puri, and Ariel and soon two more sexual partners who will participate in sexual activities with me. One was Sammy, Pito and Puri's cousin and the other, was Juan Pablo my father's brother Nelson's son, my cousin.

It started one day, when my father went to work and it was Carmen, Nelson's wife Alba and Puri, they were in Carmen's room gossiping and it was Ariel, Ariel's brothers Carlos and Raul, then it was Pito, Sammy and myself. We were all started playing wrestling and after some time, we changed the game play to Hungry Hippo on the floor, then after a couple of minutes playing the game, Pito was the one who started the sex game, he got up closed and locked the bedroom door, then he turned around and whipped his erect penis out and asked, who wanted to sword fight?, we all stood up and whipped our flaccid penises and started masturbating to make our penises hard like Pito's, Once we all had erections, we started sword fighting with each other, and after a few minutes, Ariel and his two brothers laid on their backs on my bed with their pants down onto their ankles, Pito then laid on top of Carlos and Sammy laid on top of Raul and they started dick humping each other. I on the other hand started preforming oral sex on Ariel, who didn't last long, he ejaculated blanks in my mouth and held my head between his legs with his erect penis in my mouth. We stood like that until his trembling body calmed down, then he stood up and fixed himself and since I didn't have to dress myself, I purposely unlocked and opened the door wide open, it took the other four boys a few minutes to realize that the door was open, then they quickly jumped off each other and dressed themselves and just in time because a minute after they fixed themselves, Carmen passed the room to go to the kitchen and cook us all macaroni and cheese with cut up hot dogs in it for lunch and after she served every one, she went back into her room to continue to talk with Alba and watch Spanish soaps. Afterwards we all finish eating lunch, Ariel and his brothers left the crib and the rest of us just chilled in the room and played games.

Sammy witnessing what I had done to Ariel, asked me if I wanted to suck his dick. I replied yeah but not right now, it happened the next day but at night, I was punished by my father for no reason and sent to my room. I had fallen asleep and some time had passed, when I was awakened by Sammy, he told me that he was staying over and asked me if I wanted to suck his dick. I could hear the adults in the living room talking and laughing, not caring if we got caught I answered "yes" he quickly took off his clothes, I followed suite, and we stood facing each other with an erections, we then got so close to each other where our dicks were almost penetrating our groining areas, I whispered into his ear that we should wait until everyone was sleeping, he agreed but we first we hugged each other and started humping each other's between our groining area slowly. I stopped then went onto my knees and started to perform oral sex on his dick and balls quickly, after a few seconds, I stopped and told him to wait until tonight. He agreed and we only put on our shorts and hid our underwear's in between my mattress, he went into the living room and I went back to bed and fell asleep.

It was almost morning when I felt some one pulling on me and pushing me to wake up, I woke up groggily and saw that it was Sammy, standing by the bed not only naked but with a hard on, I became fully awake and whispered to him that I was going to brush my teeth. After I was finished, I quickly went into my room and took off my short's, we were both naked, so we laid on my bed, I got on top of him and we started dick humping. I wanted to French kiss him but he refused, just as we were about to ejaculate, Sammy whispered lustfully to suck his dick, I replied in a whisper for us to get off the bed because the plastic of the bed was making too much noise, we got off the bed and we laid the pillows side by side on the floor, Sammy laid on his back with his legs wide open, and I laid in between his legs and started kissing, licking and sucking on his penis and balls. He started to moan softly, making me more lustful, after a couple of minutes, Sammy asked me to fuck him in the ass. I got up on my knees and waited for him to turn around on his stomach, I then laid gently on him because I was heavier than he was, he had spread his butt cheeks with both of his hands and I then penetrated him and started humping slowly at first, as I was humping, I was also kissing and sucking on his neck, making him

moan like a girl and making me more even more hornier than I was, that I was whispered in his ear that I loved him and wanted to be with him fucking forever, I started humping him harder and faster because I was about to ejaculate, being that I was fucking him so hard and fast it made me heavier, he asked me to get off of him because he couldn't breathe, I did breathing lustfully and just as my lust started, it instantly disappeared, we both got up from the floor and got properly dressed and laid on the bed and fell back to sleep, when I awoke Sammy was gone, he had to go home to take his Insulin because he was a diabetic.

But the next weekend, Sammy stood over and being that my bed was big, it was Pito, Sammy and I sharing my bed. I laid between them and we all went to sleep, but then after a couple of hours had passed and everyone else was sleeping, I was being awaken by Pito and Sammy, they were awakening me by them grabbing and massaging my buttocks and my dick and balls, just as I was about to get naked like they was, I mysteriously started feeling sick at first I started sweating heavily, then I became nauseous. It got so bad that I jumped off the bed and started vomiting heavily on the floor all the way into the bathroom's toilet, a couple of minutes later, my vomiting stopped and the nausea feeling disappeared, I went back to my room and saw that Sammy and Pito had gotten dressed and it was a good thing because my father had appeared by the bedroom door, Sammy and Pito was telling my father what happened to me and before he left back to his room, he told me to clean up all the vomit, which I did but the sexual moment was gone, so we all went back to sleep.

. . .

As the days came and went, sex became an everyday thing between Pito, Puri, and myself. If not with them, it's with Ariel or with Sammy when he would come to visit or stay over but then another body would soon join my sexual escape. My cousin Pablo, everything started one day, when my aunt Alba came to visit and she brought Ivy (pronounced Evee) her and my uncle Nelson's three-year-old daughter, Ivy had long silky mid back black hair and was light skinned and she had an imaginary mouse as a friend, I was in Carmen's room

to wrap itself around his whole dick, I licked and kissed on his dick and then I put his dick and balls in my mouth and I tried to suck him off until he ejaculated but he was like Pito, he couldn't ejaculate. Pablo was nine years old with a light brown skin complexion and I couldn't believe his dick was that small, Ariel's two little brothers had longer penises than Pablo, after some time, we all stopped with the sexual activity and started to play games until Pablo's mother came to pick him and Ivy up.

. . .

Days passed and the sex between Pito, Puri, and I slowed but the sex with Ariel didn't. We would go out to different neighborhoods to have sex in the building's roof or staircases. One day, we planned to go somewhere to have sex and I told him that I was not going to wear underwear that he should do the same, just in case we had to run and avoid being caught. He agreed but that was a big mistake in my part because later that day, I put on a pair of jean short's with a zipper. I was waiting for Ariel to come and pick me up, and in waiting I had to take a piss. I went into the bath room unzipped my short's and took a long piss, after I finished I put my penis back in my pants but my foreskin stood exposed, not knowing it, I zipped my pants pinching my foreskin in the zipper, I felt like my life was over for the pain that shot throughout my body was unbearable making me cry out loud at first. I lowered my cries, so no one would hear me and find out what was going with me and make fun of me, I let go of the zipper and stood very still because it made the pain subside, I looked down and saw a piece of my foreskin trapped between the zipper and it made me sob even more, after my sobbing subsided, I knew I had to do something. I did, I held my breath, clenched my teeth, and painfully grabbed the zipper handle, I then closed my eyes and without thinking about it, pulled my zipper down quickly, it worked and my foreskin was freed but it was throbbing with pain, I then put my penis in my short's carefully and zippered it, then I went into my room and laid on my back on my bed because moving my body made the rubbing on my penis's foreskin hurt, as for the sex, it was canceled for the next few days.

. . .

That experience was painfully horrific and I promised myself that the next time, I would be very careful but the next time arrived and it was in the beginning of school fall season and instead of returning back to I.S. 118, I was sent to The Angelo Patri school, on 182 street in Webster Avenue on the US-1 line in the Bronx. It was supposed to be a disciplinary school for emotional children but I didn't believe it because they had a section where it was regular kids not special ed like I was. I remember sneaking to their side one morning to use the bathroom, and I passed by a classroom, where each student had a dead frog, laying on its back in a long metal tray, I watched as one student cut the frog down from the upper chest area down onto its groin, then the kid, opened up the frog and started taking the Organs out and placing it on parchment paper with the name of each organ, I was entranced by the experience that I was thinking to myself, why wasn't the teachers who taught in my class, teach me things like this, I was standing there to long and I didn't want to get in trouble with my actual class, so I left but wishing I was in class like the one with the dissecting a frog, it had my brain on fire with wanting to learn more of what really matter but what I was taught was really nothing but the same shit over and over again.

The only time I was having fun was in sewing class, since my grandmother taught me how to sew by hand and machine I was able to make pillows out of certain wilderness characters mostly Teddy bears and Panda bears. It was to impress the girls and it worked, the girls requested for me to make them Teddy bears and Panda bears and in return they would give me hugs and kisses on my cheeks or pinching them or the girls giving me complements on my looks and saying that I was an adorable little hottie but not in a sexual way. It made me feel good.

In the school there were incidents where a selected group of girls would snatch a male student force him into the bathroom, take his clothes off, and do sexual things to the male student. I was hoping that those girls would have done that to me because they didn't know that I was already sexually active

but one day after school, there was a pretty Caucasian female student of about twelve or thirteen years old, hanging out on a short cut that I use going down a rocky hill to Webster Avenue on US-1. She stopped me and asked me if I was going to Patri school, I answered yes, then she told me to be careful in school and not get snatched because I look good for the taking. I knew what she meant and knew she was one of the girls who was snatching boys to have sex with them but with me, they didn't know that I was fucking pussy almost every night with Puri, I was going to give them what they wanted and more.

So forgetting of my last incident with the zipper foreskin experience, I started to wear my jean pants without underwear. One morning Lil' man knew why I was getting dressed and he let me use one of his Lee jean jackets, which matched my Lee jean pants. I left the jacket on my bed, while I took my socks, t-shirt and jean pants to the bathroom to put on after I showered. At that age I had two things going for me my looks and my longish curly hair. I had let my hair grow and it made me noticeable to those kids who were sexually active, whether male or female and as I was thinking that I was going to be next to be snatched into the girls bathroom, I pulled up my jean pants and thought I had put my penis completely in my pants, until I zippered my pants and felt that stinging and powerful pain shoot through my foreskin, balls, thighs and all the way up to my eyes, making it shed rivers of tears and when I looked down to the zipper area and saw that it not only pinched a piece of foreskin but the zipper managed to zipper completely over a piece of foreskin, where I could see the piece stuck in between the zipper, I started to sob loudly.

It took me a minute or two to muffle my sobs because I mistakenly moved a little and I could feel the pulling on my foreskin making me cry even more. I had grabbed the edge of the sink to use the edge of the sink and try to squeeze the pain away. Once the pain subsided a bit, I looked down at the zipper and the pinched skin and started preparing myself for what I had to do, I then with one hand gently grabbed the zipper's buckle and with the other, I held onto my waistband, and said to myself on the count of three and do it fast. I did but when I reached two, I chickened out because I was scared that the zipper would get stuck on the foreskin and not free it. I also knew that I couldn't scream out for help because I knew that my father would tell everyone in the family or

whoever, just to humiliate me. I closed my eyes and opened them quickly, then I counted and pulled the zipper down quickly, all I felt was that stinging pain and me grabbing my penis and my hands pinching my foreskin, I had even started crying loudly but after I got myself in control, I went and got a pair of underwear, put them on and never forgotten what would happen, if I didn't wear any underwear underneath pants, as the experience with the wild girls snatching boys, well it never happened because they got caught.

. . .

Now before I get into the seriousness of my life, here is another penis experience as a kid. I had turned thirteen years old, and I was wondering if my penis had grown, though it was a little longer, I still saw it small, so I decided to stick my meatus (dick head) inside any empty bottle to see if my dick head fit, I grabbed an empty bottle that happened to be rubbing alcohol, there must have been alcohol inside the bottle because as soon as my dickhead touched the edge of the bottle, it felt like liquid fire was poured on my penis, I bent down and started to jump up and down trying to give my penis air with my hands and mouth but that didn't work so I stood in front of the fan, and it took a minute or two for the air to calm me down and learning to never stick my privates into anything again on less it was flesh.

On my uncelebrated thirteenth birthday, I didn't receive anything but the only good thing about it was that we were moving to Puerto Rico, where Milagros and her husband had bought a house. They had asked my father if he wanted to live in and help them take care of the house, my father had responded yes and my father, Carmen, my step siblings and I moved to P.R. a week or two before Christmas.

Chapter 11

Puerto Rico

Milagros and her husband bought a house in Brisa de Tortuguero in the town of Vega Baja, and we lived in Calle Ocho (8 street). The house was built with brick and cement and it was a two-part of the house. The first part had two bedrooms, the bathroom, the living room and the kitchen, and the second part of the house was in the back and it had the two other bedrooms and a bathroom, which was outside of the rooms, where the occupants can share the bathroom and in between the outside bedrooms and the house, it had a little walkway that took you to the backyard which led to either the side of the house.

In exploring the neighborhood, I could see that some of the houses in the neighborhood were either built out of Tin and Wood, others were built with wood and cement or tin and cement and the rest, which were a few regular houses like Milagros. The neighborhood I was in was one of the poor sides of Vega Baja but the difference between the town and my hood, which I noticed after living in Calle Ocho for more or less than two weeks, the people in the neighborhood always took care of one another and people weren't starving because fruit and all kinds of vegetables grew either from a tree, a vine, or the ground and like I said before, the people took care of one another.

Within those two weeks, I hung out on the corner of Calle Ocho, playing grab ass with the boys of the neighborhood. It was literally a bunch of boys of all ages, chasing one another and grabbing each other's asses. At first I found it funny but then seeing that some of the boys had fat buttocks, like me, I decided to play. There wasn't any sexual influences or arousal in the game, I called it "butt tag", and after two other times of playing the game, I was getting aroused by one kid, eight-year-old Danny, who lived a house across from where I lived. He had this sexual attraction and after constantly hanging out with him, I couldn't take it, so I asked him if he wanted to get his suck his dick by me but he stood quiet for some time and asked me to play a game with him. I thought it was to have sex but it wasn't and since he didn't tell any of our friends with what I asked of him, I knew he was thinking about it.

I left him alone with the asking for sex but I had to find someone different than Pito and Puri to have sex with because it was getting boring with both of them. One night, we were left home alone and we were all sitting next to each other and as soon as my father got in the car with the rest of the adults and left the driveway, Pito and Puri both at the same time, reached down into my spandex type short's and started playing with my dick and balls. Once it stood erect, I got naked and they did too, we then sat back the way we were and they started masturbating me and I with one hand I tried to masturbate Puri and with the other Pito but it was hard, so I would take turns using both of my hands to play with Puri's vagina for some time, then I'll turn to the other side and masturbate Pito until he asked me to let him fuck me. After he pumped his thighs a little while he penetrated me, I told tell him that it was my turn, I got on top of him and fuck him until I ejaculate, it wasn't no fun just lust and I was tired of me being the only one, who could ejaculate.

Then I was enrolled in school in the town of Vega Baja and it helped distract me with my sexual feelings. The school was okay but I had to learn how to read and write the Spanish language the hard way. I wasn't getting tutored and I had to figure out what the teacher was saying or putting up on the board, though me speaking Spanish and being spoken to in that language on an everyday basis made learning Spanish easy. I was able to self-teach myself how to read and write and it became easy, I had made it look hard because my father

never passed the second grade and he couldn't read or write and if my father caught on that I was smart, he would of made me suffer more than he was already doing.

The school challenged my mind and I was taking it all in. On school days I really didn't hang out with the neighborhood kids, as I did on weekends but when the weekend did arrive, I remember one Saturday morning, one of the kids invited me to go swimming in a Lagoon, something I never did in New York, I told him I was down and followed the kid to the corner of Calle Ocho, where there were boys of all ages, ranging from six years to seventeen-year-old's, I was introduced to a couple of the boys I didn't know, we all then walked up the right side of the block for two blocks, then we made a left and walked a long stretch of distance and we kept on walking until we crossed a two way street into a forested area.

As we walked further in, we passed a chain partition that denied any cars from going inside the forest. We walked a little more and I could see the lagoon and it stretched farther than my eyes could see. I was facing the boys and was shocked by what I was seeing. All the boys were getting completely naked. I didn't know about skinny dipping until years later and I for some reason was so embarrassed to show my nakedness to all these boys that I turned to go but then the boys started taunting me that I was scare to get naked. I faced them and saw that none of them was ashamed of being naked with one another, they all had different size dicks and different colored ones, my shame and embarrassment left me and I got naked myself and all the kids starting "yaa, yeaing" me and then we all started playing swim tag or hide and seek, there was sections of floating grass, floating all over the water, where one can swim and hide in or we did swimming contest to see who can swim the farthest or the deepest.

There was about fourteen to fifteen naked boys and while we would take breaks from swimming, some sat nakedly on our clothes, which was piled up in their own personal section, we sat and talked kids talk, while others climb nakedly up a Mango tree and started making ripped mangoes fall to the ground, which we all ate, then we would go back to playing and swimming in the Lagoon. While sitting on my clothes, I briefly was thinking that New York boys would think this swimming naked as faggotty but to these kids it wasn't.

It was normal and as we all played and swam, I realized not one said or did anything gay, we just had fun and after a couple of hours of playing, we stopped and got dressed. I went into a bushy section to get dressed, where I was blocked from view, then this fifteen-year-old kid followed me in, I looked down to look at his small penis and he stood still letting me look, then I told him that we needed to get dressed before they catch us, he agreed for he too was looking at my penis and after everyone was dressed, we all left the Lagoon and went back to Calle Ocho.

I had fun at the Lagoon but then I got sick. The mosquitoes were biting me constantly on my legs from my knees down to the point that I had developed sores all over my legs and putting on socks to cover my legs and the sores made matters worse because the socks would soak into the wetness of the sore and become hard, making it very painful to take off, there were times where I would go in the shower with the socks on and let the water soak the dry areas where part of the sock glued itself but it was still painful taking the wet socks off to the point of bringing tears.

My father didn't care, he was sending me to school and after a week passed with my painful dilemma an aunt of mine came to visit us and upon looking at me, she knew that I was sick. She not only told my father but made him take me to the hospital, where we found out that I had a fever of a hundred and two and my legs became very swollen and almost being infected and when I would sit in a certain way, I could smell my sores. It had a funny smell and seeing the doctor, he told us it was a good thing that I came to see them because my legs were starting to get infected, I was given medication and told to keep the sores free from any covering, which I did but that didn't stop my father from sending me to school.

Going to school sick was hard and it took like two to three weeks for my legs to heal and for me to feel better but I managed and as time passed, I had stopped having sex with Pito and Puri because I was bored with them and as for my friend Danny who I wanted to have sex with, he still hadn't answered the question, even after I asked him a couple of times but then one night, while we were playing hide and go seek-tag with the kids in the neighborhood, Danny and I hid together. He started talking sexual things and just when I

thought that we were going to have sex, he ran out of the hiding spot to get away from the seeker, who had seen Danny but had to tag him, I was frustrated I knew that sooner or later Danny and I were going to have sex, all I had to do was be patient.

Living in Puerto Rico was fun but for some reason after almost a year of living there, my father, Carmen, my siblings and I were moving back to New York. I didn't know why but my father was the first one to leave to New York, so he could find us a place to live. It took him almost three weeks to call and notify every one that he found a place for us to live. I was a little saddened but I was anxious to leave because though I love life in Puerto Rico, it was not active like New York, in P.R. everything starts closing around six o'clock at night and by seven, it's like a dead zone no one was around, unless you go to clubs or La Cancha, the field, where there's basketball courts, a Baseball field and Hand ball courts but our Cancha only had one handball court and two baseball fields with benches and our field didn't have any lights, so I never hung out there, only in Calle 8 with the rest of the kids.

Now New York life was different, it was active twenty-four/seven and stores were open and there were people outside either selling or using drugs, hanging out with friends or dancing and other activities that makes New York-New York and when my father called and told Milagros that he found a place, Milagros husband had bought the plane tickets and Carmen, my step siblings and I were to leave in a couple of days.

The night before we had to leave, I was in front of the garage rolling up the hose I was using to clean up the ramp of the garage, when all of a sudden someone grabbed my buttocks. I stood up mad and turned around to see who it was and to my surprise, it was Danny and I asked him what was he doing and he told me that Milagros husband paid him a dollar to grab my ass. I was still mad but then a thought popped in my head. Milagros husband had given Pito, Puri, and I, a few dollars to buy candy when we arrived in New York. I asked Danny to follow me to the back of the house. He followed me into the outside bathroom, where the two bedrooms were located and I told him that if he let me suck his dick, I'll give him a dollar and without any hesitation, he whipped his flaccid penis out and I started to perform oral sex on him and after

a minute, I knew that he couldn't ejaculate but I still was sucking. We stopped because the bathroom didn't have a door but a shower curtain hooked up to the bathroom's entrance and upon hearing movement, we stopped and went to the gates in the front of the house. We chilled there for a moment, then Danny said that we can go somewhere else and keep on doing fresh stuff. I followed Danny to a house in front of mine and we went on to the backyard, where I continued to sucking him off. I was turned on by him, even though he couldn't ejaculate, he grabbed my head and started fucking my mouth. After a couple minutes of him humping my mouth, we stopped and went back to my house and chilled with Pito and Puri.

The next day, before I left, I gave all my friends handshakes and hugs and said my goodbye's, then I got in the car and was taken to the airport with Carmen and my step siblings.

Chapter 12

Back in New York

We were back in New York and my father was the one who picked us up. A friend of his had lent my father his car and my father took us to our new apartment. It was on the other side of the Bronx, we now lived on 645 East 152 street on Prospect Avenue between Union Avenue and Avenue St. John and the school I was enrolled in was I.S. 52 on Kelly Street between Avenue St. John and Leggett Avenue. This school was two blocks across from P.S.62 on Fox street, a school I used to go to and after some time passed living on Prospect Avenue, I found out that I had family that lived not too far from us.

I had an aunt named Elsa, who had twelve fingers and twelve toes and had an artistic alcoholic young son and Elsa was into that Santeria bullshit and always watched Walter Mercado. They lived across the street from P.S. 62 on Fox Street and I had three aunts, who lived on East 150 street between Wales Avenue and Tinton Avenue. One was Betsy, a dike, who I loved very much because she was a good hearted woman and she used to spoil me a lot and the other two was Maria and Anna.

Anna had four kids, one twelve-year-old girl named Pilar, who had shoulder length black hair and is light skin like her three brothers, thirteen-

year-old Nelson, ten-year-old Julio, and six-year-old Joshua and all three boys had close crop brown hair. I did not get to know them until later on.

In going to my new school, I was starting to be conscious of my body and my looks, every day before I went to school, I would take a shower making sure that my privates were cleaned especially my rectum (asshole) and my balls, why?, because I was getting the eyes of interest from the boys and girls in school and the neighborhood and since I stopped pissing in bed, I was starting to feel a little better about myself but one thing I had stopped doing was look at myself in the mirror, I been avoiding the mirror since I was ten years old and when I would fix my curly hair, I would avoid looking into my eyes because I hated what I saw. Even now as an adult I still do the same thing and feel the same way, I won't look at any one in the eyes because I am scared that they would see what lurks inside me but beyond this, I was find with myself.

By October, my father was more oppressive towards me and like always, I would escape into hardcore sex with Pito and Puri. I was getting turned on by Pito pissing in my mouth and in my rectum. I was finding ways to degrade myself. I would let him piss all over my face and body. I would even started sucking Pito's dick after he fucked me in the ass, which was something I didn't do because I didn't want to suck on a shitty dick, even though I've never had a dirty asshole but once or twice, when I was twelve something Ariel use to like when he fucked me in the ass. There were times while having sex with Pito, I would drink his urine just to feel degraded and nasty. Something I felt for myself, I really hated myself and since the moment I started to live with my father, I started to hear the distant voice again deep in the back of my mind, telling me that if I kill myself that no one would care that they would be happy with me gone but this time the voices were louder, there were moments that the urge to end my little life would confront me so strong but somehow the urge would disappear as soon as it appeared.

Halloween arrived and Pito and I were invited to a Halloween party from one of Carmen's family members. My father had taken us, and he left, we were promised that we were going to be taken back home by one of Carmen's other brothers.

The party was packed with Carmen's family and their friends, all the kids were sent to a big bedroom, there were around nine or ten boys, some were

boys that I knew like Sammy and another of Pito's cousins named Oscar, a little ten-year-old light skinned heavy set kid, with close cropped black hair, we all started playing wrestling and after some time passed, we stopped but then Pito started asking the boys in the room who had the bigger dick. All the boys except two brothers, whipped their flaccid penises out and they started making them erect. Pito then started rubbing his with Oscar, who had the smallest dick in the group, I was sword fighting with Sammy and two other boys, then Pito and Oscar joined us, Pito stopped and decided that he wanted to fuck Oscar in the ass. Pito pulled Oscar's pants and underwear down onto his knees and started fucking him. Oscar was making sexual noises, but I was busy sucking on Sammy and the other two other boys dicks but in seeing Pito fucking Oscar, I wanted to suck Oscar's dick. While Pito was fucking him in the ass, I couldn't control myself hearing Oscar moaning like a girl, so I went down on my knees in front of Oscar and started sucking him off, Oscar had grabbed my head and started guiding my head the way he wanted his dick to be sucked. I noticed after more than a minute that Oscar was like Pito, he couldn't ejaculate but I kept on a little longer, until one of the boys started saying to me that it was his turn, while all the boys except the two brothers were not having some type of sex, the two brothers were standing in the back of the room, watching everything we were doing. I took a break and went to the two brothers and asked them if they wanted to get their dicks sucked but they both responded "no", I went back to the group that was having sex and joined in, we kept on sucking, fucking, and sword fighting each other for more than an hour. Then we stopped and returned to wrestling, and after some time, an adult knocked on the door, announcing to Pito and me that it was time to go, we put on our coats and left the party.

At home I was thinking that the two brothers were going to tell but they didn't but the next night, the telephone rang and it was one of Carmen's family member who threw the party. It was Oscar's mother and she started talking to Carmen and after some time, Carmen hung up and told Pito and I to go to the room. She went to my father and Pito, Puri, and I could over hear the conversation they were having and it was about what Pito and I were doing with Oscar and the other boys, my father became so enraged that he physically

threw me out of the apartment and told me to leave and threatened me with " that if I went go to the cops, he would get freed and he will kill me", and slammed the door. The last thing I heard him say to Carmen was that he didn't create a fucking faggot. I didn't dare knock on the door because I was too scared and plus I could hear him screaming that he didn't want me living with him. So I left, dressed in short pants and a tank top on a cold November night.

I went to a bus stop and took the bus to my aunt Sara's apartment, she is from my mother's side and she lived somewhere near a highway by the Hudson river on 125 street, in the one of the many tall projects buildings. She lived on the twenty-fifth floor. My aunt Sara was one of my favorite aunts on both sides of the family beside my aunt Betsy, on my ride there, the bus driver asked me if "I was alright?" I shook my head up and down to answer "yes" and sat down by the door. I wouldn't been able to verbally answer the driver because I was fighting the tears that was building and the emotional sadness that comes with it.

It took more than an hour to get to my aunt Sara's crib. I was lucky that the bus stop was a couple of blocks from my aunt's because it was a very cold night and I was still cold when I was waiting for the bus. I took the elevator to the twenty-fifth floor and went and knocked on her door, she opened the door and hot tears burst out of my eyes, she grabbed me and pulled me into her arms and hugged me and started caressing the back of my head, asking me what was wrong. I started sobbing so uncontrollably that my aunt and uncle Angelo couldn't understand anything I was saying. it took them some time to calm me down and I told them with tears still rolling down my eyes and face, that my step brother and I got into trouble and my father threw me out of the apartment and to never come back. I was sitting in the kitchen and my aunt and uncle went into the living room to talk amongst each other and after a couple of minutes, they both came to me and told me that they were going to call the police, I panicked and started sobbing loudly begging them not to do it. They waited until I calmed down and I told them the threat my father made to me before I left his crib, they stood quiet but didn't call the cops but did call my mother and told her everything and after a couple of hours, my mother came to pick me up to go live with her.

Chapter 13

Back with My Mother

The ride to my mother's was quiet and she drove all the way to the Van Courtland section of the Bronx, she lived in 225 west 232 street between Kingsbridge Avenue and U.S. 9 and in the middle of the of the block was Goodwin Terrance. In the car my mind was running wild with my emotions, I didn't want to live with my mother and her family, I hated my mother, stepfather, and my half brothers and sister and lost in my emotions was the thought of committing murder if my stepfather touched me the way he did when I was younger.

My mother and I entered the building and went into her apartment on the first floor, which was next to the buildings elevator. I gave my brother Stefano a pound and a hug, Stefano had grown and was around twelve or thirteen years old and my little sister Patricia, who was five or six years old, hugged and kissed me on the cheek but I said nothing to Gus. I was taken to the first room upon entering the apartment, the living room, it was big and it had a big dinner table with six chairs around it and a big sofa that was occupied by my brother Stefano. My mother had brought me some quilts and blankets, so I could set them up on the floor, so I could sleep and with all the shit that happened I was tired, depressed, and enraged, so I went to sleep.

The next few days, I spent them outside walking around the neighborhood loathing everything that represented love and happiness. I would see families laughing and showing all that lovey dovey bullshit, and my body would become enflamed with a murderess intent. In my mind I would look at these families and I would envision myself killing one or more of them, just to wipe all that happiness and laughter out of their life, I wanted to make every one suffer and feel my pain, to me people didn't deserve to be happy while I continue to suffer, when these thoughts appear in my mind, I would stop walking and I would go into a daze and hear a voice in the back of my mind, whispering to me, "kill them all, your justified, look at you, you don't have no clothes, you look like a bum, why should they look well dressed, no one loves you, everyone is always hurting you, make them fear you", the last four words was said in such anger that it snapped me out of my daze, making me feel guilty for my visualizations of me committing murder to people in different ways.

There would be times, when outside by myself, either sitting in front of the building or walking around that I would imagine myself as Michael Myers from the Halloween movies. I would imagine myself with his mask, going around and committing gruesome and brutal murders, after being in this state of mind for a couple of hours, I would go home, eat whatever my mother made, then I would go to sleep.

I felt lost within myself not knowing what the fuck was going on with me and as the days passed on, Gus was always verbally and physically abusive with my mother and it wasn't until months later that I found out why there were always fighting it was because of me living there with them. I found this out one night while I was laying on the floor to sleep and Gus walked into my sleeping area and told me that he didn't want me in the apartment. I didn't bother to really listen to him because he owed me for what he did to me and I couldn't stop thinking how bad I wanted to kill him but I knew that if I did, not only would I go to jail but they would make me look like a monster, so I waited to see who Gus loved the most between Stefano and Patricia and realizing that Patricia was his pride and joy, I decided to molest her. At first, I had her masturbate me and the last thing I did to her was tried to penetrate her and all I managed to do was make Patricia cry. I stopped trying to have any

further sex with my sister because it wasn't out of lust, I just hated her and I tried to convince Stefano to even try to have sex with me but he refused. I wanted everyone to suffer but didn't know what to and how to do it. I even tried to have sex with Stefano's Asian friend, named Jimmy. One day Stefano, Jimmy, and myself, went to Van Courtland park and Stefano was way ahead of us, Jimmy had stop to take a piss and seeing his flaccid penis made me want to suck his dick and I told Jimmy. I went so far as to reach out and quickly grab his penis, he jumped back, fixed himself and told me that he doesn't do those things with boys but every time I saw Jimmy, I would ask him just in case he change his mind but he didn't, he was so uncomfortable with me that Jimmy would only hang out with Stefano.

In the neighborhood, I didn't have any friends and I really didn't want any because we always wind up having sex and though part of me wanted to have sex with every boy who was interested, but then there is a big part of me that was not only tired of having sex but disgusted with it, especially with boys but once the forbidden fruit has been tasted, it's too late to go back and plus no one was telling me that what I was doing was wrong and because I didn't have to force or trick the boys, I felt it was okay.

I woke up mad like most mornings and that mood stood throughout the entire day, I remember that evening, I will say around six in the evening, Stefano was outside playing in front of the building. I was in the living room where I slept, and Stefano came into the apartment sobbing. I asked him what happened and he told me some kid bigger than he is was bullying him and he started hitting him. I told him to go outside and show me who the kid is but to not let him know that I was watching. I went across the street from my building and waited, my little brother was playing with a toy he had and after a couple of minutes, a white heavy set kid passed by me and crossed the street and headed straight for Stefano. He started to force my little brother to let him play with the toy, the white kid who out weighed Stefano by a lot, started to man handle Stefano, I crossed the street and approached the kid and asked him, " what the fuck are doing to my little brother",, the white kid froze and turned to me and that's when I punched him on the face and continued to hit him non-stop even when I heard, his mother screaming out the window to

stop hitting him, darkness had taken over me and it didn't give a fuck, I was still hitting the white, when three grown adults pulled me off of him, one of them was his mother, they had to carrying him back home, I screamed at him " don't you ever fuck with my brother again " and Stefano and I went back home, as for the white , he never bothered Stefano again.

. . .

The winter had arrived and my birthday came and went with a little birthday celebration and a gift that I wanted, a battery-operated music organ, which was the trend back in the early nineties. I would take it outside with me every day after school and hang out in front of my building and try to play the organ in piano mode while kids were in front the building playing.

One evening, I was in front of my building and the same kids were out there playing, then this white girl of eleven approached me and asked me if I could let her play with it and no matter, how many times I told her no, she continued to ask me. I got tired of her asking me that I told her that if she let me suck her pussy that I would let her play with my organ, she stood quite for some time, then she agreed. We went behind our building, which was connected to other buildings and I went on my knees in front of Crystal, the white eleven-year-old and unbuttoned her pants, pulled her zipper down with the front part of her panties and started licking and sucking on her pussy lips. I was at it for some time, when all of a sudden someone from the building screamed at us, asking us what were we doing. I got up and ran and left her fixing herself. When she appeared in front of the building, the person who screamed at us approached us downstairs. It was one of the teen kids who was playing outside, who supposedly went upstairs to use the bathroom and happened to see us in the back of the building. The teen kid started telling all the kids that were in from of the building and they all were telling us that it was wrong for doing those things. They turned around and told Crystal that they were going to tell her mother, which they did. Some of teens escorted her into the building's elevator taking her upstairs to where she lived. I stood outside with some teen boy who was telling me that what I did was wrong. I wasn't

really paying him no mind, I'm not going to lie, but after some time of him rambling on about what I did was wrong, I started to feel guilty, so I took the teens advice and went upstairs to the floor and apartment number to where Crystal lived. I took the elevator to the fifth floor and knocked on the door to apologize to her mother. Crystal's mother answered and I apologized to her but she slammed the door on my face. I went downstairs to where I lived thinking that the issue was closed, but after an hour or two after Crystal and I was caught, Crystal's mother knocked on my door and my mother was the one who answered it. I was in the living room trying to listen to the conversation but failing, some time had passed and my mother closed the door. She came into the living room and started beating on me, punching me every where she could after she got tired of hitting me, she threw me out of the apartment. I left in a fucked up chaotic frame of mind, I questioned myself with, what the fuck did I do wrong? And all I could say was, nothing. I reviewed everything that happened, a girl of eleven years old kept on asking me to play with my battery operated Organ and after I told her "no" a few times, I decided to make a deal with her. I'll let her play with my Organ, if she let me suck on her pussy and she did. I didn't force her, I had turned fourteen years old a couple of days ago, plus I didn't do anything wrong but the fact that kids aren't supposed to be having any sexual activity.

As I was walked to the 1 and 9 train station, I was in a daze. I felt like crying but the rage in me had a lock on my tears. I felt my whole body enflamed with an inner fire and thoughts of wanting to kill people. I even caught an erection, thinking of the different ways I would kill everyone in my path, especially those happy-dappy innocent people. My vision became dark and they didn't clear until I was ringing the doorbell of my aunt/god mother Rosa, who lived in 182 street on Bathgate Avenue, in the Bronx and instead of her taking me in, she called my father's brother Nelson and made living arrangements so I could stay until they could figure out what to do with me and though they didn't ask me why I'm was thrown out from where ever I was living, I didn't offer any information either.

Chapter 14

Uncle Nelson and his Family

I walked to 183 street on Bathgate avenue building 2293 and walked up to the fourth floor, where they lived, my uncle Nelson was by the door waiting for me, I gave him a hug and told him "bendicion" (asking for his blessing), I was escorted into the hallway, which is longer than the apartment upstairs, when I lived with my father, the first bedroom was shared by my uncle, his wife Alba and their daughter Ivy (pronounced evee), then there was the living room and further down the living room was Pablo's bedroom, where I would be sharing Pablo's bed.

I was tired and as I laid on the bed next to sleeping Pablo, I still felt numb of all emotions and I was asking myself, what is wrong with me? Why am I going through this? Why can't I have a real family that would love me and protect me? And the only answer that came forth from a distance in my mind, was "you don't belong anywhere" and I fell into a deep sleep.

$$\cdot \quad \cdot \quad \cdot$$

I awoke to the sounds and smells of the early morning breakfast being made but I awoke still numb of emotions. The numbness only lasted a couple of

though I felt like ramming my penis in but I knew that I would hurt him, so we got up from his bed and went into the living room nakedly. I laid on my back and Pablo laid on top of me, face to face and we started humping on each other's penises. While we were taking turns sucking on each other's neck and after a couple of hours, we stopped and got dressed. He went into the kitchen to wash the dishes and I went into the room to get some clothes so I could take a shower, no more than ten minutes had passed, when I heard my uncle, his wife Alba and Ivy, talking in the living room. We were awfully close at getting caught but that did not stop Pablo from wanting me to suck on his rectum every night, even when his parents were home, there times they were in the living room and Pablo wanted me to perform oral sex on his penis and butt hole not caring if we got caught.

· · ·

I remember in the middle of the summer, it was me, Alba, my uncle Nelson, Ivy, Pablo, Ariel and his parents, chilling across the street from where Ariel lived, and while the adults were talking, I snuck to one side with Ariel and started flirting sexually with him. We wanted to have sex, so I told Ariel to go into my building and wait there. When I saw him enter the building, I turned to Alba and asked her if I can get the apartment keys to use the bathroom, she gave them to me.

Just as I turned around to cross the street I hear Pablo yell out that he needed to use the bathroom also. I was mad and didn't say anything to Pablo until we crossed the street heading to our building, I asked him to stay outside but he refused, as we got closer to entrance of our building, I again told him to stay back because I had to do something but he refused again and told me that he wanted me to suck his rectum. I reply okay but I didn't say anything about Ariel because I wanted Ariel to fuck Pablo in the ass.

We entered the building and Pablo saw Ariel and was about to say something but I cut him off and told him that I told you to stay back but you wouldn't. Ariel and I are going to fuck and if you want me to have sex with you, you have to do it with the both of us. The three of us were walking up the steps

with Ariel and I stopping here and there to French kiss and grab on each other lustfully. Once we reached the third floor, Ariel and I stopped so I could perform oral sex on him, Pablo seeing what we were doing started to protest against us having sex in the building steps but we ignored him. I gave Ariel's penis a couple of kisses, licks and sucks, then we continued to the fourth floor. Pablo was opening the apartment door and Ariel with his penis still exposed made me pull my short's and underwear down from behind a little and Ariel penetrated me. He humped me until the door was opened and Ariel and I rushed in and enter the living room and laid on my stomach on the sofa and Ariel laid on me and started humping me hard and fast and within a minute or so, his body trembled, stopped moving and he laid on me until he was able to catch his breath.

Pablo in the meantime was trying to get in the action but Ariel and I told him later we were preparing for round 2 and started French kissing passionately again. Ariel then got off me and stood standing in front with his penis ready to get sucked but just as I was going to start preforming oral sex on Ariel, Pablo started complaining and rushing us to finish, so we could leave before Pablo's mother decides to come up stairs, we tried to ignore him but Pablo wouldn't stop. Ariel turned around and asked him if he wanted to fuck for real and Pablo replied "yes". Ariel told Pablo to pull his pants down and Pablo did. Ariel positioned himself behind Pablo to penetrate him but when Ariel did Pablo started screaming and saying that it hurt, to take it out. I saw that Pablo was on verge of tears and Ariel stopped trying to penetrate Pablo and the sexual moment that Ariel and I had was gone, so we left the crib but later that night I had sex with Pablo.

•   •   •

One day Pablo had gone to stay at his grandparents apartment (his grandparents from his mother's side of the family), because they had to wake up early and head to the airport to go to Puerto Rico because the plan was to send him first, then the rest of us would follow right behind them but on a later date.

That night my uncle and Alba had some adult friends come over and my uncle told six-year-old Ivy and I to go to Pablo's room and watch television.

We went to the room and laid side by side watching wrestling, since Pablo wasn't home and I couldn't play wrestling with him, I decided to play wrestle with Ivy. we were playing when I got a little rough and Ivy said that she didn't want to play anymore. I stopped and we continued to watch TV but after some time passed, Ivy asked me if I wanted to pretend play, I answered "yes", then she asked me if I could pretend to be Michael, I asked her, who is Michael? and she answer that it was a boy in her classroom, who puts her to suck on his actual finger. I knew this to be true because she got caught one day in her class doing this to a boy and it was reported to my uncle and Alba. Ivy only got punished that day but I knew already what was going to happen and when I agreed to play Michael, she laid on her back on Pablo's bed and spread her legs, I noticed that she didn't have any panty's on and when I saw that she had a fat pussy, I was instantly lustful. I started to lick and suck on her pussy lips and nibble on her clitoris, her body started trembling and when I reached her pussy hole, I tried to stick my tongue as far as in as I could, her body started shaking hard while sticking my tongue in her, I then felt a little bumped inside her pussy and she grabbed my head and pushed it in, I kept sucking on that bump for a couple of seconds more and she ejaculated so hard that she closed her legs and pushed my head harder into her groin making my nose bleed. She held me there until her whole body calmed down and that's when I learned that girls can ejaculate, I didn't know the proper word then which was orgasm.

After we finished, she got on shaky legs and went into the living room. I followed right behind her and sat on the opposite side to where Alba was sitting on the big sofa. In the position that Alba was in all she had to do was look a little to one side and she could see into the room and see what was going on but being that my uncle and Alba had guest, she wasn't paying any mind to us. I myself was surprised that a girl could get an orgasm because as much times I had sex with Puri and some other girl, they never ejaculated, so I thought that girls couldn't achieve those feeling.

I remember when she caught that orgasm, I was really scared because her body went through some explosive moments and I really didn't understand what she was going through and while I sat on the one-sitter and she laid on the big sofa next to her mother but facing me, I noticed that she couldn't stop staring at me.

I knew that I was going to mess up and I didn't want too because my uncle and aunt Alba were really good to me, they treated me like one of their own kids but the doors were opened for me to have sex and I was becoming addicted to preforming oral sex with Ivy, then in the beginning of the summer, I was allowed to hang out on the roof of a store by climbing down the Fire Escape and playing with other kids, two brothers, a thirteen-year-old obese dark skinned boy, who rarely came outside and his six-year-old brown skinned boy, who were both of Dominican decent and only spoke Spanish with a little broken English. I was playing with them running around the store's roof, we then change it to talking about kids' stuff because it was hot. After we rested the six-year-old named Edgar wanted me to follow him to show me a hole on a roof connected to the store but further in the back, I followed him and he climbed down the collapsed roof by climbing down a fallen Pillar, as he was climbing up he started saying in Spanish " me Inco la chocha" ("my pussy is going to get sting), he was referring to getting his privates caught on the wooden splinters but as he kept on saying it, he would look at me and I knew that look and knew what he was doing, he was letting me know that he was gay and a few days later while hanging in the building's Hallway, Edgar was on the third floor playing with some ball and I went down to where he was and upon seeing me, he stopped playing and we sat down between the stairs of the second and third floor, he started talking and telling me how his brother would make him do sexual things at night and how he wanted to suck my dick. He even took me down to lobby floor under the steps on the side of a wall, where anyone could have sex and not get caught.

I pulled my shorts and underwear down mid-thigh and he grabbed my erect penis in his hands and started rubbing it all around his face and lips. He acted like he was hungry he then started giving me head and just as I was about to ejaculate, I stopped him because I wanted to suck on his privates. He pulled off his shorts which was the only thing he had on, his little penis was rock hard and I kneeled in front of him and performed oral sex on him. I got so lustful that I even performed oral sex on his rectum making him moan like a girl. I realized that he was like Pablo, he couldn't ejaculate and after a minute or more of me sucking on his rectum, I stopped because he was starting to moan a little

too loud and I didn't want to be caught with a boy having sex, though I didn't see anything wrong with all the sex I was having because I didn't have to say or do anything. And every time we saw each other, he would tell me that he wanted to fuck, I remember early one Saturday morning while watching cartoons, someone was knocking on the door and I quickly went to answer, so as not to wake up everyone in the crib and when I opened the door it was Edgar. I let him in and we stood in the hallway of the apartment and I let him suck on my dick and I did the same to him. He them whispered to me that he wanted me to penetrate his asshole, I told him that everyone was sleeping and that we could get caught, we fooled around a little bit more and French kissed hungrily and then he left.

• • •

Sometime later, my uncle, Alba, Ivy, and myself were hanging out on the block chilling. My uncle and Alba was talking to one of their friends. I had to use the bathroom so I asked Alba if I could get the keys because I had to urinate. She gave them to me and I quickly walk/ran into the building and ongoing up to the third floor steps, Edgar was just sitting there. I asked him if he wanted to fuck and he replied "yes", we walked up to the fourth floor and entered my uncle's apartment. As I was closing the door Edgar had already taken off his short's and we walked in completely naked into the living room, I was already turn on but by him getting naked before coming into the apartment, he made me very lustful, I followed him nakedly into the living room but told him that I had to take piss first. I finished using the bathroom and by the time I reached the big sofa, he was laying on his back with his legs wide open, playing with himself, I laid part way on top of him because I didn't want to suffocate him, we first started French kissing hungrily, then went to sword fighting. I was super horny and I got up off of him and started to lick on his neck making him moan. I continued to lick and suck on his neck, then I started going down his chest, sucking and licking on both of his nipples and the more he moaned the more I explored his chest all the way down unto his groin with my tongue. I then turned him around and started to lick and suck on his rectum, he started

moaning a little harder than before begging me to fuck him in the ass and I tried but I was only able to stick part of the head of my penis in, he started to yell to out to take it out, I wanted to ram him but I knew that I would've hurt him, so I listen to him moan as I placed my penis between his buttocks and started humping him like that.

We fucked in almost every room in the apartment with me holding on not to ejaculate because if I did, it would have been finished right there and then. After some time, I told him that we had to stop because my Aunt Alba might come upstairs. We stopped and got dressed but continued to French kissed for a minute or two. We promised to be boyfriend and girlfriend then we left the crib, I only agreed with a relationship because I didn't ejaculate and was super horny but in reality I really didn't want to have sex with boys but for some reason, I'm always on my knees pleasing boys of my age or younger and a lot of them become obsessed with me, which in turn gets me in trouble, not knowing why was I in trouble.

. . .

There many mornings before going to school I would perform oral sex on Ivy and sometimes Pablo before he left to Puerto Rico. He liked it in the night because everyone was either busy watching TV or sleeping. He like the way my tongue felt in his rectum, he also like it at night because he liked being naked. When I perform oral sex on him, he knew that I wanted to penetrate him and when I tried, he screamed out in pain and like Ivy, I wanted to penetrate her too, but I knew that Ivy couldn't take my penis it would definitely hurt her. I remember one school morning just as I preparing to go to school I had performed oral sex on Ivy and she asked me to put it her pussy, I tried and it made her cry out in pain and when her mother asked her what happened, she explained that she had fallen and hurt herself.

One night, she was kneeling on the floor in Pablo's room by his bed doing homework, I was in the living room trying to watch TV but I was horny and seeing Ivy kneeling, I went into the room and kneeled right behind her. I pulled her short's and panty's down from behind and tested if she could get penetrate

from behind, I then spit on the head of my penis and I penetrated slowly, it went in completely but it was very tight she was turned on. I humped her slowly until I couldn't hold it much longer and started to hump her quickly, she let out a little moan and that's when my body shook hard from ejaculating in her and after I empty myself in her, I left my penis in her until my body calmed down, then I fixed myself and I helped Ivy fix herself with that I was able to watch TV.

I remember Pablo would always watch me fuck Ivy but couldn't say or do anything because I was fucking him too but no one else suspected Ivy and I of having sex. there were times, Ivy would put on a dress with no panties on and sit on my lap on the one-seater while we would be in the living room and her parents would be sitting on the big sofa right next to us, I would slowly without making it obvious or draw any attention would pull out my penis of my short's and put it between Ivy's pussy lips and she'll move slowly. We'd get wet from our pre-cum mixing together. It was so slippery down there that when we both ejaculate, she would grab onto the edges of both the sofa corners and try not to blow up the spot and I would be holding both her wrist to slow my trembling and shaking too.

Other times Alba would ask me to prepare the bath water for Ivy so Ivy could bathe, and Ivy would follow me into the bathroom without her mother knowing it and get naked. I then would penetrate her in the ass and when we would finish, she would get dressed and wait for her mother to bathe her.

Then one early afternoon, Ivy and I were in Pablo's room and Ivy had a dress with panties on, she pulled her panties down mid-thigh and sat on me where my penis would be in between her pussy lips, Ivy was moving and I was matching her humps and just as we were about to ejaculate Alba walked in Pablo's room and froze at catching us having sex, then she came at us and started beating on both of us. After a minute or two, she pulled Ivy off of me and started to beat on her from Pablo's room into her bedroom, then she came into Pablo's room and started beating me over my face and cursing at me and saying that I am an ungrateful faggot and a worthless piece of shit and told me to stand by the entrance door of the apartment. As I walked to where she told to, I didn't feel none of the hits or felt the hits with her words, I was all of a sudden completely numb of all human emotions.

I felt like I was split in two. I was in the darkness looking at what my body was going to do, my true self didn't want to stop it. It stood standing numb to all human emotion with a blank mind looking up into nowhere, more than half an hour passed by when it heard Alba call our name, yelling at me "pack your fucking things and get the fuck out of the apartment". It turned and walked to Pablo's room and in a garbage bag, it started putting in the little we had, there was a money stash that Alba had in one of Pablo's dresser, it took half of the bills without counting them, then it went into the bathroom and pretended to be urinating but what it was really doing was thinking how kill everyone in the crib. It saw a plastic bathroom cleaner container that said it was poison if consumed. I saw myself, sneak into the kitchen, to where Alba had a Penil "pork shoulder" thawing and it poured the liquid cleaner around the pork shoulder, spreading it around the Penil, so no one would notice, then it pick up a knife and started making holes around the penil and putting liquid cleaner in the holes, it made sure that the Penil didn't look tampered, it washed his hands, went back into Pablo's room, grabbed our bag and left the apartment to the only place we could go to, my grandparents.

Chapter 15

My Grandparents at Age 14 1/2

It was still in control of me, when we got on the city bus, which took us to another two buses that would eventually take us to 2029 East 104 street on second Avenue in Manhattan (the actual address I've been going to since I was younger, not 102 street), on the way there I felt comfortable letting it take control, it made me feel no guilt about Alba and her family dying of poisoning or what I've done, but inside myself, I was thinking, "what hell is wrong with me? One, it is wrong to have sex with boys, but nobody tells me why, then I have sex with a young female family member and its wrong, but nobody tells me why I was confused.

I notice that we had gotten to our destination but stopped two blocks short, so we could spend some stolen money in a Chinese sit-in or take-out spot. It ordered to stay and we sat down within a few seconds of sitting down. I was back in control of my own self and that's when I felt the full weight of what happened throughout the whole day, a renewed hatred for myself and everyone around me. I felt a heavy cloud of darkness surround me letting me know that I will always be alone, these feelings birthed a loathing feeling for anything happy or innocent,.I vowed deep within myself that the whole world will one day pay for everything done to me and they will fear me before I die.

• • •

I finished eating my food and walked without thought the rest of the way but when I entered the building it was like nothing happened. How can I better explain it, it was like the events and feelings of the day happened long time ago and I got over it. I didn't feel affected by it at all. I stood in front of my grandparents apartment door and knocked, my grandmother was the one who answered the door and upon seeing me, she snatched me off my feet and hugged me. I hugged her back and we stood in that warm embrace for a few minutes, then we went in. I don't know what I told her or if I told her anything but I think they were told, when my father called them to find out if I was there.

• • •

Things were awesome with my grandparents but I was going through a whole bunch of emotions and the principal ones were my hatred and the silent rage burning in my heart, body, and soul. As the days passed, I couldn't escape into sex because I really didn't go outside to find any sexual partner because though I was lusting for male flesh, I was really disgusted by being with a boy and preforming oral sex or having intercourse. I always dreamt that I would be married in a church with a woman and our kids would be sitting in front watching the whole ceremony and crowds of family and friends filling the church but the reality of it all, is I still dream that dream and being fourteen, I didn't know who I was, if I was human or even real or if I was in a dream and because of my grandparents, I kept my feelings hidden and pretended to be normal.

But then, after being in the crib and not going outside for some time, my grandmother started to tell me to go outside and play and make some friends. I think she was throwing me out because I was constantly scare pranking her. I remember one day, my grandmother was washing the dishes and I crept up behind her and screamed "BOO", and she instinctively turned around and threw me with a butcher knife, missing me by mere inches when it past my face, the knife penetrated and stuck to the hallway wall.

I started going outside and made some friends with a couple of kids from the neighborhood, but I wasn't interested in them with play, I wanted to let my hidden emotions out. I wanted to be on my knees sucking dick or getting fucked in my ass but I knew that eventually one or all of them will start talking about sex, making us horny.

Days passed by with no one talking about sex and while waiting for that day to come, my cousin Omar came to stay for the weekend, I was thinking that he was like Chewito with the sex. I tried to convince him to have sex with me but he wouldn't do anything sexual, even after I surprised him from behind and pulled his underwear down from behind and tried to lick his buttocks. He pulled his underwear back up and told me that if I do that again he would tell on me with that I left him alone but played with him like we always did.

. . .

One hot summer day, I decided to go a neighborhood swimming pool I heard about from some kids in my Sunday school church meetings. It was a long walk but I didn't care I have walked farther. I had my towel, my swimming goggles, a mouth piece, so I could swim with my head underneath the water and pretend that I was a professional diver looking for treasure and my swimming flippers. I went through the bathroom and straight into the swimming pool area first, I placed my towel stretched long on the ground and put my swimming gear on the towel. I then walked back into the bathroom to the shower area because I wanted to wash all the grime from my body from all the sweat I accumulated from walking to the pool, in the shower was a grown male and a black kid of about my age but shorter than me, they were washing up and by the time I turned on the shower, the adult male left and it was just the black kid and I alone, he had taken off his underwear and I did the same. I was lathering my body with the liquid soap they had by the shower, the black kid was facing me lathering himself too but mostly on his privates, we started having the regular kid conversations of "where you from?", "how old are you?" I answered every question he asked me and I found out that I was older than him by a year with all the talking, I was starting to become aroused with an

erection developing. I started to rinse myself quickly but with my eyes was glued to him rinsing his long skinny penis and balls. I couldn't help it, so I got on my knees in front of him, and put his penis and balls in my mouth and gave them a couple of sucks, I then stopped and stood up quickly like nothing happened and thank God I did because as I stood a swimming pool worker had passed by the shower area to head his locked office.

Once the worker left from our site, the black kid told me to meet him in the swimming pool area, he put on his swimming trunks and left, I stood until my erection went down, then I put on my swimming trunks and ran to where the black kid was swimming, the pool area was empty it was just the both of us and the life guard. We first swam around, then we started competing with one another to see who was the better swimmer and who could hold their breath the longest, then we switch the game to tag and played until we got tired, we then went to where I had set up my towel, David, which was the name he wanted me to call him by had set up his towel next to mine, he laid on his stomach and he started humping the floor slowly, he then laid on his side facing me and whipped out his long erect skinny penis and started to masturbate slowly at first, then he started to pick up his pace, we weren't worried of any one catching us because like I said before, there wasn't any one but us and the life guard and he wasn't paying no attention to us, while David was masturbating, he was telling me that if his older brother would of see me sucking on his dick and balls, I would of gotten into trouble with him, he then stopped masturbating, fixed himself, got up, said he would be back and left into the bathroom.

I knew what he was going to do and I wanted to be part of his lust, so I waited a minute or two and I too went into the bathroom area to look for David and see if he would let me suck on his dick or fuck me in the ass. I looked in the shower area and the bath room but he wasn't there. As I was walking back to the swimming pool, I heard movement in a bath room area that was closed due to renovations, I decided to climb and walk over the lockers that were laid out on the bath room floor blocking the walk way and saw David had started walking out of the back area jerking off but with some speed. He saw that it was me and asked me if I wanted suck his dick. I replied "yes" and

instead of staying there, we climbed out and tried to have sex in the bathroom stalls but people were there either to use the bathroom or to use drugs but not the swimming pool. They kept on coming in and out of the bathroom, we then went to a section of the pool, where there was a locked door that lead in and out the pool's bathroom, it was completely dark and it was located in the locker section, so we took a chance and as I started playing with his dick and balls some Mexican guy sat on a bench that face where we were at and he was sitting down facing us but not at us, David grabbed my hand and stopped me, he then motioned for us to stay still and wait for the Mexican guy to leave from the area.

Once the Mexican guy left, we left the area and I saw that David's penis was out of his swimming trunks and it was throbbing up and down. We went back into the bathroom area and some guy noticed David's erection but said nothing. David wanted to do more than have me perform oral sex on him but there wasn't anywhere to really go, so we went to where our towels were at, and he had taken his towels with some of my swimming gear, I picked up the rest of my things and headed for the locker area and hung out until the coast was clear and get our fucking on but just as we were waiting, two older black teens who knew David started teasing his about a shitty incident on his underwear and since David and I couldn't have sex, he decided to leave with the two older teens.

I stood sitting down until my erection went down by then some Caucasian kid of my age, sat on one of the bench looking at me and after a minute or two, the white kid started a conversation and asked me what was I doing, I don't know why but I told him the truth about David and me and what we were going to do. He stood quiet and when I asked him, if he wanted to get his dick sucked and didn't answer, I knew that I could have him but I had to convince him somehow.

Once my erection went flaccid, I headed out of the pool area and onto the street. I noticed that the kid was following me, and as we were walking, he started a conversation about kid stuff and as we passed by an abandoned car. We had stopped, and I asked the white kid if I could touch his privates. He responded yes. I stuck my hand down in his pants and started fondling his penis

and balls. I asked him if we go into one of the housing projects that we were passing by, so we could have sex and he replied "no", because he lived in the area. He then began climbing up a fence that would lead to the housing projects and I followed him. We walked and talked about sexual stuff, he stopped talking sexually when we approached a group of kids. He said "what's up" to some the kids and introduced me to all of them. The white kid then asked me to stay and play with him and the other kids, I stood to see if the white would want to sneak off into one of the buildings to finish what we started but after a couple of minutes passed by with nothing happening, I decided to leave, I said that I had to leave and said my goodbyes to the kids and left.

Later that night, I was chilling in the living room waiting for my grandparents to go to sleep because I was horny and I wanted to masturbate to let my sexual frustrations simmer down, they finally went to sleep around ten o'clock. I was laying on the five piece sofa that I was using as a bed in my underwear only, I was watching television giving the moment some time to make sure that my grandparents were completely asleep. Once I was sure they were, I covered myself with my bed sheet up to my neck and took off my underwear, I started fondling myself and instead of fantasizing about the black or white kid, I started fantasizing about the Devil's son on how beautiful he would look and how a nice penis he had. Not too big and not to small, in my fantasy the Devil's son was my age and we fucked in every possible position we could think of, and in my fantasy the devil's son didn't look like a human being. He did have a human form and with his tail, it enwrapped me while he was fucking me hard and slow the fantasy was so real like that my body tremble and shook uncontrollably from ejaculating, my hand was still grasping my penis tightly and I was breathing hard. I don't know how long after my penis went limp and my breathing was back to normal, I slowly put on my underwear because I was a little weak and as soon as I put them on and laid back down and covered myself again but this time to go sleep, my grandmother happened to peeped her head into the living room to check up on me, I was relieved that it wasn't when I was in my sexual moment. Boy, I would of died of embarrassment and she would have had her preacher from her church come to her crib and had me and my masturbation ways exorcised.

. . .

As summer was turning into Autumn, I started hanging out with the kids from the park across the street from where I lived. It was a group of five other boys, two brothers ages twelve and six-year-old, the other three were friends of their for years, one was a thirteen-year-old, the other was another twelve-year-old and the last one was an eleven-year-old, we were all Puerto Ricans, we didn't only hang out in the neighborhood park, we would go to many different neighborhoods being mischievous with people or one another, we even climbed a school's balcony to see if we could break in but there was a custodian polishing the cafeteria's floor, so we decided to leave before we all got into trouble, then there were times that we would go up onto the roof in the projects, to either spit, throw things over the roof, or piss where ever we wanted on the roof's floor or the staircases.

One day, we were on the roof of one of projects and one of the boys wanted to see, who had the biggest penis, we all whipped out our limp penises out, and my was the winner but they were laughing at my penis because I had baby powder on my dick and balls. I explained to them that I did that every time I took a shower, so that my privates would smell good. They stopped teasing me but we kept on with trying to force piss on every stair case.

One day we were hanging in a different park in some other neighborhood and we sat inside one of three big cemented tubes placed in the playground. We talked about masturbation, and I began to get an erection and when my penis was fully erect, I whipped it out and started masturbating in a way that no one from the outside of the tube could see what I was doing. The other boys wanted to witness me ejaculate, some were even touching themselves. They started questioning me about the form that was developing on the head of my penis and inside my foreskin. I told them that it was pre-cum that it made jerking off slippery, making me cum faster and just as I was about to ejaculate, some older teen and his girlfriend sat on a bench that faced us and could see whatever we were doing. I stopped and the boys asked what happened and I pointed to the couple. I fixed myself but we stood there talking about kids'

stuff, then we left after some time had passed, we went back to their neigh-borhood, which was on 103 street where they all lived, the two brothers invited me to their apartment, while the rest of the boys went to their cribs.

The brothers mother was cooking dinner and she had the crib smelling awesome, the two brothers took me to their room, where there were three other children in the bed room playing, a three-year-old, a ten and eleven-year-old, I chilled with all the brothers for a while, then I told them that I had to leave home, they didn't want me to leave, even the mother asked me to stay, so I could eat with them, I politely refused, explaining that I lived with my grandparents and that they would become worried, if I came home late, I said goodbye and I left.

The next day, the oldest of the brothers came to pick me up, so we could hang out. We agreed on going to Central Park, as we walked to Central Park, we conversated about everything, I then asked him if he ever did it with a boy and he answered "yeah", he started telling me that one day he went the street hydrant to drink some water and there was a black kid dressed in girl's colored shorts and shirt drinking water too. And the black kid said he was a girl and that he/she wanted to fuck, my friend continued to tell me that they went into a hiding spot and he started fucking the black kid in the ass and when he asked the black kid to let him fuck in the pussy, the black kid surprised him by pulling down his shorts and exposing his penis, my friend finished the conversation by saying that he fuck the black kid some more in the ass and left the hiding spot.

I was glad to hear that and as we neared Central Park, I asked him if I could suck his dick he answered "yes" without hesitation. We changed the subject to kids' stuff until we reached inside Central Park, we first went to a section of the park, where there was a man-made cemented tank with live gold fishes in it, also surrounding this tank were bushes and benches with thin trees on the side, we got in the tank trying to catch a gold fish, the water reached mid-thigh, so we didn't worry about drowning but no matter what we tried to do to catch at least one gold fish, we failed. We stopped trying to catch the fish, he then unzipped his pants and pulled his erect penis out. I went to him and started sucking but water started getting into my mouth. I told him to let's do it on the bench and he agreed. We went to a bench and

he pulled his pants and underwear down onto his ankles and sat on the bench with his legs spread open, I got on my knees and started to perform oral sex on his dick and balls, he was like Pito who couldn't ejaculate. I stood sucking him for a couple of minutes, then he interrupt me by saying that there was someone coming our way, we stopped and my friend fixed himself and we both left to find another spot.

It didn't take us long to find another spot. The spot we found look like a stoned throne with a stone like table and where it was positioned, there was a chance that we could get caught having sex, we were horny and didn't care. He unzipped himself and brought his pants and underwear down again onto his ankles. He then laid on his back on the stoned table with his legs wide open. I then started preforming oral sex on his dick and balls. I sucked on him for almost five minutes. We stopped, so I could take a break from sucking because my jaw was getting tired. He sat up without fixing himself, and after a minute or two passed by, I told him that I was ready for round two. He laid back down and I started sucking again but this time it didn't last long because I happened to see someone coming our direction, so I stopped and told my friend, he sat up quickly, got off the table and quickly fixed himself, then we ran out of there.

He didn't want me to stop sucking on his dick and balls, so we looked for another spot where we could have sex and not be disturbed. After some time going from here to there, we found a spot that in the bushes, we saw some cardboards spread around, so we place them together on the ground and we got naked. He laid on his back and I laid on top of him to sword fight and French kiss. We stood in that moment for some time, then I moved down between his legs and started sucking again, not two or three minutes past by when I heard someone from a distance walking towards us, my friend heard it too and we both quickly got dressed and left the area and Central Park. We left because we realized that we passed our curfew, and when we arrived in his neighborhood, I gave my friend a pound and left to my grandparents, who were mad at me for coming home late. They told me that if I do that again, I would be grounded, I apologized and reassured them that I wouldn't do it again.

Later that night, my grandparents told me some good news, they told me that we were all going to move and live in Puerto Rico and that we will be moving real soon. I was really happy, so happy that when the next day arrived and the two brothers came looking for me, requesting that I suck on his dick and his six-year-old brother's dick, I answered "yes" and being that we were in my building, we took the elevator up to the fifteenth floor and went in between the fourteenth and fifteenth floor staircase , I first had sex with the older brother, then after I finished the older brother, I did his little brother, I desperately pulled his shorts down onto his knees and started sucking his dick and balls.

His little brother started moaning and gyrating his waist from side to side and in a humping position and after some time, we all jumped when we heard a door to one of the upper floors open and close, the two brothers fixed themselves quickly and we ran into the hallway and pressed for the elevator, once it arrived, all three of us got on and once we stopped on the lobby floor, we ran out the building and around the corner. We stopped to catch our breath, then my friend said that he had to leave but his little brother wanted me to continue to perform oral sex on him.

My friend left and his six-year-old brother and I went into a Senior Citizen Center that was connected to my grandparents' building, and we snuck into the bathroom and went into a bathroom stall. I sat on the toilet bowl and he stood on my lap, the string to his shorts got tied up making it difficult to pull down. After struggling with his shorts, I was finally able to pull his shorts and underwear mid-thigh,.I was lost in pleasing him and hearing him moaning while gyrating his body like before. I don't know how long we were in the stall having sex when the door to the bath room was opened, we froze and didn't make a sound but then someone reached the only stall in the bathroom, the one we were using, whoever it was knocked on the door and I responded that I was using the bathroom doing a number two, whoever it was left and we continued our sexual activity and after some more time passed, the six-year-old said that he had to go home. He fixed himself and we both left the bathroom and the Senior Center, he went home and I went to mine.

The next few days, I didn't hear from the two brothers or even the other three kids that I use to hang out with until one day, my grandparents left me

home alone and I was looking out the window and saw all the boys hanging out in front of my building with some older black teen of about thirteen or fourteen years old, he was taller than all of us. I screamed out from the window to the brothers, and they came to the where I was at, they told me that they can't hang out with me because his little brother was being taken a bath by his mother and he caught an erection, she had questioned him about why that happened and he told her what I did to both of them and their mother told them not to hang with me, they even told the black kid, who looked at me with interest but nothing happened between us.

· · ·

By the ending of August, my grandparents had packed some of our stuff, so we could wake up early in the morning and head to the airport and be off to Puerto Rico. The next day arrived and my uncle Angelo, my aunt Sara's husband arrived and he help us take some of our suit cases to his car, while my uncle was driving to the airport, my grandfather was telling Angelo that he had bought a house and once we get to Puerto Rico, he would be coming back to New York, to get all their property packed and shipped to the house in P.R.

We arrived at the airport and my grandparents registered our suitcases at the booth. Afterwards we chilled with my uncle Angelo until we heard our plane was ready to be boarded, we all said goodbye to my uncle and my grandparents and I boarded the plane and when the plane lifted off, I fell into a dreamless sleep, only to be awaken by grandparents, telling me that we reached Puerto Rico.

Chapter 16

Puerto Rico and My Grandparents

The house my grandparents bought was big. It was a two-story house with the second floor being the living quarters, the first floor had a locked bathroom, to the middle but on the left side of the house on the back of the house was a little tool shed built in tin and wood. The rest of the space were was for the cars, which could house three to four cars.

Now on the second floor, there were four bedrooms, the kitchen, bathroom, and living room. My grandparents didn't share the same bedroom, not out of anger or anything negative, my grandfather's bedroom was located on the corner of the left side of the house and my grandmother's was on the same side but in the middle of the house. As for me, my room was on the right-side corner of the house with an unused bedroom next to mine.

We lived on top of a hill and to the left of our house were houses made of tin and wood or cinder block and cement, the properties were separated by fences and on the right of the house, the whole area of the neighborhood was surrounded by coconut, mangoes, sour sop, tamarindo trees and many other fruits. The house next to ours lived a religious family of seven, the father, mother, two girls age twelve and four-year-old, then there were the three boys age ranging from thirteen, eleven, and a eight-year-old and since my grandmother was

a super religious woman. She became friends with the neighbor's and I with the kids. Soon after my grandparents and I started going with the neighbors to religious outing's.

· · ·

It was still school vacation in Puerto Rico schools, so I spent the days playing with my newfound friends all sorts of games. They introduced me to a game similar to snow fighting but with dried horse manure. I know your saying that's disgusting but the dried-up horse manure is grass and hay and when thrown at some one, it disintegrates into dust.

I had stayed over with the religious family, in another property they had and being that it was late, we ate and went to sleep but the next day, the boys invited me to play horse shit fight, at first I was disgusted by the game but then I got hit by one, which turned into a shitty dust cloud and the war was on, it was a free for all war between the thirteen-year-old Mateo, eleven-year-old Elias, eight-year-old Simon and a sixteen-year-old friend of theirs.

The fight was fierce but fun, we ran around the big property's yard, throwing dried horse shit at one another hitting each other anywhere in the body, even on the face, I had caught a couple on my face, where some of it went into my mouth, a nasty taste but I caught them too, we played for more than an hour until Mateo's mother screamed out the window to stop playing and go take a shower because the food would be ready. The boys invited me to take a shower with them in a small tin metal bathroom outside the house. I refused stating that I wasn't gay, the boys explained that it wasn't gay unless someone does something sexual. I joined them nakedly and we started soaping ourselves and passing the soap, as we did this, we would prank one another by putting soap on each other's hair or face. After we finished showering, we played tag nakedly until Mateo's mother caught us, she didn't get upset at us but told us to hurry up and get dressed that the food was ready. We got dressed and ran into the house to eat.

Mateo's mother served rice and beans with some meat and after we had finished eating, all the kids, the girls included, went into the living room where

they all asked me questions about New York life. I told them as much as I could about New York, plus the snow, the kids were fascinated by stories and when I described the snow and how the snow is created and what the kids in New York do with the snow, they all wished that they could be there and experience the snow.

Later that night, Mateo's mom served us a coconut custard pie before we all went to sleep. I entered a bedroom where I shared a room with Elias and the sixteen-year-old, the other kids slept in their parents room. Elias, the sixteen year old and I, talked for a while, then we fell asleep but hours later, everyone in the house was awaken by the screeching scream from a horse they had on the property. We were all frightened and Mateo's father went outside and some of the boys myself included followed right behind him. We went to where the horse was properly tied and the Mateo's father inspected the horse but nothing was wrong with him, the father told us that the horse was spooked by some thing, he and the rest of us couldn't see or figure out what scared the horse like that. Once back inside we all returned to our sleeping area and as Elias, the sixteen year old I were going to sleep, the sixteen year old was telling Elias and me that there had to be something evil around because it is the only reason that a horse would shriek like it was being killed, then we fell to sleep.

· · ·

As the days turned into weeks and the weeks turned into months, life in P.R. was awesome. I wasn't even lusting for sex, just the occasional masturbation moment but just as I was happy about not having sex, especially with boys, things changed. Early one afternoon when Mateo and Simon asked me if I wanted to play hide and seek. I answered "yes", it was Simon, who had to count. Mateo and I went into the abandoned room next to mine and hid, we could see Simon looking for us around the back of house's balcony and we stifled our giggles.

While Simon was looking for us around my house, Mateo had asked me, if I had ever done it with a boy and I answered "yes". We didn't French kiss at first but I got on my knees and started sucking on his privates with a burst of

burning lust and just as he was about to ejaculate, he stopped me from making him ejaculate and once he calmed down, he let me continue. He did this over and over again, then feeling in the mood, I got up pulled my short's and underwear down unto my ankles, turned around, bent down and told Mateo to fuck me in the ass. I could feel the tip of his penis almost penetrating me and it was at that moment, when Simon smack the metal venetian window and screamed "ustedes estan alli" (are y'all in there), Mateo and I jumped up in fright that we ran out of the room, trying desperately to fix ourselves. We ran into my room and finished dressing that's when Simon came to my room looking at us funny. I knew then that Simon knew about his brother Mateo sexuality but couldn't prove it, even after Simon asked us and we denied it.

Mateo and I were always trying to get our nut off but we were always close to getting caught by one of his brothers, who had a suspicion of us doing something but couldn't prove it or the moment would be spoiled by fear of getting caught when we hear movement. I'm not going to lie Mateo for reason turned me on, he was beautiful to look at. He was my height with dirty blond curly hair, tan skin complexion, and a skinny but not that long penis.

I remember one night, we were to meet up with his parents and his brothers and sisters at a church, I couldn't go with them because I had taken a shower and wasn't ready, so they left wanting to get to the church early. Mateo stood behind, so he could take me to where the church was located. Once I was ready, we headed towards the church, which was quite a distance but on the way there, we would stop to go into hiding spots to French kiss and fondle each other. We would stop and move on then we spotted an abandon house made of cinder and cement but it wasn't finished, we agreed to go in there and fuck hard, he had his erect penis out and just as I was about to get on my knees, he stopped me telling me that we have to finish our sexual activity for a next time because we would be late going to church and true to his word, once we arrived at the church, it was closed, so we headed back without doing anything sexual.

. . .

Days passed with Mateo and I still trying to get our sexual gratification but failing because the other two brothers were always trying to catch us in the act but they never did but one day Simon and his mother came to visit my grandmother and they told us to go outside and play until they are finished talking but instead of going out, Simon and I went into my room and watched TV for a while, after some time I asked Simon if he wanted me to suck on his dick being that Elias and him were trying to catch Mateo and I fucking. Simon without answering got completely naked and I did the same. He had erection before he got naked and his little penis throbbing up and down, I sucked on his dick and balls for some time since he couldn't ejaculate, then he stopped me and told me that he wanted to suck on mine, we were on my bedroom floor and I sat with my legs spread wide open and let him suck on my dick.

He was sucking me the way I did him but better and just as I was about to ejaculate, I stopped him because I wanted to continue having sex with him and we did. We French kissed, then I sucked on his privates and he me, then we sword fought and laid on each other humping dicks, he even was fucking me in the ass, though his penis was too small to penetrate me and after more than an hour of us having sex, his mother called out to him, to let him know it was time to leave.

He left and we never had sex again because the opportunity never arose but Mateo that was a different story, we tried to have fulfilling sex but as always there was always some type of interruptions. I remember one day Elias and his twelve year old sister Elena came to visit me, while being home alone I was busy washing dishes and Elias was on my left side and Elena on my right. as I was washing the dishes we were talking about nothing but kids' stuff and for some reason, I on the down low reached my hand behind me and started to fondle Elias, after some time he stopped me and waited to his sister to leave the house and told me that he doesn't go that way, I respected what he said and left him alone.

But days later, I was invited to an overnight church revival with Mateo's father and the rest of the family. Mateo's father was the driver of a van he owned and he uses the van to carpool families that wanted to go to church or revivals. I sat with Elena and Simon in the front seat, she sat between Simon

and I and every time Elena's parents got off the van to go the parishioners house to see if they wanted to go to the revival, Elena would whisper in my ear about the little boy that was seating in the middle back seat behind us, how every time he sat next to her he would on the low reach up her dress and fondle her privates with the last of the parishioners getting on the van. We started to head to the revival Elena then took my left hand and guided it up her dress. I was surprised and frightened of getting caught but observing that no one was paying us any attention, I started to played with her vagina until it got real wet, then she stopped me telling me that we arrived at the church's revival. I was excited by the whole encounter. What made it exciting was the fact that we were doing something sexual not only in the van but in front of everyone in the van especially her parents with no one having a suspicion of our activity.

We arrived at our destination, and everyone got off the van. We then walked the distance of half a block to where the church revival was at, and we entered some large property, where a large tent was raised in the big backyard, and it could hold at least a hundred to two hundred people.

The house on the property was a two-floor, the first floor was not completely constructed but the front bottom was being used for the cooking that was going on. The church ladies were preparing a big meal so the parishioners could eat something after the ceremony. I look towards the back and it was very dark and it looked spooky, everything around me felt empty with no life, even though there were people walking either solo or in groups or in and out of the property.

The second floor was completely done and was well furnished. I went up there with permission to use the bathroom. The house also felt empty after using the bathroom, I quickly went back outside because I felt spooked in and out of the house and property. I left the property to where only kids were grouped up and they consisted of Elena, her brothers, her little sister, the little horny boy that would always feel Elena up and myself, Elena pulled me aside and whispered in my ear to follow her. I followed her into the back of the property passing the church ladies that was preparing the meal. We walked all the way into one of the back unfinished rooms, she then place her back to the wall of the room where nobody could see us, then lifted her skirt and pulled the

front of her panty down and told me to fuck her. My dick was already as hard as a rock and when she saw how long it was, she became excited. She pulled her panty further down to her knees and told me to go ahead and stick it in and just as I was about to penetrate her, we heard footsteps approaching our direction, she pushed me back and quickly fixed herself, seeing that I was fixed too, she started talking out loud about the whole back unfinished section of the house and when we left the back section, there wasn't anyone near that area.

As we left the property, we could see that Elias was eyeing us with angry suspicion, he approached us and asked us, what were we doing?, Elena and I both answered in unison "NOTHING", he knew what we were doing by the erection that was threatening to pop out my shorts, he became mad when Elena said in front of him to follow her in the van so we could fuck. We turned around and walk towards the van, we were about to enter when Elias came charging up to us screaming "ustedes no van acer frecreia", (y'all are not going to do any fresh things), I was already getting irritated and angry by his interruption and I told him to get the fuck out of my face. He then ran across the street and picked up a half rusted can, then came charging at me, I was waiting for the right moment when he got close enough, I punch him hard on the face, the hit made him stagger and I threatened him that if he didn't stop, I was going to hurt him real bad.

Mateo seeing what was happening got in between Elias and me, Elias was sobbing and threatened me that he was going to kill me, his threat almost made my monster that I keep imprisoned come out. I walked around Mateo and grabbed Elias hand with the half rusted can and put it to my neck, I told him in a threatening voice to go ahead and cut me, I was hoping he would make the slightest movement because I was going to destroy this bitch. I was already starting to lose the colors around me and a bloodied taste in my mouth was developing, when that happens it's my imprisoned personality trying to take control of me.

Elias didn't do anything, and Mateo was the one who cooled us down. We all went to the ceremony and after the ceremony, we all ate then we all said our goodbyes to the parishioners and our God blessing to one another and left, we arrived at Mateo's house and being that it was extremely late, I stood over at their house.

The next day, we were awakened by Mateo's mother and the smells of breakfast being made she was telling all of us that to freshen up because breakfast was almost done. After I finished eating I excused myself and left to my grandparents and upon entering the house, I received a spanking on my buttocks with a belt by my grandfather, after the spanking, my grandfather explained to me that they were worried about me making my grandmother lose sleep. I wasn't mad at my grandfather for spanking me but I explained to my grandfather that we returned late and I didn't want to wake any one up. He responded that it didn't matter, I should have come home. I apologized to my grandfather, promising that I will never do that again. He gave me a hug and I went into my grandmother's room and laid down next to her and told her that I was sorry. She accepted my apology and asked me to kneel down next to her and pray the our father and a personal prayer with her asking God for forgiveness and to pray for others. After the prayer was finished, all we did that day was hang out in the house and chilled.

(I praying as a child was to please my grandmother because I really did not understand anything about God and did not believe).

. . .

Later on that day, one of my favorite uncles from my mother's side of the family, came to visit us and let my grandparents know that he and his family, lived somewhere in Fajardo. This was the uncle that has the three daughters and a son and the three daughters were the ones who performed oral sex me, when I was eight years old with me pissing in their mouths, I started to think "this time I'll give all three girls a mouthful of dick and cum ".

My uncle Dereck, my cousin's father, was built like a truck. His body was just one big rock hard muscle and because of his height people was very intimidated by him and he used that fear to bully people. He invited us to come to where he lived in Fajardo and spend some time with his family, my grandparents replied that they would come to visit, I couldn't wait I will put them to suck me off again, if they dared but after a month passed by I started to lose hope with visiting my uncle Dereck and having sex with my female cousins.

Then another uncle from New York came to Puerto Rico to visit my grandparents and stay because my grandparents had to take care of some financial business in New York and to make sure that the transfer of their property will be sent from New York to Puerto Rico without trouble. When they left my uncle and I had the house to ourselves.

This was Uncle Jay, Chewito's father, another of my favorite uncles from my mother's side of the family. He brought over his V.H.S. and his collection of Martial arts and horror movies. I remember when I was younger and I used to visit Jay and his family, Chewito and I would sit for hours, watching martial arts movies and afterwards Chewito and I would pretend to be martial artist and beat each other up.

Late that night, my uncle told me to get ready to leave that we were leaving to go to Uncle Dereck's house, the one with the three daughters and the son. I was excited, he drove for hours, he even passed Luquillo beach. We passed all kinds of food kiosks and beautiful women in bikini swim suits. When we arrived at Dereck's house, they were all there waiting for us, Dreck and his wife greeted us, I glanced at the three sisters and they were much taller, especially the oldest, she was taller than all the kids in the house and I knew then that I was going to fuck all three girls.

Louisa, the oldest girl was around fifteen or sixteen years old. She had grown up looking more attractive than when I last saw her. She had her long black hair that reached passed her buttocks and a light tannish skin complexion with a nice set of boobs.

Then there was thirteen or fourteen year old Erica, who was also developing into a beautiful girl but unlike her sister, Erica had shoulder length dirty blond hair with a milky white skin complexion with breasts bigger than Louisa, and Christina, the youngest girl, was around eleven or twelve years old and she also had shoulder length black hair and had the same skin complexion as Erica but was flat chested, and lastly Julio, who was around twelve or thirteen years old, had a darker brown skin complexion with short black crop cut hair and a shy demeanor.

Their mother aunt Clarita was a small thin light-skinned lady with black hair that reached the middle of her back. She was faithful and a resolute woman

to my uncle Dereck and while Dereck and my uncle Jay went to talk in private. Aunt Clarita was cooking dinner, and I went and hung out with my cousins and for some reason Erica was mischievously pranking me. I vowed to myself to get even. We played for a while then chilled until dinner was served around six in the evening and after everyone was done eating, the girls went into their room, the adults went outside to talk and Julio invited me to watch television in his parent's room.

The house they lived in was a one floor house with a three-bedroom, kitchen and bathroom. As you enter the front of house, you're in the living room. On the right side of the house was the kitchen connected to the bathroom, and an abandoned bedroom that was furnished also connected to the bathroom but further back was my uncle's bedroom and on the right of the house but connected to my uncle's room were my three female cousins bedroom.

I followed Julio into my uncle's room and we laid on my uncle's bed side by side, getting comfortable on our stomachs and watching TV. Once in a while, I would do a wrestling move to provoke him to wrestle with me but he wouldn't fall for it. I kept on trying for some time and he gave in, we fought playfully doing some wrestling moves on one another, and in our battle, our uncle Jay's jean jacket was on the bed and as we were wrestling, we heard something break inside his jacket Julio and I checked what it was and it was a pair of sun glasses to make my uncle Jay look cool. We didn't think it was that important so we continued to wrestle for a while longer, then we stopped and laid on our stomachs on the bed next to one another and went back to watching television.

As we were watching television Julio laid on his side and looked at me. He reached forward and kissed me on the lips. I knew why he was shy, he like dick, I responded in kind and it turned into a French kissing ceremony. I was horny but not for dick, I wanted to fuck the three girls. Especially the oldest but he started it and I will finish it. He laid on his back and I laid on top of him to continue French kissing, he then asked me to stop. I did he then proceeded to pull his shorts and underwear down onto his knees and asked me to lay on him and fuck him between his groin, I pulled my pants and underwear down mid-thigh, laid on top of him again and stuck my erected penis between his groin and started humping away.

I was sexually excited behind the fact that all it took for us to get caught was for the adults to take one or two steps from the living room and look down the hallway into the bed room and we would be busted. Jay, Dereck, and Dereck's wife were in the living room talking and the girls were outside playing with their friends and boy, if Julio and I would of have been caught the ass whipping that we would receive would of been bad. I remember one time when I was much younger, I was with my grandparents, Chewito's family and myself. We were preparing to go to the beach, so Chewito and I went into the back of my uncle's Station wagon waiting for everyone to get ready, Chewito and I started talking sexual things of what we were going to do in the beach's water, we had gotten so aroused that we both whipped our penises out and started to masturbate one another. We were so into it that we didn't see Chewito's father approaching the back side of the station wagon and busted us red handed. We first froze with each other's penises in our hands then we quickly let go, my uncle became so enraged that he punched both of us hard on our faces, we cried but that didn't stop us, when we arrived at the beach Chewito and I snuck into the bathroom and finished what we started.

Now having sex with Julio and the knowledge that we can get caught and plus my pre-cum lubricating his groin, penis and balls making it very slippery made me ejaculate a lot of sperm. It went all over his groin area and stomach, I laid on him until my trembling body and my breathing calmed down. I then rolled off him and fixed myself, Julio did the same and just as we laid side to side to watch television like nothing happened, Jay walked into the room and my heart was pounding hard and fast, I thought that he knew what Julio and I were doing but when he entered the room and picked up his jean jacket, I was relieved and as he was putting on his jacket, my uncle Jay reached in the pocket and took out a pair of broken sun glasses, he had an angry expression on his face, and I apologized to him explaining to him that Julio and I were play wrestling and we didn't know that the glasses were there, the expression he gave us was one of I should beat your asses but he didn't. What he did was tell me that I was staying over for the night because he had to take care of some personal business. I was happy at that.

Jay had left around eight or nine o'clock, since everyone else was outside Julio asked me to go outside with him. I followed him around a couple of blocks introducing me to some of his friends that were playing outside. We continued to walk around and he was telling me that the sex we had felt really good. He even asked me if I wanted to be girlfriend and boyfriend? and I replied "yes".

We walked to an area of a block, where there was a path which led into a dense forest area that eventually lead deep into the mountain. I followed him down the path and he stopped behind some trees that hid us from view, he then faced me and took off his t-shirt and pulled down his pants and underwear unto his ankles and asked me to do the same thing I did earlier. I did, but walking closer to him was difficult because the clothes on my ankles limited my walking but once we were close enough, we started sword fighting each other for a little while, then he asked me to fuck him the way I did on the bed. He bent a little and waited until my hardened penis was between his legs rubbing on his balls and he stood up, I then started humping him and it didn't take long for me to ejaculate but this time no sperm came out. We stood in that position just French kissing lustfully. After sometime passed without any words being said we pulled back from one another and fixed our clothes, then we headed to his house.

Julio and I entered the house and all three girls were next to each other sitting on the big couch watching TV. The conversation between the girls stopped as soon as Julio and I sat down on the two seater couch, all three girls were looking at me and they started to whisper to one another. I knew what they talking about, so I got up and sat with the girls, I started to fondle on Louisa's breast. she didn't complain or tried to stop me and when I whipped out my not so fat but long penis out and said to all three girls, "I'm not a little boy any more".

Louisa, being the oldest of all three girls told Erica to go behind the big sofa and let me fuck her. Erica listened to Louisa and went behind the sofa in the living room and laid on her back fully clothed. I climbed over the couch and positioned myself between her legs. As I was lifting her dress and moving her panties to the side to penetrate Erica I could see that Erica's had uncomfortable

expression on her face and I knew that she didn't want to do it, she was just listening to Louisa. I got off of Erica with my harden penis still exposed, faced Louisa and told her "let me fuck you. I am not that little boy with my little dick you were sucking on". I swung my harden penis side to side and told her "look at how big my dick got", all three girls were staring at my penis even Julio was staring. Then all three girls burst out laughing.

Julio, on the other hand sat on the other sofa with a serious expression on his face. I knew that he was not only jealous but was lusting for me, I didn't say anything to him but I was going to give Julio what he wanted, for I too was lusting for some sex and since the girls were only dick teasing me; well, Julio was open season.

While all this was going on, their parents were in their bedroom watching television but as it got late, Clarita gave Julio and I a choice to where do we wanted to sleep, either in the abandoned but furnish bedroom or the living room floor, I walked to the doorway of the room and entered it, inspecting the room I looked at the bed, which was big enough for Julio and me but there was a pile of old dried up dog shit with that I chose the living room. Julio and I fixed a mattress on the living room floor and waited for everyone to fall asleep but then I too succumbed to the sleeping virus.

I was in a peaceful sleep, when I felt some one tugging me at my side. I awoke groggily and saw that it was Julio completely naked with his little hard on. I was fully awake with seeing his nakedness and I too got undressed. He then laid on top of me, where my penis would rub against his and he started to sword hump me slowly. I was feeling the moment and I responded by matching his gyrating rhythm. While in this sexual dance, we started French kissing slowly but passionately. It felt like we were lost into each other not caring that all his parents had to do was step into the entrance of their bedroom and they would see two naked boys fucking. I was on fire by the way Julio and I was gyrating. My pre-cum was making him slippery down there, I spread my legs, so his waist could down be in between my legs, I wrapped my legs around his waist and fought hard not to moan. I grabbed both of his buttocks roughly and just as I was about to ejaculate, I stopped him from moving and gently push him off me, I then laid him on his back, I sat on his stiff little dick and

laid on him, I started to French kiss him again but then I started to lick and kissing him on his chin, neck, all of his chest and stomach, belly button, I was even sucking and licking the groin area right before reaching his penis.

Once I reached his dick and balls, my body was burning on fire but I ignored the pain. I felt something with him that I didn't feel with all my other sexual partners, it felt like hunger but not like hunger for food, I really can't explain that precise emotion but the more I performed oral sex on him, the more lustful I became. I was rubbing my face all over his precum and saliva filled groin area, I even stuck my tongue in his rectum, tasting to see if he was clean. I got off him and guided him onto his stomach, then I started sucking and licking both of his buttocks and the inner sides of ass cheeks. I continued until I was nibbling, sucking and licking on his rectum, I don't know how long I was preforming oral sex on his rectum but I couldn't take it anymore, so I stopped and positioned my body on top of him and gently penetrated him, I started humping him slowly but I didn't last long because my body started trembling uncontrollably and I lost control of my moment and ejaculated hard, it felt like I was catching a seizure and when the trembling of my body and the throbbing of my penis subsided, I stood laying on him and waited for my body and breathing to become normal, then I rolled off him and we laid naked for a while but as soon as we started feeling sleep creeping in, we got dressed and went to sleep.

In the morning Julio and I acted like nothing happened between us and though I enjoyed the sex, I felt guilty because I really didn't want to grow up sucking dick and getting fucked in the ass, I wanted to have sex with girls and be with girls, yet I didn't understand what was going on with me and why I was always on my knees.

After everyone finished eating breakfast, Julio and I went outside and I followed him down the block to where a chocolate brown skin complexion boy and girl were chilling in front of a house, Julio introduced me to the girl and boy. They were brother and sister, they both had a short afro hair style, the boy was a husky thirteen-year-old, who introduced himself as Angelo and his sister eleven-year-old Alisa.

Angelo was my height and his sister Alisa was almost right behind us in height and I found her attractive. Angelo, Alisa, and I hit it off really good and

as we chilled in front of their house. Julio had left to help his mother further down the block to a food kiosk across the street from an elementary school. Clarita cook empanadillas of different kinds and fried tostones and other snack foods to sell to the kids in school when they went for their recess.

The sun was shining a little too hard on my head, so I asked Angelo and Alisa, if they wanted to hang out in my aunt Clarita's house. They both answered "yes" and we walked to my aunt Clarita's house and entered the house. I was relieved from the heat and we sat on the big sofa, where they started to questioned me about my life in New York. I told them everything I could and told them about the snow, which fascinated them.

Angelo's mother was calling out to Alisa, and she excused herself promising to return. When she left, Angelo was explaining to me that Alisa had to do an errand for their mother, while we waited for her to return, we continued to talk about kid stuff, then he switched the conversation to his sister. He asked me about what I thought about his sister. I answered that she is beautiful. He then started to tell me how his sister makes him feel aroused that sometimes he masturbates in her name. I was already getting aroused by him talking about sex, I was wondering if his penis was bigger than Julio. Since Angelo and I was sitting on big couch, I was trying to find a way to seduce him, so I could perform oral sex on him but just as I was about to boldly ask him if I could suck him off his sister walks into the house and things got strange. Angelo told his sister to come to him and sit on his lap. She obeyed and sat on his lap in an inappropriate manner, I knew then that they were having sex with one another. She then got up and I grabbed one of her buttocks, when I did her brother had an angry jealous expression on his face, he then told his sister that they had to leave and they left without saying goodbye.

· · ·

I was home alone, when Julio and his three sisters walked into the house. They had spent the day helping their mother do some chores in the kiosk. We chilled in the living room and they were taking turns telling me stories about their father. They were telling me that they used to live somewhere else but their

father was accused of raping a fifteen-year-old gay boy and because of that incident, they moved to Fajardo to get away from the cops. They continued telling me that he loves to torture and kill puppies, they even took me to the back yard to show me, a last surviving puppy and he had an eyeball popped out of its socket, hanging down its face. The puppy just laid there, like it gave up in life. They continue to tell me that Dereck was a bully.

With all that they were telling me about my uncle Dereck, the only thing that I found wrong about my uncle was the torturing of the puppies. I didn't understand what rape was, so I brushed it off but as for the bullying, I didn't see anything wrong with that and being he was one of my favorite uncle, I wanted to be like him. Later on that day Julio wanted to show me all the dead puppies, so we walked into the area of the mountain that Julio and I had sex in but a little farther and he showed me, where the dead puppies were laying on the ground but on top of each other.

Later that night Julio came running in the house and told me that my Uncle Jay was coming. The girls told me to lay on the sofa and pretend I was asleep. I did, I laid down with my face facing the sofa so my uncle wouldn't tell if I was awake. I could hear him walking in and I felt him nudging me awake. My cousins intervened explaining to him that I was playing hard and helping with some chores and that I've been sleeping for a while, uncle Jay told them to tell me that he was coming tomorrow to pick me up with that he left.

I continued to pretend that I was still sleeping, just in case my uncle Jay returned to check and see if I was really sleeping, my cousins notified that he was gone, but I still continued to pretend that I was asleep but when my cousins started nudging me to wake up, I jumped up and playfully attacked them in a wrestling fashion, we played wrestling for a while until my uncle Dereck shouted from his room to chill out, be quiet, or go to sleep. We obeyed knowing that if we didn't chill, Dereck would get mad and beat on us but that didn't stop us from quietly taking turns mimicking him, we had to muffle our laughter or get in trouble. We joked around for some time, then we quietly watched television until soon one by one, my females cousins went to sleep until it was just Julio and me, even Julio's parents were asleep and once we knew that everyone was for sure asleep, we laid on the mattress in the living room floor,

took all our clothes off and fucked for a long time and once I ejaculated in him, I rolled off him and we laid there nakedly catching our breaths, then we got dressed and fell asleep.

The next day, everyone except Julio and I went to Clarita's kiosk. We stood behind because Julio wanted to fuck again before I get picked up by our uncle Jay. We wanted to fuck because Julio and I may not see each other again and since we didn't know when Jay was coming to pick me up, we took advantage and went into the abandoned room, flipped the mattress onto the other side, so we won't lay on the dry shitty side of the bed. Julio then laid on his back with his shorts and underwear down onto his knees, I did the same and laid on top of him, we started with the dick humping and the passionate French kissing. We were at it for a while, then my body started trembling with the beginning of my ejaculation but just as I was about to cum, we heard footsteps coming from the front of the house. We quickly and fearfully jumped off each other and the bed and fixed ourselves properly, I think we broke the world's record in getting off each other and dressing quickly because just as we finished and started walking out of the room, our uncle Jay was walking in the house, seeing us coming out of the room, my uncle questioned us on what were we doing in the room, Julio was so frighten of us almost getting caught that he couldn't answer. I jumped in and asked my uncle to follow me. He did and I showed him the abandoned room, I explained to my uncle that it was the first time coming into the room and I was fascinated because there was a venetian window on the inside of the room and not only can I see into my uncle De-reck's room but my female cousins room too and the other side of the house could be seen, I knew that it was a lame excuse but I was nervous too, my Uncle Jay didn't say anything but "it's time to go". I gave Julio and a pound and a hug and I followed my uncle into his car.

On the drive back to my grandparents, my uncle had made a few stops to do some private business. When he was through it was late at night. My Uncle Jay is an expert driver like my mother and when they both drive, it's like being inside the car with a race car driver. There were times, even with my seat belt on I would hold onto the dash board with my butt cheeks clenched and my heart beating a hundred miles per hour and it's no different tonight. My uncle

was driving real fast into the mountains with the head lights off and it was pitch black darkness. I was scared as hell but also excited. Don't forget that my butt cheeks were clenched too and I don't know if it was instinct but my uncle switched on the head lights and slammed on the brakes real hard at the same time for the car had stopped at the edge of a cliff. If my uncle hadn't turned on those lights in time, we would of hit the side of the cliff and fall into the river.

All the excitement I had felt earlier was replace with fear and relief that I was still alive. My uncle felt the same way by how his eyes were wide opened and how he was breathing. He stood still for a couple of minutes, reversed the car and drove home slowly and safely. I, on other hand was still going through the emotions, my heart beat was slowing down but the knot of fear was still stuck in my throat and it didn't go away, even when we arrived at my grand-parents' house and I went straight to sleep.

. . .

Later on that night, I'll say around midnight, I was awakened by something moving by my window. I was going to check to see what it was but a sudden fear stopped me. Then I started hearing many dogs barking. I left my bedroom and went to the front of the house and look out the window, all I saw was a bunch of dogs barking and howling in the direction of my grandparents' house. I was still spooked, when I entered the room and as I sat on my bed in fear, I could hear whatever it was by my window, jumped down into the back yard and disappeared and so did the dog noises but for a couple of nights after, the dogs would surround my house and start with their barking and howling and each night the dogs made those noises, they sounded like they were about to attack whatever it was that was on hiding in my back yard but then it just as it started, it stopped. No more dogs barking, howling, or sounding like they are ready to attack and no more whatever it was that was coming on my property and by my window. (I always felt like whatever it was by the window was watch-ing me more like observing me and while growing up I always felt like I was always being watch by something unexplainable waiting for something on my

end but what it is, I don't know. Even now, as I edit my life, I still feel like something is watching me and whatever it is, is not friendly and it won't be the last time a presence appears to me.)

.   .   .

A week or more had passed since that spooky incident but it didn't stop me from watching a couple of horror movies, and when my uncle Jay left me home alone one night and he didn't return after many hours, I still wasn't spooked. And when my uncle Jay returned he had brought someone with him, my cousin Julio. We all got comfortable in the room that Jay was sleeping in and watched horror movies. After the movie was over my uncle told us that it was time to go to sleep. Julio and I left the room and went into my room and locked the door, I was really tired and as I laid on my bed fighting sleep, Julio started unzipping my shorts, pulling out my flaccid penis and started to masturbate me. I was trying to tell him to stop but he then laid on me and started kissing me on my lips. We French kissed for some time then I pushed Julio off me a little and told him that I was tired and promised him that we would fuck in the morning, when our uncle Jay leaves us home alone to take care of personal business at that Julio kissed me a couple of times on the lips and I fell into a dreamless sleep.

The next morning Julio and I were awake and were both in the bathroom with the door open brushing and washing our faces, our uncle peeked into the bathroom and told Julio that as soon as he finishes fixing the car that he would return Julio home and left. We finished with taking care with our hygiene and ran into the living room, to see if our uncle started fixing the car. Once we were sure of no interruptions, we walked back into my room feeling on each other's erect penises and stopping to French kiss. We reached my room and we took our t-shirts off and pulled our shorts down onto our ankles. We were so horny that we stood standing and started sword fighting, then it turned into dick humping. We wrapped our arms around each other grabbing one another by the buttocks squeezing them and pulling each other closer into one another like we were trying to become one and just as we stopped to get naked, lay on

my bed and fuck hard, we heard the door to the house squeak open, we quickly, no I'll say, we magically got dressed and walked out of the room slowly like nothing had occurred between us but my heart was beating hard and fast from fear that my uncle knew what we were doing but as it turned out, it wasn't my uncle but Elias the twelve year old, who didn't like me and his eleven year old sister Elena, who is dying for me to fuck her. For me Elias was way to jealous I believe that they were having sex with one another, until I showed up.

Elias started talking to me like we were friends and I went with it. He wanted to know if I wanted to play with him, his brothers, and his sixteen-year-old friend. I replied "yes but it has to wait until my cousin leaves", I introduced Julio to Elias and Elena, I was really trying to get rid of them, so Julio and I could finish what we started. They stood around for a couple of minutes more then they left, Julio and I started French kissing and groping one another again, as we were walking towards my room and were about to entered my room, my uncle Jay called out for Julio. We walked back towards the front of the house still French kissing and once we reached the door, we kissed one more time and he left. I went to the other window, where my uncle waited for Julio and watched them leave, I was thinking about our kiss and why having sex with Julio felt like a deep hunger I never felt before.

When they left, I went into my grandfather's room to turn on the radio and listen to some Spanish music while I stare off into the back yard think of nothing. I was doing just that when I noticed some naked kid of ten or eleven taking a bath in a big plastic tub, which was situated on the back balcony of Mateo's house. Spanish music was playing and seeing the boy naked and his skinny flaccid penis and balls, I got in the mood to masturbate. I got naked and started masturbating, while the kid was enjoining his bath, I could tell that the kid's penis became erect. It would be a little long, and I started to fantasize me on my knees giving him head, then turning around and letting him fuck me in the ass. Just as I was deep in my sexual grove, I saw that the kid was looking at me. I stopped masturbating just in case he didn't see me and got dressed. I then went to the back side of my balcony and stood looking at him and he as watching me, he then took a cup and started pouring water down his chest, while with the other hand, he was rubbing the water down his body, he then opened

when I tell you Anthony and I developed super speed we did, we jumped off each other and the bed and got dressed before another uncle of mine named Sachi came to visit, as my uncle reached the kitchen, Anthony snuck out the back of the house's balcony and climbed down onto the little metal shed that was below, I went towards the kitchen and I could see that my uncle had brought his wife and their six year son too.

My uncle Sachi (strong A), asked me some questions about my grandparents and I answered them all, then they left me with a message to my uncle Jay that they would back in a couple of days. Then my uncle Sachi stood quiet, then he and his family all left, when my uncle Jay returned home, I told him about who came and the message they left, he then told my grandparents, when they returned from New York a few days later.

· · ·

Some time had passed and Mateo's mother Clarita asked my grandparents, if I could stay over their farm again they answered "yes". My grandmother turned to me and told me to pack a bag for a day and I did. I was excited because the last time, I had fun. I finished packing and ran to my grandparents gave them their hugs and kisses, as I was running out the door I could hear my grandmother scream out, "behave" she knows, I can get very mischievous.

Once I went to Mateo's house, I could see that Elias did not like me being there or going to the farm. I, seeing this, I purposely started flirting with his sister. He was so mad that his father had to check him about his attitude. I just smirked at Elias.

After a couple of hours on being on the road, we finally reached the farm and every one pitched in helping with the animals food and other things that were in the car. After we were done Mateo's parents went inside into their one story two bedroom house while the rest of us ran into the backyard and played tag, we then switched the game to dry horse shit fight and the girls wanted to play, even though we told them no but they stilled played anyway and after a few minutes they refused to play any longer due to being the only ones targeted with the horse shit.

As the three girls were leaving, I threw a dry horse shit at the back of Elena and she turned around seeing me smiling at her, she smiled back and left making Elias real mad but I was hoping that he did something so I could whip his ass. I promised myself that I was going to get even with this faggotty bitch. We continued to play the shitty game with the sixteen year old who came with us too and after some time, we lost interest.

I saw Mateo further down the yard bent over to what I thought to be an ant hill, I went to where he was and he told me to stand on the big ant hill and my stupid ass did just that, I started to see and feel the ants crawl up my legs, then all of a sudden I started to feel a burning sensations all over where the ants were crawling. I jumped out of the ant hill and started slapping the ants away, Mateo and the rest of the boys were laughing at me. After they finishing laughing, they told me that they were fire ants and when they bite, they shoot a burning venom, the boys even told me that in some instances, fire ants can kill and consume human beings.

We were walking back towards the house, when Mateo's mother screamed out to go take a shower that dinner was ready. We ran in the house got our change of clothes and towel and ran out to the small tin shower under the house and showered, as we were all showering I kept on noticing the sixteen-year-old was eyeing me and my body, soon one by one the boys started leaving only leaving Mateo and I. I took advantage of the situation and grabbed on his dick and balls, he pulled my hand away nervously telling me that we can't do anything because we could get caught, yet, while he was talking he was staring at my erection. He stood staring a little longer and quickly ran out and wrapped himself with a towel, I couldn't leave until my erection went down.

Once my erection was down and I stepped out to get my towel and to my frightened surprise the six-year-old girl was sitting by the towel, I quickly grabbed my towel and blushingly ran back in the tin shower and got dressed, I came out and grabbed the little girl by the hand and lead her into the house, where we all sat down and ate together. After dinner, the girls, Mateo, and his parents went into one room and Elias, the sixteen-year-old and I went into another, where we slept on the three beds that were placed side by side to make it look like one big bed.

started saying that she had fucked some older kid and every time they had sex, it felt good. I was getting aroused but something made me not participate in their sexual conquest. Elena seeing my reluctance took the keys from my hand and went into the bathroom with the little girl.

I left to play with Elena's brothers and some other kids. Elias for some reason didn't bother me and Elena but I was watching the bathroom door waiting for Elena to come out but she was there with the little girl for a long time and when they came out they sat on the house steps out of breath. I left the group and went straight to Elena, they were catching their breath and I asked them what were they doing in the bathroom that long, they looked at each other and smiled, the little girl said "nothing'" but Elena said "chichando" "fucking". I asked Elena if she wanted to fuck and she answered no, so I went and played with the other kids.

· · ·

In the beginning of October, my grandparents tried to enroll me in a school, but the principal explained to them that he could not accept me until my school records are sent to the principal. My grandparents understood, and the principal told them that as soon as the records arrive, he would contact them.

By the time my fifteenth birthday arrived, the principal still hadn't received my school records, though on my birthday, my grandparents celebrated it with some cooked food and fruity exotic beverages but no presents. I really didn't care because they didn't have that much money and two, they given me something that hasn't any value to it. Real love, they even invited Mateo's family for a little get together.

They all came and ate with us, afterwards we chilled in the big living room and just made conversation for everyone to participate. Mateo had whispered to me that he has a birthday present for me but he can't give it to me here but in the room. We snuck away from the group and headed to my room. Once inside he faced me and we started French kissing while hugging and rubbing on each other's buttocks, we stood like that for a couple of minutes, then we returned to the group.

Mateo and I kept on sneaking in and out of the group to French kiss and rub on each other. We slowed because Elias noticed us sneaking in and out of the group and he asked us, what were we doing, we both answered "nothing", and he left it at that but we knew he was watching us and when we were sure that Elias wasn't paying any attention at us, we snuck into my room but this time Mateo pulled his pants down and laid on the bed. I did the same but laid on him and started dick humping and kissing. After a couple of seconds of humping, he asked me to fuck him in the ass. I rolled off him and waited for him to lay on his stomach, then I laid on him and penetrated him, just as I was getting into the grove I heard footsteps outside my window and I jumped off Mateo almost falling on my ass, Mateo did the same without falling. We then quickly fixed ourselves and walked out the room, we realized that it was Elias trying to sneak up on us. He came from the entrance of the back of the house's balcony and asked us loudly "que ustedes estaban hacendo?""what were we doing?"

Mateo answered" one, nothing and two, none of your business", I smirked at him and answered "nothing". He looked at us up and down slowly, then turned around and headed for the group. We followed right behind him and chilled for a while until all the kids came together wanting to play tag but were afraid to ask for permission, being my birthday I approached my grandparents and asked them permission to play tag downstairs. She answered "yes" but on less Mateo's parents gave their permission, I turned to them and gave them the puppy eye look and asked them, they quickly replied "yes" but with laughter, we ran out the door and downstairs into the garage, where we all put our feet together and someone choose the person who would be it.

They were a few kids, it was Elena, her sisters and her brothers, two kids from the neighborhood, Anthony and his twin sister. The moment I saw his twins, I was in love and I lusted after her without her knowing it. We all played tag for a while, then we changed it to freeze tag, soon the kids started leaving for their homes and the only ones left was Elena, Anthony's twin sister and Anthony.

All three of us sat on the stairs and talked about kid stuff, then Elena excused herself saying that she had to go to the bathroom and she left. Anthony stood for a little longer and he too left, Anthony's twin introduced herself as Rosaline. I really wasn't paying any attention to what she was saying because

all I was doing was looking at her as my heart was beating fast. When she finished talking I asked her if I could suck her pussy. She replied by getting up from the steps, facing me and lifting her dress, she had no panties on. I got up and we went behind my grandfather's car and van, she lifted her dress and I kneeled in front of her and started preforming oral sex on her vagina.

I was sucking on her for over a minute and things between us was getting deeply into the mood, then Elena appeared catching us in the act. Rosaline and I jumped and I quickly stood up I could see that Elena was very angry but then Elena did something that made me real horny, she bent down in front of Rosaline, lifted her dress and started sucking Rosaline's pussy for a couple of seconds. Then Elena stopped sucking, got up, faced me and told me "that is mine" and pointed at Rosaline's pussy and she finished by saying that no one touches that pussy but her and that she was going to tell my grandmother.

Elena waited for all the adults to leave and went upstairs to supposedly use the bathroom. I waited until she went into the house and followed her. She went into the bathroom and I went into my room to wait for Elena to come out, I heard the door to the bathroom open and I snuck out of my room and tipped toed right behind her, she went into the kitchen and told my grandmother that she had a secret to tell her, as soon as she said that I came out from hiding making Elena jump in fright, she stood quiet for a moment, then she told my grandmother that she wanted to tell her in secret but in the room, my grandmother was listening but she was busy washing the dishes. My grandmother replied that she had to wait after she finishes the dishes, Elena was really waiting, then all of a sudden a car horn started honking it horn in front of my grandparents house and some male voice started screaming out to Elena and Rosaline's name that it's time to leave and hurry up and come down, they both left without Elena telling on me though I never saw Mateo's family again, I knew Elena was mad and jealous that I wasn't doing sexual things with her but it was Elias fault. He was always around messing everything up and if she would of told my grandmother about what I was doing with Rosaline, I was going to talk about what she did and said to me.

. . .

Many days passed without seeing Mateo and his family but uncle Sachi, one day came to the house and returned not only with his wife and his six-year-old son but with a mattress and a couple of bags of clothing. I, for one didn't like what was going on here, how they just come unannounced wanting to stay, I found the situation suspicious but being young, my voice would be heard but not listened to and since my grandmother has a heart of gold, she allowed them to stay.

I don't know why I did what I did, maybe it was out of anger but one thing I know for sure, it wasn't lust. I started playing with Michael and after some time had passed, we started chatting about this and that, then I changed the conversation to sex talk. I asked him if he ever did fresh things with a girl and he replied that "yes once" he continued with "his friends had made him get naked and have sex with a girl older than he was". I didn't know if it was true but to me it was ammunition for my next move. I then asked him if he ever did it with a boy, he looked confused with my question, not really understanding what I was saying, so I described what boys do to sexually have fun and he looked curious, I asked him if I could touch his penis and he shook his head up and down to answer "yes". I then laid Michael on his back on my bed and pulled his shorts down mid-thigh. I then started jerking him off making him get an erection as soon as I touched his little penis, it was small but it was longer than Elias, I then started to perform oral sex on Michael and after two or three minutes passed by with Michael not ejaculating, I lost interest and stopped. We laid and chilled on my bed and watched television until his mother called him to go to her, so he can take a shower.

Well, as soon as his mother started taking him a shower, something happened that she called her husband and a few minutes later. The mother came to my room telling me that she was washing her son and he caught an erection and she questioned Michael about it and he told her that I played with his dick and sucked on his penis. I denied it but the evidence was clear. I was guilty.

My uncle made a big deal about it, telling my grandparents that I had to be sent away back to my other family, my grandparents tried to explain that it

was just kid stuff but the motherfucker acted like it was his house, giving them an ultimatum, demanding that I be sent to New York and because of the ruckus he was making they gave in that night. My grandmother made me throw all my comic book collections and my Garbage Pail Kids card collection away, telling me that those things are of the Devil influencing me to do bad stuff.

Two days later, my grandparents took me to the airport but on the way there, I could see that they were upset that I had to leave, especially my grandmother. I wasn't mad at them but at my fucking uncle and at myself. They walked me to my gate, I hugged them both for the last time, got on the plane feeling numb and when I landed in New York and I walked the highway for a long time until I reached an intersection. I grabbed a cab and told the driver that I only have twenty dollars if he could take me to the nearest train station, he answered "yes" and drove not too far a distance. I then hopped on the train with my duffel bag, packed with clothes and headed towards my new address, I was so enraged that I didn't feel the freezing cold, I laid the back of my head on the train window, feeling the rage and hatred engulf me and as I headed to 645 Prospect Avenue on 152 street, I knew that I was going to suffer more than ever.

Chapter 17

A Place Called Home

"When one teaches a child the evil ways of humanity that child then forwards it forward, the question that remains is, who is the guilty one? when the child, becomes the monster?"

I arrived at my stop and walked through piles of snow which were on each block that I passed. I walked heading to 645 Prospect Avenue in 152 street. Once there, I saw a two-door entrance and being that it was late, I didn't want to ring the bell to the apartment 411, so I waited for someone to come down and open the door. It didn't take long, someone from the building was leaving and I told him to hold the doors for me. He did, first he opened the front door and with his keys, he open the second door, I went in took the elevator to the fourth floor and walked to apartment 411. I stood standing in front of the door for more than five minutes, hearing voices inside but I was too scared to knock on the door, so I changed my mind and went towards section A of the stair case of the building. I walked up to the roof floor, placed my duffel bag on one corner of the floor and laid in the freezing cold and since the fire of hatred and rage swallowed me whole, I fell asleep not feeling the cold.

The next morning, I kept on going up and down to fourth floor to listen to the door of 411 and see if I can hear any one awake in the apartment, after the fifth time I finally heard voices and it seemed that everyone was awake, in one of my moments of going up and down missions, I happened to hustle up some money and buy a Christmas greeting card. I asked the pharmacist, if I could use a pen, I then wrote a little something, signed it, then sealed it and went into the building.

The card in hand, I continued to listen to the voices in the apartment, I was reluctant to go with my plan but I had nowhere to go, I placed the card underneath the door, pushed it in a little, stood up, rang the doorbell and ran straight to the back stair case of section A and up to the fifth floor. I was going to continue to the roof but I heard a door open and then close, I held my breath just in case someone was looking for me, my heart was beating hard with fear of being caught, I let out my breath out slowly as not to give my position away because whoever it was that opened the door, hasn't made a move and was still standing in whatever floor they were in, then the silence of the stair case was broken by the scream of a familiar voice "Manny, papi wants you to come home", I was overcome with emotions but I stood silent and when Pito screamed out again "Manny, I know your there", in an emotional voice I called out his name "Pito", upon hearing me speak, Pito ran up the fifth floor and stopped when he saw me, then he ran to me and gave me a big hug and I responded by hugging him back. I told Pito that I had to go upstairs to the roof and get my duffel bag, he asked me, if that's where I slept and I answered "yes".

Pito followed me up the stairs to the roof and tried to help me with my duffel bag seeing him struggle with it, I took it from him and we continued down the stairs in silence. Once we reached apartment 411, I was shaking, nervous and emotional and then the door to the apartment was opened. It was my father, my eyes was running with watery tears and upon seeing him, my tears became rivers leaving me speechless. My father hugged me and I returned the hug, in that embrace I was looking for comfort and for someone to help me with my pain and suffering but I also knew that this moment was a fraud. I went inside the crib and was greeted and hugged by Carmen and Puri,

Carmen told me not to worry about school that after the winter holidays are over, she'll enroll me back.

Christmas and New years were spent okay but like I knew it would happen, my father's wickedness started, he started with words like "hey stupid" ,"you loser","you bum, you're going to amount to nothing" , and when he tries to break me down, he'll say "I wish you were never born, you disgust me", then he'll go on a beating frenzy.

He then started mixing his torturing ways with extreme workouts on a treadmill machine and pushups. By the time summer school vacation arrived my father was trying hard to break me, day in and day out, after he finished verbally abusing me, he would get a metal pole of about two feet long and he'll put it in a corner and tell me that I have to do twenty five push-ups, something I never done before and if I couldn't do it, he'll beat me to death with the pole.

At first, it took me almost a couple of days to be able to do five push-ups, what I would do to constantly do full complete push-ups was to stand up on my feet and go back down. It was to develop enough energy to be able to do one or two more push-ups. It took me some time to finish the twenty five push-ups, but when I was finished he would force me to get on the treadmill machine and force me to do fifteen minutes of either running or sprinting and by the time the summer arrived, he had me running and sprinting for half an hour or more. I'm not going to lie, every time he forced me to do the same exercise, my arms and legs were wobbling and shaking. There were times that I didn't have enough energy to even masturbate, also in order for me to complete all the exercise I was being forced to do, I would use my hatred and rage that I had towards my father and the messed up thing about all of this, is that no one intervened with my father's mental and physical abuse on me. Everyone knew that it was happening but they all gave a blind eye to the situation.

There were times that Carmen would send me outside to play just to get me away from my father's wrath. I would go outside but instead of playing, I would walk down third Avenue in the Bronx and look inside different department stores, not to window shop for clothes but for a fantasy family that would love me and in one department store, I saw a Spanish family. A father, mother and a couple of kids, the father was holding the hands of the oldest child of

about nine or ten and they were all laughing and having a good time. I started to fantasize that it was my father holding my hand but then the blackness started to overtake my vision, leaving me numb but with two emotions, rage and hatred. And the more I watched their happy dappy moment as a family, the more I hated them. It got so bad that my body felt like it was on fire and the urge I felt was to go into the store and confront the father and son, cursing them both and doing something bad to both of them, so they could suffer and feel my pain.

I felt demented and murderous thoughts erupted in my mind and the things that my mind was thinking was chaotic with torture, blood, and dismembering them piece by piece until they all died. As I watched them all I could think of was getting my vengeance on everyone and making them pay for my pain and suffering, to me no one deserved to be happy.

I awoke from my dazed fantasy and continued to walk to nowhere but with the hatred and rage burning my heart, mind, and body, I looked up to a street sign on a light pole to see where the hell I was at because in my darkness. I've walked without knowing I did so and as I looked around to figure out where I was at, I realized that I have walked quite a distance, so I took a short cut back to my crib.

I began walking and my mind started flashing with a few thoughts that appeared. I asked no one, why do I suffer so much? And when will it end? Then an image of me going into a dark corner and laying on my side but curled up in a ball and just giving up appeared and in my final dark thoughts as I reached my destination. A question appeared in the back of my head, asking me why don't I give up? Not knowing the answer, I enter my father's apartment.

. . .

Some time had passed and a lesbian sister of Carmen who I'll name Victoria was staying over for a few weeks and she witnessed my father's ruthlessness on me but like all of Carmen's family members, all they did was stay quiet and mind their own business. I believe they were scared of my father but Victoria was a little different. Though she never confronted or said anything to my

father, she found ways to deceive him so I can find some peace and escape from my father's wrath.

One day, she told my father that she needed help doing work for the super and asked if she could take me, my father thinking it was work, answered "yes". I was already dressed, so I followed her out of the apartment door and walked all the way to the back of the section A stairwell and instead of going down the stairs, she went up the stairs all the way to the roof. I followed her and sat down next to her on the top step. Leading to the door to the roof, Victoria then pulled out a fat joint, lit it, took a deep drag and held it for a few seconds, then she let the smoke out and as she did, she was explaining to me that this is how I should take a drag and then passed the joint to me and told me to smoke it like she did.

I took the joint and inhaled the smoke like she did, the first drag was a long one and I held it for as long as I could, then I slowly let the smoke out, Victoria complemented me by saying "smoking like an expert". I got a little to open and took a second drag and boy do I tell you that-that was a freaking mistake, the smoke went the wrong way and I started to cough uncontrollably. Carmen's sister started laughing hard at me and said "acting like a big boy". My coughing took some time to calm down but when it did she told me to take another pull, I did and I felt different, I didn't feel my demons, the ones hidden in my head or the screams that racked my mind every day haunting my every thought. I felt free, good and happy.

My head was completely quiet, I was so happy that when I looked up to Victoria, I just burst out giggling and every time she would say something to me, it would change to bursting out laughing. I was laughing so much that I was not only clutching my stomach but I was breathless. After a couple of minutes of me laughing uncontrollably, I calmed myself down but continue to joke with Victoria. We chilled on the roof for a while, then she mentioned that when we get back to the crib, she would make some pancakes, then she warned me that when we return home, to not laugh too much because my father would notice something was wrong with me.

I followed her down the stairs and into my father's apartment and went straight into the living room, to watch what was left of the Saturday morning

cartoons. Victoria, on the other hand went into the kitchen to blow my mind with her way of making pancakes. I was watching one of my favorite cartoons "Kid Video" and I was still in my giggling stage but it went away when out of the corner of my eye, I saw my father creeping to see what I was doing, he didn't like me playing or having fun and when I saw his bald head with hair only around the edges of his head and that fluffy mustache, I returned my gaze to the TV and concentrated as hard as I could because I wanted to laugh at him and the more he stood there, the more my urge to burst out laughing was building up in me. The more I hoped my father would leave, my prayers were answered within seconds, I again looked through the corner of my eye and saw that he was gone, I quickly grabbed one of the sofa's pillow and buried my face on it and cracked up laughing.

After a few minutes passed since my father appeared, Victoria all of a sudden appeared from the corner of the living room entrance, acting like my father and making some funny faces and movements like he does. Pito, Puri, and I, started giggling and laughing, then we all heard my father screaming from his room "shut the fuck up" at that, we stood silent, then Victoria told us that she finished making the pancakes and to go to the kitchen, so she could serve us. We followed her and she wasn't lying, when she stated that my mind would be blown; it was, she had served all three of us, one pancake each but these pancakes, where as big as dinner plates and after I ate that one pancake, I was stuff as hell.

Later on that day, Carmen and my father had finally woken up and not only was my father in a bad mood, he was starting to focus on me and before he took it out on me, Carmen told Pito, Puri, and me to go outside and play. We went to the back of the building, where there was a hang out area before heading to the building's parking lot. There were three cemented tables with chess or checkers patterns above the table and connected to the table was four small cemented benches that was made for sitting around the table. Then not too far from the chess tables, were two long regular wooden benches with a patch of grass that surrounded part of the hang out area and part of the fenced parking lot. Then there was an exit/entrance door of the back of the building, which lead to the hang out area and like twenty feet

from the door was a children's ride, which was a round metal wheel where you can sit on metal benches with handle bars and hold on to them to prevent from falling off the wheel and in the middle of the wheel was a smaller wheel, where a chosen spinner would make the whole ride spin as fast as everyone wanted, the ride was able to hold five to six kids at the same time.

Pito, Puri, two other boys and myself were on the ride. I was the chosen one to do the spinning. Instead of everyone sitting on the metal chair with the handle bars to keep any one from falling off, every one chose to sit on the metal platform of the ride and hold on to the metal pole that was part of the metal seat. I positioned myself by standing a certain way, making it impossible for me to fall off and as I spun the wheel, I started spinning the ride asking every one if they wanted me to go faster, all the kids screamed out "hell yeah", so I spun faster. It was going real fast and everyone was holding for dear life but then one of the boys decided he wanted to show off by removing his hold on the metal pole and was quickly ejected from the ride and flung a little distance where he landed onto the grass, I was holding hard to my laughter because if I did laugh I would of been ejected from the ride too.

The boy was thrown quite a distance, I'll say about ten to fifteen feet from the ride but he landed on the grass unharmed. I slowed the ride to a stop and started cracking up in laughter, so was everyone else on the ride even the boy that landed on the grass but the boy was lucky because though the ride was fun, it can become dangerous. If the boy had fallen to the right side of the ride, he would of smack the buildings brick wall, which was the distance of five or six feet and if he would of fallen off in any another direction beside the two places I've described, he would off landed on the concrete floor. After all the laughter was out of our system Pito , Puri, and I stood outside a little while longer until the curfew given by Carmen approached.

· · ·

Time moved on so slowly and my father wouldn't stop finding ways to humiliate and put me down or beat on me and since Pito and Puri were requesting sex from me, I dived into the only escape I knew; sex, but then I got bored

with them because they couldn't ejaculate, so I decided to seduce one of the boys I became friends with from the building.

While I was looking for a new sex partner, Carmen had enrolled me into I.S. 52 on Kelly Street between Avenue St. John and Leggett Avenue. I was graduating from junior high school the next year and experience the high school years.

School, like I've mentioned before, was my true escape from my father's bullshit and all the sexual bullshit too. I was free from the torture and suffering and when the school assigned art class to my schedule, I instantly fell in love with art class. The teacher was teaching the students how to draw, something I knew how to do. Not like an expert but I knew how to draw, I became bored in class so I decided to roam through the class room and see what I could find of interest that's when I found a dusty book that perked my interest, it was the Art of Calligraphy and as I went through the book quickly, I became fascinated with the different styles of penmanship

I became so obsessed with calligraphy that I started to self-teach myself how to change my hand writing style and after a few tries, I got the hang of one style and as I kept on practicing soon I was able to write different styles of penmanship. I loved that book so much that one day I asked the teacher if he could lend me the book for a couple of days and the teacher answered "yes" and for that whole week, I would lose myself into learning how to write different styles and when the week arrived, I brought the book back giving it to the teacher in his hands but then the faggot motherfucker screamed at me, accusing me of stealing the book. He even went to the Principal office requesting that he call my father and request for him to come to school and meet with him, I was so upset that the teacher was accusing me of stealing the book that I started shedding tears and it got worst knowing that my father was called to come to my school.

The next day, my father and I walked to school and he threatened to beat my ass in the school if it was something bad, I became real frightened as we walked into the school and met the teacher in his classroom and they started speaking, I waited for them to finish talking so I can retell my story and the teacher realizing he messed, instead of apologizing he told my father that it

could be true because he was real busy that day, then the meeting ended and it ended with a good note, saving me from an ass whipping.

As for the teacher, I lost all manners of respect for him even though he is a known artist whose name I won't mention but he wanted the whole class to do an art project with horns and trumpets, so he can have it painted on the side of a housing building as a mural. I refused to do anything for him but a year later, I happened to be in Longwood avenue in the south Bronx and I happened to pass a certain block and on the side of the wall of a building was a mural of the trumpets and horns that my classmates drew were up there. Ever since that day, I regretted not doing my drawing, which I had already drawn at my crib.

After school that day, I was feeling depressed and hopeless, I felt like running away and just giving up, what I couldn't understand was why?, no matter how hard, I try to be a good kid and do the right thing, so people could love me, the more messed up situations intervenes into my life, bringing me down and making me hate myself more than I could ever have and that night at home, Pito had told me that he wanted to fuck and we agreed to have sex, when everyone went to slept but I wasn't please because having sex with him made my depressed feelings worse.

It was still early in the evening, and I was in my room chilling away from everyone in the crib. I just wanted to be by myself. I couldn't sleep because of how I was feeling and as everyone started to fall asleep, I just laid on the bed depressed but when Pito appeared by my bedside naked and with his long skinny erection, I quickly turned and lost myself in sucking on Pito's dick and balls. Since he couldn't ejaculate, I just wanted to perform oral sex on him. We were so into the oral sex that I did something I never done before. Pito asked to piss on me and I let him, he peed all over my face, head, and mouth. I even drank some of his salty piss. After he finished pissing on me, we continued to have sex but doing different sexual moves, we stood fucking for more than an hour and Pito stated that he had to take another piss, so I told him to urinate in my rectum.

I laid on my stomach and he laid on me penetrating my rectum, he started humping me slow and fast for a couple of minutes, then he stopped and I could

feel his hot piss going in me and after he finished, he continued to lay on me and after a minute or so, he began humping me again. He stood humping me for more than half an hour and I just laid there, enjoining being pissed on but not sexually satisfied, one because of feelings and two, since Pito couldn't ejaculate, I couldn't have the satisfaction of hearing and feeling the Pito cum like I do to all the boys who could cum, I love it when they grab the back of the head and start fucking my mouth hard and fast, while they moan and talk dirty to me.

Pito stopped humping but laid on me. He whipped his penis out of my asshole, he laid on me and pissed all over my butt cheeks and back. We were wet from his piss, after he finished, he just laid on me for a couple of more minutes, then he got off me but laid on his side on my bed, where we just rubbed on each other's penis. We did it for a couple of minutes more, then we stopped, he got off my bed, got dressed like I did and we both went to sleep. As I fell asleep my feeling attacked me in such a way that I felt worse than ever before.

. . .

The school vacation arrived and all the kids were happy even I was somewhat happy but it was short lived, when my father received a phone call from my mother and she told him that he needs to bring me to her house because she had some bad news to tell me. The next day, my father took me to see my mother in the Bronx, when we arrived at my mother's, he stood in the car and waited for me to come out.

As soon as I knocked on the door, my mother answered quickly and we both embraced each other, she held me in her arms for a minute more, then we walked further into the apartment, all the way into the kitchen, where she asked to sit down, then she said "Macho, abuelita died", she stood quiet for a couple of minutes, so the news could register. My mind went blank and all that happened was a tear roll down my right side of my face. I didn't believe it. She continued telling me that my grandmother died happy that one early morning, my grandfather went into her room and she died in a prayer position with her hands still in a prayer position and with a smile on her face.

My mother continued saying that after I left, my grandmother got real depressed over me leaving and not only did she lock my room, preventing any one to enter it and touching the things I left behind, my mother was telling me that once in a while, my grandmother would call out my name and get depressed when I didn't respond and my mother continued saying that to add on more stress to my grandmother was Sechia my grandmother's son, my uncle, who barged in and decided to move in and stress my grandparents out.

My mother continued telling me that when she went to Puerto Rico to go to the funeral, all my family was there and while the ceremony was going on, the burial wreaths that was for my grandmother's grave, rose up in the air above the people's head and started to swirl around in the air, then they gently returning back to the ground.

My mother further told me that while she was staying over in my grandparent's house, a hurricane passed through Puerto Rico and it destroyed my grandparents' house completely, leaving only two pillars that was attached to a second-floor wall with a picture of Jesus Christ on it.

We talked for a while longer then I left and got into the car completely numb, as my father was driving us home, I felt guilty because of my grandmother's death. I blamed myself for her suffering and her dying. I felt the fire of pure hatred enwrapped my whole body and it was so bad that the colors in my eyes were being covered with blackness, it was my other personality trying to come out, I fought mentally hard to gain my control and imprison the beast that stills lurks inside.

Even now, as a 50-year-old adult male, I feel the guilt of my grandmother's death and as I edited this part the flow of tears run down my face. I still think that if I haven't done what I did, I would have been there she wouldn't get depressed and Sechia wouldn't last long living there.

I dedicate this part of the chapter to my grandparents. I love and miss y'all. I thank y'all for all y'all love and patience and because of the both of you, I knew what real love was, plus I say this for the two individuals who are in my life. I thank them for reminding me of my grandparents love. I have changed my life even though part of me wants to see the world burn, it's because of your love and belief in me that keeps from doing that "abuela and abuelo,

watch over me and ask the Lord, to bring me a piece of mind for my mind is rambling in madness".

· · ·

Before I continue with my story, I just wanted to say this: my family and society does not know what they created in me of how dangerous, perverted, and chaotically sick the other side of me wants to torture and kill everyone in every way feasible way.

· · ·

Returning to my story, I was in the car and was silent throughout the ride back home, I was silent even when my father and I returned home, I just sat quietly on the sofa for a few minutes, then I went to my room and fell numbly to sleep.

It took a couple days for me to come out of my funk, then one day it got better when Carmen asked me to do some laundry I went and that's when I met Luis, a fourteen-year-old Spanish boy with light skin complexion and short black hair, who upon seeing me approached me and asked me, who I was, if I am new in the building and if I would be living in the building. I looked at Luis up and down. He wore glasses and had a discolored front tooth and I knew by his eyes, he was a masturbator and though he wasn't handsome, he was my type and I wanted to have male sex, so I could escape and feel satisfied. So I introduced myself, as Manny and answered his questions with yes.

We were alone in the laundry room and we started to conversate about our likes and dislikes in food, school teachers and movies. I looked at him in the eyes and asked him if he ever did it with a boy. He answered "no" but that he saw a fag movie with two guys kissing. Then I asked him "would you fuck me?", he stood quiet but staring at me, he then turned around and left the laundry room.

I finished folding the clothes and placing them in a bag, then taking them upstairs. Carmen liked the way that I washed the laundry that she sent me to do three bags of laundry. I spent the whole morning and afternoon in the laundry

room, washing, drying and folding, I would take my break here there, by four o'clock, I was still doing the laundry that's when Luis appeared and approached me and said "I want to fuck", and grabbed my butt cheeks while I was folding the clothes. Then we started fondling each other but on the down low because we didn't want to get caught by the kids that were playing outside in the back yard of the building, which some were our friends. We continue to fondle each other for a couple of minutes more than Luis asked me to suck his dick.

We went behind the driers, where there was enough space for him to lean his back on the wall and for me to kneel in front of him and perform oral sex. He had a long skinny penis and I found my escape. I felt all my problems and worries evaporate as I sucked his dick, I heard Luis tell me to get up, so he could fuck me in the ass, I got up turned around, pulled my short's and underwear down from behind, so my buttocks were only exposed, then I spread my butt cheeks with of my hands and he just penetrated me hard. It didn't hurt it just made me more lustful, my body felt on fire, I had to control myself because I wanted to moan and when he started humping me harder and faster. I didn't ejaculate but I became light headed almost dizzy. It felt like I ejaculated, I didn't want him to stop. I felt him hump me hard one time, stopped then humped me quickly a couple of more times, then stopped but started kissing my neck. I let him kiss me like that for some time, then I turned around and we started French kissing and rubbing our penises against each other.

Just as I was about to ask him to do it again, he asked me to follow him and I did. We left the laundry room and made a left into the lobby hall, where we walked past five apartments into the staircase and behind the first floor flight of stairs was an embankment that could hide at least five grown adults and right next to it, was an emergency exit that led out of the building. We were in the C section of the building and I quickly took off my clothes and stood naked in front of Luis. He didn't get naked like I did but he pulled his shorts and underwear down a little to exposed his penis, balls, and his buttocks. We put each other's penises between one another legs and groin and we started humping and French kissing. We were kissing like we were hungry for each other. I couldn't contain myself and got on my knees and kiss, lick, and rubbed his dick and balls all over my face and lips, then I started hungrily to sucked

on his dick, where Luis didn't last long, his knees started shaking uncontrollably then he grabbed me by the back of my head with both of his hands and fucked my mouth hard and stopped on shaky legs, he was breathing hard, he held me in that position for a couple of second more, then told me to get up and turn around. I did and he bent my upper body forward and started humping me hard and as fast as he could.

We kept fucking for more than four hours. It was eight o'clock when we stopped and I went to check on the clothes. It needed to be folded but I left them in the drier with the drier still running, Luis and I, went back to C section of stairs and started fucking again, he ejaculated a couple of more times, then said that he wanted to fuck me on the staircase of his floor, I followed him to the third floor C section. He then opened the staircase door and showed me an apartment right next to the door and told me that's where he lived with his mother and father, he then closed the door and grabbed me and made me face and we started French kissing again.

He undid my short's and pulled my underwear down a little from behind, then he pulled me as close as he could and grabbed both of my buttocks and started finger popping me. I let him do this for a little while, then I told him that I wanted the real thing. He turned me around roughly, bent me down and started fucking me hard, my butt cheeks were up in the air and he was humping faster, making slapping meaty noises, moaning, and whispering that he loved me. He ejaculated three times, stopped and told me to suck his dick. I made him cum a couple of more times but he wouldn't stop fucking me, he told me that he didn't want the sting to stop (the sting, he is referring to, is him ejaculating), so I continued preforming oral sex and anal sex until he started whispering lustfully that he needed to go home before it gets any later yet he wouldn't stop fucking me.

As he continued humping me, he started to fondle my dick and balls and suck on my neck. I was lost. I felt alive. I didn't feel the pain from the suffering of my torturers and the nonstop screams of the demon in me, having sex with Luis made me forget about all that and just as I was about to ejaculate, I stopped his hand and let him continue to suck on my neck. Luis was giving me a hickey. He had ejaculated but left his penis in me, after a couple of more

minutes, he stopped sucking on my neck and fixed himself. I did the same but just as I was about to head down the stairs to the laundry room, Luis stopped me and pulled my shorts and underwear down from behind and stuck his dick in me again, he humped me until he ejaculate three more times, then he quickly fixed himself and opened the staircase door and knocked at the door of his parents apartment, I; on the other hand, ran down stairs to the laundry room to only find it closed, it was a little past ten o'clock, I went upside to my crib and told Carmen before she left with my father that I had to go to the bathroom and when I came back, the laundry room was closed, she said not to worry to wake up early in the morning and go get them but my father threatened me by saying that the clothes better be down there or else he was going to beat my ass.

They had left and left me home alone with Tito. I went and took a long shower. When I got out of the shower I was in my underwear walking out of the bathroom and drying my upper body, I happened to catch Tito with his erect penis exposed and upon seeing me, he positioned himself, so I could see all of his dick and balls. I stared at his dick for a couple of minutes and went into the bathroom, locked the door and masturbated to the image of Luis and me having sex with Tito's big fat penis. It was when I imagined Tito fucking me in the ass that my body shook uncontrollably and I ejaculated so hard that I stood holding tightly onto my erected penis for a couple of minutes. After my body calmed down, I let go of my penis and waited until it became flaccid, then I went into my room, got properly dressed and went to sleep. I'm not going to lie, I was so horny that if Tito would have asked me to suck his dick, I would have.

The next day, I went down to the laundry room around eight in the morning, and it was opened, I went in and checked on the clothes to see if they were still in the drier. It was, just as I was about to start to take them out and fold them, Luis appeared, he walked in and told me that he wanted to fuck me again. I put the clothes back in the drier, turned the machine on and we both left the laundry room, he whispered to me that he wanted to fuck me, on the staircase of his floor, I followed him into the elevator and he pressed the third floor button and as soon as the doors closed, we started to passionately French

kissing, we stopped once the elevator reached the third floor then we walked to the C section of the floor, passing by eight apartment doors and into the staircase where we had sex before.

I took off all my clothes and stood in front of him naked. He then whipped out his erect penis and grabbed me roughly, turned me around, bent my upper body down, and rammed me hard in my ass. He fucked me in that way until he ejaculated four times. He then told me to suck his dick and I did though I had sex with him before, I had made it a rule to myself to never perform oral sex after being penetrated in the ass but since I felt disgusted with myself and horny, I made him ejaculate a few more times from oral sex, then I decided that I wanted to fuck to Luis and do what I do with Pito, suck his rectum. I told him that I wanted to fuck him in the ass and he replied to go ahead. I stood behind him and penetrated him and as he bent forward just a little, I started humping him and as this is going on, I masturbated him until he ejaculated quickly and just as I felt the tingling in my penis, I took my penis out of him before I ejaculated, I then went on my knees to suck on his rectum but when I spread his buttocks, it was caked with feces, it left me feeling a little disgusted, so I got up and told him to fuck me again and he did. He fucked me and put me to suck him off for hours. Then he stopped, fixed himself and went home, I went back to the laundry room and looked at the clock and saw that it was past eleven in the morning, I couldn't believe that we fucked for that long. I folded all the clothes and went upstairs, I put the bag of folded laundry in the living room sofa and went to the kitchen, to where Carmen was washing dishes, I asked her if I could go outside and she replied "yes".

I decided to go to Fox Street between Intervale and Long wood Avenue, to visit Chewito and a family friend named Lucy. I don't know who she really was but she was considered as family. It took me some time to get there but as I was walking by the neighborhood blocks, I happened to glance up at the mural and become upset at myself for not putting in my Art project. I reached 855 Fox Street to see if Chewito wanted to go sneak somewhere to fuck but he was punished, so I walked over to 854 Intervale Avenue to where Lucy was living. Lucy was there and we started having a conversation about me and then she changed it to my uncle Dereck, which I heard that Dereck's family was

here. I was already making plans to fuck my cousin Julio, I asked her about Julio and she told me that he is with his real father for the summer vacation but as for my uncle Dereck. Well, he was murdered.

Lucy continued telling me that since he was built like a truck, he was using his weight to intimidate and steal drug material and beat people up. Even his friends were scared of him and one day, he was supposed to go to a drug pick up spot, to pick up a couple of thousands that was to owed to him, my uncle went with one of his friends and when they arrived at the pickup spot, two guys approached the car and shot my uncle twice, once in the head and the other in the chest but as for his friend, he was left alive with the money. "How did I feel about the news?" Nothing. I didn't believe in family any longer, so there weren't any love lost,.I spent a little more time with Lucy then I went home.

. . .

I became friends with some kids in the apartment further down from me, it was three of four brothers, the oldest was older than twenty who I saw here and there. Then there was Carlos with a creamy skin complexion just like his brothers and curly dirty blond hair, then there was eight-year-old Felix and his six-year-old brother Joselito and every time we all met in the building's yard, we would play tag, freeze tag then wrestle, afterwards we'd sit in one of the two wooden benches and talked shit and joked about everything and everyone.

Way into the summer Carlos was my playmate and we played all sorts of games but early one evening, Carlos and I was wrestling and I happened to do a real pile driver move on him, making him cry. He ran into the building and like ten minutes later, Carlos comes back with his older brother. His brother told Carlos to leave and he did, the older brother then turned to me and asked me what happened. I explained everything to him but he responded by swinging at me with his fist, I dodged the punch just in time and he tried to continue to throw punches at me and each time I manage to dodge them, then he tried to front kick me and he missed. I reacted by jumping up in the air as he was coming at me and punching him as hard as I could with my fist that first hit made him staggered back almost falling. I didn't know that Carlos was still

behind him and started nibbling, licking, and sucking on his rectum without checking if it was clean.

I continued to perform oral butt sex for a couple of minutes more then I got up quickly and rammed my dick in his ass, he was a little tight but he was enjoying it. I was fucking him hard and fast whispering to him that I love him and wanted to stay fucking him forever, I was feeling uncomfortable because it was a closed quarters, so I told him to follow me. We walked to the back of C-section staircase, where we both got naked and we started to French kiss like we were hungry for each other and dick fucking. I really couldn't control myself, and didn't know where to start in fucking him, I wanted to do everything at the same time but decided to start on sucking his dick and balls then on his rectum, it got so hot between us that we were taking turns sucking and fucking each other and though he couldn't ejaculate it was alright by me.

We were fucking like that for more than an hour and Jaelo said that he had to leave. He quickly got dressed and left but I stood naked masturbating and once I ejaculated, I got dressed and headed for the elevator. Jaelo was sitting on the lobby window looking out into the front of the window, where his aunt, his sister and his sister boyfriend were chilling, I approached Jaelo and grabbed one of his butt cheeks, he looked at me and said "what are you doing faggot, I am not gay", I stopped and laughed at him, then I got on the elevator and went home and though he claimed not to be gay. There were times that we were closed to having sex again but someone either in his side of the family or in mine appeared out of nowhere, fucking up the moment and never having the chance to fuck him again.

Then during one of my summer adventures, Pito happened to get into a fight with an older kid from our building and Pito not only did he beat the kid up but told him that he was going to get a gang after him. I didn't know about this until one day, Pito and I, were coming from hanging out and we were entering through the fenced parking lot, the gates were open, so we didn't have to climb the gate but as we reached the middle of the parking lot, a group of older teens, some ranging from eighteen to twenty one surrounded Pito and me, I had a little boom box in my hand and I was going to use it to hit the one that was blocking us from entering both the hang out area that led into the

building but one of older teens seeing what I was about to do threatened me that if I hit anyone they were all was going to beat me to death. I was scared out of my ass but I was not going to leave Pito and when they questioned us about a gang, I responded that we aren't in any gang. Pito, jumped in and told them about the fight he had with some older kid, when they realized that we weren't a threat, they were going to let us leave but they wanted the radio. I looked at Pito hoping that he got the message and I slammed the radio against the floor, shattering the radio into pieces. I told Pito to run and just as I was about to run, they surrounded me and started to punching me all over my face. I then covered my face and they started to punching me all over my sides, chest and stomach, yet, I never fell on my knees and when they decided to stop I looked at them with both of my lips busted, my nose running with blood and as they ran out of the back of the parking lot, I was enraged and hoping that one day I would see the older teen who wanted my radio. I vowed when I got older I was going to stab him in the throat and watch him die, then leave him.

I went to the crib and my father was sitting on the big sofa, when he saw my face, he asked me what happened. I answered him and told him everything that happened in the back of the building and his response was to laugh uncontrollably. he stopped laughing and said that that was good for me, I went into the bathroom to wash my face. I felt like my body was on fire, I felt so hot that I was sweating heavily. I washed all the blood from my face and I saw that my lips and nose were very swollen, I stood inside for two days, so the swelling could go down but as for the bruising that took a while longer.

My faggot ass father started to overwork me with exercise to the point that I was owing, on push-ups and minutes on the tread mill, my father would add them on for the next day, so far I was owing over forty five push-ups and over an hour on the tread mill. One day, my father made me do push-ups but while doing them he put a fifty-pound package box on my back, it was one of many boxes packed so it could be shipped to Puerto Rico, Carmen saw what he was doing and told him to stop his shit but it wasn't after I did three struggling push-ups.

My father had me still doing push-ups when the door rang. Carmen was the one who answered the door and it was Spanky, coming to visit her. Spanky

didn't like my father, especially the way my father treated me. After some time had passed, Spanky announced that he was about to leave and he told my father as he was leaving that he was doing some work in the basement and needed some help. Spanky then asked my father, if it was alright to take me so I could help him. My father answered "Yes, but work him hard". Spanky replied "don't worry, I'll do just that" and since I was already dressed, I followed Spanky out the door.

We walked the distance of twenty blocks or more into a six story apartment building. We entered his basement apartment and we passed two rooms. One of them had a weight bench with a weight bar and some weights and the other room was empty. I continued to follow Spanky down the apartment hall into another room, where Spanky and his girl Maritza slept and further ahead of me was the bathroom, splitting two rooms, the one to my right was the living room and the one to my left was the kitchen.

Spanky escorted me into the living room, where there was a ten-year-old boy sitting on the big sofa watching television. Spanky introduced me to Alfredo, a curly brown hair tannish skin boy, who looked so beautiful that when he spoke or expressed himself, it was like he was trying to hide a feminine side and it turned me on. I sat next to him on the big sofa and started a conversating about kid stuff. Spanky had left stating that he will return and he did, five minutes later with a rolled up joint, he gave it to Alberto so he could light it and share it with me. Alfredo lit the joint and watched him take a pull, hold it, and let it out slowly, like he has been doing this for a while. It had my penis erect, I wanted to fuck him and when Alfredo passed me the joint, I looked at the joint with reluctance but Spanky and Alfredo assured me that everything would be alright. I took the joint and took my three pulls and past it to Alfredo, Spanky seeing us smoking, left the living room to go to his room and smoke with Maritza.

Alfredo and I smoked and giggled about everything and when he mentioned that he had to take a shit, we cracked up like little girls. Alfredo asked me to follow him and I did, we entered the bathroom and he told me to close and lock the door. I did, he pulled his long t-shirt over his head, exposing only underwear, then he pulled them down onto his ankles and sat on the toilet, I

was staring at his long almost thick penis and hanging balls, he sat with his legs open and wasn't uncomfortable with me staring at him. I sat at the edge of the tub next to Alfredo and we continued to smoke the joint, joke and giggle, after we finished smoking the joint, Alfredo got up pulled his long t-shirt back on the right way, then pulled his underwear up. I knew that he didn't want to defecate he was checking to see if I like having sex with boys, it was a message but instead of doing anything sexual, we left the bathroom and went into the living room to chill.

I was super high wishing that this feeling didn't go away. Alfredo and I was laughing and giggling at everything, then he asked me, if I wanted to go outside and play, I respond "yes" by nodding my head up and down, he then said that he was going to ask Maritza and Spanky for permission. He left the living room and came back running into the living room with short's in his hand, saying to get ready to play tag, when he finished dressing, we both raced out of the apartment and into the back yard of the building.

We played tag until we got tired, then we just sat down in a corner of the back yard, talking and joking. After some time passed, Maritza called out for both of us and we ran back in and sat in the living room waiting for Maritza to serve us food, we all ate rice, beans and fried chicken and after we finished, we chilled for a little while longer then Spanky took me home, where I pretended to be exhausted so I went took a shower then I went to sleep.

· · ·

By the time Autumn arrived, my father was harder on me than before I think it was because of the last time, when he threw me out because of that homosexual activity with Pito. Oscar and some other boys at the Halloween party and the only time I was important to him was when he needed to put me down, beat on me, and punish me with extreme work out.

I was so depressed, confused, lonely, and angry at every one, even at myself, I was angry at myself because I wanted everyone to feel my pain but I didn't know how to do it and I was too afraid of committing suicide because of the pain I would feel. On days when I feel worthless, I taught myself how

to draw and l would lose myself into my drawings, my first actual drawing was a cartoon mouse that was in the school's paper and it was to enter a drawing contest to see who drew the best mouse. I drew the mouse perfectly but didn't enter the contest, the drawings were for my pleasure, I drew many drawings, some I finished and some I didn't, some of my finished drawings was one of a Unicorn on a the edge of a high cliff, the one I was drawing now and almost finishing was of a spooky cemetery with some disturbed broken tomb stones and empty open grave with an almost hairless figure, dragging one leg, as it enters through the broken down gates of the cemetery.

I finished my drawing and I closed my notebook and headed to the bath room, after I finished using the bathroom, I opened the door and I could see that Pito was by the eating table, where my drawing book was, I could see that he had my note book in his hands and he was doing something to it, seeing me coming he closes the note book and left the table. I reached the table and retrieve my note book, I opened the note book and all my drawings were destroyed with chaotic scribblings, I felt the blackness engulf me and I fought hard, so it won't take over me. I felt on fire and the taste of blood was on my tongue, I closed my eyes tightly fighting the urge to go to Pito and stab him, what I did was force myself into my room and lay down and wait for my rage to subside, so I could be able to fall asleep.

I was enraged because that specific drawing represented how I felt. I felt dead, empty, lonely, and I wanted to go somewhere to lay down and perish. I couldn't express myself to the real world but for what, I wasn't going to receive any help, the adults that I depended on to love and protect me hated me and the rest of the other adults, turned a blinds eye to me being abused.

· · ·

By mid-Autumn, Carmen had enrolled me into a after school program at P.S. 130, Abram Stevens Hewitt school on Prospect Avenue between Macy Pl. and 156th street, the same after school program that Pito and Puri was in. Carmen was the only one trying to help me as much as she could, by keeping me away from my father as much as she can.

Sometimes I would walk with Pito and Puri the couple of blocks to the after school spot and sometimes I would go by myself but one day, it was Pito, Puri, and I and we were assigned the same classroom with a bunch of kids of different ages. Pito and I sat by the window and Puri sat across from us, sitting next to us was a thirteen year old kid named Marvin, who had a dark brown skinned complexion who was a skinny Spanish kid with afro style hair. The other kid was a twelve year Caucasian kid with blonde hair and blue eyes named Richard and a six-year-old, light-skinned Spanish kid with a Caesar haircut.

The classroom was set up with five desks connected to each other and situated in different areas. In total there were twenty desk with all kinds of students doing homework, the teachers desk was situated in the middle of the room but in the back, where she could see what is happening in the classroom, by the end of the first week the six year old was busy fondling Pito's and Marvin's dick and balls, this activity happened one day when I didn't go to the after school program, Pito was telling me about the incident, while Pito and I were having sex. Then in the program Richard would tell Marvin, Pito and I, how he sleeps naked at night waking up with a hard on but that's all he would say for conversation. I couldn't hold myself any longer and mentioned to Richard that if I was to stay over in his crib, I would suck his dick and I stood quiet, Richard never responded to what I said, though after that day, Richard never returned to the class.

But days later; while using the school's bathroom, Marvin walks in and stands next to me at the urinal, we started a conversation of masturbating, making us both get a hard on, I asked him if he would like for me to suck on his dick, he replied that he didn't care. I got on my knees and started preforming oral sex on him but it didn't last because he stopped me and asked if we could go somewhere else to finish. We went into the school's staircase but on the basement level, he whipped out his small penis and I started to suck it. I could tell that he could cum by the way his body was moving. He was getting to the point of ejaculating but we stopped because someone had open the door on some floor scaring us to a stop, Marvin quickly fixed himself and we both snuck out of the staircase noticing that it was time to go home, we gave each other a pound, then we went to our separate ways without saying anything to each other.

The next day, I didn't want to walk with Pito and Puri, so I left the apartment ahead of them, once outside I crossed the street on my side of the block and headed straight for the after school program. As I crossed the street to the next block, a truck had stopped right by me and the passenger side door of the truck opened by the driver of the truck and some white husky heavy set man asked me if I wanted to make some money. I responded "yes, but doing what", he answered that he needs someone to help him off load some deliveries at certain places in the neighborhood and not only will he be returning me back from where he picked me up but he will pay me twenty dollars, part of me was saying go with him but somewhere in the back of my mind was saying don't go, I stepped forward towards the truck and just as I was about to get on, Pito and Puri started screaming out my name. I stopped and turned around and looked at them that snapped out of the situation and I told the truck driver that I couldn't go with him because my brother and sister were calling me, at that the driver didn't say anything but closed the door and drove off. Pito on the other hand, threatened me that if I had left with the truck driver, he was going to tell my father on me but little did we know that if I would have gotten in that truck, it would have been the last time they ever saw me.

I walked with them to the school quietly not knowing the danger I was in. If it wasn't for them, I would have been one of those missing kids on the back of a milk cartons or being used as sex slave or the truck driver would have killed me after raping and torturing me. The most dangerous thing about the whole situation is that I was never taught the dangers of the world not only of the monsters in the house but of the human beings outside the house hold how the wolves disguise themselves in sheep's clothing, to me I thought that I was the only one suffering in the world and that it was only my family that were the dangerous and evil ones.

(If the parents hide the dangers of the world to kids, how are kids supposed to defend themselves or watch out for the dangers of the human monsters).

We entered the school but for some reason I didn't follow them into the classroom. I went into the auditorium and looked around. The two back exits, one that lead to the back staircase of the school, which lead to the upper floors of the school and the other one, lead to the outside of the school. I hung out

in the auditorium for a couple of minutes more and headed straight to the classroom but on the way there, I happened to bump into Marvin who was late. We started talking about our last time together so we agreed to do it again. I told Marvin to follow me into the auditorium and he did. We walked onto the stage, which had the curtains down blocking the view of any one coming into the auditorium from the entrance, I wasn't lustful but I wanted to finish what I started, I got naked and so did Marvin. At first I started preforming oral sex on him, then he asked to penetrate me in the ass, we fixed our clothes on the floor, so I could lay on my stomach and not feel the cold of the floor, once on my stomach, he laid on me and I could feel the tip on his penis, going in and out, after a couple of humps, I told him to stop that I wanted suck him off and make him cum, he did, he stood standing in front of me and I was lost myself into sucking his dick and balls, feeling his excitement, I stopped and told him, to piss in my mouth, face and body, he responded that her couldn't because he had to defecate, it almost killed the moment but I went back to sucking off, just as he was about to cum, we heard an aide from our classroom call out our names. We didn't respond but quietly picked our clothes and shoes up from the floor and sneaked out into the back section where it lead to the schools stairs. We quickly got dressed and Marvin and I waited a couple of minutes until we were sure that the aide wasn't around looking for us, Marvin left through the stairs` that lead into the hallway of the first floor and I tried to leave through the door that led outside of the school but it was locked with a chain and lock, just as I was about to leave the way I came an urge to defecate hit me, so I defecated by the entrance door. I ripped off my underwear and used it to wiped my ass with it. I then fixed myself and I started to leave the area, when the aide from the classroom appeared by the door that I was exiting, he stopped and asked me what was I doing?, I responded "nothing", he then let me go but he stood behind, I heard him entering from where I can from and as I was leaving the auditorium, I could hear him make a gagging noise.

The last time that Pito, Puri, and I went to the after school program, the six-year-old was there, he has been coming off and on the kid and I were seated side to side but in Puri's side, as soon as we got comfortable, the six-year-old started fondling me on the down low. I let him do it until I couldn't take it any

longer and just whipped my penis out, since it was cold outside, I used my jacket to cover myself while he started masturbating me, I uncovered myself and whispered to the kid to suck my dick he stopped jerking me off and was about to suck my dick, when Puri stopped us telling us that we could get caught and it wasn't a lie because as soon as I put my penis away and fixed myself. The six-year-old's mother walked in to pick him up. They left and I sat somewhere else, near some older kid and started to masturbate, the kid saw what I was going and I asked him, if he wanted to jerk me off or suck on my dick, the kid said "no" that if I ask him again, he would tell the teacher, I stopped bothering him but continued to masturbate until I ejaculated.

. . .

At home things were very hot with me because I was on the Graduation roster and my father didn't want to buy me the graduation clothes, pictures and ring. The day after day Carmen went into a heated conversation with my father, over buying me graduation clothes and after more than a week, my father gave in and gave Carmen a hundred dollars to get my clothes but it back fired on him because the pants, dressing shirt, and tie she got me was to my liking. The dressing shirt was of a black silky texture with silver lining that when standing in any form of light, it shines brightly. The dressing pants, were a silky silvery color with black lining and the tie was a silky black with little silver lining. I really loved those clothes, now, as for the shoes, well that was another story.

My father had given me thirty dollars to buy me a cheap pair of shoes. It was late in the evening, I'll say around five or six o'clock at night. I remember some time ago, I had went window shopping down on 3rd Avenue and seen a shoe store that had a very nice pair of shoes that would go perfect with my clothes, so I decided to take that long mission. I left the crib and got on the elevator and headed down. Once in the lobby a thirteen-year-old African American kid with dark brownish skin complexion and a low afro style haircut, stopped me and asked me where I was going, I knew the kid. He lived on the fifth floor of the building I lived in but I only seen him here and there, I told him where I was walking to and the reason he asked if he could come along

and I responded that it was a long walk, he replied that he didn't care, so we walked down to 149 street on Prospect Avenue and walked down the 149 street line, by the time we got on Cauldwell Avenue on 149 street, the African American kid named Michael started a conversation with a sexual encounter with a cousin who stood over Michaels' crib. He was explaining how an older cousin started fondling his penis, while they were in bed then the older cousin sucked him off, he stood quite but I could see that he wanted to tell me something more, at first, I thought he was talking about a female cousin but when he broke the silence with, "have you, ever done it with a boy", I already knew, what this was leading to, I answered "yes" and he let out a sign of release.

He asked to enter the park on Cauldwell Avenue. As we entered the park I noticed that it was empty of people. I also noticed that Michael had whipped out his dark brown skinny long penis and started masturbating as we walked deeper into the park. I already had an erection from the beginning of his sex talk and I too, whipped out a longer and a little fatter penis than him. He quickly grabbed it and started jerking me off. I was super lustful so I got on my knees and started performing oral sex on Michael by a big tree that covered us from street view, he started moaning and holding my head with both hands, moving my head in certain positions, making louder moaning sounds. We stopped and with our penises still exposed, I pulled his pants' and underwear down unto his ankles and suck on his dick and balls more comfortable, he stopped me every time he would about to cum, I stopped and stood up, pulled my pants and underwear down unto my knees, turned around and told him to fuck me in the ass. He didn't waste time, I could feel a part of his penis entering and it made me feel crazy. We were fucking in broad day light with no concern of getting caught, what made me stop him was the fact that it was already starting to get dark, we fixed ourselves and he asked, if I wanted to French kiss and we did for a minute or two, then we left, the same way we came through on the Cauldwell Avenue and 149 street side.

We walked down to 3rd Avenue to where the shoe store was located, I purchased the shoes for twenty dollars plus tax and we left. On the way back Michael was telling me that he wanted to finish what we started. I agreed but told him that we would do it in the roof of our building, we walked in silence and

when we reached our building, he started getting excited, we got on the elevator and started fondling each other and French kissing, once the elevator stopped on the last floor, we quietly walked to C-section of the building's staircase and walked up to the roof, we quickly undressed ourselves with me laying on my back and him on top of me, we were sword fought and French kissed, we were getting into the grove, when we heard a door open from one of the bottom floors, we became frighten so we stopped and quietly but quickly got dressed and ran down to the fifth floor steps and into the hallway, then into section A stair case, where he went home and I went to mine.

In the apartment I gave the change to my father. as I was heading into Pito's and Puri's room to put my shoes away with the rest of my graduation clothes, I heard my father speaking with Carmen about when they will leave to Puerto Rico. Carmen asked him how about going to my graduation ceremony but he replied that he'll be there. I knew with a sinking feeling that he was lying and on November, my father moved me to one of his sister's apartment on Fox street, my aunt Elsa who had twelve fingers and toes and was into Santeria and followed Walter Mercado faithfully.

She was taller than my father with light skin complexion and long curly black hair. She put a cot behind the stand in the living room, where the television was situated in with figurines placed everywhere else on the stand.

She didn't like me and she made it known to my father by telling him that she wasn't spending any money on food for me. What he did was go to the supermarket, come back with a big bag of chicken legs and a twenty-pound bag of rice, some cans of beans and a couple of dollars for anything else and left without giving me a hug or saying goodbye.

I really didn't feel anything I was so used of him disappointing me that I've became immune to his bullshit. My aunt Elsa hated me and to make matters worse, I had to deal with a school bully, who started focusing on me. It was some eighth grader who was the tallest kid in the school and because he had an extra skin coming out of one of his ears, the kids in school behind his back called him "The Elephant boy", "Elephant head" and many other names.

Chapter 18

My Aunt Elsa

"Who loves the child that is unloved."

Elephant boy, like I said before, for some reason, every time he saw me, he would always put his hands on me like he was kneading dough or put me in wrestling moves and when I'd tell him to stop, he'd smile and continue with his bullshit.

One day while in the gym, I was doing my own thing, when I noticed that he was there. I stood far away from him but once in a while he would draw my attention and have his penis exposed. I looked around to see if anyone notice but nobody acknowledged what just happened. I knew then that he was going to do something sexual to me, I was scared and I was too embarrassed to tell anyone.

Then in the lunchroom one day, he made it his business to sit across from me, take my pint of milk, drink the whole thing, then place the empty carton back on my tray. I looked at him for a minute, then without saying anything to him, got up, went back to where they were serving the lunch and told the lunch lady that my milk spilled, if I could please have another. She smiled at me and gave it to me, then I turned around and started opening the pint of milk completely, as I headed back to where he was, I also looked around to see

if there was any teachers around spotting them, I reached and stood to the side of the sitting bully and poured the whole milk contents all over his head and face, then I ran to where I saw the teachers, he was fast on my ass but I dip to the side to avoid the bully from grabbing my sweater, I reached the teachers and they came in between us holding him back from coming after me, he started yelling at the teachers that I threw milk at him but didn't say why, I did it but the teachers grabbed us both and escorted us to the principal office, where they sat us down right next to each other, the principal waited until the teachers left and asked the bully what happened. He responded by saying that I poured milk over him and stood quiet, the principal looked at him and asked him, why did I do it. He looked at me and said nothing, I was scared but I was more scared that if I didn't tell the teacher everything, he would do something bad to me and get away with it, so when the principal turned to me and asked me, why I did it?, I told her everything, especially the gym incident.

The principal told us that she was going to suspend us both for a week from going into the lunch room but that she was going to suspend him for two days more for what he was doing to me. Though I was grateful I was still scared because he had to come back to the school. I was already preparing myself by bringing a steak knife in my book bag every day to school but on the day that he was supposed to come back, he was beaten up in the school yard by three other kids and because of the beat down the bully never returned to school.

With one problem ending, another quickly began, on the last day of my lunch suspension, I was hanging out in the park across the street from the school and as I was sitting on the park bench waiting for the lunch period to be over, when suddenly an older teen of about eighteen or nineteen-years-old, entered the park and approached me with a baseball bat. He was a tall African American kid, who I had to look up at his face to look at him in the eyes, he then threatened me by asking me, what would I do, if he was to beat my head with his bat?, I didn't answer him but an image of me, being his size whipping his ass emerged but my thoughts were broken by the ringing of the bell announcing that the lunch period was over, I got up and proceeded to walk out the park giving the teen my back, hoping that he understood the meaning of

it and not caring if he bashed my head in but he didn't do anything as I walked out the park and I continued to my school and after that incident, I never saw that teen again.

· · ·

At my aunt's apartment, she did not show me any emotion but hostility. I remember one night, I had a sweet tooth and on top of the refrigerator was a pack of chocolate chip cookies. Those cookies which are two for one dollar. I took out three cookies and ate them, later on that night my aunt started screaming at me for touching the cookies, saying that those belong to her nineteen-year-old son to not touch anything in the house, I didn't respond, I just went to bed.

Being in that hostile environment, I would leave the apartment and hang out outside the building. Elsa lived in 663 Fox street between Avenue St, John and Leggett Avenue, across the street from P.S. 62 and I made friends with a couple of the boys in the neighborhood. And we would hang out on the little yard of the side of the school and watch handball matches between kids in the neighborhood or from other neighborhoods.

My regular hang out friends were a group of eight to nine boys ages ranging from eleven, twelve, and thirteen-year old's. There was a ten-year-old obese kid and an eight-year-old, who was sexually active and having sex with his six-year-old sister and I was trying hard to get him to let me suck his dick.

We would all hang out in the school's little side court yard taking handball lessons from a thirteen-year-old boy named Ulysses, he was an A player in Handball (an A player is the highest category in handball, they're the best, there are categories that ranging from A to D players, after D, its I suck status.), I was really fascinated by this physical combative nature of the game, I got up and asked Ulysses if he could teach me how to play hand ball, he replied that if I was really serious and I answered back 'yes', after he finished a match he was in, he told me to get on the court, which I did, he then started explaining the rules of hand ball, I listened carefully at everything he was saying and when he finished his explaining the rules, we started to play.

As we were playing hand ball, he was making me bust my ass. He would explain how I should respond to his serves. I would try but I would miss. He then showed me different serving styles, seeing that I was trying, he would let me serve the ball, just to show me how to respond. We played four games of 21 and I became tired, I told Ulysses that I couldn't play anymore because my legs was becoming wobbly, he laughed a little and told me to chill. I went and sat next to his twelve-year-old brother named David, a light skinned kid with dirty blond hair like his brother but there was a difference. David had straight hair, while his brother Ulysses had curly hair. David was a shy kid, while his brother was somewhat popular. David and I used to chill a lot, we sat next to each other saying nothing but just watching what's going on in the block or whatever its happening on the school's little court yard. I didn't mind the quiet for once there were some peace in this quietness, some times before I would hang out with David, I would be with the other kids pranking one another or daring one another to do something crazy, the boys dared me one time to masturbate right before entering the building's lobby, I told them no but they responded that it was the only way to join there group, first they checked to see if they were any adults around the area, being told that it was clear, I entered the first door of the building in our block, whipped out my flaccid penis and started masturbating, I was looking at them looking at me and it made me horny for some reason and as the pre-cum made my penis slippery. I started masturbating faster until my penis started shooting out cum hitting the floor.

The boys were fascinated and after I finished ejaculating, I put my erect penis back in my pants, we then walked to the school yard to talk about my masturbation and how they would be doing it that night, we played tag until David came out and hung out with him, we then sat down together and watched as the other boys played different games and until the grown up's started calling us to go home.

. . .

By the time Spring arrived, I made myself invisible in the my aunt's apartment because my aunt Elsa would get in one of her moods and starts her verbal assault

on me just to put me down. She'd tell me that I am unwanted child and that nobody wants me and though her words hurt me, it didn't hurt as bad as it should have, I was immune to the bullshit, thanks to my father and everyone else before Elsa.

I hung out more outside than being inside and it was fine by me, I learned how to play hand ball a lot better. Not an A player but able to beat some regular players and as I played, I started to learn their weakness and what's their limitations and since I was a hustler, it was hard to get me down.

One day it was all the kids from the block and we challenged each other either in teams or singles, to see who's the best, Ulysses and I were partners and we won three straight games of 21. I was tired and I told Ulysses that I wanted to take a break and just chill. He replied "okay". I went and sat next to David. We sat quietly as usual watching the handball game, David broke the silence by saying "you know, every time that my brother takes a shower, he comes to the room and once he is in the room, he takes the towel off and starts swinging his dick and balls in my face, while I'm on the bottom bunk", I asked him "how do you feel about it?, he quickly replied that "his penis starts to stand up", then we stood quite.

I then asked him, if he wanted to fuck and he answered "yes". We were sitting crossed legged on the school floor safe away from getting hit by either the player or the ball, I acted like I was passing something to someone and put my elbow between his legs closed to his crotch, I could feel his erection and he started to gyrate slowly in and out, he then told me that we could go into his building and up the roof and fuck.

We left the school yard and on the down low snuck into his building. We took the elevator and as soon as the elevator doors closed, we started French kissing. He whipped his penis out and I quickly got on my knees and started performing oral sex on him but after a minute of me sucking he stopped me and put his penis and balls away, I stood up and stood on the other side of the elevator and in just in time because his father was waiting by the elevator on his floor, waiting to go down, David's father asked him, what was he doing and he replied nothing that we were going to hang out by the stairs on his floor. David's father looked at us and entered the elevator, we waited five minutes

and ran all the to the roof, we both then got naked, fixed the clothes on the floor, so we could lay down. He laid on top of me and we started to French kiss and dick humping each other, he stopped and stood up and I started to suck his dick and balls and rubbing them all over my face and lips, just as he was about to ejaculate, he stopped me and asked me to fuck him in the ass.

He got in front of me in a doggy style position and laid his head and chest on the floor, I could see that his rectum was clean, so I started licking, sucking, and nibbling on his rectum. He started moaning like a girl and I liked it. I don't know how long I was at it but after some time, I stopped and I penetrated him hard making him make girl noises, I ejaculated in him and all over his rectum but that didn't stop me from preforming oral sex on his rectum. I continued for a couple of minutes more, then we stopped and got dressed, as we were walking down the steps, David started telling me that a female cousin was coming over and the three of them were going to have sex that what we did on the roof will not happen again and he entered his living quarters, I left the building and went to the school yard with the other kids and just chilled like nothing happened.

A couple of days later, I was chilling with some of my friends in front of Ulysée's building, when some old man in his mid-fifties early-sixties pulled me aside and told me that he saw me masturbating the other day. I looked at him and growled angrily at him, then turned around and went back to my friends but later on that night. I was hanging out in the school yard with Pete, the eight-year-old that was having sex with his sister and we were talking about sexual things and I asked Pete if I could suck his dick and he replied "yes". We headed out of the school yard to sneak into the buildings back yard but as we were leaving, I happened to notice a dark figure sitting in the back of the school yard, it was looking at me and it was the second time, I noticed a dark figure sitting in the exact spot, I didn't know if it was the old man because it was at night and all I can see was a form that I paid no mine.

· · ·

Graduation day arrived and I was dressed to impress. Everyone was complementing me on how I was dressed and the only one who appeared at my ceremony

was my aunt Betsy, a dyke, who had close cropped blond hair slick back style, looking like a man, she was high and drunk but she was one of my favorite aunts. I didn't care, I was really happy that she came.

After the ceremony, my aunt Betsy escorted me happily to her sister Elsa's apartment and once we entered the crib, my aunt Elsa told me that I couldn't live with her any longer that I had to leave. My aunt Betsy got into an argument with Elsa but Elsa didn't want to hear anything, my aunt Elsa had my things packed already with the cot that had wheels closed and ready to be rolled, I took my bags and Betsy took the rolling cot and we left.

As we were walking to my next destination, I walked in numbness, while the blanket of darkness, slowly enwrapped my soul vowing chaos on everyone.

Chapter 19

Life in Tin Tin Avenue

I always and still do love my aunt Betsy and as we walked to Tin Tin Avenue, she tried to cheer me up by letting me take a sip of her nasty beer. She told me that I had two other aunts living in the same building that she lives in. One is Anna with four children, three boys and one girl and my other aunt Maria.

We passed my old block on Prospect Avenue and walked behind the building on a cut street, passed an Elementary school and onto Tin Tin Avenue, and we stopped in front of building 799, which was on East 150 street. It was the only standing building, all the other buildings connected to 799 was either abandoned or falling apart.

There was an abandoned fenced block across the street from the building with an abandoned truck container. We entered the building and Betsy first took me into a first-floor apartment, where she lived with her female lover and her lover's two boys, an eight-year-old and a thirteen-year-old. Betsy introduced me to all of them and proudly told them that I had graduated today, after every one congratulated me Betsy asked the oldest boy to help her take the cot upstairs to the fourth floor.

We walked up to the fourth floor to the first of the apartments on the left side by the stairs. We entered and Maria quickly embraced me giving me a

hug and a kiss on each side of my cheeks, Maria then introduced me to her kids, first was thirteen-year-old Nelson, he had short dirty blond straight hair style and like he's brothers and sister, they all had tannish skin complexion, then there was ten-year-old Joseph, who had curly dirty blondish hair and then there was six year old Joel, who also had curly dirty blondish hair and lastly, twelve year old Pilar, she had long black hair that almost reached her buttocks.

Betsy, Edwin, the thirteen-year-old and I entered further into the apartment, passing the kitchen and into the living room that only had a big sofa, a floor TV and now, the rolling cot, I could see into the first bedroom and it only had a bed and a wall closet. I was welcomed by everyone and was told by Maria not to worry about anything that everything was going to be fine and that she'll contact my father. I knew by the dirty almost crumbling poor condition of the almost empty building, the lonely tenants and the tenants with families were struggling with some escaping into the life of hard core drug usage, I knew then that shit was going to be different for me.

My aunt Maria's apartment was really empty. The second bedroom was small, and it had a dresser and a bed. The bathroom was connected to the kitchen and there were hardly any dishes, the refrigerator was empty but with an empty milk container, the whole apartment looked like someone left the crib and left a few raggedy furniture behind.

I remember Maria cooking dinner one time but after that my cousins and I were left on our own, I found out why there wasn't any food or things in the apartment. One afternoon I decided to look for my aunt Maria, I asked someone from the building that was hanging on our floor, if he saw my aunt and he told me that Maria was in the apartment across from hers. I went and knocked on the door but no one answered, I turned the door knob to the apartment door and it opened, I walked further in the crib and stopped by the kitchen, where there was two women, one was my aunt and the other was her friend and they were both sitting across from each other sniffing something powdery from a small aluminum foil.

She was joking with her friend and wasn't at all disturbed by my presence. She kept on sniffing and told me to go back to the apartment and wait for her. She never appeared that night my cousins and I went to sleep without eating and without seeing my aunt Maria until the next day and while playing with

my cousins and some of the kids from the building, I found out that the white powdery substance that Maria was using was cocaine and it seemed that all the adults in the building were hooked on this drug.

Since there wasn't any food, sometimes my cousins and I would go into grocery stores to steal cakes, chips, and drinks, sometimes we would fight in the store to distract the store owner, while the rest of my cousins took edible stuff without the store owner knowing, then we'd go somewhere to chill and eat our prize.

Pilar, their sister, would be with us some times but it was always the boys and me. She hung out somewhere else. As for my male cousins and I, if we weren't stealing snack food, we would go into different neighborhoods to play with other kids or start trouble. Sometimes we would throw rocks at apartment windows to break them and run, then when the swimming pool season opened, my male cousins and I would spend the days swimming and by the time we went home, all we were in the mood for was sleep, hunger never really register in our stomachs.

By the middle of the summer eating regular food was nonexistent. All we ate was just junk food and that was a maybe, we spent the days just playing and not eating anything, we were too tired to eat and since all the adults were lost in their addiction. My cousins and I needs were unimportant, there were times that we didn't see the adults unless they came early in the morning or waking up late in the evening to get ready to hang out and get high again, the only nightly company my cousins and I had were the rats that used to run on top of us as we slept, though they didn't bite us, we used to be scared to go to sleep but as time passed, we became immune to the big rats nightly activities where falling asleep wasn't a problem.

This became a way of life with my cousins and I until one night the activities changed, it was my male cousins, Betsy's lovers two sons and two sisters from the building, we were chilling in my aunt's crib unsupervised, the two sisters a thirteen-year-old, where all the boys called her in the building "two tits in one" because the girl's breasts were big for her age and her six-year-old sister who was a wild one, they both had long black hair that reached their buttock and they both wanted to get fucked by thirteen-year-old Edwin.

dick, we stood in that motion for some time and since he couldn't ejaculate, I sucked until he moaned that he wanted to get fucked in the ass but not in the living room.

We went into the back bedroom and picked up sleeping Joel and took him into the bed in the first room, he then helped half-awake Joseph into the same room and bed, he was fast asleep. Nelson and I ran into the back room, got naked but this time Nelson laid on top of me, we French kissed and dick humped. It got so lustful that I started to put one finger in his rectum and seeing that he like it, I put in a second one, feeling that he was lose in his rectum, I wanted to see if I could stick my hand in his rectum. I had half my hand in his rectum, so I started hand fucking Nelson for a minute or more, he then asked me to stopped and I did but then he sat on my dick and started riding me, we were into our lustful grove when we both heard the door to the apartment open, we quickly and fearfully jumped off of each other and the bed and got dressed.

We laid back down on the bed next to each other and were pretending to be in a whispery conversation, when Betsy pops up at the bed room door way asking us what were we doing. When we both replied nothing, Betsy was satisfied with the answer but as she was about to leave Nelson asked Betsy where was his mother and she answered "downstairs", he got up and left the room, I chilled with Betsy in the crib for a few minutes and I too went downstairs.

Maria was downstairs sitting in front of the buildings stairs chilling with her coke fiend friends eating a chicken salad. I was left dumb founded by her eating food. My cousins and I haven't eaten anything in days and weeks but cakes, potato chips, and sleep and here she is eating while we were all sleeping, Nelson begged his mother for some of the salad though half of the salad was gone. She gave it to him with an attitude, seeing how hungry Nelson was I didn't bother to ask him for any, so I went back upstairs and went to bed.

· · ·

A month had passed by and all I heard about my father was that when he was ready to send for me he'll let us know, I was becoming somehow immune

to my hunger pains, if I felt hungry I'll steal a bag of chips or a cake or some cookies and that ends the hunger though I wasn't thinking about food, I was too busy hanging out with my cousins having fun and being mischievous and sleeping.

It was a sizzling summer day when my male cousins and I decided to go to the swimming pool. It was quite a distance, so we cut through different neighborhoods playing tag, racing or throwing bottles just to watch them burst and as we passed a neighborhood's garbage pile, there was a pile of glass window frames laid on the fence. Joseph dared me to punch one of the frames. I did not get cut but feeling really good I decided to punch two more frames consecutively but this time cutting myself but not badly. Nelson said that if we went to the pool that they won't allow me to enter because of my cut, so we went to the nearest grocery store and begged the store clerk for a free band aid, which he gave me and I put it on.

As we neared the pool area, I took off my band aid and I noticed the bleeding had stopped. We entered the pool with no problems and played tag or competed on who could swim the fastest or who couple hold their breath the longest under water, then we switched it to racing one another after a couple of hours in the pool. We decided to head home, where we played until it was fully dark outside then we went upstairs and went to sleep.

The next day, while everyone was sleeping I awoke to use the bathroom and as I was returning back to bed, Joseph was walking towards the bath room in his underwear. I wanted to have sex with him and since I did it with Nelson, I wanted to see if Joseph was down with it but I didn't want to straight out and ask him, so I asked him if he wanted to see me fuck the wall. He shook his head up and down and I whipped out my penis, made it erect and started humping the corner of the bath room door entrance, I saw that he was catching an erection and that his penis was way longer than Nelson's. He kept his penis unexposed, while walking in the bathroom, I asked him in a lower voice, if he wanted to fuck me in the ass, he answered "yes", I sat on the edge of the inside of the bath tub with my short's and underwear off, making it easier for Joseph to penetrate me, he was about to ejaculate when Nelson and Joel walked in the kitchen and saw us, Joseph stopped, putting away his penis and I got

dressed, we all left the kitchen talking about something else not mentioning anything of what Joseph and I were doing.

Later that evening, I'll say around seven or eight o'clock at night, my male cousins and I were home alone and Joseph asked us who wanted to play "the naked party". He explained that it was us running around naked playing different games everyone but Joel agreed to play because he was tired and wanted to sleep. Once he fell asleep we didn't have to worry about him, we then took off all our clothes and started running around chasing each other until we started to wrestle and things turned sexual.

Nelson sat on the big sofa with his legs spread wide open as Joseph knelt down in front of Nelson and without asking Nelson started preforming oral sex on his brother. I laid down behind Joseph and began preforming oral sex on Joseph's rectum. Joseph continued sucking on his brother's dick and balls for a while. I asked Joseph to suck my dick but he ignored me and kept on sucking on his brother's dick like he was hungry and couldn't get satisfied and as soon as Joseph started masturbating while sucking his brother's dick his body shook, then Joseph stopped sucking as his body started shaking a couple of times more. Joseph then stopped and put back on his underwear and went into the room with his sleeping brother, I tried to have sex with Nelson but I was turned off, I wanted to fuck and get fucked by Joseph but it didn't happened, I pretended to be exhausted and laid on my cot watching television, Nelson went to sleep with his brothers and I too fell asleep after some time but I don't know how many hours later, I was awakened by the sound of someone opening the apartment door and people talking, they entered the living room and I noticed that it was my aunt Betsy, Pilar, and Pilar's twelve year old female friend, who I knew from the neighborhood when I was living on Prospect Avenue. She had a slutty reputation and they were all true, she like to have sex with boys but they had to be older, I was thinking to myself why was she here?, I really didn't know and didn't ask but Betsy said to me that Pilar's friend was staying over to not do anything sexual with both girls, I giggled and replied that I wouldn't do anything but that was a lie.

I wanted to have sex with both girls. I wanted to suck on their pussies and fuck them both hard but as soon as they laid next to me, they went fast to sleep

. . .

After almost two months passed by when my father contacted Betsy and told her that a plane ticket was waiting for me at the airport. The next morning Betsy told me to be ready that she was looking for someone to take us to the airport. She was gone for a while and everyone was leaving the apartment to hang out, Nelson and I stood behind making sure that everyone was gone and not coming back. We ran into the last room, took our clothes off and laid on the bed and dick humped and French kissed. It was feeling so good that I was about to ejaculate but stopped myself when we both heard the door to the apartment open and Betsy was screamed my name.

My heart was beating rapidly with fear of getting caught. We jumped off each other and the bed quickly and got dressed, I heard Betsy footsteps near the first bed room, so I pretended to be going out into the fire escape, when she reached the room, she asked us what were we doing. I responded that we were going up to the roof and she stated that I didn't have enough time for stupid and dangerous shit that my ride was downstairs waiting for me that it was one of her closest friends. She grabbed my bags and I gave Nelson a hug and left Maria's apartment, I walked down the stairs not seeing any one else to say goodbye to, I continued to walk to the car that was waiting for me. Betsy got in and we drove in silence. Once we arrived at the airport, Betsy and I entered the airport and waited by a certain gate until it was boarding time, we spoke for a little bit and Betsy left as soon as it was time for me to board the plane, I was tired and I fell asleep on the way to Puerto Rico..

Chapter 20

Puerto Rico

"Who is the true Monster when all created me."

Before I continue with my story, I want to mention that my sexual experiences aren't to arouse any one. It was my escape from everything that was going on with me. Since no one told that having sex with the young was wrong only that homosexuality was wrong, hearing their pleasurable moaning was what turned me on to the point where was it was the only thing that made me feel alive/human, plus the fact that all my sexual partners in this book were already corrupted by someone and being that we were all being corrupted by those we trusted, it was what drew us together in a sexual way. I really didn't want to write about my sexual experiences, whether good or bad but then how would y'all understand me and though I was having homosexual experiences, like I said many times, I not only hated it, I was repulsed and disgusted by it and it wasn't because I hated homosexuals, I didn't give a flying fuck what he thought, it was one of the reasons why I was doing it and because it was wrong. No, it bothered me because I wanted to be with girls, but boys seem to just need to whip out their dicks out ready to stick it into me when I'm around them.

I don't really have to tell my story of my life but I want to expose those who pretend to be decent in society, while hidden within them are their true selves. Wolves hunting for its next prey. To me at that age I believed society being decent was a fucking lie. I want everyone to know what was done to me and what I fight to keep imprisoned in me. If it would take control of me put it this way, I would put every serial killer to shame, don't get me wrong I thirst for revenge for not only what was done to me but to all the people I betrayed and hurt. I want them to know why my wrath struck their doors and as I continue to write about my life experiences, I've come to imbed in my mind that telling the truth of what was done to me, will be revenge enough because the other alternative is to torture every single one until they die but then not only will they win but I would go to hell.

Anyway, back to my story, I was awaken by the stewardess informing me that we're about to land. I knew how life was going to be living with my father, Carmen, Pito and Puri. My father picked me up with my cousin Pablo, I hugged and kissed my father on his cheek and greeted Pablo. I put my bags in the back seat with me and waited for both of them to get on. Pablo asked me a lot of questions of New York, mainly of Bathgate Avenue, where he used to live. I told him the truth that I wasn't really there but on the other side of the Bronx, where our aunt Betsy lived and after I was finished speaking, everything stood quiet which was what I wanted.

My father drove for more than an hour to reach my old neighborhood, Calle Ocho in Brisa de Tortuguero in the town of Vega Baja. It's been more or less three years since I've been there and I could see some of my old friends hanging out in the corner talking and playing, as my father was nearing the house, he stopped in front of a secured metal gate and Pablo got out unsecure the gate and my father drove and parked inside the garage that is connected to the house and the rest of back rooms.

I got out and went in the house and greeted Carmen, Pito and Puri. Carmen had cooked and she asked me if I wanted to eat, I answered "yes" and I waited by the table. While waiting for the food to be heated and served, I stood up from the chair and looked out the door. It was late and the only people who were hanging out in the streets were the kids from the neighborhood, I

didn't want them to know I returned because they would want me to hang out and chill but I was exhausted but the next day that was a different story.

Early in the morning I helped my father clean out the little duck and chicken pond and feed the ducks and chickens, then I went to the other side of the house and fed the rabbits that were in a homemade cage. Afterwards I chilled sitting in the front porch of the house on a rocking chair, I left Pito doing the rest, I stood staring up at the Dawning sun enjoining the sounds of the Roosters crowing and all the other animals.

I went back inside the house because Carmen announced that it was time to eat breakfast. Breakfast was a delicious homemade coffee and buttered Pan de agua (Italian bread made differently). I then sat in the living room with Pito and my father watching some Spanish TV show. I was watching a couple of shows until my attention was drawn to outside the house, and saw that there was a group of kids in the corner of Calle Ocho, the usual hang out spot.

I knew some of them, so I went back inside the house and asked my father if I could hang out with my friends he answered "go ahead". I was excited to see them and as I left the house and out of the gate, the ones that knew me started to cheer my return. I approached the friends that I knew and we hugged and shook hands, they introduced me to the new kids of the neighborhood, then they invited me to go skinny dipping, I followed them to the nine blocks that led to the Lagoon.

As we walked to La Laguna, we joked and pranked one another, then we talked on missing times and what's been happening in the neighborhood. We reached the entrance of the forested area and walked over the chain that is used to stop any car from entering, then we walked some more until we reached the Lagoon. Then everyone got naked and ran into the water.

We swam and raced and challenged each other to see who could swim the fastest and the farthest, then we took a break while the younger boys would climb the mango trees, sour sop trees and/or tamarindo trees. After we all energized ourselves we went back to swimming and playing Tag, then we challenged each other on who could hold their breath the longest, then we finished it by swimming around, we got out and went to our clothes spread them out side by side and sat on them nakedly just talking shit and joking.

Sitting around without clothes didn't make me uncomfortable or even sexually aroused seeing all those different sizes dicks. The long and fat ones or long and skinny ones, then there was the small and fat ones or the small skinny ones and in different colors, I didn't feel aroused by all the asses I saw even though I had sex with one of them. The last time I was in Puerto Rico as we sat no one said or did anything homosexual, after we dried up and decided to leave the Lagoon and hang out in La Cancha "the court yard".

The courtyard was big, it had two separate baseball fields with wooden benches on each field and in the middle of both fields, splitting the fields in two, was a two-sided hand ball court and an area with wooden benches just to chill and it was a close distance to the Lagoon. I'll say like half of block and once we arrived, we all went to one of the wooden benches in the baseball field and just talked and joked.

Once nightfall arrived, I told my old and new friends that I had to go home and I left them. I arrived home and all I did was shower, eat, watch TV for a little while, then I went outside to one of the two bedrooms connected to each other and the outside bathroom that was not fully finished and it didn't have a door but a shower curtain was used to prevent anyone from seeing inside the bathroom. I entered the first bedroom and it only had a bed and one small dresser, my room had three windows, one behind the head board of my bed facing the door and the other two were on the side of the room, where I could see Pito and Puri's bedroom and the living room, I was tired so I went to bed.

· · ·

Within the week I got sick and developed a heat rash and because of the rash, I had sores on my arms and legs, my friends then named me "Jagoso" "sore" but in Spanish and it became what everyone in the neighborhood knew by, the heat rash took more than a week to go away and it was good because Carmen took me to my new school, Escuela Intermedia Angel Sandin Martinez in the town of Vega Baja, to enroll me and since the school system is different in Puerto Rico, classes starts from six or seven in the morning and it ends at

around twelve in the afternoon, then there is lunch and that's the end of the first shift and those students go home.

The second shift is from one in the afternoon until five in the evening and it's for a different set of students. I was in the morning shift, my friends was telling me that I had to wake up at five in the morning and wait at a certain corner for the school bus to pick up Intermedia and high school kids. My friends told me that they went to my school, I was happy but I was upset because in New York, I had graduated and I was to go Morris High School but in Puerto Rico instead of starting in ninth grade, I had to repeat eighth grade again. Once enrolled I was told that I won't start school until another few weeks, until then all I did besides helping my father with the animals or skinny dipping and hang out with my friends, I hung out with Danny, the kid I had sex with, he was older but that's about it, he was still small and skinny and though we hung out, we never spoke about our sexual encounter.

· · ·

At home, my relationship with my father didn't change but he didn't start his bullshit yet, we really didn't speak to each other. We only spoke when he wanted me to do work, which I didn't mind because it involved the animals.

My father's property was big like the house. The house had four bedrooms in a two part one story house. The front of the house had two coconut trees on each side with a nice patio on both side, the right side of the patio went around the house up to the back, where there was part of a bread Fruit tree from another property that over shadowed the back side of the yard, the inside of the house was well furnished, my father's room was the first bedroom facing the front of the property, then there's the bathroom that connected the second room, which Pito and Puri shared, then there's the living room and a long counter with four chairs that split the kitchen and the living room.

Like I described before the house was to the garage, then further in the garage was an empty room where my father kept a big cage with rabbits. As you walk further into the second part of the house, there's the two bedrooms and the unfinished bathroom, also there is a little hallway that splits the house

and the outside bedrooms which leads to the back side of the house and under the Bread fruit tree was six homemade cages built by either my father or with my help and it house two fighting roosters and where the rabbits will be moved too.

Then connected to the cages was a chicken wire fence that was built to block anyone from going further into the back of the house and it housed the free ranged chickens, ducks, and the two geese and a goose from getting out the back. On the left side of the house but in the back corner of the house was the homemade cemented pond for the birds, the garage wall up to entrance of the garage was block the birds from further roaming around and in order to get in from that side, one had to open a homemade chicken wired fenced door, the only two animals that roam freely around the property was two adult turkeys, a female and a male.

The neighbors on the right side of our property were a family of four, the father, a mother and the two teenage boys. Alex a fourteen-year-old and twelve-year-old Alfonso and they lived on a one story house, now the neighbors on the left side of our property was a family of five, a father, mother, two daughters Alicia age thirteen and twelve-year-old Lissie and a six year old boy named Chapote and both families were good families, as all other families in the neighborhood.

Every morning I would be awaked either by Pito to help him feed the animals or my father to do the job solo. I loved the animals and I loved feeding them. Sometimes I would play with the turkeys, I would make sounds like the male turkey making him mad, he would warn me that he was ready to fight for his girl by dragging both his wings on the floor and making threatening bird noises while following me until he realizes that I'm no longer a threat.

Then the two geese and the goose were hilarious, one of the geese was actually gay and the only one with a name. We called him "Bebe" and he had a nasty attitude towards humans. I used to let them out of their area just for them to chase me around the front of the house, Bebe would be the instigator, he would lower his head and charge after me, the other two would follow Bebe's lead in honking and chasing me, after I provided enough entertainment, I put them back in with the chickens and ducks where I would spread feed on

the dirt floor and talk to the birds, after feeding them I would scrub and clean out their pond and put in fresh water.

Taking care of the animals kept me out of trouble plus the experience with them was awesome but like everything in my life the solemn of peacefulness was shattered by Pito and Puri and their corruptive ways. One night while sitting on the one sitter sofa in the living room, which faced the window where I could see the second part of the house and anyone who enters the two bedrooms or the bathroom.

Sometimes, when someone is using the bathroom in the house and someone else needs to use the bathroom, the outside house bathroom will be used, Puri was using the outside bathroom to take a shower, when all of a sudden she appears completely naked on the bathroom's doorway. She was making movements to draw my attention, it did but I carefully had to look at her because my father was laying on the big sofa which faced the window, my father's back was towards of the window and not noticing what Puri was doing and her seeing that she had caught my attention started touching her vagina letting me know that she wanted me to fuck her.

I was sexually aroused to the point where my lust factor was beyond high. It wasn't only at seeing Puri's naked body and how her body has grown, no, it was also because we were taking a chance of my father catching us and the fear of getting caught was what made me super lustful. As I continued to look at Puri's ten-year-old body I could see that she was big-boned like Carmen. Puri had a body type of a fifteen year old girl but with no breasts, she stood playing with vagina for a couple of seconds more, then she went back into the bathroom and got dressed, as she entered the house she smirked at me that night I didn't fuck her but before I went to sleep, I masturbated three times with the image of her naked body and me fucking her hard, as for the next day that was a different story, my father had to go somewhere far and wouldn't be back until the early evening, as for Carmen, she was too busy doing stuff in the house and when she finished, she left into town to go shopping but before she left, she told us that she made something for us to eat.

Pito, Puri, and I waited. Earlier in the day, I told Pito while we were feeding the animals about what Puri did and what she wanted to do, Pito

We laid nakedly next to each other for a couple of minutes, then we got dressed and chilled in the house watching television but from that moment on, Pito and I would have sex almost every day but as for Puri, only when she's in the mood and that's like once or twice a week. I was getting tired of having sex with Pito because he couldn't ejaculate but then I didn't have to look far because while hanging out with my old friends and new friends, I found out that were having sex with each other and age didn't matter and their ages ranged from six-year-old's to seventeen-year-old's.

A couple of days before I started school, I had my first friend fuck. It was some six year old named Manuel, he was one of the boys that had sex with all of his friends, and it didn't matter the age. I was sitting on the rocking chair on the porch when this six year old enters and approaches me and sit on the porch's banisters edge and started asking me questions about New York and what I like but instead of answering any of his questions, I just straight out and asked him, " can I suck your dick", he answered "yes" and we entered the house and went into my father's room. He got naked and I laid him on his back on my father's bed and started sucking his dick and every time he would ejaculate his body would not only thrash every which way but he would piss in my mouth and I would drink every last drop. After I made him cum a couple of more times, he wanted to stop and get dress, then he left.

But doing that was somewhat a mistake but a blessing because he went and told all our friends that he be having sex that we had sex. Not only did they all wanted to fuck me but I turned down at first though Manny was coming around every day just so I can suck his dick. We would go to different hiding places and I would suck his dick and drink his piss, then he would go his way and I mine but as for the other boys, I didn't pick and choose, which male friend I was going to have sex with until I started school.

• • •

Now the school I was going to was as I said before is Angel Sandin Martinez and it was a school with three sections, the front section is the front and entrance to the school, this front side of the school took the whole block. It had

319

three floors the office and on top of the office but on each floor was the bathrooms and next to the bathrooms were gates that locked the floor, behind those gates were five to six classrooms with more than twelve students in each of them and if any student needed to use the bathroom, they had to ask the teacher and she'd give them the keys to lock the gates. Also on middle but on the bottom floor was the cafeteria and when you pass the lunchroom further down a long hallway was a locked bathroom with the vent broken in, and across from the bathroom was the back stairs that lead to the second and third floor classrooms, it also had locks on the gates.

Now separating the back of the school is a green grassy patio with a basketball court and two sections with wooden benches. Moving on further back of the benches was another gassy patio and connect to the patio was another section of the school with three floors with the upper two floors were also locked with gates and in order to use the bathroom one had to go through the back locked gates which was connected to the back staircase.

My classroom was the third classroom on the first floor and in front of the side section where my building was-was a cemented patio but with two large trees with small wooden benches around them. Further down the trees was a third section of the school, where the building had a long section which curved onto the other side of the front of the school, also in the front section of the school but in the back area was another basketball court which is called "Cancha de Baloncesto Brisila Vega Baja" and it had single little benches surrounding the basketball field, and on the back of the Basketball field were houses.

● ● ●

Since I started school, my father would wake me up not only for school but to feed the animals too. Our relationship returned to the way it was but with a new twist, he would hide certain items or equipment he needed to deal with the animals and tell me to look for it. I would search but I wasn't be able to find them. What he would do was wait for me to come from school and order me to continue looking for the item or the equipment missing, Pito, and Puri would even join to help me but after long hours of looking and not finding

anything, my father would start cursing at me and threaten to beat my ass and seeing that I couldn't find the item, he would to go to the back of the house and all of a sudden he'd find the item or equipment that was missing, claiming he found it in a spot that Pito, Puri, and I looked multiple times.

I remember another time, my father asked me to look for the machete. I did but after more than two hours, I still couldn't find it. Pito knowing what I was doing approached me and told me on the down low that my father had the machete hidden just like all the other times and my father punishing me for not finding the missing items but I did get so fucking even with my father.

One night, he had told Carmen that he was going to take me somewhere far to cut a specific grass for the chickens, ducks, and rabbits. I knew where he put the machete, so I on the down low took the machete from inside of the back seat of his car and put on the roof of the house, early the next day my father knocked on my door waking me for the trip. I told him that I needed the machete to file it and sharpen it for me, I thought that he was going to send me to get the machete but after five minutes of me getting ready, I could hear my father swear in Spanish and slam his car door.

My father was a quick to anger and boy was he furious. He started yelling curses out loud, he even woke up everyone in the house, Pito and Puri came outside to help look for the machete and when Pito caught me on the lonesome, he asked me if I had something to do with the disappearance of the machete I just smirked at Pito. He caught what I meant and he started laughing that whole day my dad was in a foul mood, one because the machete disappeared and two, because he had to buy other machete but after that incident he stopped hiding anything from me.

· · ·

Going to school early in the morning wasn't as stressful, since I taught my father a lesson. Every morning I would do my chores with no problems afterwards I would head out to the corner of Calle Ocho, where some of my school friends were waiting for me and the other kids who were going to the same school I was going to or going to the high school that was across the street

from my school and once every one that was going was there, we then headed to one of two bus stops, one which was by Escuela Manuel A. Padilla Davila, an elementary school and the other was located, a block down almost heading towards La Laguna de Tortuguero.

We were all waiting for the yellow school bus that kids in New York called "the yellow submarine" or "the banana boat" and were to ashamed to get on but in Puerto Rico kids didn't feel ashamed, we didn't have time for stupid things like that. Don't get me wrong we did stupid stuff like joked and pranked one another while waiting for the school bus and even in the school bus and while we're on the road, some of the teens decided to moon drivers that were behind the school bus, making everyone else laugh. The ride wasn't very long, and we were dropped off on C. Marginal, right on the block where Lino Patron Rivera High School is situated. We walked to Calle Tulio Otero and turned on Cll Julian Blanco Sosa and into my school Angel Sandin Martinez and unlike New York, we were all required to wear school uniforms. My schools uniform was a light blue shirt with beige khaki pants, I felt uncomfortable wearing a uniform because I was used to wearing regular clothes to school, the teens that went to my school, all went to the cafeteria to eat breakfast, eating the food in school was like eating at a restaurant and it didn't matter if it was breakfast or lunch, New York schools couldn't come close to Puerto Rico's school food, I ate my breakfast and went to class and all that other stupid shit that New York kids are embarrassed about, like eating school food, we didn't a fuck about nonsense.

My school taught every subject even English class, which in my mind I thought I was going to ace. As for the rest of the classes, I was up to the challenge in learning how to read and write in Spanish and being that I was being challenged I never felt bored with school. I started to self-teach myself on how to read, write and spell and soon I was getting the hang of the Spanish vocabulary and I was able to do some schoolwork and homework.

I had three things that helped me escape my father's wrath and his darken abuse towards me. They were school, feeding the animals and having sex with some of my male friends and with Pito and Puri.

My father had bought a wild horse and every day after school, he would tell me to change my clothes that he was taking me somewhere to cut grass

for the horse and though there were places very close to home. My father would take me many miles away to spots that had large areas of tall grass and before he left he would tell me that I had to cut enough grass to pack not only the trunk but above the trunk too and throughout my time cutting grass, I would use my hatred and rage to cut more than he asked but there were times that he would leave me alone cutting grass and a new thought and urge would appear more and more in my mind, I wanted to kill my father and every time I was left to cut grass, my father would come and pick me up late in night.

I remember one day in one of his moods, he took a big empty glass jug and with both hands and he started to beat me with the edges of the jar. His reason for the beating was because I forgot to clean out the chickens and the ducks homemade pond, then he figured that he was going to break me by volunteering me to work with some old timers in helping them mix cement to build houses or extensions to rooms on top of houses and I was to do it for free.

On weekends, I would be awakened by my father so I could go down the street on Calle Ocho to meet with the old men. They would then teach me what was needed and how to do it. There were men assigned to do specific things, like some would deal with the buckets of sand and others would deal getting the buckets of gravel, while others would get 50 lb. bags of cement, I would volunteer to help in everything.

I would help get twenty-seven buckets of sand and gravel and lay the sand first on the street and then the gravel on top of the sand, then I would help in getting and spreading a hundred and twenty bags of cement on top of the sand and gravel, once that process was completed, someone with a hose would pour water on the cement. While the men and I would mix the sand, gravel and cement together until the mixing was done and ready to use, some of the men and I would shovel cement in empty five gallon paint buckets and take them to the other men, who would be the ones actually building whatever it was we were building. By the time lunch arrived, we'd done the cement process around three times, now the person we were doing the construction for would make a big meal for all the workers. The meal consists of rice and beans with chicken but other days until we would eat different types of meats with the rice and beans or sometimes delicious soup with rice.

After all the workers ate and chilled for some time, the men I worked with expressed and complemented me on the way I worked and to top it off, I was the youngest person working with the men. All day until the early evening, we would be doing construction work, afterwards I would help clean out the equipment and the street floor that was use for the mixing, then I would head straight home completely exhausted, where my father would be sitting on the rocking chair in the front porch with a sadistic smile on his face, in my mind as I passed him by a would envision myself murdering my father with the machete.

Envisioning murdering my father wasn't enough to keep me from actually doing it, so I started killing my father's favorite pets, I would take a syringe fill it up to a hundred units of my father's insulin and inject the pet with it and watch it as it dies. Some animals died within half an hour but others took a couple of hours to die and the more I did this the more I wanted not only to kill my father but to kill people too. As for the sex, well it wasn't really working because my hatred and rage was an constant emotion engulfing me on an everyday basis.

If it wasn't volunteering to help build rooms or houses, I would hit the books and study harder than before because, get ready for this, I was failing English class. Everything else I was barely making it. I made some school friends in school that didn't live in Calle Ocho and we were excited because of the Christmas, New Years, and the Three Kings day celebration and to impress my new friends, I told them about my father's stash of a box of nine, one gallon of Bacardi rum liquor, they told me to bring some to school for the next day, I replied that I would bring enough for everyone.

The next day, Carmen and my father had to go to an appointment somewhere. Pito ,Puri and I were left home alone and they too had the early shift at Escuela Manuel A. Padilla Davila, when they left I stood behind and quickly looked for a container to put the alcohol in, I found a big empty container that use to hold powered Tang, then I went into my father's room took a gallon of Bacardi and filled the container, I then seal the container and put back the gallon of alcohol back in the box.

I was already dressed so I put the container in my bookbag and left to where my friends were waiting to catch the school bus, the picked us up and

we arrived at the usual bus stop that led to my school. I split from my neighborhood friends and met up with my school friends at the back entrance of the school, we chilled in the back section of the school and I took out the big container filled with the alcohol and we all took a big gulp of alcohol but that one sip left me breathless for just a second. I wanted to drink with my friend to celebrate my early sixteen-year birthday that fell on a Saturday. I asked them if they were going to take another sip but they all said that the alcohol was too strong, so I asked them if they dared me to drink the whole container, they all answered "yes". I took the big container and gulped down half of it quickly, I stopped drinking because I was left breathless for more than five seconds and I felt a burning sensation going down my throat and all the way down into my stomach, after the side effects of drinking the alcohol quickly wore off, we all headed to the school's cafeteria and as I reached the entrance of the cafeteria everything went dark for me.

All I remember was regaining my consciousness and collapsing on the front of the cafeteria entrance again, then I got up and everything went dark again. I awoke standing in front of the staircase that led up to the third floor of the front of the school and the classrooms. I walked up to the third floor, turned around and threw myself head first down the flight of stairs. I got up on wobbly legs and looked down the second floor stairs and I threw myself again down the second flight of stairs head first and screaming in Spanish "yo me quire muerir"", "I want to die". I continued to throw myself down the stairs until I reached the main floor, I remember getting up feeling and seeing that the school was completely empty, I walked all the way back to entrance of the cafeteria and collapsed, not regaining consciousness until I reached the hospital waking up with tubes down my throat pumping my stomach, then I passed out again.

I awoke a day later in a Manati hospital with an I.V. in one arm but no tubes down my throat. I was in the children section of the hospital with a thirteen-year-old as my roommate. We didn't talk to each other and I didn't pay him no mind, later that night my father and Carmen came to visit me in the hospital but I didn't speak to them, they stood for a little while and left, they came two more times as I stayed for more or less than a week in the hospital

and on their last visit, my father gave a couple of dollars like that when I was discharged I would get transportation to go home.

I was in hospital for a week and I was discharged, I took the minivan that served as a public bus and took it home to Vega baja. I got home and it was like nothing happened to me, no one asked me if I was okay or why did I do what I did and the next day in school it was like nothing happened, I wasn't provided with any counseling by the school but I managed to meet up with my three school friends who I drank with and all three of them took turns in giving me a hug and a hand shake, they told me the whole story of what happen that day. They were taking turns telling me that I looked possessed and as I kept on falling and getting up to reached the first floor steps and up the flight of stairs to the third floor, they tried to stop me from continuing up the stair case but that I fought them off and when I finally reached to the third floor and started throwing myself head first down stairs, they tried very hard to stop me but they failed, as I continued to fall and get up heading to the cafeteria. They stood behind me and told me that I passed out in front of the cafeteria that I looked dead, seeing me in that condition, they started punching and kicking me on my chest. I vaguely remember waking up in the ambulance and a female paramedic telling something but not understanding until my three friends told me that the paramedics thanked them for saving my life because the kicks and punches to my chest area was what kept my heart pumping and kept me from dying, when they finished with what they were telling, my reactions were like, I really didn't a give fuck if I died because part of me already felt dead, plus dying was what I wanted.

We hung out until classes started and after school. I didn't get to see them and as I was about to leave to go to the bus stop and meet up with my friends, I happened to go to the water fountain that was situated on the first floor, where I had thrown myself down the steps and saw one of my friends from Calle Ocho, a twelve-year-old named Pipo. He was drinking water, when all of a sudden I approached him from behind and grabbed his penis above his pants then letting go, I stood back and he turned around. I could see that he had a long erection, he asked me why I grabbed him. I responded because I wanted to suck his dick. I sat on the third step of the first flight of stairs and

he walked up to me and whipped out his penis, he started guiding me with both hands around the back of my head, we were getting into the grove, when suddenly we heard grownups talking and walking down the steps, we stopped and he put his penis away and in good time because as he put it away, he took a few steps back and a group of teachers were coming down the stairs, not seeing anything suspicious, they kept on moving but Pipo said that we needed to leave so we could catch the bus and we ran and made it at the nick of time.

I finished what with Pipo and I started two days later but before then, I was being enticed by Danny, my neighbor's thirteen-year-old son. Danny kept on throwing me sexual hints of sexual interest with me and I did want to fuck and get fucked by Danny, who was beautiful to look at but for some reason, something prevented me from having sex with him. Danny would wait until we're alone and he'll start a conversation of him masturbating and how good it feels, I would respond "especially when it gets slippery", he would bite his lower lip and make a moaning sound and agree with me or he would tell me that he had a crush on the ten year old girl, who was my neighbor on the other side of my father's property and how he wanted to have sex with her or he would tell me an sexual experience he had when he was six years old. While going to kindergarten, all the other kids were returning to class from being in recess, Danny continued saying that he stood behind with some other kid, he never mention what sex was the kid but they had sex in the school's backyard. I assumed it was a girl but then a couple of days later, Danny came to my house to hang out with Pito and me and we were in the garage area of the house where we couldn't be seen but heard, Danny started grabbing my butt cheeks and Pito's and in return I did the same. I was starting to get very aroused, so I grabbed on Danny butt cheeks and with the other hand fondle his dick and balls gently. He stopped talking and looked straight into my eyes biting his lower lip. I was so turned on by him that I was about to grab his face with both of my hands and French kiss him but when he whispered in a sexual manner asking me "tu eres pato" "if I was gay". It broke me out of my lustful emotion and made me stop playing grab ass with him. The funny thing about this is that when I decided to actually go through with giving my body to Danny, his family had moved out and a family of five moved in, it was two boys ages five

and twelve and a ten year old girl, they lived with their mother and father. And at the same time a female friend of Carmen moved into the next room with her fraternal twins and her little dark grey and blackish fur Benji type dog which was tied to a small concrete shed behind the house situated below the bathroom, and it also held a lot of my father's tools and other worthless junk.

One night while I was taking a shower, I happened to look out of the bathroom window and I was surprise and frightened by what I was witnessing. In the house it was illuminated by a red lights and I started hearing some type of chanting that I couldn't understand. It frightened me so much that I rolled the venetian window shut, I knew for some reason that they were practicing black magic and I was right with my suspicion when the next day I happened to see the twelve-year-old and I started a conversation with him by first introducing myself, then I asked him how did their party went and what were they celebrating, he looked at me and replied "we didn't have a party", so I left the subject alone because I didn't believe him and I do believe that what I witnessed the night before wasn't meant for me to witness because a few nights later, I was awakened by a sense of fearful danger, the fear was so deep that I was frozen in my bed, I was completely awake but didn't dare to move even though I slept with a sharpened machete by my side, I felt that if I let whatever woke me know that I was aware of its presence, it would have been my last act.

My bed's headboard was facing the back of the window which faced the back yard and in the corner of my eyes I watched the two windows on the side of my room which I could see the living room and Pito's and Puri's bedroom. I slowed my breathing and didn't move at all and it's when I heard an animalistic breathing and growling. I felt its hatred beyond I ever felt, as it was breathing and growling, I was trying to figure out what animal could be outside behind my window, when all of a sudden, the breathing and growling stopped but it appeared on the side windows of my room and at the front of the door. It was like it was appearing and disappearing from window to window and back to the door, this activity continued for at least ten minutes and the funny thing was as it kept appearing and disappearing. It was doing it faster and faster than it stopped and I felt whatever was out there vanished. I was still scared out of my ass and after some time passed I finally fell asleep.

The next morning, I was still a little frightened still but I didn't tell anyone about the incident. When I went in the first part of the house to eat some breakfast, my father told me to go feed Amelia's dog and give him food and water, I had forgotten about the dog, and while preparing the dog's food, I was wondering why the hell didn't the dog bark at whatever was out there. I started to doubt that the incident, thinking it was a nightmare but when I went to the concrete shed and saw why the dog didn't bark, my question was answered. The dog was not only dead but his fur which was a mixture of blackish and greyish fur, was completely white.

Whatever the dog saw outside that night, killed the dog by its presence. I went into the house and told my father that the dog was dead and he went outside to go check the dog, I followed right behind him and reached the concrete shed. He saw the dog, then told me to get a garbage bag put the dog in it and throw the dead dog into the garbage and when my father told Amelia, she wasn't that upset about her dog.

Seeing the condition of the dog, I became frightened again and I started thinking that whatever it was outside my windows and door that night wasn't a human being or any known animal. All I know was that in sensing its presence, I not only felt its hatred for me but I felt an evil so strong that I still have a little of it in me. I knew then that it's the same form that I saw when I was a child in North Carolina and it will not be the last time, it will present itself to me.

I wanted to tell Carmen and my father, but I knew they wouldn't believe me. Plus my father lately had been treating me like I was taking up space. If I told him, he would have wished the presence into existence, so it could do whatever it wanted with me, I just didn't know the hell was wrong with my father. I don't know if he tried to break my will but he tried extremely hard and there were days that I thought that he would break me but I managed.

I remember one of many incidents, where he thought that he would break me by putting me to make a water path from the corner of his property to across the street to the other property, where it would connect with other water ditches. He gave me a pick axe and he told me that the water ditch had to be six inches wide and five inches deep, I looked at whole area and there wasn't any problems with the flow of the water ditch on his property, I was going to

question him but I knew it would make matters worse, I asked him about the working gloves and he answered "there isn't any". I turned my back to him because I didn't want him to see what had flash in my mind, it was me burying the pick axe in the top of his head.

I started breaking the road around ten in the morning and as I broke the road chip by chip I felt something wonderful happen to me. I felt an anger so powerful that it engulfed me completely. It felt like it was burning and numbing my body with a burning fire (like it feels now as I write and edited this part) then I felt the blackness take control of me and by the time I came to my normal self, I felt the anger completely drained out my system, leaving me physically and emotionally drained also and not only did I completed my task but I noticed that it was after six in the evening and when I looked at my palms. They were completely bloodied even the handle of the pick axe was covered with my blood. I was also noticing that both of my hands hurt opening and closing them.

I went and took a shower in the house and the water stung my hand so hard that tears were burning down my cheeks and I held back the scream of pain that wanted to come out of my mouth. As I continued to let the water fall on my hands, I'll watch the blood wash away leaving chunks of pieces of hanging skin, after the shower I painfully struggle to put my clothes, finished I left the house to go to my room and throw my sweaty and dirty clothes on a corner floor and returned to go eat, I sat and could hardly hold the spoon to eat, my tears started running down my cheeks mixing with my food, I then stopped eating, got up and put my plate with food in the sink, then I went to bed and I tell you this, that the first three days with my palms damaged was even hard for me to do my school work.

My father waited until my hand was completely healed to one day while I was in school to bring an item and place it behind the back of my window to my room and when I returned home from school, my father asked me to follow him into the back of the yard and I did. We walked from around to the left side of the house. I could see a boulder half my height behind my window and as we got closer, he told me that I had to break the boulder down until it's all gravel size so he could use it to build his house in Arecibo, where his mother

and other family members lived. He then gave me a hammer with a wooden handle and threatened me with death if I didn't come from school every day and use the hammer to break down the boulder and he then said to hurry up and change my clothes that I had to start right now. And like he ordered, every day after school I would change my clothes and go out in the back with the hammer and started pounding the boulder. I did it not because the threat of death or his fucking scare tactics, it wasn't working any longer, I did it because I wanted to show the piece of shit that nothing he does to me can break me down and as the days turned to many school weeks and my hand becoming bloodied blisters after many hours of me pounding on the boulder, my blood and skin was always on the handle but I persisted with the hammering and every time I would start, I would let the darkness take over me. I would not come to until Carmen would call my name and break me out of my trance. She would tell me to stop and take a shower and go eat. Sometimes I would eat and sometimes I would go just to sleep and to make matters worse, he would take me every weekend to Arecibo in Hatillo, Pajuir, somewhere called a El Cerro de Maravilla, on a steep mountain hill going up or down.

He started the outline for the house which was going to be built next to his mother's but below her. After the house was built, the roof would even out on the mountain side, where you could walk on it without climbing on it but first I was following my father helping him measure certain areas were tall structures for the house were going to be build. He said something which I couldn't hear and I knew that he was going to start with his bullshit. My father had a habit when he wanted to start bullshit with me, he would whisper softly making it hard for me to hear him and when I continue to question him about what he said, he would start cursing me out in English and Spanish until he started to beat on me. And that's what he did but this time he took a machete and hit me hard with the back of the machete on one of my legs. I walked away enraged and went looking for another machete finding one in my uncle Nelson's house, who lived across from his and my father's mother's house. I began to walk back with one plan, to hack my father to death, my uncle witness everything that went on between my father and I, and he stopped me and asked me what I was going to do with the machete, in my rage I told him that I was

going to kill his brother, he stopped me from going to my father and told me to leave my father alone and go play with my cousins and not to worry about anything that he'll deal with my father.

I left but with murder on my mind. My uncle didn't tell my father what I was going to do to him but my father not knowing how closed he came to being murdered, he continue his job alone. He finished all the measuring and digging. I watched from a distance, while chilling with Juan Pablo, my uncle was doing a little digging and cutting wooden panels and hammering them to each other and placing Rebar in them. A lot of this work I did with bloodied hands, they only finished what I had started. The next weekend I returned to Arecibo to prepare the cement with gravel mixed in with it.

Now this motherfucker wanted me to get twenty-seven buckets of sand and twenty-five buckets of gravel. I can't remember how many fifty-pound bags of cement I had to get but I know it was more than twenty but before I started getting the full buckets of sand and gravel, I watched him take the empty five-gallon bucket of paint and cut the white plastic handle, leaving the metal handle bare and when I asked him about some working gloves, he told me that there wasn't any.

I was going to start at the top of the hill, where the street surface was flat enough to do the mixture and closer to his property. My father seeing what I was about to do he asked me "what the fuck are you doing?" And when I told him what I was going to do, he responded "no you have to do it at the bottom of the hill", I looked down at the bottom of the steep hill and how hard it was going to be, I then knew that my father was really trying to break me but I grabbed two empty five-gallon buckets and went to the top of hill, at the two big piles, one of sand and the other with gravel, my father wanted twenty seven full buckets of sand and twenty five buckets of gravel, so I started with the sand going up and down the hill until I had all the sand and gravel done. I then did the same with all the fifty pound bags of cement needed. I placed them on top of each other but to one side, while I spread the sand and gravel together. I took the bags of cement and broke each one pouring and spreading its contents on the sand and gravel, after the pouring I would make an opening in the middle of the pile, so water could be pour in the middle of the cement mixture as

I mix the cement, my father's lob was to only hook up a couple of hoses and attached them together, so the hose would reach the bottom of the hill and he could poured water in the middle, I started to mix the cement mixture with a shovel, when I was done I had to take half a bucket of prepared cement and pour it where my father told me to pour it.

I wasn't tired doing this torturous labor because I was overcome with a profound hatred for my father and the rage that burned my body. It gave me the endurance, I needed to deal with the work at hand. I managed to do three more piles of the cemented mixture and taking it to wherever my father directed me to pour. By the time I was finished with the third pile, it was already dark, I didn't realize that I was in my darkness until my uncle Nelson called me over to his house to eat some food that his wife Alba prepared for dinner, as I ate in my darkened silence I started to feel my emotions calmed down and feel extremely exhausted. When my father decided to leave and head home, I fell asleep as soon as I got home and went to my room and laid on my bed.

Those were my weekends and as I mentioned before, every day after school I had to beat on a boulder with a wooden handle hammer. When I was finished for the day, everyone had already finished eating and were sitting in the living room chilling like a family. I would sit alone and painfully eat my food feeling like I was invisible and at those moments, I would envision myself killing my father in different ways and boy, the urge to murder him was getting stronger, and in order for me to stop the urge to, I would inject a hundred units of insulin into one of his favorite animals mainly his fighting roasters, going down the line ending with his chickens and as I watched them died slowly and painfully, I would feel soothed making feel at peace and in a sleepy state.

· · ·

In school I was struggling real hard even in English class. The teacher would teach us about nouns, pronouns, and adjectives but I couldn't pay attention because my mind was going crazy with all the shit my father was putting me through plus the murderess urges that were getting stronger and stronger and the disgusted feelings I felt for having sex with boys that turned me on, I didn't

want to be a homosexual but every time I would have sex with a boy, I would promise myself that I wouldn't touch male flesh again, yet, I was always either bent forward getting fucked or on my knees sucking dick, while lost in my chaotic racing mind. I was trying to figure who the fuck I was and why the hell am I going through this hell, and the hatred I had for myself mixed itself with secret thoughts of suicide swimming in the back of my subconsciousness.

Then one day after school as I was getting off the school bus and the all the kids were whispering to one another, one of kids said as he was pointing a taller and bigger older teen, that he wanted to fight me because they all wanted to know how a gringo could fight. The older teen rushed towards me and tried to sucker punch me but I was ready for it. Living in New York, I had to learn how to fight, so I could prevent bullies from coming for me and other kids who wanted to test my fighting skills.

I was bopping and weaving every punch he was throwing at me. Missing every time, I could see that my dancing around him was getting him upset because he couldn't land a punch. I even put both of my hands down to my sides putting my face forward taunting him but he still missed. I really didn't want to fight but he persisted and when he got lucky and managed to land one punch on my face and all the kids started cheering for him, I became enraged and took off my school shirt, leaving me bear chested and started beating his ass. I was getting tired of torturing him, so I hit him with a right and knocked him on his back. As he sat up I told him that I didn't want to fight him but the kids were cheering for him to get up, he let them put a battery on his back and as he started to get up, I happened to wipe sweat from my forehead and saw blood mixed with my sweat, at that I started to feel the darkness cover my eyes. I knew that if I didn't stop the fight, I was going to do something bad to him but he charged at me again and started swinging at me but every time, I would smack his fist away from me. I then wanted to break his wrist so I matched his swing with mine and our fists connected head on, my hit was so hard that we both fell on our asses, I jumped up before he did and waited until he got up, we fought for more than forty minutes until some adult broke us up. Nobody cheered for me but they cheered for him, like if he won the fight, I knew who the older teen was and

where he lived, he lived in the corner of Calle Ocho and after we fought, a few days later we became friends.

. . .

The school vacation arrived and I would sometimes disappear from my neighborhood with certain boys ranging from the ages of eight to fifteen-year-old's. We would either go to the benches in the baseball field, La Laguna or into other people's properties just to have sex with another. It first started with Pipo, we would go into a two floor house at one of the corners of Calle Ocho, and we'll enter an unfinished room, Pipo would lower his short's with no underwear down unto his knees and I would suck on his dick and balls making him ejaculate multiple times, we would stop when his dick couldn't handle getting sucked any longer and as we fixed ourselves, he would tell that I sucked dick real good, if I wanted to do it again some other time, I answered "yes".

One of the other boys I was having sex with was Pipo's little eight-year-old brother Manuel. He was the kid I performed oral sex on when he was six-years-old, it was "The Three Kings day" and he saw me hanging out in the corner with my friends, he approached me and asked me on the down low so none of the other kids could hear if I wanted suck his dick. I answered "yes" and we went into an abandoned house. He got naked and I sat on the floor and sucked his dick, balls, and drank his piss every time he ejaculated, I continued to preforming oral sex until his dick couldn't stay erect.

Later that night, a twelve-year-old named Fleje, started rapping in Spanish at me, he then stopped and started to tell me that he was in love with someone. When I asked him who it was, he stood quiet and answered that it was some girl but by the way he said it, I knew that it wasn't girl, I knew that he was trying to bait me to open the doors so we could have sex with him though we didn't have sex, he told some boys that we did.

If it wasn't escaping into sex with boys, I started to hang out with one of my father's friends named Carlos. We formed a friendship due to him witnessing some of my father's abuses, he would then ask me if I wanted to go with him "land crab fishing", something I've never experienced and to get out the

house and stop having sex with boys, I answered "yes". He then ask my father's permission for me to stay over and go crab fishing with him and my father allowed me to go, we walked to the corner of Calle Siete to a one story house. It was a nice property with a fence surrounding his house and a back yard that led to a lagoon. I followed him into his house and he introduced me to a light skinned thin woman, who was his wife and his two children, a four-year-old tannish skinned boy with dirty blond curly hair and a little three-year-old light skinned girl.

We all chilled for an hour or more, then Carlos showed me a second bedroom, where there were two cribs situated with one in one corner and the other in another. He fixed a thick quilt on the floor between the cribs and I went to sleep but then I don't know how many hours passed by when I was awaken by Carlos. He said in a low voice that it's three in the morning and that the crabs were hungry. I got up with excited anticipation but careful as not to wake up the kids, I went into the bathroom and just splashed water on my face and goggle and spit out some water, I then left the house went and sat on the passenger side of his car, he had a thermostat filled of some awesome coffee and a loaf of agua de pan bread, the ride took over an hour and a half but the drive there Carlos would act like my father and joke on himself. I would laugh hard and long, we arrived in a wooded area where within a mile from where we were was a beach.

I got off and followed Carlos behind his car, where he opened the trunk and he had over twenty handmade wooden crab traps that were placed side by side of each other and on top, he also had two five gallon empty paint buckets with their tops. Carlos had explained to me what needs to be done, so I grabbed ten wooden crab traps and a bucket and he did the same. As I followed Carlos deeper into the woods I was examining the wooden crab traps, each one was the size of a sneaker box, above the traps but in the middle was a slated opening where a plastic cover would fall down once the crab enters from below the front section of the trap and it pulls a piece of bait that is attached to a nail as the crab pulls on its prize, it also pulls on a string that's connected to the pointed edge of the nail when that happens, the plastic cover falls in trapping the crabs.

We went further into the woods and arrived at the area we needed to be. He went his way and I went to mine, I was looking for holes on the ground near grassy areas or in certain hidden spots, I then would put the front of the trap with the entrance on the bottom on the hole in the ground, so the smell of the bait can go into the crabs hole. Once the crab is enticed it would enter the trap and pull on the bait. When that happens the plastic cover falls trapping the crab in. You could hear the plastic hit the bottom of the wooden trap but for the crabs to get trapped it took hours, meanwhile Carlos and I waited in the car and drank the coffee with the bread and waited until dawn, as dawn arrived we got out of the car and I headed to where I placed the traps with a bucket in hand and as I was nearing the traps, I could hear the plastic covers falling in the trap and every time I would grab a trap crab, I would take the cover off of the empty five-gallon paint bucket and put them inside securing the bucket with the cover. I then placed the empty traps on the ground, to be picked up on the way back.

Once Everything was collected, we would return the traps the way we got it, then we placed the sealed buckets of live crabs in the trunk. He then would drive back to his house where in the back yard there was a hard to described handmade wooden crab tank made with plywood. He lifted the locked chicken wire gate and poured the live crabs inside, he then closed and locked the gate, and with a hose he filled the wooden tank with enough water not to drown them, the water was mixing up with rice, corn, and regular beans from the can, Carlos was explaining to me that reason he won't eat the crabs now is that they were too skinny. He opened the tank again, grabbed a crab and showed me the crab legs that had little hairs on them, he further explained that when crabs are fat, the hairs on the crab falls off, he then returned the crab back in the tank and we went inside and went to sleep.

Every weekend Carlos and I would go crab land fishing but on this day it was a special day because it wasn't only to go crab fishing but to catch the crab he named "Hercules". He had built a crab trap three times the size of the regular traps and it was the same with the width of the trap but with a metal trap door, Carlos took out only the trap for "Hercules" and I followed him into the same wooded area as the first night but farther where it was more terrain, he

stopped and showed me a little hill with a hole almost a foot wide all around. He then placed the trap and made sure that Hercules wouldn't be able to push the trap a side.

We then went around and placed the rest of the traps around the crab holes that we haven't hit yet, then we returned to his car to drink some coffee and eat homemade Cubanito sandwiches. Carlos began telling me of a season when the crabs are growing. They cover their holes to hide because their shell becomes very soft and they become food for predators, he continued saying that when their like that you could break into their holes and grab them, fried them with shell and all and consume the fried crab as a sandwich.

After many hours passed by we decided to go check on all the traps, and as soon as we entered the area where the traps are set. We could hear the trap doors falling trapping the crabs as we were collecting the traps and putting the crabs in the bucket, we heard the sound of wood crackling and breaking almost like an explosion. I looked Carlos and He looked at me and he started saying "no, no, no" and started running towards Hercules hole. I followed and when we arrived, Hercules had completely destroyed the trap, Carlos was mad but he told me that he has respect for Hercules for representing his name that he would no longer be hunting for him.

. . .

Hanging out with Carlos was cool, when I wasn't under the oppressive tortures of my father, my father had bought two little Collie type dogs (Lassie the in-famous entertainment dog of all time), he loved those dogs so one day I asked Carlos when was he going to go crab fishing again because we had stopped crab fishing for a while. He responded in two weeks. I couldn't wait and when the time came and he asked me if I was ready to go crab fishing, I answered "yes" but told him I would meet him at his house. I waited until he was out of eye sight then I went into the house, I grabbed two syringes, inserted it inside my father's insulin and filled both syringes to its capacity, a hundred units, then I went back outside into the garage, where my father kept two Collies inside a metal kennel. I took one dog injected with a hundred units of insulin, then

put it back and then I did the same to the other one, I close the kennel's door and left to Carlos's house, I was sitting in Carlos's living room not really paying attention to him or his family, I was waiting for the outcome of my actions and after an hour or more, I heard the first dog start to howl, the howl of death and then I heard the second puppy start to howl in unison with its mate. Ohh the pleasure I felt hearing them scream the screams of death, (I still feel the same pleasure as I'm editing and proof reading this part).

As the hours went into the late evening, the puppies were still howling their death song but in a higher volume and it continued until a little after midnight when they went silent, letting me know they were fucking dead. I felt a relief that I was over swept away with a calmful peacefulness. After that incident, I knew how to really get to my father, I would wait for him to get attached to his chosen pets, and when he wasn't around, I would inject half of my usual dose, so it would take longer for them to die. Only the other dogs died howling as for his prized fighting roasters, my father started out with five fighting Roosters, so far he had two left, as for the fowl, they died dragging their wings on the ground and continue to walk around until they're sit down and close their eyes and die since my father couldn't explain how his animals so he stopped buying any more favorite pets.

I stopped killing his animals but was trying to find ways to kill my father by mixing different things into his insulin bottles, so he could die slowly and in pain but somehow, he noticed that his insulin bottles were being contaminated, so he'd throw that insulin bottle away.

My father had a habit of humiliating me in front of his friends, people, family and Carmen. I knew that see he was jealous of me because I've become taller than him thicker and stronger than him but he liked to show Carmen how much dominance he had over me. One day, I was helping my father clean out the chickens, ducks, geese and goose area and pond but no matter what I did, it was wrong and he would start with a barrage humiliating insults to me while Carmen was watching me doing all the work and my father started whipping me hard with his mental whip but then he had the balls to ask me to prepare him a cup of coffee. I went in humiliated and enraged, I went into the house and heated up exactly a cup of coffee but instead of putting his sweet n

low, I took two pills from a pill bottle that he uses to check his sugar through mixing the pills in his urine. The pills started bubbling in his coffee, even shaking the cup to the point that the cup cracked on one side, I looked at the pill bottle and saw two bones making a cross and a skull, I didn't have to continue reading any further because I knew it would kill him if he consumed the whole cup.

I cleaned the cup from anything floating on the coffee or anything spilled on the side of the cup, then I went outside and gave the cup to my father, he took it and said in Spanish " where did you go to Africa to get it", I didn't answer him or didn't look at him because I knew he would know that I put something in his coffee alerting him that I was trying to kill him, so I directed my attention to the fowls but out of the corner of my eyes. I watched as he took a big gulp, swallowing it, then taking another smaller sip but spitting out the rest, he asked me what did I put in the coffee salt, I responded by describing a small jar that had salt but saying that I thought it was his sweet n low, he threw the rest of the coffee in the cup on the ground and gave the cup to Puri and told her to make him a real cup of coffee. The next day, he was bedridden and he vomited blood three times but didn't die though he was sick for a couple of days.

The second time I tried to kill my father was like a week or two after the last incident. I was sitting in the front porch on the rocking chair, sharpening a machete and reminiscing about how my palms are messed up with the tor-turous labor of building his house and how bloody and painful my hands were and how I did everything in my power to avoid my father seeing me in tears, I waited until I took a shower and do it in silence. I could feel tears burning down my face and feeling nothing but hatred and rage heat my body like fire.

Then everything went black, my vision returned but it was like I was look-ing through someone else's eyes and everything was in black and white, all I can see was me standing over my father, while he was laying sideways on the big sofa sleeping with both of my hands wrapped around the machete's handle and raising both my arms, I watched through secondary eyes and couldn't stop what was about to happen. My arms were as high as they could and I was about to come down with the machete, when we "my controller of my body" and I, saw out the corner of our eyes the door to the front of the house opened and Carmen walked in and froze, my we both turned our heads to the side and

looked at Carmen, and stared at her eyes for a few seconds, then we turned our attention to my sleeping father and slowly lowered the machete, turning and walking away and out of the other side of the house without killing my father, and as soon as I entered my room, I stopped and everything went dark few a few seconds and I was back to normal but extremely exhausted to the point of passing out, as I walked to my bed. I knew that if I didn't make it to my bed, I was going to pass out on the floor and as soon as I laid on my bed, I went into a deep sleep.

This hidden personality was activated when one day I had lent a shrimp net to one of my father's friends. The motherfucker told me that my father told him that he could pick the net up, so I gave it to him and he returned a few days later with torn up shrimp net but gave it to my father. My father was so mad that he started to beat me with the net and finish breaking the net all over my head and body. It was later that evening while I was eating food, when my father was telling me that he never gave anyone permission to use his property. I didn't reply but just kept on eating my food, then all of a sudden I felt something of me disappearing briefly and returning and that's when I knew "it" was going to kill my father.

· · ·

I realized that my father wanted me to get hurt when one day he built a stable in the backyard, where his fighting roosters used to be. They all died of mysterious circumstances, and he actually bought a wild horse but wouldn't let me help him tame or ride the horse claiming that I was to fat but it backfired on him because all the men he was paying that claimed to be horse tamers were afraid of being around the horse because the horse was too wild to tame and they didn't want to get hurt. My father then assigned me to ride and train the horse.

The horse would jump up and down wildly like in a rodeo, sometimes he would jump over fences with me on him and there were close calls where I had to jump off the horse, in order to prevent from any one of us from getting any injury, all the tactical bullshit my father was telling me to use on the horse wasn't working. When I would ride the horse away from view, I would let the

horse do whatever it wanted to do and it was running and running real fast, I would let him burn himself out, then I would start to teach the horse Paso Fino steps (short steps with the horse's head at a certain angle) letting him do him made him respond better with my commands, I knew then how to tame the horse.

I was doing good in training the horse but one day, I wanted to show off to my friends and make my father angry, on how I trained the horse but as soon as I got on the horse it started acting weird, it started jumping up and down like he did in the beginning of his training. He ran out of my father's property and towards another property that had a cemented fence, the horse jumped over it with me on him and he started running towards another fence but I knew that if he jumped over, he would of broken his front legs, so I jumped off him and started to whisper and talk to him to calm him down. Once he was calm, I told that I had a sweet treat for him, when we get back home. I walked him unto the street and mounted him again and rode him to the front of my house. All of a sudden the horse stood up on his two hind legs and I held on and it felt good, I held him by his mane and I could hear everyone that was outside cheering and applauding me on but I knew my father wasn't one of the cheerers and after a minute or two of the horse on his hind legs, he took a step back and slipped on a green moss, we fell on our sides, he stood up first and I followed quickly right behind, just in case the horse decided to start kicking wildly.

I stood up unhurt only dusting my side, I was lucky that the horse didn't fall on me because he would have crushed me and probably killed me, I noticed when I grabbed the reigns of the horse and checked to see if he was injured that everyone was silently quiet until they saw me walking the horse back to the house, then they all cheered my name like I won a competition. At home I bathed him and waited until he was completely calm, then I gave him water, fed him, and gave him a whole apple.

The thing with horses is very complicated, I was told that as a horse owner, I had to make sure that I don't give to the horse water after you just rode it because it would kill the horse. I didn't believe it until I witnessed an incident in front of a store, two blocks above Calle Ocho. The owner had gotten off

his horse and with a hose, he lifted it up and let the horse get his drink on but all of a sudden, the horse stopped drinking water, stiffened up and fell sideways dead. I don't know if that's what killed the horse but I was always careful when I fed the horse.

. . .

So much shit was happening to me from everywhere that it was affecting my schooling. I couldn't concentrate in any class and I started to feel darkness wrapping itself around my whole being. I happened to form a friendship with some older teen in school and he one day invited me to cut school with him. At first I was weary of cutting school because of my father but then I said fuck it and hung out all day in the school grounds or to the town and when classes were over, he would go his way and I would go to the bus stop and wait for it to pick my friends and I up.

On the bus, I notice some older teen known as Popi looking at me with an hostile eye and one day after the bus driver dropped us off at home, Popi decided to come from behind and snuff me, he didn't stop the assault on me, only giving me a chance to cover my face and run away and go home but the next day in school, I saw him acting tough playing basketball. I approached him and told him to meet me outside the other basketball court outside school grounds and I turned my back to him and walked away, I could hear him and his friends talking shit about how I was to be knocked out as they were following me. Once we arrived, his friends and school kids made a circle around Popi and me, he lunged at me and I ducked and moved to the side and punched him on the jaw, the hit was so hard that it lifted him off his feet, throwing him backward between two of his friends, almost knocking all three of them to the ground. Popi fell on his back, I went towards him and stood above him for him to stand up, one of his friends pulled out a brass knuckle and threatened me to stay back, I already knew what was going to happen, when Popi got up.

They were going to jump me, I looked at him as he got on shaky legs, he was one step to going to sleep but not wanting to get hit with the brass knuckle, I turned my back and just kept on walking away from the crowd but Popi didn't

want to leave it like that he started hitting me from behind as I kept on walking away, really ignoring his punches because it felt like a baby was hitting me, he stopped after he realized that his hits weren't affecting me but in the school bus, everyone was cheering for him like he won the fight. I really didn't care because I knew that I could whip his punk ass any time because his weakness was having a glass jaw, I learned that some of the kids on Calle Ocho were afraid of him because of his height, weight and because he had supposedly a trophy for boxing, okay if that what he told my friends.

Then at home one of my father's friend had it in his mind that I was messing with his wife. It happened one day, when my father threw a party and invited his friends and their wives. My father provided alcoholic drinks, even though my father didn't drink. Everyone was in the house hanging out in the living room, one of my father's friend, left to fix himself another drink and his wife started a regular conversation with me, he heard his wife speaking to me and turned around and started screaming at me to get away from his wife, I tried to explain to him that nothing was going on but he wouldn't hear it.

He then started becoming threatening with his body and I expressed to him that I didn't want any problems but he wouldn't liste. My father was standing right there but he didn't do anything but just watched the confrontation. The guy lunged at me with a fist and I quickly ducked to one side and hit him with a right, then a left and he fell, knocking him onto his knees. He got up on his feet and came at me again, I tried to plea to him that I didn't want any problems but he rushed me quickly, hoping to get catch me off guard, I was expecting his move, and I counteracted by ducking and hitting two more times, knocking him down again.

My father yelled at me to stop and sent me to my room, Pito, Puri and some of my neighborhood friends came to the side window of my room, hyped that a sixteen-year-old beat up a twenty-eight-year-old, we were talking excitedly when I heard a banging on my door, it was the same guy I just finished beating up, he kept on banging hard at the door until he broke my door down and rushed me putting me in a bear hug hold, I wriggle away and as I was hitting him, I was going to make sure I tortured him physically for being a bitch. I started punching him on the face, changing strategy by hitting him all over

his body, I was hitting him so hard that every punch that made contact on his body, he would moan out in pain. I was beating this bitch down for over four minutes and its, when I noticed my father running into my room, stopping me from continuing assaulting his friend, he had yelled at me that I was punished and not to come out of my room. He escorted his friend away and allowed him to stay in the party.

．　．　．

I was going through so much shit and feeling guilt for having sex with males and young boys, I even had sex with a three-year-old with down syndrome or rape shock, the three-year-old would walk around the neighborhood naked. I realized that he was being abused by adults when I penetrated his rectum, his rectum was stretched so much that it made it very easy to fuck him without hurting him or using any lubrication. It felt like I was fucking a hole, the kids in the neighborhood whom I had sex with many times before told me that the three-year-old liked dick and it was what led me to stop him one day and have sex with him.

One day while cutting classes, I bumped into Pipo and he wanted me to suck his dick. We decided to go to an abandoned bathroom that was connected to one of the benches in the basketball court. The gate to the abandoned bathroom was broken off, so we both entered the bathroom stall. He pulled his pants and underwear down unto his ankles and pulled the front of his t-shirt over the back of his neck. I was just watching his erection stiffly move with his body, I couldn't take it any longer and I got on my knees and started sucking on his dick, making him ejaculate within three sucks. He didn't want me to stop, his body was moving side to side every time I made him cum, we would whisper sexual things to me, I had whisper that I wanted him to fuck me in the ass and he'll promise me every time I made him ejaculate that he would.

Pipo had gotten older and he was long with a skinny penis. I've sucked many boys off, who would cum many times but Pipo was different. I was sucking on his dick for more than an hour making him cum multiple times but he

still didn't want me to stop. Neither did I, as I sucked on him I kept on mentioning to Pipo that I wanted him to fuck me in the ass but all he wanted me to do was perform oral sex on him. We didn't take a break I just kept on sucking and making him cum when all of a sudden everything went black. When I came too I felt like I was in some else's body and being a second viewer I was horrified, as I watched my hands wrapped around Pipo's neck choking him and him trying to get out of my hold. While I was doing this, I didn't feel anything but a peaceful calmness rush all over my body and mind, all I wanted to do was take this kids life, he fell on his knees trying to free himself but failing, he starts falling backward slowly and I was following his lead, as his back was about to touch the floor, I could see that he was losing consciousness but then I heard a screeching scream and it woke me up, I quickly let him go and watched him struggling to get air, I kept on watching him after his gasping moment was over, then I walked out the bathroom as if nothing happened and every time we would bump into each other in the neighborhood. He would fearfully run away from me but long after that I made his little brother Manuel into my almost every day fuck buddy.

When I decided to say "the hell with school" was on an day that I was in class and some older teen ran into my classroom and punched me in the face. I quickly got up from my desk and ran after him before he managed to leave the classroom. I grabbed him by the back of the shirt, pulling him back roughly, as he was trying to get his footing, I grabbed a desk nearby and hit him on the face with it. He stumbled out of the classroom and I let him go. And every day after that I decided to stop going to class and hang out with the older teen, whom I first cut class with. At first it was fun and exciting but after a couple of months of doing the same shit, it was getting boring.

One day the older teen and I snuck into the third-floor classrooms peeking into each of them when on the last classroom, the older teen stood behind me and started yelling to the female teacher nasty sexual things and even threatened her and since we were locked in on the third floor, she sent for security. The older teen then climbed down unto the second floor and

onto the ground floor abandoning me, I was arrested and accused of harassing the teacher and since I wasn't a snitch, I stood quiet. The judge gave me a choice, either go to a job corp for a year old or go to juvenile jail and since I heard in the neighborhood from the kids and teens that if you get locked up, you'll wind up being raped, so I chose the job corps and I was sent to La Catalana in Barceloneta.

Chapter 21

La Catalana

La Catalana was hidden by trees on top of a mountain in the town of Barceloneta. The job corps had over twelve to thirteen cabins but seven were being occupied as sleeping quarters by the students. Upon entering La Catalana, was the first cabin on top of the mess hall, which fed everyone in La Cata. And that cabin was reserved only for the girls continuing to the left of the job corps, was the mess hall which was connected to a boys and girls bathroom and a five-foot-deep swimming pool and five or ten feet from the swimming pool area were two wooded cabins side by side each other but with a large room with two pool tables in between the two cabins attaching them both together and on the right to the cabins was the staff's cabin.

Now entering the right side of La Catalana was way different, on one right side but going up a hill was a grassy patio area with one big tree, and next to it was an abandoned cabin with a big shaded porch. Connected to this cabin were two more, which were sleeping quarters, I was in on the last cabin at the end, cabin A. Across from us were more connected cabins with a building connected to it which was used for an agricultural class (what I chose to study) of the cabins in that side only three were occupied. One was for cooking, the other for construction and the last one was for electric study students. Next

to these but going down the hill was the actually cooking class where the students learned how to cook professionally. The second one was for the mechanic study room and it was filled with car parts and car tools and these cabins where attached to the mess hall and the girls cabins now the difference between the right side was that all the cabins were made of brick and cement, while the left side of the job corps was built of wood.

On my first night in cabin A, the older students explained to me that later on in the night I had to go through a ritual, which were for all the newbies. It was a hazing, they continued explaining to me that a selected few would take a pillowcase and fill it with junk, like construction boots and haze the new comer. I was a little nervous but I didn't let it show and as darkness fell, the chosen ones started to arrive in my cabin, one of them was giving orders to the others to get the other newbies and bring us to them one by one. I watched them haze three newbies, now on the fourth newbie, I saw one of the initiators put a lock inside his pillowcase, and they started hazing this particular newbie so bad that he defecated on himself. They even made him cry. I watched as the one with the lock in his pillowcase took it out the pillow and threw it into one of the rooms, I looked at them and I was kind of weary. I gave them the look if you hit me with a lock, I will put your lights out but they assured me that they have no locks in any pillowcase. I stood in the middle of the six of them and let them haze me for a minute or so. After it was finished, they all gave me a handshake and welcomed me to La Catalana.

They explained to me that the reason they hazed the last person bad was because he wasn't a newbie. He knew how the townspeople hated all the students at the job corps and how the townspeople didn't want us in their town but that this motherfucker went down there and started getting drunk and starting problems. They continued saying that they were impressed by me for not running, then they asked me my age and I replied sixteen. They all laughed and said that for my age I was strong, as for the teen that got hazed bad, well he left by the next morning.

I went to my agriculture class, where the instructor introduced himself and all the students that were attending at that moment, the teacher explained to all of us that he would be teaching us about the magic of dirt and how to

cultivate the land and how to fuse one plant species with another. He concluded as time move on, he would teach us how to deal with farming and taking care of the livestock, which were mostly of cows. He then asked all the students to follow him out the classroom. We did and followed him down the paved road of the Cata behind the two cabins with the pool room, past a basketball court, and not much further was a big locked greenhouse. Once the teacher opened the gate, we all walked in, I could smell nothing but dirt , fresh cut grass and clean air, there were three long tables with empty flower pots or some being used, while other flower pots looked like they were half done.

The teacher explained to us the fusing process and gave us an example of a fruit. He shows us a fruit that was bigger than a volleyball and said that the reason that the fruit is that big was because it was an orange fused with a grapefruit known in Puerto Rico as "Chinronja".

After spending the day with the agriculture class I headed for my cabin but was approached by a staff member telling me that I had to move from cabin A to cabin E, which was the cabin attached to the pool room and cabin F. After being in the cabin E for more than a month, I had my first fight, it was some heavy set seventeen-year-old, who was trying to impress his older brother and thought that he found a victim. He sneak snuffed me and during our battle he managed to break my nose, I didn't noticed until another student broke us up and told me to look at myself in the mirror of the bathroom, the fight was in back of our cabin on the basketball court, I went into the bathroom of my cabin and man was I mad when I saw the front of my nose pointing to the left.

The same friend who told me to look at myself tried to place my nose back in place but to no avail. Then we went to see the nurse where I told her that I fell from the top bunk and hit my nose coming down, she checked my nose and said that she couldn't do anything about the nose that my nose will stay bent in that position forever. I said to myself, don't worry your nose won't stay like, it will be fixed one way or another and true to my word I did just that.

I went to the teen that I had fought and told him that he had to fix my nose, he asked me how, and I responded, "by punching it back in place", I put my face forward and his fist connect onto my nose you, afterwards we gave each other hugs and shook hands out of respect and went our separate ways. I

was laughing to myself when I asked him to punch me on the face, he looked at me like I was crazy and joking. I convinced him that I wasn't joking and I reassured him that I won't hit back. He agreed and we went to the back of our cabin and onto the basketball court, where I watched as his punch connected to my nose, his hits was hard rocking my head sideways and that's when I heard the crunch sound and that was it, the teen said that it looked straighter and we went into our cabin's bathroom and I checked for myself, it had gotten back to normal but you could see a slight crookedness to my nose that but night the teen, his older brother, and I got drunkenly hammered.

· · ·

La Catalana was a job corps for teens ages sixteen to twenty-one and every teen had a fucked background with families who got tired of them after someone corrupted their innocence making them unmanageable. Then you had the court appointee's like myself "we were the fuck ups", and to have the townspeople hating us. It was like we were the unwanted everywhere. The occupants of La Catalana were afraid of going into the town because they were getting beat up. I promised myself that I was going to change how the townspeople saw us but didn't know how at the moment. There were still some rotten apples messing it up for everyone else but I had to wait for an opportunity to do so and it came.

I was moved back to cabin A and a female student who was a student assistant to the instructor in the agriculture class was hanging out with all cabin A inhabitants. She was trying to find someone to go down into town and buy a half a gallon of Bacardi liquor but everyone was shaking their heads no, because they were too scared to go into town and since I wasn't scared, I volunteered to go, the female assistant gave me the money and asked me how am I going to bring the liquor up here, I only responded by requesting for her to give me the greenhouse keys, she responded with "what am I going to do with the keys" and I just looked at her without replying, she gave me the keys reluctantly.

I left through the front of the job corps and followed the instructions which led me through to a shorter way into town. It was a dark journey but

thank God for the brightness of the moon I made it down the mountainous hill to where people was hanging out or just walking. When they saw me they knew I was from La Catalana and they all tensed up, I went into the store and two men followed me into the store, even the store worker was looking at me like "go ahead do something stupid and we're show you how much we hate you" but when I opened my mouth and started speaking in a broken down Spanish requesting for a half a gallon of Barcardi, and I noticed their whole attitudes changed and when they spoke to me, it was in a welcoming tone, they knew that I was a New York Rican.

I approached one of the two men that enter the store, and whispered to him, if he knew where I can get some weed. He asked me to follow him and I did, we went outside the store and walked further down the block. He then turned around and said in Spanish, "yes that he sells weed but in joint form". I asked him the price and being that they were cheap, I bought more than five joints.

Now going back, I didn't go the front way, I had to follow a trail that led deep up in the first part of the mountain passing some private houses and onto the second part of the mountain going up the path that led into the back of La Catalana. I was told by some of the students that its very scary at night but I brushed it off like I wasn't scared but now as I am going up the dark forested mountain, I started to get paranoid and scared every noise made by the wooded mountain. I would imagine some type of creature lurking for a human meal. I approached the broken fence, which surrounds La Catalana and walked up a little further towards the greenhouse, I unlocked the door went in and started looking for the biggest flower pot that the liquor can go in, finding none, I decided to tuck it in my pants waist, once secured, I took two flower pots that had dirt and a plant on each one, I used those flower pots to cover the bulge that the liquor bottle was making, I locked up and headed to cabin A, I was walking pass the staff headquarters and a staff stopped me and asked me what was I doing with the two plants, I replied that my teacher had asked for one of the students to get these two specific plants, to teach us how to hybrid plants, and as I was speaking to the staff, out the corner of my eyes, I saw some of the students that sent me to the store, they looked scared when I was stopped but

when the staff was satisfied with my answer and let me go, the students started walking towards cabin A and on the down low with a smile on their faces.

I passed cabin A and headed to the locked agricultural classroom. Once inside, I put down the two plants on one of the tables, the assistant and all those who chipped in walked in right behind me, they all cheered, congratulated me in not getting caught and when they all saw where I had the liquor, they all laughed saying that they wouldn't of think of doing that but when the celebratory moment was over, they were telling me that they were scared I was going to get caught and snitch on them to get out of trouble. I didn't reply because I knew that I wouldn't snitch even if I did caught but that night not only did I earn their respect and love but we all got drunk and high.

· · ·

After a few months in La Catalana, I wasn't counting on how many days I had left to do of the one year given to me, I was too busy enjoying myself and having fun but one day I woke up in a bad mood and as the teacher drove us to La Finca (the barn) and teaching us how to drive a tractor trailer as well as on how to round up and deal with the cows and bulls. I was extremely irritated by all of them. The teacher gave us a break and all the students decided to jump in pond to cool off, I went and even tried to be part of the horse play but it still didn't change my irritation.

After an hour of either swimming or walking around and viewing the scenery, which resembles the old western days with nothing but mountains, hills, and low stretches of grassy land, my teacher told us that it was time to go back to the job corps and that I would driving us to the barn. I told him that I didn't know how to drive especially stick shift, the teacher reassured me that everything would be okay, as I got on the driver side, the teacher explained to me on how start a stick shift vehicle and use the clutch, gas and breaks and I being gifted with being a fast learner, understood the instruction and started to drive, I started weaving in and out the road at the beginning but then I got the hang of it.

The students started making fun at my driving and even the teacher had joined in too and though I was proud of my learning how to drive, I was still

irritated by the teacher and the students. I really didn't want to be around human beings, so I decided to get even, the road I was driving was split by thorn trees on both sides with fenced sections belonging to the farm we were heading to return the tractor. I drove to one side, where some of the students were either sitting or standing and let the thorny branches brush their upper body and face, then I did it to the other side, where the teacher and the rest of the students were. I then returned to the road, the teacher and all the students were yelling in pain and complaining. I had a smirk on my face and when the teacher told me to get off and let another student drive, I responded "no that everything is alright and it won't happen again", I drove without incident into the barn, as I was waited for everyone to get off. I felt someone staring at me. I got off the tractor and turned to where I felt the staring from and I saw a thirteen or four-teen-year-old boy staring at me, as he continued to stare at me and I stared back. I knew what that looked meant, it was the "I'm interested sex" look. I tried to ignore him but I liked the way he looked. He had a tannish skin com-plexion with long dirty blond curly hair that almost reached his shoulders and I knew that he would do anything, he awoke my lust and by the way I continued to stare at him, it was to let him know that if we were alone, we're be fucking, I heard my teacher call out my name and telling me to get on the pickup truck, I left and wished that the kid and I would have had a chance to have sex.

That kid awoke my lust and it almost took over me. One day, when I awoke from an afternoon nap in cabin A, across from me was a dark brown hairless eighteen-year-old on the top bunk, naked masturbating slowly and speaking to someone on the top bunk of my bed, I caught an erection just watching his actions, I fantasize him putting me to suck on his big dick and him fucking me slowly, I was watching as his body started trembling and shak-ing and his sperm started shooting out landing on his chest and stomach, I wanted to get on top of him and lick all the cum off his body, I held to my urge and waited until everyone in the cabin was gone and masturbated until my penis hurt but that still didn't work.

A few days later, it was the same dark brown teen who was taking a shower and I, I lay on my bed sideways and started to masturbate slowly and fantasiz-ing that I was in the shower with him having sex. I ejaculated so hard that the

first squirt of cum hit the wall behind me and as I empty myself on my chest, stomach, and groin, I felt like I was going to faint from the pleasure. I relaxed for a few seconds more and quickly fixed myself, wiped my sperm filled hands on my blanket, and laid there to gather my breath and relax and I did it just in time because the brown-skinned kid appeared on the front door of the room, naked and with an erection. It was like he knew I was doing something sexual and I'm not going to lie, If he would have walked in while I was masturbating, we would have been having hardcore sex.

There were a couple of teens my age or older that if they would have exposed themselves to me or asked me if I wanted to either have sex with them or perform oral sex on them, I would have, but not only did I fight the homosexual urges with the teens in the job corps but in town too.

I befriended three adult males ages ranging from their mid-twenties to their early thirties and because of how I represented myself, they started to let students from La Catalana come down without the townspeople intimidating them but in the town was a group of ten to twelve teens, all ranging from twelve to fifteen-year-olds, and I looking very young with a husky body would hang out with them until my three adult friends arrived in town, so I could hang out with them and chill. I noticed them giving me the eye of sexual interest and though I was lusting badly, I fought hard even when the same thirteen-year-old would always approach me and pull me aside to tell me on how he would fuck a male in the ass, he was making it hard but once my adult friends appeared, I would quickly leave and go hang out with my three adult males until dark.

My presence in the town was an everyday thing, as soon as the agriculture class was over, I would go down and hang out with the townspeople, especially my three adult friends, they would tell me why they dislike the kids of La Catalana. It boils down to this, every time the students would come down, they would steal and start problems with the townspeople, so the townspeople put a stop to the bullshit and since my presence in town. I changed their look on us were I managed for nothing to happen to the students but one night, six months into my stay in La Catalana, some black skin seventeen-year-old who stood in my cabin named Quakula, had gone down to town and after hours later, he came back to the cabin and stood silent.

Something like fifteen minutes passed by when a staff knocked on the cabin door requesting to see me, I open the door and a short fiftyish man was speaking to me nervously, telling me that there was three men with guns looking for Quakula and that they were going come in and search for him if they had to, the staff asked me to please speak to them. I left my cabin without replying to the staff and as I headed to the front gates. I noticed that the job corps area was completely deserted. I could see everyone looking out the window of their cabins, I reached the front gates and it was my three adult friends and they were explosively angry, they were yelling at me about a teen they were describing as Quakula went into town and started drinking, as he was getting drunk, he was flirting sexually with women and disrespecting the females in town that he even disrespected some of the males and they wanted justice. I spoke to my friends for a while calming them down, I reassured them to leave it up to me that justice will be done. They agreed to let me deal with the situation, then I walked them half way down the mountain talking shit, I gave them all a ghetto handshake and I went back to La Catalana, as I entered the gates, all the students and staff were cheering on me and thanking me. I went into my cabin and told the students what Quackula did and they all gave him such a bad hazing that he fled never coming back to La Catalana, the next day I went into town and announced that justice was served and he fled for his life and everything went back to normal and it was a good thing that he left because if that situation didn't happen, I was about to lose on my lust and let him fuck me.

Quakula was an ugly seventeen-year -old skinny dark skin kid and one day while we were in the barns field, there was a thirteen-year-old light skin boy, who was the instructor's nephew riding a house and telling us where we should make holes in the ground, so we could start building fences. As some of the students and I were working, the thirteen-year couldn't keep his eyes off me. I wanted to have sex with him but there wasn't anywhere we could hide but after the students and I were finished, we all headed back to La Catalana and to my surprise, the instructor asked me if the thirteen-year-old could take a shower in my dorm, I replied with a "yes" and it was Quakula, the thirteen year old and I alone in the cabin. Quakula went into his room and laid down, the thirteen-year-old spoke to me for a minute while I was in my room, he

wasn't talking about anything but after he finished, he went to the bathroom and went into the shower. I was in my room lusting to have sex with him and wondering if he was giving me a signal. I had a hard on and I couldn't take it any longer. I went into the bathroom and pulled my shorts and underwear and sat on the toilet that faced the shower, the thirteen year old was in, I sat back and let see my erected penis and boy he not only was staring at it but he started getting clumsy. I knew then that he wanted to have sex and just as I got naked and was about to enter the shower he was in, when the instructor knocked on the door, I couldn't answer because I had a massive throbbing hard on, I went into another shower and faced the wall letting the cold try to bring my erection down, Quakula was the one that answered the door and the instructor yelled the thirteen-year-old, if he was finished, the kid replied "almost" and the Instructor left, I still had an erection but I started masturbating slowly, while lathering my body with soap, the was watching and I could see the burning urge in eyes but he quickly dried up and got dressed and told me goodbye and left.

I was still in the shower masturbating slowly while fantasizing the kid and I fucking in the shower. I was still facing the wall when Quakula walked in naked with an long erection masturbating slowly. I couldn't take my eyes off his long black skinny dick. He sat on the toilet that faced my shower and continued to masturbate and look at me. I was giving him a hint that I was horny by me lathing my fat butt cheeks and opening them, while I stuck my soapy finger in my rectum, he started masturbating faster but stopped and told me to leave the bathroom. I finished showering but left the bathroom and into my room, where I finished masturbated, then got dressed and went to sleep.

• • •

Then one stormy night while hanging out with the townspeople, it started to rain hard with thunder and lightning. Everyone ran to their homes, but I had taken another shortcut that lead me to the front of the job corps. In doing so I had to follow a trail that led through other people's properties. As I was struggling going up the trail, I happened to glance at something that made me stand

still and stare. It was the most beautiful girl I've ever seen and she was smiling at me struggling up the trail. I was completely drenched from the heavy rainfall and as I stood stuck on her beauty, my focus was broken by her mother inviting me to sit with them until the storm calmed down. I did and I was given a sitting space between them.

We were quiet for some time just watching the rain fall and for some reason I knew that they knew I wasn't a native of Puerto Rico, they asked me where I was from and I responded with my funny accent, I told them where I was born and how life is in New York is. The mother changed the questioning by asking me how I liked Puerto Rico. I answered "I like it but the bad thing about everything is that everything closes early". I explained to the things were different in New York, there were stores and businesses that were twenty-four hours open. They both started laughing and the mother replied "don't worry you'll get used to it". Every time I would speak, I would glance at this beautiful brown-skinned girl with mid-back long black curly hair and light brown eyes. It made my heart jump and beat fast, I was actually in love, and as the rain started to calm down and as I was preparing to head back to the corps., the mother told me to pass by anytime.

I did, every day I would go down to this families house and hang out, the family had introduced themselves to me but I always used to forget the girl's name, whom I found out was two years younger than I was, I was not sexually in love, I really wanted to be with this girl for the rest of my life and when the girl and I spent time alone together on the front porch, I would be lost as she held my hand and looked into my eyes while talking to me, she made me forget my pain and suffering and when we started an actual relationship, the mother invited me for dinner.

I accepted her invitation for the next day and I arrived at a certain time, so I could spend it with my girlfriend on the porch. When dinner was ready the mother came outside to the porch and told us to go inside an eat. I followed the girl into the kitchen where there was a big dinner table able to seat six people, I sat next to my girl and waited for everyone to be seated, the mother was serving everyone- one by one, she introduced me to her husband and her fifteen-year son, who was as beautiful as his sister.

The father wasn't bothered by my relationship with his daughter. He was very friendly about it and as we all sat and started eating, we all spoke idle conversation and after dinner, I excused myself to everyone except my girl, and we went back into the porch and sat down quietly holding hands looking down to the scenery below us, I loved her and it wasn't sexual, I would wait until she made the move or was ready. I wanted it to be special but her brother was jealous of our relationship and he wanted to have quality time with me to get to know me but as time passed I knew that he was interested in me sexually. he would flirt with me some times in a way that if someone would of been paying attention they would think that something sexual was going on between me and the fifteen-year-old. He was starting to making it tough for me because he acted like a regular fifteen-year but with a hidden feminine side and that shit turned me on and every time I hung out with the fifteen-year-old, my lust and my past was slowly creeping up on me.

Everything that my girl erased was coming back and I was losing the battle with my homosexual urges. I remember one early afternoon I invited her brother to come to town and play some pool with me. We played a couple of games and in one of the games to let him know I wanted to have sex with him, he stood at the entrance of the door to the pool room and I stood so close behind him that my flaccid penis rubbed between his buttocks, I even held him a from behind with my arms wrapped around him in a tender embrace.

He was interfering with his sister's relationship and it was going to do was end up in embarrassment, humiliation, heartbreak, and pain, and to avoid all that I started to hang out less and less in town and with my girl until I just stop going down into town but when I did go into town, I would do so on the down low to avoid bumping into anyone I know it pained me in doing this but she deserved to be with someone who wants to be with her, not in a hidden gay relationship.

· · ·

Behind that necessary break up, it took a toll on me and my past was coming in and out of my mind in mental pictures. I was starting to get so stressed out that I had two fights and on both of them I didn't do anything to defend myself

but just take the beating, feeling nothing as the punches hit my face and upper body. The last fight was because someone was preaching the word of God and I snatched the Bible from his hands and threw it on the floor and spat on it.

I was so stressed out that I didn't want to be around human beings, so when the staff mandatory sent all the students to wherever they were living, for the weekend. I stood alone and hungry in my cabin until the weekend was over and everyone returned to La Catalana but when I did decide to go to my father's on the weekends and deal with his torturous bullshit, I would spend the day having gay sex with whoever was willing and ready. I remember one incident, where my father took me to Arecibo to his family in El Cerro de Maravilla to chill and I started hanging out with my half-sister's from a different mother two brothers, a nine-year-old named Joel and his six-year-old brother named Bebe, at their request, we went down to the mountain side road, where I sat on a big boulder and BeBe stood standing right beside me. We were watching another mountain across from us with plans of hiking there, when all of a sudden I noticed Bebe standing right next to me but with an exposed erection. Seeing that it was long like Pito when Pito was his age, I wanted to fully pull his pants down and suck his dick but I didn't because I didn't want him, I wanted Joel and I was trying to find a way to persuade Joel to let me suck his dick. I've asked him many times before but he rejected me. Joel had also witnessed what his brother did but didn't pay mind to him after chilling on the boulder for a while, BeBe put his erect penis back in his pants and we went back up our mountain.

Joel went home to watch television but Bebe told me to follow him. I followed him into a shed that is supposed to be a bathroom, when my father finishes building the house, we entered the shed and closed the door, I asked Bebe if he wanted me to suck his dick and he replied "yeah" and got naked. He put his clothes on some cinder blocks that was piled and I kneed in front of him and started to suck, kiss, and lick on his penis and balls. After a couple of minutes of me preforming oral sex on Bebe, I realized that he couldn't ejaculate but I continued to suck him off as he stood. Bebe then stopped me and laid on his clothes that were on top of the cinder blocks and told me to continue suck him off, we were down in the shed for more than an hour, I even lick and

sucked on his outer and inner butt cheeks and his asshole but after some time, we stopped and I help Bebe put on his pants, we both then exited the shed together and he went home and I went to hang out in my aunt Wanda's house with my cousins.

Another of my cousins approached me and stated that a movie was going to be watched at Bebe's house and that we were all invited. I only went to Bebe's house to see if Bebe and I could sneak out and go for round two but just as I was about to get comfortable in Bebe's house, his mother approached me and confronted me about how she was bathing Bebe and he caught an erection, she then asked him what made him like that and he responded that I was sucking on his dick. Joel hearing the conversation jumped in and said that I too had asked him to suck his dick, Bebe's mother asked me if it was true but I was so embarrassed and humiliated that I left the house, the hill and headed straight for the job corps.

I walked part way to the La Catalana but the rest of the way, I hitch hiked a ride and ever since then on every mandatory weekend, I would stay hidden in the cabin and go two days without eating and by Monday morning I would wake up shaking from the hunger.

Then one mandatory weekend some church people came to do one of their church revivals for their flock and since all the students of the job corps had to left for the weekend, the church people slept in cabin F. They didn't know I was there until Saturday night when I was moving in secrecy and I happened to bump into two teenagers. I quickly disappeared but they had told the churchgoers about me. I decided to show myself early Sunday morning and the churchgoers weren't bothered by my presence and after answering a couple of personal questions, I hung out with the two teens at their request.

I walked them around the job corps giving them a tour and telling them what life is like here, I walked them up the hill almost heading towards my cabin but stopped on the abandoned cabin with the big porch that overlooked the bottom part of the job corps. The teens and I sat on the porches cemented banister just having idle conversation and watching the churchgoers prepare for the church's ceremony and dinner. I asked them if they wanted to see the inside of my cabin and they both shook their heads up and

down, saying yes without words, I snuck them into my cabin and showed them the three bedrooms, one bedroom had three double bunk beds, the other one had two double bunk beds and the last room had one double bunk bed, then I took them to the bathroom and showed them the two shower stalls without curtains and the two toilet area with a wall in between the two toilet bowls. We then went to one of the rooms and sat on the beds and talked about nothing important and after a couple of minutes longer, we left the cabin and walked back to the abandoned cabin with the porch that over-looked the bottom half of the job corps.

The two teens, a fifteen-year-old that was over six feet tall and over three hundred pounds, had a handsome face but that was it and the other teen was a thirteen-year-old, who was of normal height but on the verge of being obese and we were having a nice chat when the thirteen-year-old changed it to mas-turbation, and how one time, he went to a school trip and while he was sitting down, some female passed by him and tripped falling on his lap. When she got off of him, he had an erection. All this sex talk was making me horny want-ing to have sex, the fifteen-year-old left and it was the thirteen-year-old and me and he wanted me to take him to the back section of my cabin to sit down on the grass.

We laid on our backs on the ground having idle conversation but I was super horny. I interrupted the thirteen-year-old and asked him if he wanted me to suck his dick and balls he didn't reply, all he did was unzip his pants and pulled them down to expose his erect penis. I sucked on his dick and balls until he was on the verge of ejaculating but he stopped me and fixed himself. He then asked me if there was somewhere he could go and wet his erect penis, so he could pour cold water on his penis and make it flaccid. I took him to the side of the agricultural class, to where there was a hose connect to the water valve. He whipped his erected penis and I quickly pulled my shorts and under down and asked him to fuck me in the ass, he approached and penetrated me hard, he banged me for a couple of seconds, then stopped and went to the hose and watched him pour water on his penis making his erection go down. He fixed himself and he and I went into different destinations, I went to the cabin to masturbate and he went with the churchgoers.

Later that night I went looking for the thirteen-year-old to see if we could finish what we started but I couldn't find him but I did see the fifteen-year near the patio tree area which led to the abandoned cabin with the porch. I approached the fifteen year old and he had his erect penis out of his pants, his back was towards the churchgoers that was either walking around or sitting on wooden benches near the gate or around the front of the job corps, anyone looking in our direction could see we were doing something sexual, I didn't care and I whipped up my penis which was way longer than the fifteen year old, even Pito's penis was longer than the fifteen year old, we started rubbing our penises together, while we were getting ourselves sexually aroused, I noticed the thirteen year old sitting on a bench with his father crying, they were talking for some time, then they stood sitting down quietly but with the thirteen year old still crying.

The fifteen-year-old and I were rubbing our penises against each other faster and faster and I told him to follow me into my cabin so we could fuck, we put our penises away and started to walk further up the patio area to not draw any attention to us, as we headed towards the back section of my cabin I noticed the thirteen-year-old's father glancing at us. I knew then that the thirteen-year-old told his father. It was confirmed when the father approached us midway to my cabin and the father asked us what we were doing and we both answered nothing. The father of the thirteen then told the fifteen-year-old to go with the churchgoers, when he left the father turned to me and called me all kinds of names and told me to stay away from his son, I did but later on that night before the churchgoers left La Catalana, the fifteen-year-old snuck out from his congregation to my cabin to tell me what the thirteen-year-old told his father, the teen told his father that I forced him into gay sex, which was a fucking lie.

· · ·

The father didn't tell staff about the incident but I was upset by the teen's lie, he started the sexual conversation and he allowed me to perform oral sex on him, I guess by being in church, he felt guilty of having gay sex or having homosexual

tendency but I didn't give a fuck and as the days turned into weeks and months, I would hang out with a small group of paint thinner sniffers, and participate in their activities and every time I sniffed cine (pronounced ceene last letter is almost silent, its Spanish for paint thinner), I would feel all my problems and stress in my life and mind disappear, I felt at peace with myself, so I made sniffing paint thinner my escape from my problems and reality but one night everything changed and I crashed mentally and emotionally.

I was sniffing paint thinner with my get high group when all of a sudden I blanked out and the most craziest shit happened, I woke up standing by the side of a bunk bed watching my body conversing violently and screaming I wanted to die, as this was going on, I saw everyone in the cabin run outside, I returned gazing at my conversing body and I started thinking that I must not only be hallucinating but dreaming as well but the screaming that was coming out of my mouth and how my body was thrashing this way and that way on the bed made me think something spooky was happening to me, I then saw the residents that ran out return with staff and the female cook, who liked me as a son, she started crying as soon as she saw my body going crazy yet no one knew what to do, then I watched as my body stopped conversing, get up from the bed and walked into a living room like area of the cabin and stand in front of all of us, and started to scream that I wanted to die to everyone. I then saw one of my cabin mates stand behind me and punch me on the back of my neck and everything went black.

I regained consciousness on the floor with a crowd of students and staff around me. Two of my cabin mates helped me up from the floor and I went to sleep, nut the next day while eating breakfast, I was looking down on my tray and the figure that appeared, when I was dreaming about the water slide, when I was ten-years-old and tried to pull me under, appeared again, I forced the rest of the breakfast down and went back to my cabin and slept the whole day.

I stopped sniffing cine but continued to hang out with the paint-thinning sniffing crew, one night one of my get high friends invited me to sniff some paint thinner with him. I declined but he went into the cabin's bathroom to get high. I stood outside with two other residents just chatting and after some time passed by, I heard my friend in the cabin say hoarsely "I can't breathe",

but I didn't pay him no mind because he was always pranking people and I thought that since he was getting high, he was going to start with his pranking games but then I heard a thud like someone falling and I ran into cabin's bathroom and saw that my friend was on the floor unconscious, I picked him up in a cradle position and took him outside to the front of the cabin and laid him on his back on the concrete floor and tried to feel a pulse on a specific spot on his neck area but I was doing it wrong since I couldn't find a pulse. I then checked to see if I could feel him breathing and he wasn't, I then position his head upward to stretch his wind pipe and I administered mouth to mouth, on my first breath into his mouth, it felt like I dislodged something in his throat because when I did that he awoke coughing uncontrollably and gasping for air, the ambulance was called and they arrived, my friend was too weak to stand up, so the paramedics helped him onto a stretcher. As the paramedics were putting him in the ambulance I volunteered to ride and go to the hospital with my friend.

In the hospital, I explained to the doctor what happened and he started getting ready to take blood from my friend's arm but the doctor was having trouble drawing blood and when the doctor pulled out the syringe from my friends arm, I could see why my friend's blood was coming out his arm almost like a jelly-like substance. The doctor continued to physically examine him, then he left the waiting room. It wasn't until hours later did the doctor return to tell me that there is evidence around his throat that there was a blood clot and that he was lucky for me for providing mouth to mouth but he also said that my friend wasn't out of the woods because his blood is starting to harden, my job corps was called and I was picked up hours later and headed for La Catalana and as for my friend, I never saw him again, I don't know if he survived or died.

My friend was damaged like everyone else in this story and after those who took our innocence and threw us away after they drained us completely and we became uncontrollable. Some of us choose to commit suicide to escape from the pain and suffering and others escape into the world of drugs making their life even worst. I am not including the small percentage of those that lives a productive life who managed to survive. Where do I fall in these categories,

just put it this way, I wake up and go to sleep every second, minute, hour, day and year of my life, wanting to die and sometimes in my nightmares the feeling of wanting to die feels even stronger.

. . .

One weekend, I decided to go home and things were quiet between my father and I for a while but I knew that a storm was brewing between us and it didn't help with the strong feeling of not wanting my presence around. I did everything not to be around my father's surrounding, if it wasn't having sex with the boys in my hood, I would be smoking cigarettes that I stole from my father's pack in secret with some of my friends. I noticed that across the street from where I lived, a family of four moved in, a couple with two sons, a thirteen year old skinny kid with black curly hair and a twelve year old cerebral paisley kid in a wheel chair.

That night Pito and I were invited to chill with the two brothers, while the parent went out on a date. My father allowed us to go over there. The parents had left and Danny the twelve year old was put to sleep in one of the rooms, Junior the thirteen-year-old, who everyone in the neighborhood called "Ganzo" was sitting on a big sofa with very short pants, Pito nudged me and with his lower chin, pointed towards Ganzo, who had his legs spread wide open. We noticed he wasn't wearing any underwear and no matter how he position himself, he would always be exposing his fat penis and big balls, I tried not to stare but I was sexually interested, he was pretending to be asleep and I wanted to grab on his penis and jerk it off. Ganzo woke up catching Pito and me looking at his groin but didn't say anything, we three chilled and watched a movie, then Pito and I returned home but the next day, my father volunteered me to cut the grass down around the Ganzo's family property.

I was cutting the grass with the machete and as I got around the house I could hear Ganzo telling someone to dance like that, I looked into the window and he was laying on his bed, while two little girls dancing over him in their panties, I didn't interrupt him because I was getting turned on to the point of wanting to masturbate in their names. I fought my urges by working on the

yard harder and it work by the time I finished cutting the grass around the house, the urge to masturbate was gone.

I knew then that Ganzo was sexually active and damaged and because of that, I was had a reason to come home every mandatory weekend, and every time I came to stay for the weekend, the more I got to know Ganzo. I knew he was like me but different. He told me that his little six year old female cousin Chapita, came to his house one day when he was home alone and he got her to get naked with him and he rubbed his penis all over her vagina wanting to penetrate but they got caught and he was punished for having sex with her.

Now his two little sisters were sent to other family due to Ganzo trying to have sex with them but not soon after, his family allowed a ten-year-old female, an aunt to Ganzo, stay home alone with Ganzo all night and when I woke up in the morning getting ready to eat breakfast, I could over hear my father telling Carmen and one of Carmen's friends, how all night he could hear the girl screaming painfully piercing screams and how some of the neighbors were screaming out for them to stop the screaming, yet no one had the decency to check what the fuck was going on with those screams.

I knew why the little girl was screaming, because Ganzo was raping and penetrating her all night. I was snapped out of my thoughts, when all of a sudden the little girl appeared in the front door. I went to her and opened the screen door. I noticed that she was shaking very bad, I asked her what was wrong and she asked if she could have some pancake mix so Ganzo can cook. I felt a rage engulf my body and mind, I fought hard to not go into the same darkness I was in when I tried to kill my sex buddy Pipo and my father. The moment was broken when my father told the girl to come on in, she entered but stood next to Pito and me. Carmen gave her a cup and asked the little girl, if she was okay and the girl still trembling answered "yes". I was going into a daze staring at a kitchen knife that was on the table, what I wanted to do was go into the house and cut his penis off but when I glanced at my father, I saw an evil gleam in his eyes, as he was looking at me, I knew then that if I did anything to Ganzo, my father would give me up, so I decided to get Ganzo in another way.

Ganzo was starting to show sexual interest in Pito and I used Pito as bait so I could get Ganzo and make him sexually dependent on me but I had to wait until the next weekend. Mandatory or not I was coming and knowing that my father didn't want me around, made me want to come home more.

The next weekend arrived and I was at my father's house. My father and Carmen had to go out early that day and they left us home alone. Pito, Puri and I, knew that our parents were coming late, while Puri chilled by herself, Pito and I took care of the animals, making sure that they had fresh water and were fed. After we were done with the chores, Pito and I went straight to Ganzo's house, something we already planned, we entered the house and chilled in the living room with Danny the cerebral paisley kid. Ganzo appeared from doing whatever it was he was doing in one of the rooms. Pito and I told Ganzo if he could put his brother in another room because we wanted to talk sexual things. Ganzo quickly rolled his brother into a back room and closed the door, as he did that Pito and I got naked, Ganzo returned to the living room, he saw that Pito and I had an erection and we were slowly masturbating, then I started jerking Pito off, Ganzo thirsty like a fiend went straight for Pito. Ganzo was rubbing his penis on Pito's buttock, Pito stopped Ganzo and told him that in order for Ganzo to fuck him, he had to fuck me.

I thought that I was lustful but seeing the way Ganzo was acting, I knew that if an animal would have been in front of him, he would have had sex with it. He too got undressed and sat with his legs spread wide open. I went in between and started preforming oral sex on Ganzo. When I felt he was about to ejaculate, I stopped and got up, I was feeling the fire of lust burning my body and I just sat on his penis penetrating hard and making me not only jump in pain but scream out too, I continued to ride him and when I felt him ready to explode. I got off him and got dressed, Pito also follow suit, Ganzo was begging us to let him finish but Pito and I said "no, next time", he was embarrassingly begging for either Pito or I to let him fuck us and cum. We still replied no and we left.

The next day, Pito and I did the same thing again and we again denied him sexual pleasure but the fag got even, he saw Pito and I smoke a cigarette and he asked if he could have one, I stole a whole pack of cigarettes from my

father's stash, so I gave one to Ganzo, after we finished smoking, Pito and I left Ganzo's house and I stashed the pack of cigarettes in Ganzo front lawn, Ganzo saw me but I knew he wouldn't touch them.

Pito went home and I went and hung out with my friends until after dark, I return home and my father tells me to sit down next to him, I did and my father was telling me how Ganzo was caught smoking and he said that you gave him the cigarettes. I couldn't respond, I couldn't even deny it because the cigarettes were my father's and he bought somewhere else and it's a brand not found in the neighborhood stores, he then pulled out the pack of cigarettes I stashed in Ganzo's front lawn and my father ordered me to eat each cigarette with the filter included and threatened to kill me if I didn't, I don't why I ate them when all I had to do was say no and if my father tried to get physical just beat the bitch down. I knew for a fact that my father wouldn't be able to withstand my physical assault on him but his control on me made me eat every single cigarette, the taste was disgusting making me extremely nauseous. After I was done, I went to my room and fell asleep.

]The next morning my father took me to La Catalana and dropped me off at the front gates and left without saying anything to me. I started to get nauseous, so I put my middle finger down my throat to make me vomit. What came out was cigarette filters and tobacco. After I vomited everything and the nausea feeling went away. I entered La Catalana like nothing ever happened.

The next weekend I went home. I awoke early and my father and Carmen had left us home alone, Pito had disappeared for hours and when he came back, he had a box of assorted donuts, which we never had. I asked him where he got the donuts and he replied that Ganzo traded the box so he could fuck Pito in the ass, Pito even let me know that Ganzo wants to fuck me in the ass.

Late at night, I went to take a shower on the outside of bathroom across from my room, I finished taking a shower and peeked to see if anyone in the house could see me, seeing no one, I ran nakedly into my room, I was startled by Ganzo standing inside my room with his erect penis in his hand, I bent in front of him and let him penetrate me, he was ramming me hard and fast. When I felt he was about to ejaculate, I stopped him and got on my knees and perform oral sex on him, and just as he was about to cum, I stopped him and

told him something to make him run out my room in fear, I told him that I thought I heard my father open the house door to come outside and Ganzo was gone, he went through the back of the house climb into someone else's property and into the road and went home.

I had Ganzo going crazy wanting to fuck me. It got so bad that he had tried to rape Pito in the garage even though they had sex, Ganzo was really trying to violently rape Pito. I intervened by punching Ganzo on his face making him stagger backwards. After the hit, I just whooped his ass, he ran out of my property crying like a bitch but as time passed, he called the cops on me, the cops questioned me and I told them a lie and the cops told us to chill the fuck out, I don't know why I didn't tell the cops that Ganzo tried to rape Pito but I defended him yet Ganzo still was going sex crazy wanting to fuck me.

The next day, I went an hung out with a boy that wanted me to suck his dick, so we walked a block away from my house into an abandoned house and property. We had sex until he couldn't ejaculate any longer and his penis couldn't stay erect, we stopped, got dressed and left the property, I looked down my block and saw Puri entering the property, then as I was walking slowly towards my house, I saw Ganzo look both ways of the street not noticing me and run into my property. I ran as fast as could because our parents weren't there and I knew he was going to rape Puri, I reached the gates and Ganzo had locked the gate. I jumped over the fence and ran into the house but the motherfucker had managed to run through the other entrance of the house, jumping into two other people's property.

Puri told me that he had her dress lifted and was about to whip his dick out but stopped when he heard me jumping the gate. I told Pito what happened and to watch Puri. If Ganzo comes for her that to stab him but we didn't have to do anything because Ganzo couldn't control his sexual appetite, so his mother sent him somewhere to the United States with his father.

After Ganzo left, I didn't go back for the weekend, whether mandatory or not, I had three months left to do in the job corps and two months left to graduate from my agricultural class. I was thinking of staying another year but then I started hanging out with Abel, a student in the mechanic class, we got real close like brothers and he asked me one day, since he is leaving in a couple of

a days to his house, if I wanted to live with him and his family, I replied yes and Abel told me to give him a couple of days and he will give me an answer.

While waiting for Abel to get an answer from his father, I and some other teenager got into some trouble and our punishment was to pick up every cigarette butt around the whole job corps and to cut down two big trees that were interfering with the job corps gate. After the older teen and I finished picking up all the cigarette butts, I told the teen not to worry that I have the keys to my agricultural class and I'll get the necessary tools to make cutting down the trees easier. I went and got two tree saws and gave one to the teen. We cut the two trees down in no time and since we were both in the mood, we agreed to cutting the trees all around La Catalana, it took us two days to do it but while we were cutting trees around the mountain we found a little cave with a blanket covering the entrance, we checked inside the cave and we saw was a tin tray that held candles to give light inside the cave but after the work was finish, La Catalana could be seen for miles and miles away.

Abel approached me a few day later and told me that his father didn't mind me living with them and after some days passed, Abel's father came and picked us up. I was staying with Abel and his family just a few days when early one morning, I woke up and went outside the tin and woodened one-story three bedroom house to the water faucet and brush my teeth and wash my face, when suddenly a car stopped in of Abel's family front gate. I walked outside and approached the car, there were two big well-built men in the car and one of then asked me if I knew Arnaldo Montero, my stupid ass not knowing anything amiss, replied "si, eso so yo" "yes that's me", they both got out of the car and told me that I was under arrest for violating the courts order. They put me in handcuffs without giving me a chance to say goodbye to the family and once they put in the car, they drove for a few hours and I was taken to Hato Rey, juvenile detention center.

Chapter 22

Hato Rey

I dedicate this chapter to the prisoners of Puerto Rico who fought and still fight against oppression from prisoners and correctional officers please forgive me for violating the code of silence but motherfuckers in New York are using what y'all sacrifice and stand for, to oppress people and I need to expose the true story of Neta to society, so they could understand that Neta is not a fucking gang, it's an association for prisoners in Puerto Rico.

"PERDONAME PRISIONEROS HUMILDE"

Hato Rey is a juvenile detention processing center for under twenty-one kids, and while going to and from court until our conviction is given, Hato Rey will be the jail where all the kids will be staying until we are sent to another juvenile jail to complete our sentence.

The cop car entered an unfenced long driveway and when we got out of the car, we walked through a locked gate on the side of a wall. I was taken through these gates and escorted into a small room right next to the entrance of the jail. There were four humungous correctional officers, two on each side of a staff that was sitting in the middle of the room behind a desk. The staff ordered me to take my clothes off, turn around squat down, stand up face the staff and lift my balls and pull my foreskin back, I felt so very uncomfortable

and embarrassed by doing this, I couldn't refuse because those correctional officers looked ready to pounce on someone, I was given some clothes for the processing procedure and once I was dressed, one of the C.O.'s escorted me out of the room and we walked a distance of twenty feet, to another locked gate, where I could see some kids playing basketball in a paved basketball court, the C.O. escorted me past the second gate and said something to one of the teen prisoners, then escorted me to the left side of the jail to side A. I was heading to a box-S.H.U "Special Housing Unit" like environment, which also served as a protective custody unit and a processing unit, and as I headed into the Calavoso, (the box), I was looking around the jail but in fear, I was thinking about the things I heard from my neighborhood friends, how juvenile jail is not safe and how prisoners like raping other prisoners but I knew for sure that any motherfucker tried to rape me, it would be a fight to the death or if they knock me out.

As I walked into the calavoso, there was another locked gate and another by a shower area with two shower heads and no curtains, I could see that there were twelve cells, six on one side and six on the other. I was placed on the second cell from the entrance with a fifteen or sixteen-year-old cellmate and as soon as the C.O. locked me in the cell and left, the teen asked me if I was a homo. I replied "no" but then a few other prisoners asked me the same question from their cells and I yelled out 'no" and they left it at that. I was provided with a thin form mattress and two bed sheets. As I prepared my bed I was scared to fall asleep and for the first two days I slept but lightly, because I wanted to be ready if my cellmate tried to rape me because if he did, he won't be able to run from me as I beat him to death but it didn't happen and after more than a week had passed by, I started secretly sexually enticing an older teen from across my cell.

It started one night while my cellmate was busy chatting with another prisoners in the same cell as the older teen, as my cellmate and the other one sat by the cell gate, I would stand further back in the cell and pull my underwear down from behind, then I would bend down showing my butt cheeks and rectum to the older teen and he would do the same to me and every time the teen and I did this, I had to be careful that my cellmate and the other kid didn't

catch me, as I exposed my buttocks to the teen, I would watch as he would masturbate desperately and shoot cum in a pine shape cup. The teen would show me an almost half filled cup of sperm, I had to control myself from asking him to send me the cup, I wanted to drink some and use his cum as a lubricant to masturbate and rub it in my rectum, I was really turned on by what we were doing so every night we would single each other and see if we were down to sexually excited one another, it all stopped when I was sent to population.

There were two units for a population like there is two units for the S.H.U./calvoso, one was connected to the calavoso on section A and the other two were in section B. The unit I was sent to had two sides with eight beds and in between the dorms was two television facing each side of the dorms and a desk for the staff that would be doing there shifts, the C.O.'s were not present, they stood on the roof and sometimes did rounds either inside or outside the jail.

The fear I had of being in the juvenile jail was gone and since I didn't commit any crimes unacceptable for population, I was good. I was put on the left side of the dorm, the C.O. who opened the gate for me to go in said something to a prisoner and then he left. I didn't know what was said but I do believe the C.O. told the prisoner that I was good, meaning that I didn't commit any sex crimes, robbery of old people, women, and children etc., etc., the prisoners began to introduce themselves one by one and when they heard me speak as I introduced myself, they knew that I was a New York Rican. They asked me questions about life in New York and I told them everything I could about New York and all the fun that can be had in the City, I even told them some funny experiences I had growing up in New York and they all started laughing, they even asked me to say certain words in English making them giggle and laugh, they enjoyed my presence and so did I, then some of them asked me if I wanted to play a game at night and I answered "yes", then they asked me for permission to wake me up, if I was sleeping and I gave it to them.

My bed was by the toilet and the shower area and there was a three to four foot cemented banister that divided the two sides with a passage to enter either the toilet section or the shower area and there was a wall that separated the showers from toilet, now the toilet section had four toilet

stalls with cement walls dividing them, preventing from anyone looking at whoever is using it, now two toilet stall were only for defecating and one was for urinating, as for the last one, it was not used for nothing but it had a plunger stick in the water, which it had become swollen from being in the water for a long time. As for the shower area it only had four shower heads with no partitions and no shower curtains, the bed frames where around two feet or three feet in height and they also were made of cement and bricks, I placed my thin form mattress on the brick frame, fixed my bed and chilled with the kids, teens and older teens by the gate watching TV.

Later that night, I fell asleep around ten at night and I don't know how long I was asleep, when I was awakened by some kids tying my legs and arms together with bedsheets, as they were tying, I noticed other kids who wanted to play and gave permission to wake them up, those that were being tied taken into the shower area like I was, then one by one the group that was doing the tying tied up kids were being untied and taken somewhere into the toilet area. I was the last person to be untied and the one untying me had cut me with a shank by mistake and got scolded by the team leader.

I was taken to the toilet area, where they kneeled me facing a wall by the last toilet and covered me with a blanket from the head down. Then three teens who took me into the bathroom, all kneeled behind me and pressed shanks on my back, ribs, and neck, they wanted me to admit and confess to the question they brought forth and if I refused, well you know what would happen. They asked me about my crime and I told them everything, then they started questioning me about other crimes and how I felt about them. Most of the questioned was about sex crimes and other unacceptable crimes. I responded honestly, then they asked me how I feel about oppressing other prisoners, and I replied like I did to the last question. I hated it, they uncovered me and told me that I can go to sleep with no worries that the leader of section A, will be speaking to me in the morning, which I did.

The next day, the leader approached me and asked me to follow him into the bathroom so we could talk. As I was following him, I was thinking what is he a leader of, we entered the bathroom area and sat on the floor by the toilet area so we could have some type of privacy. The leader which was a fifteen-year-old

handsome kid with straight long black hair that reached his neck, and when he spoke to me it was with respect. He told me that he represented a movement made for prisoners, a movement named NETA. He explained to me, where the Neta word derived from. He was saying that it derived from a certain native of Puerto Rico, when a child is born, the warriors take the child to the top of the mountains, raise the newborn to the sky and scream out "NETA" multiple times, to introduce his innocence and purity and it's the reason why we use it in juvenile jail and adult jails, to promote peace and tranquility.

He continued saying that the word came about in the jail, when corruption between inmates and Correctional Officers was at its highest and most dangerous, they were into raping, stealing, extorting, and even killing the weak and defenseless by both C.O.s and inmates until one man decided to stand against this condition and went to other prisoners, who were suffering like he was and wanted the same thing as the man did, he lifted their courage.

They came together and stood up against the oppressive and deadly conditions and a bloody and deadly riot ensued with many deaths. Then a C.O. gave a gun to an inmate who was into oppressing other inmates and killed the leader and founder of the group, who called themselves "NETA", since then changes in the prison system happened, now prisoners are free from oppression from both inmates and C.O.s, he also explained that where there's a positive, there is also a negative and that certain parts of the jails, were run by those who still believe in oppressing inmates.

He continued by saying that because of the sacrifice of these inmates who died to bring normalcy, a homage is done on a certain day of the month and to continue to keep the peace and tranquility rules were made and had to be followed. He then showed me a list of two hundred rules that I had to follow in order to live in population and asked me if I will abide by the rules. I answered yes. He explained to me as he gave the list to study them and that I don't have to be a Neta to stay in population, just as long I abided by the rules, I told him that I wanted to be in the Neta community and he asked me if I was sure, I replied "yes". He then said that when I learn some of the rules by heart, he will test me, if I pass, I'll be put on probation, I was so excited in being into something that brings order.

He finished with when a prisoner doesn't matter if it's a Neta or a regular inmate violates the rules, there is punishment to receive and pointed to the plunger stick in the toilet bowl. He said that there were two forms of receiving the punishment on the buttocks with the plunger stick, one was called fuego "fire", which is a harsh punishment for certain violations and then there were the mild ones and after a week I memorized all two hundred rules by heart, I was tested and I passed with flying colors but I was still on Probation.

I was told by the leader that in order to reach the leader position, one has to start from a certain rank and climb by performing your duties and showing that you are able to deal with every and all situations unbiased, and when one becomes the enforcer of disciplinary, he, before he inflicts any punishment has to investigate and determine, what violation was committed and the level of punishment and all the physical discipline will be done in the late evening. Also after one shows good communications when dealing with the prisoners and all situations, then one is promoted to right hand man for the leader, he is above the enforcer and his duties are one to make sure every everyone follow the rules, it doesn't matter who it is, Neta or a regular and the right hand makes sure that inmates who can provide clothes, food and toiletries provide whatever they can where the items would be placed in grocery plastic bags and hung on the wall for incoming prisoners and prisoners, who are less fortunate also the right hand man makes sure that the donated items are properly distribute evenly to those less fortunate.

Once one becomes a leader, which is two, one in each dorm, he has to make sure everything is running correctly in all the dorms and in the Special Housing Units. The leader also teaches everyone not to be only followers but how to be leaders and when the time comes, someone could take their place and continue keeping things in order because leaders do come and go due to being freed from the courts completing their time or being transferred to their sentencing/ jail, it's a big responsibility but it teaches us discipline, change, and respect for not only one another in jail but for society too. I felt gladdened by all of this because I didn't have to deal with adults and my father and all the other bullshit. Now school in the juvenile system is mandatory, this was made mandatory by the leaders of the dorms, the only way you don't go to school,

is either you're sick or in court also there was one rule that if broken not only will you get a beat down but you will be sent to the box and you're finish your time there.

This rule is, when staff and selected COs takes chosen prisoners to trips outside of the juvenile jail to beaches and other fun and educational places, those prisoners are not to use that opportunity to escape or the beat down that the prisoner would get is severe, I'm not going to lie I really loved the whole juvenile setting. I felt right in place and when Saturday mornings arrive, man were they fun.

Every Saturday morning when everyone is awake, we prepare the cleaning of the whole dorm with games, we take all the mattresses, and other properties into the bathroom area and put them where they won't touch the floor, we then wet the floor with water first, then pour liquid soap all over the floor and we start slipping and sliding from the shower area unto the dorm's gate and back. We even played a game where a team of two with four prisoners on each team, four prisoners line behind each other, holding unto each other's waist and bending your upper body onto the other prisoner, as the first person hangs on to the gate, then the rest of the prisoners start running one by one from the back of the bathroom to a certain distance and jump on the backs of the bended prisoners. Once every one is on the prisoners back, then the bent ones has to do everything to knock at least one prisoner down and that team loses, then the teams switched positions.

We would play different games for some time, then we would start the scrubbing of the floors and drying the floor with the mops. After all the floors are done, we all together help putting everyone's mattresses and property back in place, then we're scrub and clean the restrooms and the showers floor. Afterwards, we would take turns in the showers, in the showers there were rules to follow. One of them was to be in underwear or boxers in the shower, no one is to look at the groin area or the buttocks, this rule applies to those who takes showers naked and no one is to invite anyone to their private areas, these violations are "el fuego" punishment.

Now gay people are treated with a certain respect because they played a part in the battle, when the oppressors killed the leader and founder of the

prison movement. Once a gay person enters population, they are asked if they are a gay person or want to be one, if they reply "yes", then they will be treated with respect but a gay person cannot become a leader, and if you reply "no" then you are expected to act according to the rules of the dorm. Now if you were a homosexual in the street but not conducting yourself in any homosexual activities in jail and someone recognizes you from the streets and exposed you of your homosexuality, the inmate is asked what he wants to be, a gay person or a straight person, if chose straight, they had to behave like a straight person and if they chose to be gay, well you know the rest.

But sometimes endurance collapses and you begin what you were doing in the streets, like this heavy-set thirteen-year-old boy who decided to be straight but after two weeks, he began to offer blow jobs for cigarettes. Later that night, the gay kid was sucking on almost everyone's penis in his side of the dorm and some the prisoners on my side of the dorm asked the active staff, if he could allow some of us to go to the other dorm and the staff would open the gates and lets us go over and get our dicks sucked, I didn't go because they were some teens that turned me on and I didn't want to fall into temptation that was already burning throughout my body and be the one on my knees.

The gay teen had sucked everyone dry and drunk every drop of cum and when the sex activity was over and everyone was sleeping, the gay teen started moaning and groaning in pain, holding his stomach. The staff ignored him and the prisoners told him to shut up before he gets some rule violations. He was in pain because he consumed the sperm of more than twelve teens raging from the ages of thirteen to nineteen.

The gay teen was performing oral sex every day to whoever wanted to get pleased until one day, the thirteen-year-old got married to a fourteen-year-old virgin who was curious and got turned out, the ceremony was done at night and some of the prisoners helped the thirteen-year-old get dressed for the marriage ceremony. Man, the show was funny to me. The prisoners used two bedsheets, one was to wrap around the thirteen-year-old's head like a headdress and the second one was to wrap around his waist like a dress, then an assigned prisoner would go around and collect cigarettes from prisoners that smoked, then place them in a cup-like object and give it to the gay teen as a gift.

Now even though the gay teen had performed oral sex on almost everyone in that dorm and my dorm, prisoners who wanted to have sex with the gay teen had to ask the so-call husband permission first and if he didn't approve, prisoners had to respect that decision. As for me, well, I struggled hard with my lust and desire and I didn't give in until two months into Hate Rey. I was still waiting for the judge to sentence me but then two brothers a fourteen-year-old and a twelve -year-old were sent to calavoso waiting to be processed so they could go to population, once they were processed, they were sent to my side of the dorm.

They were put through the same thing I went through the night they tied me, they passed and the older brother wanted to be in the Neta community. The two brothers were in jail for attempting to rob a bank. The two brothers had slightly darkish tan skin complexion with straight close crop hair. The older brother was called Chaparro and his younger brother Chaparrito, as the days passed I got to know both brothers but then I started noticing Chaparrito would be staring at me from a far or would always be around me looking into my eyes. I knew what the look was but I was really trying not to fall victim to my lust and desire, yet one day, I overheard some older teen telling Chaparrito that he was going to escape the juvenile jail and that he should go with him. I don't know what got into me but I became emotional to the point of tears, Chaparrito seeing this asked me what was wrong, I answered "that I didn't want him to leave", he then told me to follow him into the shower area, where we knelt down away from view and he gave me a kiss on the lips, I broke me down and I returned his kiss, then we started French kissing for more or less two minutes, we stopped and left the shower area like nothing happened between us.

We sexually taunted each other for more than two weeks and when we finally decided to have sex was one day everyone on both sides of the dorm went to school except Chaparrito and me. We pretended to be sick and once we were alone, we went into the showers just to sit in the shower and chill, we were talking when he stood up and asked me if I could let him urinate in the shower, which is not allowed, I told him to go ahead and he whipped his penis out and peed into the drain hole but Chaparrito was looking at me, when he

finished, he went into the toilet section and sat on one of them, I followed him and I saw that he was masturbating. I got on my knees and started to suck on his dick and balls. I was lost pleasing him and though he couldn't ejaculate, I just stood sucking him off. We stopped after more than fifteen minutes, then we went into the showers, where I continued to perform oral sex on him for a while then I went doggy style and let him fuck me in the ass though all I felt was the head but it brought me pleasure.

We continued to have sex for more than two weeks until we got caught, we were having so much sex that we would sometimes do sexual things in their faces until one day we went to see television by the dorm gates and I sat down and Chaparrito sat between my legs with a blanket around us, and after some time passed by, I made sure that no one was paying attention to us and I started to masturbate Chaparrito slowly and while I masturbating him, I would massage his balls and his butt hole. We were so into it that at one point Chapparito spread his legs and it uncovered us, I quickly covered us but someone from the dorm across from us, who was sitting down by the gates watching television saw us. Chaparrito realized that we'd been caught red handed and fixed himself, I uncovered us and we stood sitting in the same position.

The next day, the teen who saw us told the leader of my dorm and they confronted us, first to find out if anyone forced anyone into doing sexual acts, when they found out it was consensual, then they asked us if we were fags or wanted to be fags and we both answered "no". After that we were left alone, I was so embarrassed and humiliated that I stood a sleep and covered myself from head to toe until the next day but Chapparrito came to me and spoke to me in such a way that it brought me out of my funk and everything went back to normal but late one night while I was taking a shower, Chaparrito followed right behind me and I sat on the cement banister connected to the shower, Chaparrito took off his underwear and had me lather his body with soap. I lathered every part of his body except his dick, balls, and buttocks, which was what Chaparrito wanted and to get fucked in the ass. Don't get me wrong, I wanted to make my form of love to him, he was the only pre-teen that I was willing to turn gay for and because he and I was in love with one another and to me he deserved someone better than me and it was the reason that I didn't

answer back the way Chaparrito wanted, plus, we would of have been caught in the moment but then he was sent to population section B and every night, we would sit by the gates and the open doorway, which lead to the basketball court and look at one another with sexual wanting but after a couple of days passed, we stopped looking for each other.

. . .

I've been incarcerated for three months when I experienced two things. One was supernatural and the other, well, you're going to figure it out. It was late one night and some of the prisoners asked me if they could play the night game for fun and if I wanted to play. I answered "yes" but somehow we were all too exhausted, so we decided to put our mattresses on the floor by the dorm's gate and watch television and as one by one fell to sleep, I was the last one to fall asleep and I don't know how long I was asleep when I felt someone grabbing my feet and pulling me. Still sleeping I kicked my feet so how ever was pulling me could lose his grip on me but the motherfucker wouldn't stop pulling me. I kicked forward a few times to tell let the prisoners know that I changed my mind and didn't want to play, and it stopped but as I was falling asleep, it happened again but this time, my mattress was being pulled down towards the bathroom with me on it, I turned with my eyes half closed and told them that I didn't want to play and it stopped, still half asleep, I got up and dragged my mattress back closed to the dorm gates, and just as I got comfortable and was falling asleep again, it happened again but this a little faster. I was going to wait for the appropriate time and jump off the mattress and scare the pranksters but when I opened my eyes, I could see all the sleeping prisoners. I was still being dragged, I looked down to see who the fuck was pulling me and saw no one there, I was still being dragged deeper into the bathroom. I could see into the bathroom and it was completely black in darkness, I rolled off and jumped to my feet and snatched the mattress and went back to the gates, but this time, I wrapped one arm around the iron bar of the gate and went fearfully a sleep but I was awaken again to the pulling of my feet but this time I was lock around the bar and it

was what kept me from being dragged into the blackness of the bathroom and though I was scared for days, it never occurred again.

I don't know how much later when the second thing occurred. A pastor from some outside church came to the jail and asked kids if they wanted to come out into the yard and hear a few words of God and pray. I went out because I wanted some air, I didn't want to hear God's word, why? Because I didn't believe in God, I blamed God for all my pain and suffering, where the fuck was God when all things were done to me by stepfather? Anyway, the pastor managed to gather eight kids and we stood standing in two groups of four facing each other, the pastor started to preach his sermon and my mind wandered off. I don't know how long I was in my daze but I came too, the pastor told us to bow our heads down so we could pray with him, I bowed my head but didn't close my eye, I watched as everyone bowed the heads and closed their eyes as the pastor did, and as they prayed, I looked up at the clear night sky, which was full of stars but then I saw something that was not quite right, I was seeing stars being blocked out by an rectangular object and by the shape of the darkness, whatever it was up there was big, I stared at it for a minute or two, then I looked down at the others and the pastor, I was tempted to interrupt the prayer service but I didn't want the pastor to think I was trying to disrespect him though I was thinking mentally, what the fuck was that in the sky? I looked up at the sky again and the rectangular object was still there. I stood fixated on this dark ominous rectangular object, I must have been staring at it for more than five minutes because I heard the pastor finishing his prayer, I broke my gaze and quickly lowered my head. I closed my eyes and repeated the "Amen" with everyone, I then opened my eyes and looked up into the sky and the dark rectangular object wasn't there any longer, the sky was bright with the burning stars, as I went back to my dorm, I was thinking to myself that it looked like it was watching us and trying to hide but failed but and I continued to ask myself, what was it watching and another thing I knew was for a fact that whatever it was up there, humans did not create it.

. . .

Days turned into weeks and somehow a known snitch was sent to my dorm. He was over six foot medium weight nineteen-year-old. He was asked by the leader, the right hand man and three other big teens to follow them into the bathroom area. He went with no suspicion. Once the snitch entered the toilet section, they started beating and kicking him, while some would climb the three foot banister that blocked prisoners from being seen using the toilet or showers and start throwing themselves on the snitch. They beat him for a long time. He was on the floor curled up in a ball, trying to stave off the harder hits, after they decided to stop and leave the bathroom area, he got up looking unhurt and place himself with his back on the wall, where my bed was by the three sinks and the banister to the shower, he had bruises or wasn't bleeding, all he did was look at all of us, I walked to him and stood in front of him, I looked up at him with fear and when I become fearful, I become fully enraged and before he could even move, I swung a quick right to his jaw and I stood back. I waited for him to defend himself but by the look in his eyes, I could see he was dazed but then he fell forward flat on his face and he was left there bleeding from his forehead. It was sometime later when CO's came in our dorm and told us to stand away from the knocked out snitch. They came in and took the snitch away on wobbly legs, hours later the snitch was shown on the television news not only talking about his attack in Hato Rey but his crime, which was a fucked up crime, I can't really remember what it was but it was bad. Also on television we could see him on tv and see that his face was swollen and had blood all over his face with stitches on the front of his head, we all screamed "Neta" three times, why? To let all those know we don't except "insectos" (insects), and to all those who are into oppressing prisoners and living foul in the streets, that we rule and will stand for what is right and just.

Talking about oppression, days later, while we were watching the news a special report was being conducted about a riot in a juvenile jail in Mayaguez and what was being shown was dead bodies or decapitated heads and blood all over the inside of the jail, the jail was painted in blood with a battle that no one would understand but those in Puerto Rican jails. It was a battle between the Neta's and Lo Insecto's. Everyone in the juvenile system knows that in Mayaguez it is predominately run by Lo Insecto's. There were two or three dorms

that was run by Neta's, society calls us criminals but in that battle it was young children and teens sacrificing their lives to change for a better way. Remember this, children aren't born evil, it's what adults do to them and all the fucked influences that makes them evil and it matters what adults does to children because the children wind up living a life of oppressing or letting themselves be oppressed or bullying others or letting themselves be bullied or doing something much worse to others or themselves, like the insecto's. As I mentioned before Insecto's are into all types of oppressive cruelty even rapes and murders and this deadly battle was to stop all that. I became emotional because I understood both sides of their pain, we are the product of what the adults have done to us, creating the future monsters.

Some of us began to cry and we all screamed out as loud as we could "NETA" three times. The leader said to all of us "this a reminder for what we stand for, free from oppression" but then something happen in the dorm of section-B, my leader that ran both sides of the dorm met with other leader of section B and what happened. An older teen asked a younger one to follow him into the bathroom, the older teen then pulled out a shank and made the young teen perform oral sex on him, after the young teen finished pleasing the older teen, the kid told the leader and they investigated.

The leaders confronted the older teen and he tried to lie that he didn't have to force him because he knew him from the his neighborhood and he's a dick sucker by time the leaders question the thirteen-year-old, he responded that, "yeah he like sucking dick in the streets but he doesn't want to be known like that in Jail". The older teen was moved to calavoso but then one late day, an older teen in my dorm and I were outside in the basketball court just chilling, when the front gates to the juvenile jail gate opened and the teen who raped the thirteen-year-old walks in and instead of being escorted by a C.O., he heads solo to calavoso section B. We also found out that the older teen was in jail for molesting two little girls, I was given a green light by the leader to invoke justice who was looking out the dorm's window bars.

The nineteen-year-old that was with me followed me. I got up and walked slowly until I got closer and closer to the entrance of the calabozo. I started to lose the colors in my sight, and then I saw my body enter the calavoso, it beat

the kid until it decided to knock the rapist out, then it stood above him, it waited until the rapist woke up and then it continue to punching the rapist all over his body as punishment, and it knocked the rapist out again. It kicked him up again and the rapist tried to scream but it punched him straight on the mouth to keep him from screaming. Then it lifted the staff desk and was about to smash it on the rapist's head, when the nineteen-year-old screamed and grabbed on me, stopping me from not only bashing his head in but killing the fucking rapist. Once I was my normal self, I lowered the desk and the nineteen-year-old and I left the rapist crumbled up on the floor. We went to the front of our dorm and waited for the staff to open the dorm's gate and let us in.

In the jails of Puerto Rico being convicted of a sex crime, especially on a child is like a death sentence unless you go to protected custody. The adult prisons and the juvenile jails in P.R. are more dangerous than the prisons and juvenile jails of New York city, in one juvenile jail, it was reported a prisoner was missing and it is because they had crushed all his bones and skull and flushed everything down the toilet, then in another juvenile jail, the staff found the head of one teen in the garbage of the dorm but didn't find the body. Prison life is a totally different lifestyle than living in a society.

. . .

As time continued to move on, the kids and teens started to get homesick, so some of us developed a plan to cause a riot and help those who wanted to escape and go wherever they wanted to go. I didn't plan to escape because I knew my father would give me up. We received some tools to help us cut the bars to the window and the dorm's gate, how and who gave us the tools, well that part I cannot say but two to three teens were assigned to cutting the fence which was attached to the bars of the window which leads to the outer gates of the jail, then another two were assigned to cutting a bar from the gate of the dorm, which would lead us into the basketball court and the whole inside of the juvenile jail.

At the same time, some other kids were mixing toothpaste and ashes to make the mixture look like the bars color. What we were doing, the kids from

the other dorm were doing the same thing but only to the dorms gate. This was an all-day process and by the time it was all completed by eight at night, we all chilled until the staff turn the light off, then my leader sent a signal, and the bars were being taken out but the kids had some problem with the window, so I tied a bed sheet on the iron bar and pulled with everything I had. Some kids put mattresses underneath me just in case I fell, but I was having trouble myself, so I put both of my feet on the wall and pulled as hard as I could and the thin piece of the gate that was preventing those who wanted to escape into the street, broke free. I fell on the mattress with the piece of gate and bar on my chest, everyone laughed and they started climbing out the hole of the window and climbing a fence and escaping into the street. I then went through the hole cut through the bars of the dorm's gate and helped some prisoners take staff as a hostage and take their keys. I opened the gates to the other dorms for those who couldn't fit through the dorm's gate, then I went into one of the calaboso's and open all the locks for some prisoners. There were some prisoners that couldn't live in population that begged me to leave the cells locked, I did but as for the others they ran towards the gate that led to the process room and the actual exit of the jail, the CO's opened the gate and let those who ran towards the gate enter, then some of the prisoners that were rioting took a few mattresses and place them by the gate and lit the mattresses on fire preventing anyone from further escaping and denying entry for anyone coming in, leaving only one snitch behind. We chase him towards the gates that were on fire, the fifth teen year old snitch stood on the burning mattress screaming for the C.O.s to open the gates, they did, then shit got really real, the C.O.s extinguished the fire, open the gates and they rushed in with their shields and baton sticks that was the size of a ten-year-old child and to make matters worse, the C.O.s were built like trucks, not one of them were fat. They rushed at us and we surrounded ourselves over some staff in the basketball court and told the C.O.s that if they came any closer, we would kill the staff, then we parted a little to show them that we had hostages.

The C.O.s surrounded us, then told us that if we let the hostages go, they won't whip our asses, we were scared but we let two go and stood with one and just as the C.O.s were about to rush us, the hostage told them to stop and they

obeyed him. Then the hostage asked us what was wrong and the leader of my dorm started explaining issues with the hostage about certain conditions and treatment by certain staff. The hostage stood up, told the COs to go and secure the dorms with the escape route. The C.O.s left us and the leader and the hostage spoke for more than an hour and once the C.O.s finished securing the jail, the C.O.s escorted us to calavoso, where we spent the next few days in S.H.U.

The next day someone from population came to the calabozo's window and told us that we were on the news and that more than half of the juveniles in jail had escaped, after a few days in calabozo, I was back in population but I didn't last long because one day a thirteen-year-old prisoner was arguing with a staff known to bully and set up prisoners so the C.O.s could beat them down. I heard the staff tell the kid "fuck your mother", the kid began to sob uncontrollably and after we calmed him down, he told us that his mother had just died in Puerto Rico prison. One's mother is sacred for the prisoners and it is a violation if you mention or even speak about someone's mother, your many "El Fuego" punishment, then an opportunity arose when another staff opened the dorm's gate to pick up a prisoner who had an appointment. I pushed passed the staff and went out into the court yard, where the shit talking staff was bent rinsing a mop, he saw me coming at him but it was too late for him to do anything because I punched him two to three times on the face making him collapse on the floor. I stood back looking down at his crumbled body. The gates to the jail itself were opened and a few C.O.s and some staff came running towards us. A C.O. who was respectful to the prisoners escorted me with a skinny male staff to the calaboso in handcuffs and were taken off by the cell. The skinny staff turned me around and pushed into the cell and slapped me on the face, then taunted me by saying "what the are you going to about it", I went at him but the C.O. stopped me and told the staff to back up so he can lock the gate. As they were walking away, I screamed at the staff and called him an "insecto" but he didn't respond, even some of the prisoners joined in and started calling him a coward and other names. I was in the box for two or three weeks and I was sent back to my dorm, the prisoners congratulated me for standing up for the kid but I really wanted to fuck that skinny fucking staff and he was lucky because he made sure to never come around me.

. . .

Days later, I was given a weekend pass to go home but nobody came to pick me up, so a staff was assigned to take me part way and the staff that was assigned was the staff that I assaulted for disrespecting the kid, I didn't want to refuse because I knew that my father was trying to forget about me and with my presence there well, you know the rest, anyway, the staff and I got in the car and the ride was silent so far but then after some time had passed, the staff broke the silence by asking me why did I assault him, I answered "the kid's mother had just died and we hold mother's in jail sacred" and we stood silent until he dropped me off halfway but on a highway. He told me to keep walking straight down the highway that eventually someone would pick me up and take me the rest of the way and he left.

I began walking and walking with my thumb out and it seem like it was days, then a car stopped by the road and offered me a ride. I got on without thinking of any danger, and told him that I was heading to Brisa de Tortuguero. We sat quietly for a couple of miles, and as he drove I looked at the male driver from the corner of my eyes. He looked in his mid-forties to early fifties, then he broke the silence by telling me that I should be careful with hitch hiking because it could be dangerous and he continued to talk about shit that didn't concern me and he switched the conversation to girls and I knew what this fag was attempting. I didn't reply but I started to prepare myself just in case he tried something sexual because if he did, I was going to put my foot on the gas pedal, while I'm punching him in the face, so we could crash, even if the crash killed me.

But then the driver asked me if I wanted to make fifty dollars. I asked him doing what and he responded that all he wanted to do was suck on my dick. I responded "no" and told him that he should drop me off right now. He stood quiet as he drove and I was preparing to assault him, when he stopped the car and allowed me to get off and he drove off. I walked the highway trail for miles and hours until it had gotten dark and a passing police cruiser happened to pass by and asked me where were I going. I told him where I was going and he told me to get in. As he was driving, he was explaining to me that I was

lucky that I didn't get hit by a car because that part of the highway is known for getting hit and run over or that I could get kidnapped or worse, we arrived at the entrance of Brisa and I got off, the cop told me to take care of myself and I just nodded in response.

By the time I arrived at my father's house, it was well past ten at night and my faggot father was laying on the big sofa like nothing was wrong, I was so enraged at seeing him that an image of me grabbing a knife and stabbing my father in the head but all I did was go to my room outside the house without saying anything to my father and that weekend all I did was hang out with my friends, have sex with some of them, have sex with Pito and Puri or just chilled and when it was time for me to return to Hato Rey, my father wouldn't take me. He gave me money enough to travel and get food, snacks, and toiletries.

I took many buses that led me close to Hato Rey. Once I was there, I went through the asshole check, and was escorted to my dorm. I gave the leader most of my money to help get food for those less fortunate and the rest of my money was enough to get me a joint which I smoked it with a few kids, getting us very high.

More time went by and I was sentenced to six months in juvenile jail, but before I was taken to my new jail, I was taken to an appointment to see a psychiatrist but after hours of waiting. I got impatient and I left the staff and went out of the facility onto the streets, at first I was thinking of going home but for what, so I decided to take a stroll and head back to Hato Rey. Once I arrived at the gates, the CO's let me in and asked me what happened. I told what happened and they all laughed but I still got punished and sent into calaboso for a week. After I did my time in calaboso I was sent my dorm where I stood there for a couple of days and I was taken to Ponce juvenile jail where I did the remainder of the month of two that I had left. I chilled and things went smoothly, my only problem was my lust for male sex. I took showers alone or avoided certain prisoners in the shower because if they were to be alone, I would be on my knees sucking and getting fucked and on my last day in juvey, all the prisoners of my dorm screamed out loud "NETA" three times to me, I said my goodbye's and since my father didn't pick me up, a staff made sure that I got all the way home safely.

Chapter 23

Back home, I was enrolled back at Angel Sardin Martinez Junior High School and I was going to classes and doing all right but at home shit with my father was the same and it got worse. I truly believe my father set this up on purpose but he allowed a male relative of Carmen to live with us and I had to share my room with a fortyish dark skinned long haired Spanish man.

It was one of Carmen's homosexual older brothers, who was dying from the complications of the AIDs virus. My father bought a new bed for this faggot ass bitch and gave me a foldable metal cot to sleep in. One night, while I was sleeping, all of a sudden I felt a presence standing over me. I opened my sleepy eyes and it was Carmen's brother standing over me jerking off, when this fucking faggot saw that I woke up, he fixed himself and left my room. I fell asleep but the next day I awoke to find that my father, Carmen, Pito and Puri gone to Arecibo. I went back outside, grabbed the machete and went back into the house where the homo was sitting on the big sofa, and threatened the motherfucker that "if you ever do that again, I will hack your faggot ass into pieces", I was two feet from him, and I could see the fear in his eyes but I also saw that he got the message loud and fucking clear, so I left the house and went to hang out with my friends. When I got back home late that night, Carmen's brother wasn't there. I don't know if it was because of me but I really

didn't care and I didn't care where he went but since that incident, I would sit on the porch of house everyday sitting on the rocking chair, sharpening a machete that was already sharpened.

Darkness was slowly consuming me even though the faggot left, my father was still treating me like shit and was beating on me but one day it all stopped when Puri and I got into a heated argument, she threatened me on telling my father about our argument, and I threatened her by saying "go ahead, if he puts his hands on me ever again, I will kill him", later on that day when my father had returned home, I watched his every move, while I sharpening the machete and rocking on the rocking chair. Puri came outside and told my father about the argument we had and my threat, he looked at me and started to scream at me "you're going to kill me, go ahead, I dare you", I got up from the rocking chair and raised the machete in his direction and stood standing quietly looking at him with the machete still raised. I stood like that for a few seconds, then I went into my room and laid on my bed with a strong urge to kill my father, I was lost with many different thoughts but one in particular always came up and I couldn't understand why didn't I take his fucking life but the motherfucker got the message because he never put his hands on me again though my father continued treating worse than ever.

With everything going on around me, I felt my world was coming apart and I was completely lost within the darkness that was quickly engulfing me. It had affected me in such a way that I would wake up every day with hatred and rage in my heart, it drove me and because of this change, I hated school and I was getting tired of going to it, then an opportunity arose, when one night I came home from hanging out with my friends and my cousin Juan Pablo and my father's mother was there. My father told me that they were both going to sleep in my room, I got mad and told him, why not put them to sleep with Pito and Puri, he responded angrily "this is my fucking house, and what I say, goes", I replied "fine" and I got up and left the house and went to sleep on the street, actually in an abandoned striped car, which was very uncomfortable because of the mosquitoes and the other nightly critters but after some time, sleep overcame me and I passed out.

The next day early in the morning, I left and went to where some of my friends that lived across the elementary school and La Cancha was located, and it was also a block away from La Laguna, now La Cancha has two baseball fields with bleachers, a two sided handball court, and a patio with wooden sitting benches. I saw my usual group of friends of ten boys and teens ranging from the age of twelve to nineteen years of age. I was hoping they would want to hang out in La Cancha. I told them what happened and a twelve-year-old who approached me one day and told me that he wanted to have sex with me but I always refused him. Sonny was his name and I'm not going to lie, I wanted to fuck Sonny but something made me keep my feelings hidden and play straight. He brought me an egg sandwich with some homemade juice, I ate, then another of my friends asked me, if I needed soap and I replied "yes", he went into his house and returned a few minutes later with a Irish spring soap and announced to everyone to go to La Laguna and we all went.

We all went skinny dipping, and I took advantage and quickly soap myself and then I went in the deep part of the lagoon water and rinsed off, my friends started making fun of me that I haven't cleaned my shitty ass appropriately. I joke fully responded "you should know I use the same ass cleaner as you do", then one of the boys asked "what is it?", I answered "plantano leaves" and everyone started laughing, then they jumped in and we swam and played until nightfall. Afterwards I chilled with them until one by one they started heading home. I decided to see if there were any stores open so I could go steal something to eat.

I found one but it was quite a distance from where I lived. It was on the middle of a mountain with tin and brick houses around the store. Upon entering, I saw a bunch of old timers sitting around a table playing dominoes and some others playing billiard's. I chilled at first with the old timers, who were playing Dominoes when I felt that they were comfortable with my presence, I snuck to a metal bin with shelves and different kinds of cakes and cookies taking one item at a time and sneaking outside without anyone noticing and stash the items in a shopping bag I found outside by the pillared structure of the store and that's where I was stashing my stolen edible items.

It was very late at night and I was hungry and sleepy, so I left the store and headed to the Cancha to eat and sleep. After I ate all the cakes, I fell asleep

in a brick and cement kiosk that was underneath the baseball field bleachers. I awoke the next morning and hung out with my friends and when it got late at night, I went back to the store and chilled and repeated my thievery actions, when I decided to leave, I took my bag with the goodies and went back to the cancha's baseball field's Kiosk to eat and sleep, I don't how much after, I was awakened by a presence standing over me, I looked up groggily at a dark figure of a man but being too tired, I fell back to sleep, the next morning I made a mental check not to return to the cancha to sleep again.

By the fourth night, I was back at the store and I had managed to steal more than before but this night was different. An old man who was a regular, realized that I didn't have anywhere to go and he invited me to stay in his house. I was reluctant but I was tired and I wanted to sleep on something soft, I followed him not to far from the store, to a little one bedroom house made of tin metal and wood. Once inside, the old man prepared the sofa for me and told me not to sleep just yet because he was going to make us a sardine sand-wich. I never ate a sardine sandwich and when he prepared four sandwiches, he gave me two sandwiches and I wolfed them down with a homemade juice he gave me, then the old man put on his little radio to an oldy Spanish station and as I laid on the sofa, I fell asleep with the old music lullabying me.

The next day, the old man woke me up and I left his house to go hang out with my friends until they all went home. I went back to the store but the owner refused to allow me to enter, explaining that he found the bag of stolen cakes and cookies. I had forgotten about the bag and without arguing I left, I had slept sitting down on the steps of a closed for the night store, by sonny and his two other brothers live at with their parents and the elementary school.

Sonny was the one who woke me up and brought me an egg sandwich with some juice, then we were just talking about bullshit. I was still sitting on the store's step and Sonny was standing in front of me with both of his hands in his shorts and after more than fifteen minutes went by, Sonny whipped out his erect penis. I just stared at his dick with a longing that ignited my burning lust within me but I held on to the temptation of wanting to suck his dick right there or anywhere else. He knew that I wanted to suck his dick and he kept on tempting me but when his brothers and our other friends arrived, Sonny

stopped, the reason I didn't have sex with him was because I had two sets of friends, my friends from Calle Ocho, majority of them were my sex buddies but the ones by the elementary school were regular friends, only Sonny was the only one that wanted to fuck me. We hung out either in the Laguna skinning dipping or in the Cancha just hanging in the bleachers just talking or joking on one another by the time early evening arrived my friends went to their houses and I walked the many miles to my school so I could climb the school gates and go somewhere to sleep.

One night, I arrived at my school and began to climb the front gates, when I heard someone scream at me to get down from the gates. I looked at the direction the voice came from and saw that it was a security guard for the school. I got down and I don't know why I didn't run but I didn't and I walked to where he was standing. He asked me to follow him to the front of the school and he asked me why were I sneaking into the school, I answered him truthfully "I'm looking for somewhere to sleep", and we both stood quiet as we walked to his parked car, he opened the trunk of his car and gave me half of a hero sandwich and something to drink, then told me to go to wherever I was going to go and sleep.

I ate the sandwich and drank the juice quickly, then I climb the front gates and disappeared into the middle of the school, I walked to a section of the school, where there were no gates for the second and third floor but with locked classrooms and a balcony on each floor, I went on the second floor and walked towards the back where the balcony was located, it had a section on the corner of that was dark keeping the school lights and the brightness of the moon from reflecting into the dark corner, which looked like it was daylight. I was on the verge of falling asleep when all of a sudden I heard footsteps, I was laying on the floor so I peeked to see who it was and all I saw was a man form walking towards my direction, I tried to see if it was the security guard but all I was seeing was a reflection of a dark figure walking towards me, even the lights from the school and the moon couldn't illuminate the figure. I felt my instinct tell me that I was in danger, so I got up and jump from the second-floor balcony and ran towards the back of the school and climbed the school gates and kept on running as fast and far as I could, even to this day I

still don't know if it was the guard or something else, and if it was the guard, how the fuck did he know where I was and what did he want. All I know is that lights of the school and the moonlight wouldn't shine on the dark figure. I scared out of my ass, I went somewhere else to sleep and when daylight arrived, I went to school that day and after school, I decided to return home.

My father allowed me to return home but the room I used to sleep in, was given to Pito and I was given the room connected to Pito's, which was the room that housed a German Shepard, and the dog used to shit and piss in the room and I was the only one assigned to clean up after the dog. My father and I didn't speak and we kept it that way though I still did my chores, and I really didn't care about the room's condition because it was how I felt about myself but worse with all the chaos going on in my head. I could hear the whispers of suicide whispering seductively into my soul, I was depressed but I also was going through something that I couldn't understand, the urge to kill, I wanted to kill yet something, I wanted to connect with my personality and be free but something was stopping me from doing it, then my thoughts were broken by a soft knock on my door, I went an answer the door and it was Pito, he wanted to fuck, he was thirteen and he still couldn't ejaculate but his penis has gotten fatter.

He enters my room and I close my door with the lock, then he helps me take my top mattress onto the floor, we got naked and laid on the mattress and we tried to French kiss but it was impossible because he didn't know how to kiss still, so I decided to suck on his longer and fatter dick. Pito was lucky that he couldn't cum because if he could, he would have fallen in love with me because as soon as I put his dick in my mouth, I lost myself and didn't stop sucking until my jaw became exhausted, then I asked him to fuck me in the ass and I laid on my stomach and he got on top of me and rammed me hard in the ass, he was fucking hard and fast, which was something new on his part and after he fucked me for a long time. He told me to lay on my side so he could fuck me again and jerk me off. I did and it didn't take long for me to ejaculate. My body spasmed uncontrollably and I started shooting cum all over Pito's hand and on my mattress, Pito was using my sperm to finish jerking me off, knowing that he made me cum, he left his penis in me until my body stopped shaking

and he pulled out, got dressed and went into his room. I laid on my mattress until my body fully recovered and some of my energy returned. I got up naked and I went to Pito's door and knocked softly, I wanted to go for another round but he was either faking that he was asleep or he actually he did.

Then one day my father took Carmen and the rest of us to one of Carmen's relatives to visit, when we arrived Carmen introduced us to whom I believe is her sister or cousin. The lady introduced us to her two kids, an eight-year-old boy with tannish skin complexion and black crop hairstyle and a ten-year-old girl with the same skin complexion as her brother but with long blond hair that reached her buttocks. The lady had a big land with a three-bedroom one-story house, while the adults were talking, the two kids took Pito and I to the backyard, where they said they had two hogs and a lemon tree. We walked the distance of half a block. Once we reached the hogs den, I could see two full grown hogs and they were in separated in singular dens, I looked further and saw eight other dens but they were empty. The two kids left us and Pito and I stood behind to collect some lemons, we had a plastic shopping bag and we started to collect the lemons, it was a painful job with the prickly thorns and after we finish filling the bag, Pito and I went to an empty den, where I sucked on his dick, I kept preforming oral sex until Pito and I decided that we were there for too long and we didn't want my father sneaking up on us, we stopped and went to where everyone was in the front of the house, and after an hour or so, my father told us that it was time to go.

We return on another day and things got freaky. Pito and I were chilling with the ten-year-old, her brother and one of their female friends. We were chilling in a swing set for kids but underneath the swing set were two benches facing each other and anyone inside was hidden from view, Pito's cousin the ten-year-old girl was exposing her ass cheeks to Pito and me but I really wasn't interested in her. I was interested in her eight-year-old brother, who was evilly wild. I overheard his mother tell Carmen and my father that he was very wild and uncontrollable that he one time went so crazy that he took a kitchen knife and cut an upside down crucifix on his fore head. When the eight year old's mother said this, I was instantly aroused I wanted to have sex with him because he represented evil. Just thinking about me and him fucking made me so horny

me, then laid on my back and without using spit, I penetrated him, he was very loose in his rectum and I knew that he was being molested by adults like the eight-year-old and a majority of my sexual partners whether they were young or teens. We were all corrupted and we found pleasure with others like us, I didn't see nothing wrong with fucking the three-year-old and no one ever told me that fucking the young was wrong, they made a big deal because it was homosexual activity, and when I ejaculated inside the three-year-old, we both fell asleep, we didn't wake until we heard Pito calling out my name, we awoke and the three-year-old quickly got off of me. I got dressed and stood by the entrance of the abandoned house. Pito went through the open gates and approached me but upon seeing the three-year-old, he asked me what were we doing, I told him the truth and he took the three-year-old back inside and I followed, Pito put him on a doggy style position and was about to penetrate him, when the three-year-old started crying and didn't want Pito to fuck and though Pito tried a couple of times, the three-year-old would continue to refuse, so Pito stopped trying and all three of us and the horse left the property and headed to my father's house.

Then there was Tony, one of Pito's friends, who lived across the street from us but on the corner of the block on a two-story house, Tony almost caught me and another of Pito's friends named Pedro masturbating, and just as I was about to suck Pedro's dick, Tony appeared on one side of my bedroom's window. Pedro and I were in a part of my room that Tony couldn't see us. Pedro quickly fixed himself and left the house but Tony asked me what was I doing and I told him the truth that I was going to suck Pito's friend's dick, he stood quiet and I told him that if he wanted me to suck his dick too, but he stood quiet without answering and change the subject.

Days later, it was Pito, Puri, myself, Tony, his older brother Julio, their sister, and their mother. We were invited to hang out in the house, while their mother went out to do an errand. I was right behind Tony in a single file with the others, Tony and I were the last ones in the line and as we walking up the back staircase which led to the corner porch side of the house, when all of a sudden Tony grabbed one of my hands and had me fondle his privates, and let go of my hand before anyone can catch us. Tony and I slowed our pace to a

point that everyone was clear from view. We then snuck down the side steps that lead to the garage and went into the garage's bathroom, we closed and locked the door and got naked, I got on my knees and started pleasing him, he would moan here and there and I would continue sucking him off, he couldn't ejaculate but he was enjoying it. I got up and I started sword fighting my big long dick and his little one, then we French kissed and I went on my knees again and started to suck on his dick and balls again. We were in the bathroom having sex for a long time that when we left the bathroom to go and hang out upstairs with the others, Pito and Puri had left and when Julio saw us, he asked us where were we. We replied nowhere but after many times that Tony and I were having sex, I found out that it was Julio who sent Tony to get sexual with me, so Julio could use it to black mail me but there was something that I was told about him. Julio was in his back yard playing with some type of dog and the witness said that Julio had a hard while playing with the dog and that it looked like, Julio was going to fuck the dog. I confronted Julio and told him that if he ever say anything to anyone of me sucking his brother's dick, I was going to tell everyone in the neighborhood and school that he was going to fuck a dog with that I left but he kept his mouth shut.

I was seventeen years old and I felt like I wasn't going to last long alive, to me everything was going too fast and the things I hated doing were the things I did the most, like having not only male sex but male sex of young boys. I figured that if they were willing, I'll take them to places with my sexual hunger, like one day, my father had dropped me off in an abandoned property with waist high grass near a short cut that led to La Laguna and as I was finishing cutting all of the grass for the horse, a thirteen-year-old dark chocolate complexion boy passed me by to urinate across the street from where I was at. The first time, he didn't act strange but when he returned to supposedly piss again, he stood standing sideways exposing his penis as he was pissing. Then he would look at me for a few seconds, then look down at his penis, when he looked at me again even though no urine came, I knew that he wanted to fuck.

I was aroused the first time he came, I was wishing that he would of come to want to have sex and the shit happened. I approached him and asked him if he wanted to fuck and he answered "yes". We walked a long stretch of road

where on each side was like a boggy swampy type with crabs and other creatures. As we were walking, we were jerking each other off. We walked half the
long road into a grassy dry area and away from the road's view, we undressed
each other, then we stared French kissing slowly then it turned into a passionate
moment and as we kissed, we jerked each other off or we sword fought, stopping every time we were about to ejaculate, I then whispered lustfully to him
that I wanted to fuck him in the ass, and all he did was turn around bend down
a little letting me try to penetrate him, I was too big and my spit wasn't enough
lubricant. I stopped trying and told him it was his turn. He penetrated me with
his skinny penis and would stop with his penis in me just as he was about to
ejaculate, after some time of him fucking me, he stopped and said that he had
to go home. It was then that I realized that we were at it for hours and it was
getting dark, I was nervous hoping my father didn't come looking for me and
as we were dressing, we would quickly kiss each other on the lips or suck on
each other's lips, we were even doing it as we got on the road and headed back
to where we met, then the kid left as if nothing happened between us and I
waited for my father who didn't come to pick me up until way after dark.

· · ·

In doing the things I didn't like, I had started cutting classes again, then it was
cutting the whole school day. I was going to school to hang out with many
school cutters, some who were teens from Calle Ocho and from where Sonny
lived. I got so addicted that I had cut half a semester of school and things ended
when one day the principle rushed me and screamed at me, telling me that I
was expelled from his school because I had jumped a student, who sustained a
broken arm and a head wound, I responded with the truth that I didn't anything to anyone but he didn't want to listen, I waited until he went into his office. I then looked and found the biggest rock I could carry and walked partway
to his car and threw the big rock at his window but only managing to hit the
car's wheel, I was walking towards where his office was kicking garbage cans,
there were some students standing outside the school office area, so I decided
to leave from the back side of the school, when all of a sudden the principle

came charging at me with a hammer. I wasn't going to run and have him hurt me, so I waited as he got near me and I two pieced him, knocking him down flat on his back. I then turned to run to the back of the school, I had gotten half way towards the gates, when I felt someone grab me from behind scratching the side of my neck. I turned around elbowing however it was trying to stop me and it was the principle. He fell on his back and I looked around and noticed that the whole school was watching what I've done and I could further see that they were all in shock, I ran to back of the school, climbed over and ran into town.

I stopped as I neared town and walked normally to not to attract attention and catch the van bus that led into Brisa's. I got on the bus and as the bus was nearing Brisa de Tortuguero. I saw a motorcycle cop and a regular cop car pass by I was scared that they knew I was on the bus but when they kept on going, I was relieved. I arrived at my stop and the bus dropped me off four blocks from Calle Ocho but instead of going to my house, I went to the Cancha and stood there waiting for my friends to return from school. I sat on a bench on the patio of the Cancha, which was towards the back section of the elementary school, I was trying to calm my racing thoughts but it overtook me and it started flashing moments in my life, like the fight I had when I was fifteen against the twenty-five-year-old. Then my mind flashed to another fight I had, when I was on a Hato Rey juvey trip. I and a group of eight of us were chosen to go to the beach with some staff and a C.O. who was cool with the juveniles, I was the last juvey to get off the bus, I really didn't feel the trip and being around many people, I slowed my paced trying to think and all of a sudden, two tall older teens approached me and tried to snuff me. I dodged his blow but then they separatedl One went behind me and the other was in front of me. The one from behind would act like he was going to charge at me, while the one in front was the one attacking me. Then they took turns doing the same shit. At first they were fucking me up but then I caught on to their strategy. I reversed it on them, as the one behind me was keeping me busy, I would entertained him a few seconds until I knew it was the right time then I'll turned around quickly and rushed at the actual attacker making the attacker freeze up in shock and that's when I connected two quick punches to his jaw,

dropping him. Then I turned around quickly again and charged at the other attacker but with this punk, I was hitting him all over his chest, stomach, and rib areas just to punish him and his body. I caught a glimpse of the other one getting up, I didn't wait, I charged at him and hit him one time on the chest taking his breath away, I didn't want to knock this bitches out, I only wanted to punish their bodies, the funny shit about all this is that the fight was on the beach's parking lot and instead of people getting out of their car and breaking the fight, no one did they just stood still and watched as I was busting these two bitches up, even the beach goers that were walking towards the beach had stopped walking and stood watching the show. I was fighting them for more than fifteen when the C.O. returned probably looking for us and ran toward us and broke up the fight. I didn't have one bruise and nor was I bleeding but them, they had busted lips and knots on their foreheads, I'm not going to lie after that fight, I actually enjoined the day in the beach and even played some games with the rest of the juvies.

I was trying to control my racing mind but the rage was building and thoughts of how my father used to beat me made my hatred more pleasurable, especially remembering how my father had gotten a pair of brass knuckles and if it wasn't for Carmen watching him and stopping him, he would have beaten me with them, my thoughts were interrupted when over the elementary school speakers it was broad casting a special report in the news. The news reporter was interviewing the principle, who I could hear the crying and playing victim on the news, saying that he was assaulted for no reason and that he was closing the school for the whole afternoon up and half the next day but the afternoon sessions will opened, then the lying motherfucker continued by saying that all he tried to do was ask me a question.

Rage burned throughout my whole body. I wanted to rip the lying motherfuckers head off but I stood in the Cancha for some time, then I headed to Sonny's house, and to my surprise, all my friends were there and they all cheered and congratulated me for not only closing the school but for beating the principle up. My friends continued telling me that I had to be careful because on their way here from school. They saw multiple cop cars heading to Calle Ocho, I was not planning to go there anytime soon, then one of the

teens asked everyone who wanted to go to La Laguna and celebrate by skinny dipping and more than twenty kids and teens yelled "yes" and we all went to La laguna.

We quickly took all our clothes off and swam and played and though I acted like I was happy but I wasn't. I felt darkness surrounding me and depression so profound that my self-hate was intensified, plus I was worried about the cops catching me. I put on the mask of enjoinment and swam and played until early evening, we all sat nakedly on our clothes and talked shit about the principle's ass whipping, while we were talking, I interrupted and asked Sonny's nineteen-year old-brother and Sonny to go to my father's house and tell him to get me a plane ticket to New York, I told them where I lived and as they were leaving, I repeated myself with the message.

The rest of us were still sitting nakedly on our clothes talking about our dick sizes, there was an eight-year-old kid, we all called El Potro "the horse" because he had a big fucking dick. Even I was scared at the thought of him trying to stick that big monster in me, we all made friendly fun at him that no girl will touch that thing. Then turned around at a fifteen-year-old who had a small dick and told El Potro "if he could donate some dick to Sonny's other brother" and we all laughed, then they turned to me and asked me what's wrong with my penis and balls. I told them that I was a chameleon that my body and privates turn to different colors and again we all laughed, after some time had passed, we got dressed.

As we were leaving, I noticed a thirteen-year-old heavy set kid, who I had a problem with, I felt like exposing his snitch but I knew if I did, they would beat the shit out of him badly. My problem with the kid comes from, one day Pito had stolen a bike from someone's property and the fat kid witnessed the thief and watched as Pito rode it around the neighborhood and instead of asking for the bike back, he went and got a relative and they drove to the front of my father's gate, I approached the car and saw who it was, the driver tried to get tough towards me and I let him know that I wasn't the one for the bullshit and all that tough shit went out the window and he threatened me with the police. I told them to go ahead that I didn't give a fuck and they left.

I went looking for Pito, who was busy enjoying the bike not knowing the problem he's in. I manage to find him a couple of blocks away and I told him about the whole situation and that we needed to stash the bike. We took the bike to an abandoned factory that was across the street from La Cancha area and we headed back home. Some time had passed when a cop car and the guy in his car with the heavy set thirteen-year-old was following right behind the cop and stopped in front of the house, Pito and I were sitting on the Porch and we walked outside the gate. The officer told Pito and I what the two in the car said, at first I was going to deny it but I told them what Pito told me, that he found the bike by a gate by the garbage cans and he thought that the bike was being thrown away, the cop asked me what I did with the bike and I told him the truth, he replied by saying that to get the bike before I can get in trouble. I told the cop to meet Pito and I at the factory, the other two followed the cop. We arrived there at different times but I went into the abandoned factory and brought out the bike and gave it to the two snitches, the cop offered Pito and me a ride back but we declined.

I looked down at the thirteen-year-old snitch sitting on a boulder looking down to the ground, looking depressed and lonely, I made sure to grab his attention and look him in the eyes, letting him know that he is safe from all of us and we left leaving the fat kid alone him alone, we chilled in front of Sonny's house and waited for Sonny and his brother to return. It was around six in the evening, when they returned and told me that my father said to go to the house at eight o'clock at night. I went home as soon as darkness fell and packed the little clothes that I had, I then went to Tony's house, the kid from the two story house and chilled in front of his house with Tony and some other kids.

This white skinned kid that I never saw before introduced himself to me and told me that he was from London and that he was thirteen-years-old, I found him sexually attractive and his blue eyes and blondish curly hair didn't help either I started to head to my father's house to see if he was ready and the thirteen-year-old followed me into my father's garage. We faced each other looking into each other's eyes and we started to French kiss like we were hungry for each other and just as I was going to take him into my room and give him the best sex he would ever have in his life, my father screamed out for me

and I knew that it was time for me to leave. I told the thirteen-year-old that I had to leave and I would never be back. He became upset and left my house and left to where ever he lived. I got in the car with Carmen and my father and we headed to the airport, once there, we waited by the gate and once my plane was called, my father gave me twenty dollars and told me that he spoke the my aunt/godmother for me to stay with them. I gave Carmen and my father an emotional hug, then left and boarded my plane.

Chapter 24

Hell

On the plane, I promised myself that I would start from the beginning and change everything about me, even having sex with boys or any male. I was going to show everyone that I can change. As the plane started to take off, my mind wonder off to something I did to a family and it was the reason for my promise to change, I had said that when I was released from juvey that I went straight to my father's house but it wasn't true. I went to Abel's family's house, the teen's house I was staying at when I left the Job Corps.

I remember walking up to the front gates of the Abel's family's property calling out for Abel. His father saw me and started to freak out in fear, he looked like he was about to run but he was frozen scared. All he did was scream out for Abel, who ran outside and froze upon seeing me, I said what's up and asked why is everyone freaking out, Abel answered still unsure of what he is seeing, that they thought I was dead. He explained that two teens died in their cells doing a protest that went wrong, they lit their mattresses on fire in their cells and they both died from burns and smoke inhalation. Abel continued by saying that one of the kids that the news people described that died matched my physical description, the father interjected saying that being we all thought you died, seeing you freaked me out. I thought that I was seeing a ghost. I

laughed at them and reassured them that I wasn't a ghost, seeing their relief I asked the father if I could live there with them, he replied "yes", I thought I had to explain why I didn't want to go home but I didn't and I felt good.

Week after week passed by living with Abel and his family, I was starting to adjust to their way of family life. I was not use to the politeness and caring being shown to me, it took some time for to get used to it and not feel uncomfortable, Abel's father was teaching me how to repair the barb wire fences surrounding his property and other manor work around his house. I enjoined living with them and as for my sexual appetite was gone, I didn't need to escape.

There was one other family living next to us but everything else was either mountains or Pineapple fields. Abel and his family lived in a one story three bedroom Tin metal and wood house, the biggest bedroom was made into two, one side was for the parents, the other side was for the five sisters who shared a huge bed, the second room had two beds, which was shared by Abel and his little eleven-year-old brother Petro and the last room also had two beds shared by Abel's other two brothers, a fourteen-year-old Alexis and twenty something Jorge, who was rarely around only to sleep.

Abel had a big family. I didn't know if all was his father's because there was a big boned thirteen-year-old with a body of a grown woman and she was very attractive. She had long black hair that reached the middle of her back and she had a creamy skin complexion. Then there were two twelve year old's, one was brown skin with black shoulder length hair and the other was white skin like her father and had long blond hair that reached her buttocks and then the two six-year-old's, one who was brown skinned with black shoulder length hair and Nancy, who had shoulder length straight black hair and had white skin.

It was the same with the male children. I didn't know if they were all his but I knew that the fourteen-year-old was hiding his true sexuality. I realized it every time he would see me, he would have a massive hard-on, and would look at me, I was aroused but not to the point that I wanted to have sex with him, I didn't have any sexual urges with him, his little brother Angel or any of the girls, though I did have a secret crush on the big boned thirteen year old but I kept those feelings hidden, I felt that I didn't need to escape into sexual activity but things do change.

After two month or so, I told Abel that I was going to the Job Corps to see if I could get the money they owed me. I left and actually walked to the Job Corps, which was a couple of miles away. It did take a couple of hours to get there but when I arrived everyone who knew me, it didn't matter if it was staff or the students, they all freaked out upon seeing me just like Abel and his father. I laughed as they realized that I wasn't a ghost and the staff that I went to see, told me the same thing that Abel and his father told me about the two kids that died, the staff gave me the check and I left and cashed in town and instead of saving the money and giving it to Abel's father, I spent it on some bullshit head phones, when I returned back to Abel's house, I saw the disappointment on Abel's father's face but I didn't understand the look, why until decades later.

But I made up for it by working hard, helping him with his house and property. He even with my help, built a little room outside the house by a fence on the side of the house and property. He provided a cot and a dresser and blankets. It was a very cozy room, and Abel's eleven-year-old brother Petro would hang out with me in the room fascinated and wishing he could have my room to himself.

Petro was the one who took me to the mountains around his property. We would hike to just either explore or get fruits for everyone. One early morning everyone except the two six-year-olds were sleeping. They were hiding somewhere in the back of house having sex with each other. The dark skinned one had just finished sucking and making Nancy ejaculate, when I caught them. Nancy gave me an attitude but went away, later on when she realized that I didn't tell on them, she was friendly to me. Then one night, I was chilling in the house watching television with Abel and his little brother, I sat one in corner of the sofa and Petro laid with his head on the other corner with his feet on my lap.

Abel sat on a love seat with his back towards us. The lights were off and we all were watching a movie. Petro was covered with a blanket, and as we all watched the movie, I slowly went up Petro's leg and since he didn't stop me, I continued slowly by the half-side of his thighs and into his shorts. He didn't have no underwear on so it made it easy to masturbate him slowly. I was trying

413

and his half-brother let me suck on their dicks, balls, ass cheeks, and rectum. We even French kissed. It got so hot that I tried to penetrate Petro but I was too big and when I tried with the dark skin kid, it went in halfway, and he told me to take my penis out and I did. he didn't say it hurt like Petro did but he did want to fuck me in the ass and I let him. Since both couldn't ejaculate, we were sword fighting, sucking, kissing and fucking for hours and when they decided to stop, they left my room. I heard the dark skin kid asking Petro if I was gay. He replied that he didn't know and they walked on into their house.

Then with my lust in full blast, every time I was alone with Abel's fourteen-year-old brother and I was about to ask him to have sex with me, someone would appear or there would be an interruption. Petro and I would find moments where I would suck on his dick, balls, and asshole or having me masturbate him. I remember one early morning, I went into the house to watch television and I was watching the news when Raymond came out of his room and sits on my lap. I caught an erection and he felt it. I placed one of my hands on his lap and slowly went up the side of his thigh and into his shorts. I gently grabbed his penis and started masturbating him slowly. I even played with his balls and rectum. While we were having our sexual moment, all of a sudden my name was mentioned on the news as a missing person and since no one was up to hear it, I stood quiet about it.

After more than half hour passed by and Petro was still sitting on my lap getting masturbated. We were trying to calm our breathing but we were lusting and when I lustfully whispered into Petro's ear and told him that I wanted to suck his dick. We left the house and went into one of the mountains behind the house, where I pulled his shorts down and performed oral sex on his penis and balls, then I would stop and we would French kiss and since he was sitting my lap facing me. He let me rub my penis all over his butt cheeks and rectum but just as I was about penetrate him, Petro told me that he didn't want to get fucked in the ass and I respected that though he let me continue to rub my penis all over his back side as we French kiss. Afterwards, he put me to suck his dick and balls again, then we stopped fixed ourselves and went home.

I went and took a shower and started masturbating. I was in the heat of the moment, when all of a sudden one of the six-year-old's stood in the entrance of

the latrine and watched me masturbate. As she just stood there looking at me, it made me so excited that when I ejaculated, it was like a fountain of cum shooting out of my penis and when it was finally over, my hand was gripping my penis for dear life and I was catching my breath. The six-year-old seeing that I was finished left and didn't mentioned it to anyone.

After a couple of months of having sex with Petro and his half-brother it was starting to get boring and I was becoming guilty that I couldn't stop having sex with them. A day arrived when I decided I was going to have sex with them one last time, especially with Petro's half-brother, who was a defecator on himself. He had defecated on himself and hid his shitty underwear behind my dresser. Then later on that day, Petro and him got caught playing a pissing game. They had grabbed some type of tube and they were on either end trying to piss each other through the tube and they got caught by their older looking thirteen-year-old sister. They didn't get in trouble but was told that they were disgusting. I approached them further in the day and told them that I wanted to have sex with them one last time. Petro answered quickly yes but his half-brother hesitated to answer but after thinking about it, he said he would be down with the sex play.

The plan made, I went to chopping wood for the open fire pit, which was the only way for Abel's mother to cook all the food she cooks. As I was chopping, I could see Petro's mother, his half-brother, all his sisters and Petro leave the property and walk around the property towards the mountain side. I had managed to chop enough wood to last a few days and I went into my room to get ready to shower and have sex with the boys. Just as I grabbed my stuff to head into the shower, the six-year old that watched me masturbate entered my room, laid on her back, pulled her dress up and spread her legs open, wanting me to fuck her. I realized then the twelve-year-old told his stepmother what we been doing, the six-year-old upon hearing this, ran to my room so I could fuck her.

I was embarrassed, humiliated, and scared and I didn't have any sneakers because I lent them to Abel for an appointment. I decided to climb the rocky mountain connected to the house and hide in a cave I found one day exploring. I was hoping no one saw me because I was going to wait until nightfall, sneak out the cave and leave but after some time had passed, Abel climbed to where

I was and told me that his six-year-old sister told him where I was. Abel asked me how it started but I was too embarrassed, ashamed, humiliated, and guilty to answer his question. Abel continued to tell me that the twelve-year-old told his stepmother that he will not come back to visit them if I'm still here because I was having sex with him and Petro and that he didn't like to have sex with me. Abel further told me that I had to leave because if the twelve-year-old would tell his father, I would have to fight the father. I put on my sneakers and left feeling like shit.

I returned a few weeks later to pick up my property and the mother told me that all my property was thrown away and that I better leave before her husband arrives because he was enraged and if he saw me we were going to fight or worse. I left and no more than three blocks from where Abel lived. I spotted Abel's father, we locked eyes for a breath of a moment and he continued to drive away. In order to avoid any confrontation, I started to cut through neighborhoods to lose him just in case he decided to turn around and come after me. As I headed back to my father's, I was thinking what the fuck did I do wrong, I didn't force the twelve-year-old to have sex with me. It is fine when I was sucking, licking and French kissing but when it was getting penetrated, I had finally penetrated the twelve-year-old and he was moaning like a girl.

· · ·

My racing mind was interrupted by the pilot's announcement that the plane was about to land. At first I was feeling depressed, lost, and lonely. I was even asking myself, why was I getting into trouble over sex? Why does my family hate me? And why does it feel like I am the only one going through the bullshit but no answer emerged. I vowed that I would change and prove everyone wrong but the devil had other plans for me and as the plane landed and I got off, the feeling of me not having human emotions and all the other feelings I felt had just disappeared like it never happened. I got on a taxicab and told the driver that I had only twenty dollars, if he could take me to the closest subway station and he did.

I arrived at 183 street and Bathgate Avenue around midnight and being that it was late, I didn't have the guts to go to either my uncle Edwin's apartment on 2292 in 183 street on Bathgate Avenue or my Godmother/aunt Rosa, on 2239 in 182 on Bathgate Avenue and knock on their doors, so I hung out in front of my uncle's building until the morning. As I sat there, some guy came out of the building and upon seeing me, asked me if I was all right. I didn't respond but he assumed that I was homeless, he asked if I wanted to make some money, and I reluctantly answered "yes".

I didn't know what this thirtyish to mid-forties man had in the plan but life was about to teach me new lessons of life. The guy pulled something out of his pocket and showed me small vials of little pieces of a white rocky substance in each one of them. He told me that it was crack and asked me if I ever smoked it. I answered "no" and continued saying that he will give me a certain amount to sell and he would bring the customers.

I didn't know anything about the world of drugs besides what I experienced by watching my aunts and an uncle use whatever it was they were using. He didn't lie about bringing the customers and the crack was selling like hotcakes. He again asked me if I ever used crack and I responded "no, is it like weed/cannabis". And he answered "yes that later, he would give me some to try". I was excited because money was being made and I was going to try something that was like weed and weed always made me deal with the things in my head. After two or three hours passed by, I had a few vials of crack left and the guy told me that it was enough for now. He then took out a cigar, cracked it through the middle and threw out the contains inside the cigar, he then took out a five dollar bag of cannabis, spread it inside the cigar leaf, then he took out a vial of crack and sprinkle pieces of rock all around inside of the cigar with the weed. Then he rolled the cigar with the weed and crack and told me that we were about to smoke something called a Wolly blunt.

He then lit the blunt and passed it to me, on my first drag, I felt a cold numbing tingling sensation on my lips, tongue, and mouth. By the third drag, my heart was beating a million miles per minute and I started sweating, my thoughts were racing faster than the speed of light making me feel manic and as I continued to smoke the blunt mixed with crack, I started to feel an empty

calmness leaving me with no type of emotions. After we finished smoking the blunt, he asked me if I ever smoked in a pipe, I answered "no". He then pulled out a pack of cigarettes and took out a small glass pipe, then he took out a vial of crack and put the whole rocky contains in one end of the pipe, put the other end in his mouth and lit the crack end. I watched as smoke was building up in the pipe and he was inhaling as much as he could and then exhaled slowly. He repeated this process until no smoke was developing in the pipe.

Once he finished showing me how to smoke crack in a pipe, he filled one end with crack, then passed me the pipe and told me to do it like he did. The emotions that overcame my body were more intense than smoking the Wolly blunt. I felt like my heart was going to burst from how fast it was beating and as I continued to smoke the pipe, I became completely numbed mentally, physically and emotionally. I really didn't feel human and the strangest thing about it, it felt like I was in my right aura, I can't completely explain it but it was more like I felt in place.

We had smoked four or five vials of crack, when he said that it was time to make some money. We made some money and he went and gotten more crack. While we were smoking, we would go inside the front lobby of my uncle's building and smoke crack then go back in front and chilled. We were just chilling in the front of the building, when the guy pointed to some older male that was walking toward us and told me to follow the older male into the building, the guy then gave me a big double O seven pocket knife and said that he had problems with the older male and that the older male didn't want to pay the guy. He continued to tell me that when the older male comes closer to us to stab the older male because he would have a lot of money. Feeling numb of emotions from smoking crack I nodded my head in a yes motion to let the guy know that I understood, what he didn't know was that I was a hundred percent serious and that an evil in me which has been awakened, was wide awake and it was hungry. The victim got close enough and I flipped the double O seven knife open and was about to stab the older male, when someone's screams broke me out of my trance like state, it was the guy, he grabbed my hand before I could plunge the knife into the older male. The guy was screaming at me to stop that he was only checking to see if I would do it. I stood silent

and looked at the older male with the thirst of stabbing him to death, I could even hear a voice in my head saying to go ahead and shed blood but the guy still gripping my hand had positioned himself between me and the older male and told me that it was actually his brother. I wanted to stab both of them to death and as the guy was explaining to his brother what test he was putting me through. I was starting to calm my bloody thoughts, the older male had looked at me and stood frozen. I could see the fear in his eyes and it made me excited. After the guy reassured his brother that everything was all right, we walked into the building and smoked some more crack. When we finished the guy's brother's crack, the older male left.

I was thirsty to smoke some more crack and the guy saw me fiending. He told me since he didn't have any money that he was going to make fake crack. He looked for as many empty crack vials he could and I followed him into the lobby's hallway, where pieces of sheet rock were falling off a side wall. the guy started to explain to me which sheet rock to use and how to break it up into little pieces of rock cocaine and how much to put in the vials to make it look official. We were selling the crack vials like hotdogs on the Fourth of July. The guy told me that it was enough for the moment and I followed him to another crack spot, where he spent all the money we made on crack. We left the crack spot but as we were walking, we began smoking crack, we arrived at my uncle's building and we smoked inside.

We continued to sell fake crack vials and smoke crack all the way until the morning hours. We stepped out to the front of the building and the guy saw some older teen walking down the block and he gave me the knife and told me to go rob him of his headphone's and his wallet. I nodded my head in a yes motion and left. I managed to sneak up behind the teen, wrap one arm around his neck and with the other hand stick the knife in his back but not to pierce him, I whispered into his ear in a threatening manner "don't move or I'll stab you to death and the same goes for if you turn around to see my face, do you understand?", the teen nodded yes that he understood and I told him to pass me his headphones and wallet. The hand wrapped around his neck was where he gave me the items nervously, then I told him to keep on walking straight and don't look back, he started walking straight

and turned a corner without looking back and disappeared, I just stood there watching him disappear.

I walked back to my uncle's building where the guy was waiting for me and gave him the headphones and the wallet, which only had twenty dollars. The guy told me to wait by the building that he was going to the crack spot to buy and trade the headphones for crack. At that he left, I sat on the front the building's entrance and waited for more than an hour and he still he didn't come back. I continued to wait but a deep sleep overcame me. I didn't know how much longer after I fell asleep when I heard someone tell me to wake up. I heard whoever it was repeat itself again. I was struggling to wake up and see who it was talking to me, the voice didn't have a male or female identity. I opened my eyes into the glaring bright sunlight and waited for my vision to clear. Once it did, I could see that there was no one anywhere near me or any one on the block. I closed my eyes again and fell asleep again. I heard the voice again but this time it was more of a scream and it told me "to wake up that I had to leave the block", Whoever it was, screamed at me again but this time my sleep was completely erased and I looked around again and like before no one was around. I was sitting down in the front of the building when I felt danger. I got up and looked around but didn't see anyone around the block and on the other blocks, it had people walking here and there. I listened to whoever it was and left my uncle's building and headed to my godmother/aunt Rosa's neighborhood. As I neared her building, she was sitting in front of a three-story building with some brown skinned older lady.

I approached my aunt Rosa and we greeted each other and she told me that my uncle Edwin is up that she would call him and tell him that I arrived. My aunt asked me if I was hungry and I answered "yes". She went in and brought out a plate of food for me to eat. Tt was in the ending of summer and the weather was still hot. I ate and waited for my uncle to come pick me up. While eating there was a drive by shooting on 183 street. A friend of my aunt's happened to come from down there and he told my aunt that someone got shot for selling dummies of crack and that they were looking for the other one that was involved too. My aunt's friend left by saying that the guy who got shot was hit nine times. He didn't know if the guy died but later on I heard a rumor

that he survived. I was thinking about whoever that voice belonged too, it was giving me a warning and lucky I listened to the voice because if I didn't, I know for a fact that I was going to get shot up or probably killed.

Anyway, after some time passed my aunt told me that my uncle Edwin was expecting me. I said my goodbyes to my aunt and headed to my uncle's apartment. On the way to my uncle's crib, I was thinking about who or what warned me but once I arrived at my uncle's crib, the questions I had asked myself were erased from my thoughts. My uncle embraced me with open arms and gave me the big sofa in the living room to sleep on. My uncle Edwin was like my father and the rest of their brothers illiterate, none of them passing the first grade but they were all skilled mechanics. They never had a problem getting off the book jobs as mechanics either in professional settings or in the ghetto garages but the difference between my father and the rest of his brothers were that my uncles weren't child abusers like my father though soon I realized that my uncle was a drug addict.

My uncle had three kids, ten-year-old Pito the oldest with close-crop black hair, a little chubby kid with white skin complexions like his father and siblings, then there was Pito's sister, eight-year-old Cali with long dirty blondish hair that reached the middle of her back but slimmer than Pito and lastly a three-year-old mischievous boy with dirty blondish short, cropped hair, and this little motherfucker would wake up every day, run into the room that Pito shared with his sister sit on her face and fart on her. I don't know why he did that but the shit was always funny and though Cali tried to have their parents stop him, he would always manage to commit his acts before she wakes up with Cali waking up screaming with disgust.

• • •

Things were good for the first week and a half, I would chill with my uncle and his family or I would go to my Godmother/aunt's on 182 street and hang out with her and my cousins thirteen-year-old Junior, a skinny light skinned kid with close crop black hair, who was shy with the girls. Then there was ten-year-old Anthony, chubby light skin with a black hair cut in a Caesar style haircut.

Then there was fifteen-year-old Emma, who of all the kids was the good one. She had long dirty blondish hair that reached her buttocks and was the prettiest one of her siblings. Emma was a shy girl and her mother used to treat her like shit and my aunt's last child was Maria who was nineteen-years-old, who didn't live with her mother because she was living with some guy that my aunt disapproves and because Maria lived with him, my aunt was always telling people that Maria was a slut, a puta, and a bitch, who opened her legs to every dick that Maria sees.

Hanging with my uncle and aunt, I was feeling good about myself and the change I was going through. I didn't have any need to escape into sex and I didn't have any sexual urges or didn't have lustful feelings for any males either young or in my age group or I didn't get blamed for things I didn't do or get into trouble. My only problem was finding a way to make money and buy clothes and sneakers because the few clothes I had was not fit for New York weather especially for the coming winter.

By the middle of the second week, things were starting to reveal themselves. Pito was telling me how his sister had performed oral sex on him, Anthony, and some other boy in the basement of where my Godmother/aunt lived. Then Pito told me that he likes to masturbate. He asked me to wait until everyone was sleeping, so I could sneak into his room and watch him masturbate. I did, and later on that night while everyone had fallen asleep, I snuck into Pito and his sister's room. She was sleeping but Pito was jerking off nakedly like he was racing. He had the bedsheet covering his waist down, I was starting to feel my lustful ways awakened by watching Pito. I wanted to see how big was Pito's dick was, so I reached down and grabbed his hand and tried to pull his hand away from his penis but he stopped me and I took the hint, so I left the room and closed the door to his room and went to sleep.

By the third week, I had returned to my uncle's crib from hanging out with my Godmother/aunt and my cousins and my uncle told me that I couldn't stay with them any longer and that I had to leave his crib. I asked him why and he didn't answer, so I left without asking any more questions. I was confused with worry, I went to my aunt Rosa and told her what happened and asked her if I could stay with her and she replied "no" with no explanation. I

sat on the stoops of my aunt's front building thinking what the hell am I going to do now and why my family just denied me a bed in their crib. While thinking of what to do, Anthony sat next to me and told me to follow him that he had something to tell me.

I followed Anthony to the corner of 182 street and walked down 182 street past Bassford Avenue onto Washington Avenue into 2183 an abandoned six-story building. We entered the building and walked the first flight of stairs but on the second floor the steps they were missing, so we walked on the edge of what used to be a flight of stairs, holding onto the handrails climbing up to the third floor, we entered a messed up abandoned apartment with a bed that looked like someone was sleeping on it. I followed Anthony and sat onto the edge of a window that led to a fire escape. The abandoned building was connected to another building, which was occupied by tenants and a grocery store, as we were sitting on the window with our legs on the fire escape, Anthony and I could see some of the tenants of the other building looking out of the window and a couple who was looking at us and warned us that to be careful because the building was unstable, we thanked them and stayed sitting down.

Anthony began telling me that the reason that our uncle Edwin and Rosa didn't want me to live with them was that his mother, my fucking backstabbing betraying lying bitch of a Godmother/aunt was telling everyone that I was not to be trusted because I was a fag, who liked to suck dick and get fucked in the ass. I was stunned, Anthony asked me "Manny is it true". I stood quiet thinking of a way to respond because I didn't want to open sexual opportunities. Then he asked me another question "Manny, my mother told everyone that you like raping boys, is it true?" I was enraged and very upset that my aunt was talking shit behind my back but in the mean while acting like she was family with dedicated love for me. I looked at Anthony and I decided to tell him the truth, I told Anthony "I never raped anyone but I did have sex with boys, who agreed to fuck". We stood quiet for some time, and looked around out the window to the trash filled back yard. After some time passed, Anthony broke the silence by saying that one day he thought he had the AIDs virus because he had a big bruise on one side of his upper leg and that he was going to cut that whole section of the bruise but Emma had stopped him. He continued telling me

"Manny, my mother told me that when I was born, she had asked the doctor to cut a piece of my dick off", I looked at him in disbelief and he got up and entered the crib, he then unbuttoned his pants and exposed his little flaccid penis. Anthony then said "look at this", he showed me a penis with no meatus (the head of the dick), it was just the rod. I was stunned silent. We didn't talk as he fixed himself, then we agreed to leave the building and go back to our block and as we were leaving Anthony told me not to tell his mother what he told me. I reassured him that I wouldn't, we went down the same way we climbed up and was leaving the building, when a African American teen of about fourteen or fifteen-year-old male was entering the building, he pulled out a double O seven pocket knife from the back of his back pocket and pointed it at us, asking us what were we doing in the building, I grabbed Anthony and pulled him behind me, just in case the kid decided to attack us and answered "nothing just chilling", he replied in a threatening manner that he didn't want us in the building again and didn't state why, I on the other hand knew why, he lived not only in the abandoned building but the bed Anthony and I saw was the teen's bed, the building belonged to him, we left and respected his wishes and never returned to the building.

. . .

We returned to 182 street on Bathgate Avenue and I could see my aunt hanging out in front of the building with some skinny brown-skinned Spanish lady. Anthony and I chilled in front of the three-story building and pretended not to know what my aunt was saying about me behind my back, my aunt pretended to be nice to me and introduced me to her friend. Margarita was her name, then my aunt introduced me to her new man Pete. In my head I was saying "this bitch is worse than a prostitute", she has gone through so many men and she treated every one of them like shit. Like Pipe, he used to get her mad and the grimy bitch would do something bad to his food, like one time, Pipe had gotten my aunt mad and what the bitch did was make him a cup of coffee and put a dead mouse in his cup. As he was drinking his coffee, he purposely swallowed the mouse to show my aunt that she didn't faze him.

I was mad at my aunt and confused as to why would she be lying about me raping boys and exposing my family's knowledge of my past of having sex with males but because of my love for my aunt and what my grandmother told me that adults were to be respected, I let the incident die with no response.

Then I noticed that my aunt became jealous when Margarita started talking to me like we were family, introducing me to some of her family that lived with her. I pretended to not notice her look of dislike for how Margarita was treating me, my worries were where the hell am I am going to sleep but Margarita spoke to some old Spanish guy, who had a yellow van that he was using and was parked in front of my aunt's building, she introduced me to this guy and left us, the old man's name was Jose and he explained to me that I could sleep in the van but I had to sell Heroine/dope for him plus I'll be getting a cut for selling his product. I didn't think about it because I never sold drugs and didn't understand the consequences behind the selling of drugs.

I agreed because I also needed clothes and food, he then gave me a brick, it's a small wrapped package of five bundles and each bundle had ten dope bags, each bag was ten dollars and if someone came to buy a bundle of dope, I was to give the buyer a special price of seventy to eighty dollars for each bundle and I'll still get my P.C., the name of the dope bags was called Salsa. Jose wasn't the original owner of Salsa, the original owner lived on 183 in Bassford Avenue, and in the earlier years of the mid-'80s the original owner made so much money that he renovated some of the buildings in his neighborhood. He even owned a building on Bassford Avenue but I don't know if it was out of jealously or just a drug life thing but he was gunned down and the dope brand died with him.

Jose had taken the Salsa brand to exploit the brand in hopes of making money and once he gave me my first brick, I started selling the dope like it was hot cakes and being that I lived in the van, my shop was open twenty four hours a day. Sometimes I'll be finished within two to three hours, Jose seeing my dedication and my loyalty, would give me four to five bricks. I would take my twenty to twenty five bundles and stash all but two bundles. I would then tie the two bundles around the string of my sweatpants' and put the two bundles inside my sweatpants and walk around the hood and sell to my customers on the down low.

At first, I was selling the bundles to a few of my dedicated bundle buyers at seventy dollars but since I was getting only twenty dollars out of each bundle, I started to wise up and change the prices of my bundles from seventy to eighty dollars and for others a hundred dollars, I was pocketing forty to fifty dollars not counting the other bundles I was selling to customers, who would buy one to two bags of dope.

I was making some money and I started to buy clothes and sneakers. I was constantly buying new sneakers because I would be in them all day and even sleep with them and by the time a couple of days pass when I decide to air my feet, the sneakers would have a smell so bad that to me it smelled like death. As for my hygiene, my aunt would sometimes let me take a shower in her apartment and once in a while she would feed me after my shower but my aunt Rosa became even more jealous when she realized that her best friend Margarita was not only letting me take showers in her apartment but Margarita would feed me also and on the days that I don't take showers, I try not exert to much body movement so as not to sweat and develop body odor.

. . .

I started to feel the stress of living in the van and dealing with the two face bitch of my aunt still telling people that not only was I a fag but that I love raping boys and the funny shit about it was that some people really believed it but I didn't let her lies stop me from keeping my promise to change my ways. While selling dope, I started to observe my customers physical demeanor changing as they returned to me every night and day to buy heroine from me, and since I didn't understand what they were going through or why heroine makes people be depended on it, I continued to sell not really give a rats ass about what I was seeing or doing to them. I continued to deal the Salsa dope brand to my customers, and to my exclusive bundle buyers who would rarely up come up short, I would bless them but to the other buyers that comes to buy one or two, they had to come with the full amount and I never fell for the dope fiend sob stories but I had this European customer who would come at night to buy three or four bundles. On the first night, when he came to cop

from me, he pulled out a knot of money the size of a Big Mac hamburger and it was the first time I ever saw thousand dollar bills and he never paid the seventy dollars I charged him. He paid full price and I want to thank him for helping me out in those moments that was fifty dollars I was making from each bundle giving me a chance to buy clothes, sneakers, get my haircut and food, he even gave me some good advice concerning trying it, he told me "don't take this poison, it's no good" and after six or seven times that he came to purchase heroine from me, I never saw him again.

But as for the other customers well, they were becoming desperate and looking haunted with dark circles either already formed or are in the process of becoming dark circles around their eyes. One day another European customer came to me with a six-year-old son to cop from me, I became enraged with him and told him that I will not serve him in front of his son. He told me to calm down and left but came back like five minutes later, I was still mad because I knew he left that little boy alone and unprotected around the corner. The European approached me to cop one fucking bag, I told him angrily to never bring his child to cop drugs and the father replied "yes sir" and left never seeing him again.

. . .

My eighteenth birthday was about two months away and still none of my family helped me with any housing but like I've mentioned before, my godmother/aunt was playing devil's advocate with me, telling everyone in her building and in the hood that I was a fag, who liked to rape boys, she even told Margarita's kids, nephews and nieces, then one day I didn't know my godmother/aunt saw me stash my bricks of dope under a car's front tire inside a small paper brown bag. She had asked me to go down to 183 street in Bathgate avenue and check out about the shooting that had happened a couple of hours ago. As I was about to go, I saw Margarita shook her head side to side on the down low warning me not to go. I pretended not to see Margarita's warning and told my aunt "nah, I'm not going for what to get shot up" and stood around selling where I had an eye on my stash.

Now I had to worry more than the rumors my aunt was putting out in the street, I didn't have enough time to cry when I spent my eighteenth birthday in a cold van lonely with no friends or family to celebrate with, why because I was worrying that my Godmother/aunt was going to set me up and get me killed.

I even spent Thanksgiving, Christmas, and New year's alone but the only difference was that Margarite fed me on the three holidays and even gave me a Christmas card. I gave her one and I gave my aunt one but she took her's and tore it up in pieces and threw them on the hallway floor of the building's first floor.

When winter became spring, I awoke early one morning I'll say around eight or nine and was ready to make some early morning money, that's when the dope fiends are on "E." (empty, dope sic), with the money I'll be making in the morning, I was gonna buy summer clothes and sneakers and if I had any money left over, I'd spend the rest on cannabis. I had put on a pair of sweat pants and a t-shirt, then tied a bundle of heroin to the string of the sweat pants and put it in my pocket. I then tied the last five bundles underneath my balls until I found enough time to secretly stash it, then I began my business of selling. It was a good morning and after making a lot of money, I went and stashed my cut and my boss's money.

I was selling across the street from where my aunt and Margarita lived and after some time of selling heroin, I laid my back on the fence that was connected to a three-story private family house that circle an abandoned parking lot, when all of a sudden a four door Dodge car stopped in front of where I was chilling and four men came out from each car door running towards me, they pretended to be cops but when they didn't showed me their badges, I was preparing to fight them, one of them had a lead on the other three and as he got closer I charged at him, so I could not only punch him on the jaw but use my body to knock him down and hurt him badly and deal with the other three but shit didn't go as planned because to guy knew what I use about to do and as he came towards me he pulled his shirt up and showed me what appeared to be a gun handle.

At that I stopped in my tracks because I knew I wasn't Superman and they would kill me if they were forced too, the other men quickly surrounded me and forced my back on the fence and requested that I give them the drugs, I

told them that I just handed my boss everything I made and he gave me a bundle as my payment, I went into my pocket and pulled out the couple of bags I had left tied to my sweat pants string and as they continued to search me, I happened to look at my aunt's front window and saw that she was smiling at what was happening to me. I knew by that look that she had something to do with what was happening to me right now, they stopped searching me and ran into the car, and sped away. I ran to someone I was cool with that lived two buildings away from where my aunt and Margarita's lived, I went into the basement apartment, and I knocked on his door and when he answered the door I told him what happened, I continually told him that they didn't rob me of the five bundles I had stashed, he told me that we'll deal with it when we come back, so I followed him outside and into his car, we went searching for the robbers but after like half an hour and I couldn't see any one of them that I could identify. We returned to his apartment and we split the money. He told me that he could get all five bundles sold somewhere else and I gave them to him, splitting the dope money fifty-fifty. He then told me that he will back up my story with his older brother Jose and when I told Jose what happened and his brother backed me up, he just took it as lost.

My friend became my partner on another heist I did but with my cousin Anthony, it was dark outside and I saw some crack dealer stash a big brown bag in a section of the garage, where I had the supernatural car experience when I was twelve. The drug dealer didn't see that I saw him stashing his drugs as I was heading to store, I bought some snacks for me and headed to look for Anthony. Once I found him, I told him what I saw and described to him where it was, he replied that he knew where it was and we waited until no one was around. We walked half a block and he walked the rest of the way into and out of garage and back to where I was waiting at, he had it stashed under his shirt.

We then walked into the back of the building where his mother lived and into the basement, the first room was filled with all kinds of fiery items but the second room, had two large sofas laying on its side on one side of the room and on the other side, it had a weight bench with no bar or weights. He took out the bag and I counted twenty-seven bundles of crack with a hundred and twenty crack vials in each bundle. I told Anthony that we'll stash it here until

I can give it to someone who could sell it for us but we'll have to give him half of the money after everything is sold. He agreed and I also told him not to tell anyone but he did. He told one of his friends, when they came into the basement as Anthony and I was smoking a blunt though Anthony didn't tell him where it was but the kid wanted P.C. Anthony and I told him to go piss off but sometime later, Anthony and I found out, the kid told his parents but they didn't give a damn about it and after all the crack was sold, I gave my friend his half of the payment and I split the rest with Anthony but what we did was very dangerous because if the owner would of found out that it was Anthony and I that stole his drugs, we would have been gunned down.

. . .

Margarita had gotten into the dope game and had me selling "Old Fashion" heroin brand. I was making more money with selling her brand and my boss's brand. I was young and I was feeling like Scar Face and one early afternoon I selling and my aunt, her man Pete and my cousins where hanging out on the front of the building's steps. I saw my boss come out of the building he lived in and walk towards me and when he approached me, he slapped me on one side of my face. I became enraged and took off a fanny pack that I had around my waist and put it on a car and went back towards him to beat him down, he had taken a small revolver and pointed the gun at my head, it made me more enrage than I ever felt, I told him in a threatening manner to shoot me, if he had the balls and as I repeated myself a few times, I walked up to the gun and placed my forehead on the nozzle, he was shaking with fear. His hands were shaking and I was hoping and taunting him to pull the trigger. I wanted him to end all the fucking bullshit with me, I wanted to die, I was tired of everyone treating me like shit, I told him that if he doesn't pull the trigger, I would on him but the coward motherfucker put the gun away and ran into his building, I ran into my friend's crib and told him what happened but excluded that it was his brother, he gave me a fully clipped hand gun and I ran out of his apartment. He had followed right behind me, I spotted Jose crossing the street of 182 street heading towards third Avenue, he was across the street from the

fenced abandoned parking lot, he was on the side of the block where there was three five or six story buildings. There were parked cars in front of the buildings and he must of saw me creeping towards him but when my friend realized it was his older brother, he begged me not to do it I stopped with the gun to my side and watched as Jose walked away and glanced at me quickly and disappeared around the corner.

The darkness had taken over me and my friend's continuous pleading not to kill his older brother brought me into an angered state, my aunt was lucky too that I didn't gun down Jose because she and her man were going to get it also. When Jose had slapped me on my face and I put my head on the nozzle, she was smiling at me. She had told my boss that I was selling for someone else and he didn't want me to sell for anyone else but him, after the incident I only sold for Margarita.

Then one night, while playing two-hand touch football with my cousins, Margarita's thirteen-year and fifteen-year-old sons and some older teens were playing on the corner of 182 street but on the street itself and having fun. When I noticed a small Toyota car heading towards us at a great speed, I told the kids and the teens to get off the street and go on the sidewalk. When I made sure everyone was off the street. I was going to head between two cars and get on the sidewalk with the others but the small four-door Toyota skidded sideways in front of me and I saw the window in the passenger seat go down and someone pull out a sawed-off shotgun, cock a shell and pointed the shotgun at my face. I couldn't see who was pointing the gun at me, it was completely dark in there. I didn't even feel fear, all I felt was a calming numbness and after a minute or two with the gun pointed at my face, the gun went back into the car, the window closed and they drove away.

I knew that my Godmother/aunt had something to do with whoever was in the Toyota with the gun pointed at my face. I wanted to kill her so bad but I thought of my cousins and how they are innocent to all I'm going through with their mother but I was trying to find a way to get even and one day I did. I started to notice Anthony looking at me with sexual interest, he asked me again if the rumors that his mother was telling everyone was true of being gay

and raping boys. I responded by saying "Anthony, I fucked a lot a boys my age and younger than me, some had gotten jealous of me for having sex with other boys or for refusing to have any sex with them because they stunk, they would tell on me, getting me into trouble". I continued telling him that I would also get into trouble, when I would go for boys who would say they would never let a fag touch them but after I finish sucking their dicks and making them cum, I would turn around and ignore them and when they came around wanting more sexual pleasure from me, I would say no.

Anthony and I was in the basement smoking a blunt. When I told him the truth, he then asked me if I wanted to suck his dick. I answered "yes" he then pulled his pants and underwear down onto his ankles and laid on his back on the weight lifting bench. I got on my knees between his legs and sucked his headless dick, I realized after a minute or two of me preforming oral sex on him that he couldn't ejaculate. I gave him around ten minutes of sexual pleasure and though he couldn't ejaculate, he was addicted just to the fact that he was getting gay sex and after some time passed Anthony started to notice that I was getting bored with him, so early one night, when we were supposed to meet up in the basement for our sexual fuck, he had brought Margarita's thirteen-year-old son Nini. He had a dark chocolate skin complexion, and was a heavy set kid with a round hard fat stomach.

Nini had a baby dick and stole money from his mother's drug stash. Nini was able to ejaculate and every time we would meet up, I would suck on Nini's dick more, Anthony would ask Nini if he could suck his and Nini one night in the basement, after I made him cum, Nini allowed Anthony to suck on his dick but after a few seconds, Nini stopped Anthony and told him his mouth was too cold, then Nini would put me to finish what Anthony started.

On another night, Nini wanted me to suck his dick across the street in the abandoned parking lot but behind the back of the three story house and their fence, which led into a grassy area of the empty parking lot. I went on my knees sucking on his dick and balls and just when he was about to cum, a light from one of the three story floors turned on and people started talking though no one was looking out the back window I stopped of fear of getting caught but he said to me" one more second and I would have cum". Then he quickly

masturbated, ejaculate and quickly fixed himself, then we both ran out into the parking lot, climb the fence and hung out in the front of his building.

Soon after, Anthony had invited Fofi, Nini's eight-year-old nephew, who had a lighter skin complexion than Nini's and when he whipped out his erect penis, it was longer than Bebe's and when he put me to suck his dick, I was able to make him ejaculate. One day before I started sucking his dick, I decided to measured his penis and it was going into the six inches range. I would suck on his dick, when he was horny or in the mood to have sex, a few nights later before going into the basement to suck Fofi and Anthony's dick, Anthony wanted a thirteen year old friend of his to hang out in the abandoned parking lot with us, the skinny light skin kid's named Ralphie, joined Anthony and me in the parking lot. We were in the lot no longer than fifteen minutes, when Anthony started sexually flirting with Ralphie, Ralphie whipped out a baby size erect penis and was trying to penetrate Anthony's rectum, never succeeding but after a few second's more of Ralphie humping Anthony, Anthony turned around and told me to suck his dick. I got on my knees and sucked on Anthony's headless dick and while I was doing him, he was telling Ralphie that it felt good that to try it.

Ralphie with his little hardened penis throbbing up and down came close to me and told me to suck him off. I did and after a few seconds, I knew that he couldn't ejaculate but I continued as he wanted, he grabbed my head from behind with both of his hands and as I sucked on his dick and balls, he would whine his body in tune with my sucking, after a couple of minutes of this, Anthony told us that we should all go into the basement and have some more sex, we agreed and they took turns letting me perform oral sex on them. We stood in the basement for over an hour, then they fixed themselves and went home and I went to my van.

Now I had four sexual partners but Nini and Fofi didn't know about me sucking either one of their dicks. The way it went, one night it would be Anthony, Ralphie, and Nini and the next night, it would be Anthony, Ralphie, and Fofi. None of the adults suspected anything going between any of us, though I was getting tired of having sex with them, then there was a part of me that I kept imprisoned, wanting to do more than have sex with the boys, it wanted everyone to feel its pain and suffering by torturing and killing everyone

in its path and it got even harder to control, when late one October night around eleven forty, Margarita had come outside in the sneak tip and whispered for me to follow her upstairs quietly that she had something to show me. I followed but I was alert and weary about her intentions being that she is my Godmother/aunt's friend. I continued to follow her on to the third and into a room which face the front of the building and a view of the van.

Margarita told me to peek out the window and just watch the van and don't let anyone see me. At first I didn't look because I didn't trust her but after few minutes past by hitting midnight, she had looked at her watch and told me to peek. I peeked down at the van and saw two men in waist goose down jackets with a baby Uzis guns, stand by the passenger side door and the other stood by the side van door, the one by the passenger side door said something into the van but when no one responded, the guy by the side door of the van, opened the side door, reached in and yanked my quilt out of the van and searched it. Then I could hear one of them ask the other where could I be. No answer was given but they started looking down and around the block and when I saw that one of the men was going to look up, I slowly let the curtain close and stood back and looked at Margarita and without asking her, she explained to me that she went to visit my Godmother/aunt's apartment and she overheard my aunt speaking with someone on the phone and telling whoever it was that she would pay him five thousand dollars if he could kidnap me, take somewhere far where no one could find me and kill me. Then she continued telling me that my aunt was the one involved in the first attempt on my life, when the four door Toyota skidded to the side on me. Margarita said that my aunt was the one who sent the fake cops to rob me and she continued saying that my aunt told Jose about me selling for Margarita, things I already knew, I was so enrage that my throat was knotting up and I felt like letting my personality take over me and fuck everyone and kill them all but then Margarita told me not to worry that I could live with her and her family and it was what brought me back to my regular self but I was still angry and depressed because I wanted my aunt to be like Margarita treating me with love and kindness but instead, the fucking dirty no good for nothing bitch was trying to kill me and something was always protecting me without me realizing it.

Not only did my Godmother/aunt hate me but what made her more mad at me was the fact that I was taking her heroin customers. She was selling heroin and crack but she was having Anthony and Emma serve her customers and since she closed at twelve midnight. I on the other hand was open twenty four hours a day. My customers had the permission to knock on the van door when I used to sleep in it, yet they still were faithful and came into the building's second floor and I would serve them and my aunt's customers. After the third attempt on my life, I woke up at six in the morning, got dressed, and went outside not only to sell drugs but to physically let my aunt know that she failed and I survived again. Later in the morning my aunt came outside and was surprised with disbelief at seeing me, I stood on the front of the building selling heroin all day and part of the night and promising myself that I would take all her heroin customers and make her suffer by breaking her pockets.

But things were about to get much worse for me and everyone who was helping me. I remember on Halloween, I was sleeping in Nini's room. Nini wasn't there, he wanted to sleep over a family's members apartment for Halloween, so I had the room to myself. I locked the room from the inside, put my crocodile Dundy knife on Nini's dresser, smoked a blunt and went to sleep on the form mattress that was place on the floor by the dresser. When I awoke the next day, I was facing my knife that was buried sum what three inches deep into the wooden floor, I got up and I had to use both of my hands and a great amount of strength to pull the knife out from the wooden floor.

By November, I decided to visit my mother one night, even though she calls me the devils son, and I took Fofi with me. My mother didn't act up, so we stayed a little longer. She was cooking food and fed us as soon as she finished cooking, we then chilled for a while with my mother, brothers, and sister until Fofi announced that he was tired and wanted to go home. We put our coats and said our goodbyes to my family, then Fofi and I headed back home. Once we arrived, everyone was in Margarita's bedroom hysterical with panic, fear and in tears, it was Nini, his mother, one of his sisters who lived there with her small little dead beat boyfriend and their infant baby. I asked Margarita what happened and she responded by saying that five minutes after Fofi and I left to see my mother, two men in ski mask and guns rushed into the

apartment, pointed a gun at the baby's head and requested that all the heroin I was selling be given to them but since I never kept the drugs in the crib, I always kept it stashed in the basement not even Margarita knew where I had the drugs and when everyone professed that they didn't know where I put it, the two men threatened to shoot the baby if they don't give up the drugs but when everyone repeated what they first said, the two men searched the apartment. Not finding nothing, they left the crib, after everyone calmed down, we talked and we all agreed that my aunt was the cause of this attempt of robbery.

. . .

Now I've mentioned that I was sleeping in Nini's room and throughout that time Margarita allowed me to stay with them until December. I was preforming oral sex on Nini when he became sexually aroused which was on a every other night basis, then he slowed down and let me suck on his dick two to three times a week but Fofi, I was sucking on his dick almost every day, after he came from school or when he would stay over and when Nini would sleep with his mother leaving us alone. Fofi even fucked me in the ass a few times, he even wanted me to fuck him in the ass but I knew that if I did, I would hurt him, so I would kiss, lick, and suck on his rectum. I was rarely having sex with Anthony and one day I had made money, so I decided to take Fofi to a movie with two of his uncles. We all went to watch "War of The Roses", Fofi's two uncles decided to leave due to having to work early in the morning, so Fofi and I stayed until the movie was over then we to headed for home and when we arrived and entered the apartment, everyone was in Margarita's room in the same state there were when the two masked men tried to rob them before but this time, two masked men told them to look for my dope stash hoping that I would have changed my ways and stash the drugs in the house but when nothing was found, the two masked men left a message saying that they would catch me and the drugs. I was so enraged that I screamed down the stairs to my aunt and said "if you have the balls why don't you do it yourself", the urge to kill someone was so strong that I felt the color in my vision flicker from darkness back to normal and back to darkness. I felt my head shake three times

feeling like it was cracking and I could hear my personality screaming at me saying "fuck these insignificant beings, they created us, it's time to let me take control and show these motherfuckers, what they created." The voice had me entranced and the urge to kill was so powerful that I was sexually aroused and just as my head felt like it was going to explode. I felt someone tugging on my arm bringing me back to normal and making all the thoughts and feelings disappear. It was Fofi, who had stayed over and told me that he felt safe sleeping with me, we curled up together in a nonsexual way and fell to sleep.

I don't know how many hours later when I was awakened by a sound coming for somewhere. Once I was fully awake, I concentrated hard to tried and identify where the noise was coming from and I jumped off the bed. When I realized the noise was coming from the roof and whoever it was-was trying to get down from the roof's entrance, I grabbed the wooden bat I had in the room and left the room and started banging hard on the stairs banister, the roof's iron or steel latter that led up and down the roof and even on the walls. And at the same time, I was screaming to whoever it was up there, which sounded like there were two to three people up there but I screamed "any motherfucker who comes down, know I will kill you", then I screamed out that my aunt is a coward bitch sending punks to do her dirty work.

I was so enraged that I was prepared to let my personality take over, I was really hoping that they tried to come down. I screamed at them again to come down and because of my racket, everyone in Margarita's apartment woke up. Margarita opened the door that lead further into the apartment, her bedroom, the kitchen and the bathroom. I could see fear in her eyes and everyone who sat together in Margarita's room. I walked in and went straight to the kitchen window, I opened it and screamed out "come down you punk motherfucker, let's see where your balls are". I was taunting them and as I walked from the kitchen to the hallway, I taunted and dared them to come down but after half an hour had passed, I didn't hear anymore footsteps and I stopped screaming and reassured everyone inside that shit was okay, to calm down and go back to sleep and as soon as everyone went to sleep one by one, I was the last to fall asleep but to reassure my safety, I put Nini's bed by the door and fell asleep right besides Fofi.

. . .

I started to see that things were getting oppressive for Margarita and her family because my Godmother/aunt didn't want them to show me love and have me live with them. I started to see things falling apart for them, and as well for me too, I was going through all kinds of emotions and not knowing what to do with myself, I'd escape into sex with Anthony, Fofi, Nini, and Ralphie. I knew that if I kept on having sex with them that eventually I was going to get busted but I didn't care, the stress of everything had me so fucked up that one night I didn't realize that I blanked out and I had grabbed my crocodile hunting knife and started walking down the stairs. Once I reached the first floor, we saw my aunt, Ariel and his older brother talking side by side unaware that we were walking silently towards them. I could hear a voice in me, telling me to stab my aunt first in the back, then the other two. I was at least six or seven feet from them, when I stood still in a daze but staring at them, my trance was broken when Ariel turned around and screamed and jumped back out of fear. It made my aunt and Ariel's older brother turn around and respond the same way, Ariel asked me, if I was alright. I looked at him and a thought appeared in the back of my head, when he tried to rob of twenty dollars I gave him, I realized then that all that gangster shit they were all portraying was a croc of shit, I responded nothing and left to throw the knife into the sewer.

Then some things were happening to me that I couldn't explain. Like one day, I awoke early in the afternoon and went down stairs to hang out with Margarita and her family and for some reason they didn't know who the fuck I was. Even after I identified myself, they still didn't recognize me and when my aunt came outside, she even asked me who I was. I decided to take a walk and figure out what the hell was happening. I returned to the neighborhood and everything was back to normal, it was like the incident didn't happen.

On another night, Fofi and I were sleeping on Nini's bed and all of a sudden I was awakened by Fofi's fearful and tearful screaming cries. Even Margarita had wakened and entered the room to see what was going on. She asked Fofi what happened and he replied that he awoke to use the bathroom and

when he looked at my face, my eyes were glowing red like if it was on fire. I laughed at him and told him that he had a bad dream but he swore that he was awake, Margarita then took Fofi to her room to sleep for the night.

After that incident Margarita tried to get me to see a Santero, which she invited many times but I somehow managed to elude him. But late one night, it was in control of me and we walked up and down in the middle of the street but in front of my aunt's and Margarita's building. We spotted the Santero looking down at us from Edwin's bedroom window, and after more than half an hour of pacing up and down, we walked upstairs into Margarita's apartment and sat down in the kitchen. By the time the Santero came into the kitchen to talk to me, it was gone and I was back to normal. He sat across from me and looked at me quietly. I really didn't care with what he had to say because I knew that Santeria is actually worshipping Demons, the Santeros and Santeras didn't know that. He broke the silence by saying to me "I noticed you've been avoiding me". I didn't respond but look at face and at a hand that was in a splinter, seeing my interest in his injured hand, he told me that he was charging people to do Santeria cleansing and other jobs and that the Saints/Angels got mad and punished him and that his injury is permanent.

I still remained silent and he continued with "I know about the love letter to your cousin Emma and I know about you getting sick and not telling anyone. You even gave someone the rest of your work to do". He caught my attention with the last thing he said, as for the love letter, well that was common knowledge. I had written a letter to Emma professing my love for her and wanting to make a family with her. I was going to give it to her when I saw her. I had gotten up to use the bathroom and when I came back, the letter was gone and it mysteriously appeared in my aunt's possession. My aunt yelled and screamed but I didn't pay any attention to her stupid bullshit.

What caught my attention was him saying that I was sick, that was all true and the person that finished what I had was Edwin. I was real sick but for some reason I didn't want anyone to know about it, Then the Santero started telling me that my aunt had some dolls made in the form of her kids and her man and it was to be in control of their lives and that she had some buried in the back yard and the freezer, I really didn't care about that but when he said that I have

a second part of me that isn't me and its angry and dangerous, I wanted to ask him what it wants but I still didn't trust him. He advised me to do whatever I can to keep it imprisoned. I was finding him a fake. When he didn't advise me to stop having sex with the boys, I let him speak to me for some time more, then I excused myself and went into Nini's room, turned on the TV, pulled out the form mattress that was underneath Nini's bed and I laid down and watched TV until I fell asleep.

A few days after my uncelebrated birthday, everyone was waking up for either school, work, and I, for my drug selling schedule. As I left Nini's room I noticed one of my aunt's dope fiend customers coming out of Edwin's room, I knew that my aunt was up to something but didn't know what exactly, then I saw fifteen-year-old Edwin coming out of his room half asleep but with a noticeable erection, I joked with him and asked him "how's that pussy", he looked at me and responded that he didn't do anything with her, I believed that my aunt sent the dope fiend to spy on me and see where I was stashing the drugs. I was getting tired of all this and I was thinking about just disappearing from the hood but I needed to think of what can I do that would make me leave permanently but nothing came to me just then.

A few days after Christmas I started to feel like I was an outsider and it was making me really depressed, so later on in the evening, Fofi and I were in Nini's room by ourselves, while everyone else even the dope fiend were in the apartment with Margarita. Instead of us staying in the room so I could suck Fofi's dick, we went into Edwin's room. I locked the door to the room, whipped out his long erect penis out and started to perform oral sex on him. He was about to ejaculate when someone knocked on the door. While Fofi was fixing himself, I noticed that someone was peeking through the key hole, which could actually see into the whole room, I opened the door and it was the dope fiend.

The dope fiend took Fofi by the arm and escorted him inside the apartment and locked the door. I went into Nini's room in fear and I knew that someone was looking through the peek hole of Margarita's apartment door to see what I was doing. I waited for more than fifteen minutes to go by and to make sure no one was by the apartment door. I put on my jacket and went

down the stairs as quietly as possible as I could and left the building. I knew that if I stayed, I was going to get in trouble. I headed into one of the buildings on 182 street between Bathgate Avenue and Third Avenue and hung out on the stairs of the roof. By midnight I went onto the roof to look down at my aunt's building. The thing in my head was telling me that it was time to get even with everyone. I went back in the roof's stairs and continued down until I was out of the building, I then started to look for a container big enough to fill with gasoline. After some time, I found an empty antifreeze container and walked down to Washington Avenue to a gas station a few blocks down that side of the Avenue. I told the gas attended that my car broke down and I needed a little gas to start the car and drive it here, the attended me told that I needed a gas container in order to get gas, I told him that I didn't have one to please help me out, he reluctantly allowed me and all I spent was three dollars of gas, as I walked back to my Godmother/aunt's and Margarita's block, I was thinking of pouring gasoline in the first room with the fire hazard materials in the basement and on the front entrance of the building and lighting those sections on fire and watch them all scream and burn to death. As I stood in front of the building, a quick picture of Grandma and her two mentally ill children flashed through my mind and it broke me out of my darkness. I then started thinking of my cousins and Margarita's young children and instead of burning them down, I went to Pete's brand new car that my aunt bought him, poured gasoline all over the car making sure that majority of the gas went into the hood area, soaking the engine with gasoline. Once I finished pouring the gas on the car, I lit the car on fire and backed away, as the fire started consuming the car, I gave the burning car my back and started heading towards the building I was in before, as I was walking I heard a whoop sound and I knew that the engine and the car was engulfed in flames, once I reached the roof's stairs, I laid on the floor and fell asleep.

The next day, I awoke feeling depressed and questioning my life, I was thinking why should I continue living when no one in my family ever loved or cared for me. I stood up, opened the door to roof and saw that it was raining. I continued walking until I was on the edge of the roof, I was hoping for someone to stop me but all I heard was the howling wind, so I let go and moved

forward to fall to my death but then someone grabbed me from the back of my sweater pulling me back from the edge, I quickly turned around to fight off whoever it was that pulled me from my jump and I froze because there wasn't anyone around. Suddenly all of a sudden, I could hear many voices whispering in my ear that it wasn't my time and something else I can't remember and for a brief moment, all the pain and suffering I felt was gone and whatever it was that saved me, was not there anymore.

I went back into the roof's stairs and chilled there until the rain stopped. I was thinking of how peaceful I felt when whatever saved me was talking to me and how I felt an emotion that I was craving for, " love of a loved one". Some more time passed and I checked if the rain had stopped raining, it did and I went to the roof's edge to see if my aunt and her man had awakened to see their car totally destroyed, I was happy to seeing both of them looking in disbelief at their destroyed car, I could hear my aunt screaming at one of her dope fiend customer that she would pay anyone fifty dollars, if they found out who did this to their car.

Hearing that, I devised a plan on putting my aunt against Margarita in order to gain favor of my aunt but shit didn't go as plan as I envisioned it would be, everyone in Margarita's apartment knew what I did with Fofi, except his uncles and my aunt. That's what I thought anyway, I walked back in the roof and continued walking until I was outside and standing beside Pete as he was looking at the burned engine. I was smiling inside not only because he didn't know I was the one who destroyed his car but because he was in hot water with my aunt because he was caught sexually flirting with one of Margarita's daughters who I actually had a crush on but one day I caught them French kissing in Edwin's room, so I pulled back from trying to form anything with her but then they got caught this time by a fat ugly nineteen-year-old kid name Charly, who also had a crush on her and upon catching them, he went and told my aunt. They fought verbally for days and I knew that Pete was going to regret what he did one day.

Charly almost had me stabbed by the dead beat husband of one of Margarita's daughter, who lived with Margarita's daughter and their child. The dead beat had it in his head that his wife and I were having a thing. I couldn't

believe that he thought that I would violate like that and the funny thing was that she wasn't my type. She was going on being obese and she was ugly to me facially and she had some type of disgusting rash that appeared off and on-on the side of her neck. He confronted me at first verbally, then tried to swing at me. I dodged his fist and told him that I didn't do anything with his wife and that I didn't want any problems but this little skinny man that compared to me physically, I could make two of him. Again came at me with fist flying for my face, I dodged every single blow, he then ran out of Edwin's room and into his room and came back out with an homemade knife that was sharp as hell, he first stabbed my Elephant skinned trench coat a few times, which was laying the hall's banister. Then he charged at me. Luckily, I knew how to fight and I was able to slap the knife away from me and grab the hand with the knife and with my other arm put the dead beat in a head lock. I warned him that I didn't want any problems that if he kept on, I would get in defense mode and fuck him up but the faggot continued with trying to struggle free from me.

I then let go of him and pushed him away from me quickly. I planned the push, so I could punch on the jaw and knock him the fuck out but his girl intervened and I hit him on the face. I quickly went for his jaw again and this time I connected my fist to his jaw, stunning him. The family seeing us fighting decided to stop us and he was lucky because I was about to throw him out the fucking window, though they broke us up, the dead beat, his wife, and I continued to argue and after half an hour of cursing each other out, his wife broke down and admitted that she had a fling with the ugly nineteen-year-old snitch. He was called to the crib and I smacked the living shit out of him and told him to never come around the apartment again.

Now as I was standing by Pete and he was cursing the shit out of whoever did this to his car, I knew one thing for certain that Pete was going to pay dearly for betraying my aunt with another female. Pete and my aunt asked me if I knew who did this to their car. I responded "no" but promised them that I will find out. What I didn't know was that she was told about the Fofi incident and that she was setting me up.

My aunt knew that I was sleeping on the streets somewhere but didn't know exactly where. What she did was apologize for how she treated me and

said that if I helped her sell the last few bags of dope that she would have one of her friends let me move in with him in the basement. Hearing that brought my guard down and I was finally feeling like part of the family. Something that I always wanted, she went so far as to give me five bags of her heroin brand and told me to keep twenty dollars and give her thirty. I was able to sell the five bags of dope and give my aunt the thirty dollars, she then told me to go inside her apartment and chill until she spoke with her friend and I did.

I went and chilled in the living room with my little female cousin Amylee watching television. The television was on a stand that blocked Anthony and his older brother Junior's room with a curtain behind the stand to block anyone seeing in or out of the room. We were watching the TV, when all of a sudden the curtains were being parted to one side, and Anthony appeared standing with his erect headless penis jerking it off. I watched Amylee's reaction and I realized that they were having sex with one another. I watched how she tried to wave at Anthony to stop but he kept on, she tried hard not to look at his penis but she couldn't take her eyes off of it. Seeing the lust between the two made mine my lust explode like wild fire throughout my body but just as I stepped out of the apartment to go to the other side and suck and fuck Anthony quickly, when my aunt appeared in the entrance of the building, stopping me and telling me that her friend said that it was okay to stay with him. he finished by saying that he was a super of a building, two buildings from where she lived.

I went to the super's basement apartment and he let me in. The Spanish man was around his mid-fifties. He showed me the room I was to be sleeping in and then he showed me the bathroom. I told him that it was good timing because I wanted to take a shower and go to sleep but in reality I really wanted to masturbate in the shower. Anthony had gotten me aroused and I wanted to quench my lust. I stood in the bathroom and I started to take off my sneakers and one sock, when I heard voices whispering to one another outside the apartment. I quickly put my sock and sneakers back on and walked to the front door of the basement apartment and I could hear more than three people whispering to one another. I was starting to get scared and when I heard a gun being cocked, my heart felt like it was going to explode with fear, at that moment the super came out of his room and was about to open the door. I stopped him

physically and threatened him that if he tries to open the door, I was going to fucking kill him. He stopped and I could see that he believed me. He stood still where he was at and we heard like three or four people banging on the door, screaming at the super to open the door, the super was scared to death of my threat and didn't move. As they continued to bang and demand for the door to be opened, I told the super to go to his room and don't come out, he did and locked his door.

I wanted to panic but I knew that if I didn't find a way out, I was going to die. I went to the back of the basement to see if there was another way to leave, all I saw was all kinds of furniture stuff, mechanical equipment and a couple of used doors leaning upright on the middle of the back wall. I felt panic creeping in my mind blinding me, when I couldn't find another way out but then I started to think that this basement is like my aunt's and there has to be another door. I went to where there were four or five doors leaning on the wall and looked and saw that there was a door that lead out back but it was being blocked by the doors. I had no trouble of moving them aside enough so I could go through.

I was in the back yard and I could see that all I had to do was jump two fences across from where I was at and I would be in my aunt's backyard. I couldn't go the other way because there were vicious dogs. I jumped both fences that led into my aunt's back yard and I saw her standing there looking down to me with a smile on her pudgy fat face. As I looked at her, I swore to myself that if I get out of this situation out alive, I was going to torture her to death. I broke out of my trance and was going to jump another fence to go to hallway ally of a building next to my aunt's building, but something made me stop in my tracks and hold my breath that's when I heard someone breathing heavily on the other side. Now I understood why my aunt was smiling, she had me surrounded.

Panic and fear were starting trying to take over me. I had nowhere to go but into my aunt's basement and I did just that. I went in and hid inside two turned over large sofas, the ground was cold, and I no longer had I hid under the sofa. When Pete and Edwin walked in, Pete had a knife and Edwin had a two by four. They passed my area into the boiler room, they checked a small closet that was underneath the stairs and moved on further into the front of

the basement. I could hear them knocking on the one room that was being rented to a lady. She opens the door and Pete asked her if anyone was there with her, she answered "no" and they left her alone, she closed and locked the door, they came back through the way they entered passing me again and kept on moving out of the basement, suddenly an urge of me popping out and scaring them ran through my head but I knew that if I did that, my body would never be found.

They left the basement and I didn't move from my hiding place just in case they came back and they did but not to look for me but to seal the basement entrance. Someone was hammering the door but they had forgotten to seal the little window on the side of the basement that Anthony and I used for no reason. I stood under the sofa until I thought it was safe enough for me to do so. I went into the boiler room and entered into the little closet that was under the stairs. I was planning to stay there until I thought it was safe enough for me to escape but hours turned into days, in the meantime, I could hear my aunt screaming at Pete and everyone else for not getting me when they had the chance.

Then I was overhearing Margarita tell my aunt how Fofi described how I sucked on his dick. I even heard my aunt scream and smack Anthony for not telling her that I had sucked his dick. My aunt was so desperate to get me that she was telling everyone in the building that she had seen me entering one of the buildings on 182 street between Bathgate and Third Avenue. I remember hearing her scream at Margarita's older sons that there I was across the street entering the building. They all went after the guy and when they came back, they told my aunt that it wasn't me.

I was starting to feel thirsty, hungry, and weak. I knew that if I didn't leave from my hiding place, it was where the cops would find my rotten corpse. That's if they did, I didn't know how many days had passed or if it was day or night. I muster all the strength I had and got up from the floor. I was feeling dizzy and woozy, I held on to the edge of the closet door entrance for a few seconds, then I climbed out. I stood still so I could listen to what was happening upstairs and outside. Everything was quiet so far, so I headed to the little basement window that wasn't sealed, and saw that it was dark outside. Still not hearing anything of suspicion, I proceeded to climbed out of the window as

quietly as I could. Once I was out, I stood still again and waited to make sure the coast was clear. I then climbed the gate and was in the ally of the other building, I then walked through the hallway but instead of leaving through the front of the basement, I climbed a gate that lead to a building that faced 182 street and where Fofi's two uncles and one of their wife lived. I knew that they weren't going to be outside because they were all pot heads and being that it was dark out, they had to get ready to go to work the next day. I exited the final building and walked down Washington Avenue into a building on 181 street. I was going to walk up to the roof and fall asleep and leave to Manhattan. As I reached the third floor of the building, I saw on the corner of an apartment door, an aluminum foil with food in it, I picked up and saw that it had ash on a corner of the food. I ate where the ash wasn't present and put the rest down and continued the two more floors until I reached the roof's stairs case little hall. I laid down as comfortable as I could and fell asleep. I was alone in the cold with no one by myside and nowhere to really go. All I felt was the burning rage of hatred for every single human being. The next day the super of the building woke me and seeing how young I was, politely told me that as soon as I fully wake up that I had to leave. I got up and went down the stairs, and left the building and as I headed to Manhattan, I vowed that society would pay for everything done to me.

The End of One of Two.